Fodor's '94

Cancún,

Cozumel,

Yucatán

Peninsula

Parts of this book appear in *Fodor's Mexico '94*.
New York • Toronto • London • Sydney • Auckland

Fodor's Cancún, Cozumel, Yucatán Peninsula

Editor: Paula Consolo
Editorial Assistant: Amy Hunter
Editorial Contributors: Kathryn Bonn, Edie Jarolim, Caroline Liou, Maribeth Mellin, Erica Meltzer, Marcy Pritchard, MaryEllen Schultz, Frank "Pancho" Shiell
Creative Director: Fabrizio LaRocca
Cartographer: David Lindroth
Illustrator: Karl Tanner
Cover Photograph: Peter Guttman
Design: Vignelli Associates

About the Author

This book was originally written by freelance writer and translator Erica Meltzer, who first set foot on Mexican soil, in the Yucatán, back in 1967. She later lived in Mexico City for three years, and from her current base in New York, she now gets back to the country as often as possible. This year's addition was updated by Edie Jarolim and Maribeth Mellin.

Special Sales

Contents

Maps

Foreword

We acknowledge, with warm thanks, those who helped us in researching this guide: most especially, Mexicana and Aeromexico, as they have made this edition possible. We also express our indebtedness to Mayaland Tours; Turismo Aviomar, Meliá Hotels; the Cancún and Cozumel Hotel Associations; the Hotel Krystal, the Cancún Playa, the Posada del Mar; Posadas de Mexico; Teresa Borge of the Mérida Tourism Office; Stouffer Presidente hotels; Continental Villas Plaza hotel; Costa de Cocos; the tourist office on Isla Mujeres; and Edelman Public Relations Worldwide.

While every care has been taken to ensure the accuracy of the information in this guide, the passage of time will always bring change, and consequently the publisher cannot accept responsibility for errors that may occur.

All prices and opening times quoted here are based on information supplied to us at press time. Hours and admission fees may change, however, and the prudent traveler will avoid inconvenience by calling ahead.

Fodor's wants to hear about your travel experiences, both pleasant and unpleasant. When a hotel or restaurant fails to live up to its billing, let us know and we will investigate the complaint and revise our entries where the facts warrant it.

Send your letters to the editors of Fodor's Travel Publications, 201 E. 50th Street, New York, NY 10022.

Highlights'94 and Fodor'sChoice

Highlights '94

The Yucatán peninsula is undergoing two opposing trends that mirror what is happening in other tourism destinations worldwide: a continued explosion of development and a growing concern for the environment. **Tour operators** are capitalizing on these trends by selling packages that focus on the Mayan ruins, wildlife, and natural beauty for which the peninsula is famous.

The **Ruta Maya,** a five-country venture to develop impoverished regions and promote low-impact tourism to the Mayan sites in Mexico, Belize, Guatemala, Honduras, and El Salvador, is now being covered by several tour operators.

Campeche   Until recently, the modest State of Campeche offered little to tourists aside from its flourishing wildlife and the genial, pleasant attitude of its native population. But as other areas on the Yucatán peninsula become increasingly congested during tourist seasons, Campeche remains attractively uncrowded. Restoration continues on the ruined Maya city of **Edzná,** the most accessible archaeological site in the state.

Cancún   Almost since its inception, Cancún has been Mexico's most popular destination. Judging by the numbers of package-tour takers, college students, and weekend vacationers who flock to its white Caribbean beaches and warm turquoise waters, Cancún is now almost synonymous with Mexican tourism.

The devastation caused by Hurricane Gilbert in 1988 is far in the past. Countless hotels have been made over, and new ones are springing up, although as the authorities become more concerned that Cancún is approaching the saturation point, the growth rate is slowing down. Among the deluxe international properties to open recently is the 370-room **Ritz Carlton.**

As the hotel inventory plateaus, however, **time-share condominiums** are going up at a feverish pitch — not just in Cancún, but all along the Caribbean coast and on Isla Mujeres as well. In an effort to keep pace with the nearly constant flow of visitors, the vast majority of whom are North Americans, **charter airlines** have been boosting their service to Cancún and Cozumel from a growing number of gateways.

To attract a more diversified clientele, in 1991 Cancún launched what was to become an annual **Jazz Festival,** which opened with Wynton Marsalis and Gato Barbieri. At press time, the '94 lineup was still in the works. The **Cancún Convention Center,** the original venue for the area's cultural events, was razed by Hurricane Gilbert and is being rebuilt. Although it was scheduled to open in 1993, at press time its doors were still closed. In addition, two megaprojects — comprising an "eco-archaeological" park, aquariums, yacht marinas, golf courses, hotels, and commercial space — are in the works in and around Cancún.

Cozumel The offshore island of Cozumel, Mexico's largest cruise-ship port and a favorite among honeymooners and scuba divers, is taking steps to curb progress's toll on the environment. Although the new Diamond Resort opened in early 1993, development of several deluxe hotels has been halted; the island museum has embarked on a serious save-the-turtle campaign; and Isla de Pasión — a tiny island off the west coast, previously used for picnic cruises — has been made into a state reserve.

Isla Mujeres Fans of Isla Mujeres (an offshore island much smaller and less developed than Cozumel) can be reassured that it has seen relatively little change, either physically or temperamentally. An attempt is being made to stop development by having the government declare the entire island a national park. (If that happens, you'll be charged a fee to come ashore here.) Still, there have been some new additions, including the **Condominio Playa Norte Nautibeach,** the **Cristalmar** condo- hotel, and the cozy little **Na-Balam.** The all-inclusive resort **Costa Club** is scheduled to open by 1994, but it probably won't.

Although there is talk of rebuilding the town dock to accommodate cruise ships and of operating an air charter service to Florida, Mérida, Chichén Itzá, and the Guatemalan ruins of Tikal, actual planning has not begun. In the meantime, Isla remains a backwater, beloved by backpackers and other budget travelers.

Mérida and the Mérida, the charming and friendly capital city of Yucatán, **State of Yucatán** is becoming increasingly popular with European tourists. Although the city is often used only as a stopover for visits to the archaeological sites, its impressive architecture and numerous cultural events are beginning to draw travelers who stay for a week or more. A new toll road linking Mérida and Cancún is partially completed (Mérida to Valladolid); it reduces driving time by one hour.

Amateur archaeologists are now able to visit the Mayan site of **Oxkintok,** about 51 kilometers (31 miles) south of Mérida, though the ruins are still buried in the jungle and just barely excavated. A display at the **Mérida Museum of Anthropology and History** of the artifacts found at Oxkintok provides an overview of the current work being done at the site.

Mexico's Caribbean The Caribbean coast is attracting growing numbers of in-**Coast** dependent travelers. **Ecotourism** is on the rise here as well, thanks to the exotic birds, marine life, and lagoons of the **Sian Ka'an Biosphere Reserve.** The Boca Paila peninsula, virtually all of which is contained in that reserve, is earning a glowing reputation for flatfishing, fly-fishing, and bonefishing. Small resorts catering to scuba divers and fishermen are gaining in popularity along the **Xcalak peninsula** at the southern base of the Quintana Roo coast, near the Belize border. The final frontier of this vast, sparsely inhabited, and beautiful region, Xcalak has miles and miles of deserted, undeveloped beaches (though rumors of impending construction abound). The northern part of the Caribbean coast — generally known as the Cancún-Tulum Corridor — has undergone the most dramatic transformation along the coast, as resorts and time-share communities multiply and sprawl in competition for the time-share dollar. The changes are particularly visible at **Puerto Aventuras,** a 900-acre development with marinas, a golf course, hotels, condos, and all the trappings of a self-contained resort.

A similar project is under way at Playacar in **Playa del Carmen,** where the arrival of cruise ships and the development of first-class resorts have altered the town's appearance and character. A long-time favorite of budget travelers looking for isolated beaches and low-cost accommodations, Playa is gradually becoming a paradise for investors with visions of luxury condos and limitless profits. Time-share and resort developments are under way all along the corridor, where the government is building a four-lane highway for easy access from Cancún to Tulum.

Fodor's Choice

No two people will agree on what makes a perfect vactation, but it's fun and helpful to know what others think. We hope you'll have a chance to experience some of Fodor's Choices yourself in Cancún, Cozumel, and the Yucatán peninsula. For detailed information about each entry, refer to the appropriate chapter.

Archaeological Sites

Chichén Itzá (Mérida)

Cobá (Mexico's Caribbean Coast)

Edzná (Campeche)

Tulum (Mexico's Caribbean Coast)

Uxmal (Mérida)

Attractions

Historical Buildings and Churches

Palacio del Gobierno (Mérida)

Casa de Montejo (Mérida)

Ermita de Santa Isabel (Mérida)

Ex-Templo de San José and Cathedral (Campeche)

Mansión Carvajal (Campeche)

Museums

Hecelchakán (Campeche)

City Museum (Mérida)

Museum of Anthropology and History (Mérida)

Museo Regional (Campeche)

CEDAM Underwater Archaeology Museum (Puerto Aventuras)

Beaches

Akumal (Mexico's Caribbean Coast)

Boca Paila peninsula (Mexico's Caribbean Coast)

Paamul and Xcacel (Mexico's Caribbean Coast)

Xcalak peninsula (Mexico's Caribbean Coast)

Playa Cocoteros (Isla Mujeres)

Punta Chiqueros and Punta Celerain (Cozumel)

Boat Trips

Chinchorro Banks (Mexico's Caribbean Coast)

Isla Contoy (Isla Mujeres)

Isla de Pájaros (Mexico's Caribbean Coast)

Río Lagartos (Mérida)

Dining

Chez Magaly, Isla Mujeres *(Expensive)*

Arrecife, Cozumel *(Expensive)*

La Bella Epoca, Mérida *(Expensive)*

La Cabaña del Pescador, Cozumel *(Expensive)*

Café Amsterdam, Cancún *(Moderate)*

Casa Cenote, Mexico's Caribbean Coast *(Moderate)*

El Capi Navegante, Cozumel *(Moderate)*

El Pescador, Cancún *(Moderate)*

La Habichuela, Cancún *(Moderate)*

La Parilla, Cancún *(Moderate)*

La Piqua, Campeche *(Moderate)*

Pizza Rolandi, Isla Mujeres *(Moderate)*

Pórtico del Peregrino, Mérida *(Moderate)*

Rincón Maya, Cozumel *(Moderate)*

Rosa Mexicano, Cancún *(Moderate)*

El Moro, Cozumel *(Inexpensive)*

Festivals and Special Events

Billfish Tournament (Cozumel)

Cancún Jazz Festival (Cancún)

Carnaval (Campeche, Cozumel, Isla Mujeres, Mérida)

Equinox at Chichén Itzá (Mérida)

Fiesta of San Román (Campeche)

Mérida en Domingo (Mérida)

Lodging

Fiesta Americana Cancún, Cancún *(Very Expensive)*

Meliá Cancún, Cancún *(Very Expensive)*

Na-Balam, Isla Mujeres *(Expensive)*

Posada del Capitán Lafitte, Mexico's Caribbean Coast *(Expensive)*

Costa de Cocos, Mexico's Caribbean Coast *(Moderate)*

Gran Hotel, Mérida *(Moderate)*

Osho Oasis, Mexico's Caribbean Coast *(Moderate)*

Villa Arqueólogica Cobá, Mexico's Caribbean Coast *(Moderate)*

Mesón San Miguel, Cozumel *(Inexpensive)*

Sports

Bird-watching Celestún (Mérida)

Punta Celerain and Colombia Lagoon (Cozumel)

Río Lagartos (Mérida)

Fishing Billfishing (Cozumel, Isla Mujeres)

Bonefishing (Mexico's Caribbean Coast, Cozumel)

Deep-sea fishing (Cancún, Cozumel, Isla Mujeres, Mexico's Caribbean Coast)

Flatfishing, fly-fishing (Mexico's Caribbean Coast)

Sportfishing (Cozumel, Mérida)

Scuba Diving and Snorkeling Akumal (Mexico's Caribbean Coast)

Banco Chinchorro (Mexico's Caribbean Coast)

Palancar Reef (Cozumel)

Xcalak (Mexico's Caribbean Coast)

Nature Reserves and Natural Beauty

Celestún (Mérida)

Cenote Dzitnup (Mérida)

Chankanaab (Cozumel)

Isla Contoy (Isla Mujeres)

Laguna de Bacalar (Mexico's Caribbean Coast)

Río Lagartos (Mérida)

Sian Ka'an Biosphere Reserve (Mexico's Caribbean Coast)

Nightlife

Carlos 'n' Charlie's (Cozumel)

Dady'O (Cancún)

Excess (Mérida)

Calypso (Isla Mujeres)

Shopping

Bazar García Rejón (Mérida)

La Loma (Isla Mujeres)

Los Cinco Soles (Cozumel)

Mercado Municipal (Mérida)

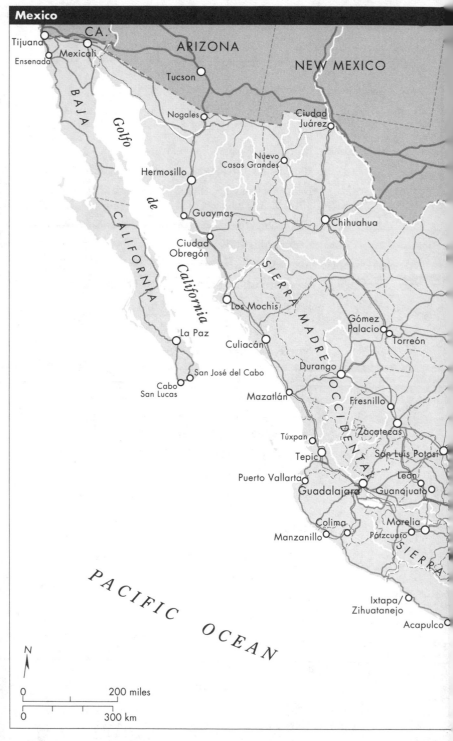

Mexico

Yucatán Peninsula

Golfo de México

Dzilam de Bravo

Dzilan González

Progreso

Yucalpetén

Punta Baz

Dzibilchaltún ⦿ Motul

Ter

25 261

80 Tekantó

Mérida ✪ Citilcúm

Izamal

Celestún 281 180

Punta Nimun Umán Hoctún Holca

180

Maxcanú **Mayapán** 18

Muna YUCAT

Santa Cruz **Uxmal** Ticul

Kabah 184 Ozkutzcab

Sayil

Tenabó 261 Labná Tzucacab

Campeche Tinúm

180 261

Punta Seybaplaya Hopelchén

Edzná QU

La Joya

Champoton CAMPECHE *Río Champotón*

Sabancuy

180

Escárcega 186 Río

186 Xpujil 186

186

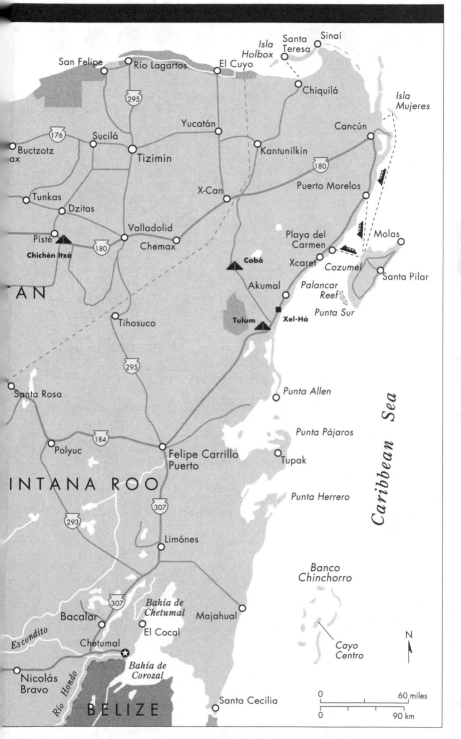

World Time Zones

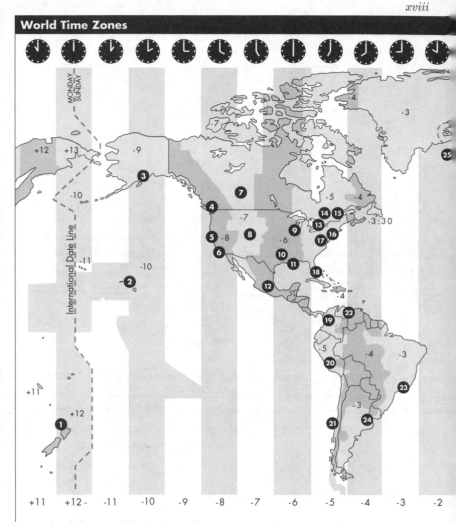

Numbers below vertical bands relate each zone to Greenwich Mean Time (0 hrs.).
Local times frequently differ from these general indications,
as indicated by light-face numbers on map.

Algiers, **29**
Anchorage, **3**
Athens, **41**
Auckland, **1**
Baghdad, **46**
Bangkok, **50**
Beijing, **54**

Berlin, **34**
Bogotá, **19**
Budapest, **37**
Buenos Aires, **24**
Caracas, **22**
Chicago, **9**
Copenhagen, **33**
Dallas, **10**

Delhi, **48**
Denver, **8**
Djakarta, **53**
Dublin, **26**
Edmonton, **7**
Hong Kong, **56**
Honolulu, **2**

Istanbul, **40**
Jerusalem, **42**
Johannesburg, **44**
Lima, **20**
Lisbon, **28**
London (Greenwich), **27**
Los Angeles, **6**
Madrid, **38**
Manila, **57**

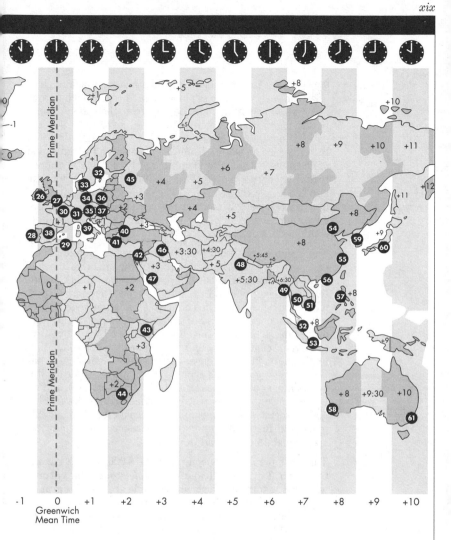

-1   0   +1   +2   +3   +4   +5   +6   +7   +8   +9   +10
Greenwich
Mean Time

Introduction

By Erica Meltzer

The Yucatán peninsula has captivated travelers since the early Spanish explorations. "A place of white towers, whose glint could be seen from the ships ... temples rising tier on tier, with sculptured cornices" is how the expeditions' chroniclers described the peninsula, then thought to be an island. Rumors of a mainland 10 days west of Cuba were known to Columbus, who obstinately hoped to find "a very populated land," and one that was richer than any he had yet discovered. Subsequent explorers and conquistadores met with more resistance there than in almost any other part of the New World, and this rebelliousness continued for centuries.

The Yucatecans of today as a whole are honest and generous, perhaps more than their countrymen in other parts of Mexico. Largely because of their geographic isolation, they tend to preserve ancient traditions more than many other indigenous groups in the country. This can be seen in such areas as housing (the use of the ancient Maya thatched hut, or *na*); dress (*huipiles* have been made and worn by Maya women for centuries); occupation (most modern-day Maya are farmers, just as their ancestors were); language (while the Maya language has evolved considerably, basically it is very similar to that spoken at least 500 years ago); and religion (ancient deities persist particularly in the form of gods associated with agriculture, such as the *chacs,* or rain gods, and festivals to honor the seasons and benefactor spirits maintain the traditions of old).

This vast peninsula encompasses 113,000 square kilometers (43,630 square miles) of a flat limestone table covered with sparse topsoil and scrubby jungle growth. Geographically, it comprises the states of Yucatán, Campeche, and Quintana Roo, as well as Belize and a part of Guatemala, though the latter two countries are not discussed in this book. Long isolated from the rest of Mexico and still one of the least Hispanicized (or Mexicanized) regions of the country, Yucatán catapulted into the tourist's vocabulary with the creation of its most precious man-made asset, Cancún.

Mexico's most popular resort destination owes its success to its location on the superb eastern coastline of Yucatán, which is washed by the exquisitely colored and translucent waters of the Caribbean and endowed with a semitropical climate, unbroken stretches of beach, and the world's fifth-longest barrier reef, which separates the mainland from Cozumel. Cancún, along with Cozumel and to a lesser extent Isla Mujeres, incarnates the success formula for sun-and-sand tourism: luxury hotels, sandy beaches, water sports, nightlife, and restaurants that specialize in international fare.

Cancún has several advantages over its Caribbean neighbors: It is less expensive; it can be reached via more nonstop flights; and it offers a far richer culture. With the advent of Cancún, the peninsula's Mayan ruins — long a mecca for archaeology enthusiasts — have become virtual satellites of that glittering star. The proximity of such compelling sites as Chichén Itzá, Uxmal, and Tulum allows Cancún's visitors to explore the vestiges of one of the most brilliant civilizations in the ancient world without having to journey too far from their base.

Yucatán offers a breathtaking diversity of other charms, too. The waters of the Mexican Caribbean are clearer and more turquoise than those of the Pacific; many of the beaches are unrivaled. Scuba diving (in natural sinkholes and along the barrier reefs), snorkeling, deep-sea fishing, and other water sports attract growing numbers of tourists. They can also go birding, help save sea turtles, camp, spelunk, and shop for Yucatán's splendid handicrafts. There is a broad spectrum of settings and accommodations to choose from: the high-rise, pricey strip of hotels along Cancún's Paseo Kukulcán; the less showy properties on Cozumel, beloved by partying college-age scuba divers from Texas; and the relaxed ambience of Isla Mujeres and Playa del Carmen, where most lodgings consist of rustic bungalows with ceiling fans and hammocks.

There are also the cities of Yucatán. Foremost is Mérida, wonderfully unaltered by time, where Moorish- inspired, colonnaded colonial architecture blends handsomely with turn-of-the-century pomposities. In Mérida, café living is still an art and the Maya still live proudly as Maya. Campeche, one of the few walled cities in North America, possesses an eccentric charm; it is slightly out of step with the rest of the country and not the least bothered by the fact. Down on the border with Belize stands Chetumal, a ramshackle place of wood-frame houses that is pervaded by the hybrid culture of coastal Central America and the pungent smell of the sea. Progreso, at the other end of the peninsula on the Gulf of Mexico, is Chetumal's northern counterpart, an overgrown fishing village turned commercial port. Hotels in these towns, while for the most part not as luxurious as the beach resort properties, range from the respectable if plain 1970s commercial buildings to the undated fleabags so popular with detective novelists (one thinks especially of Raymond Chandler) and movie makers.

Wildlife is another of Yucatán's riches. Iguanas, lizards, tapir, jaguars, deer, armadillos, and wild boars thrive on this alternately parched and densely foliaged plain. Flamingos and herons, manatees and sea turtles, their once dwindling numbers now rising in response to Mexico's newly awakened ecological consciousness, find idyllic watery habitats in and above the coastline's mangrove swamps, lagoons, and sandbars, acres of which have been made into national parks. Both Río Lagartos and the coast's Sian Ka'an bio-sphere reserve sparkle with Yucatán's natural beauty. Orchids, bougainvillea, and poinciana are ubiquitous; dazzling reds and pinks and oranges and whites spill over into countless courtyards—effortless hothouses. And while immense palm groves and forests of precious hardwood trees slowly succumb to forest fires and disease, the region's edible tropical flora—coconuts, papaya, bananas, and oranges-remain succulent ancillaries to the celebrated Yucatecan cuisine.

It is the colors of Yucatán that are most remarkable. From the stark white, sun-bleached sand, the sea stretches out like some immense canvas painted in bands of celadon greens, pale aquas, and deep dusty blues. At dusk the sea and the horizon meld in the sumptuous glow of a lavender sunset, the sky just barely tinged with periwinkle and violet. Inland, the beige, gray, and amber stones of ruined temples are set off by riotous greenery. The colors of newer structures are equally intoxicating: Tawny, gray-brown thatched roofs sit atop white oval huts. Colonial mansions favor creamy pastels of bisque, salmon, and coral tones, again highlighted by elegant white: white arches, white balustrades, white rococo porticos. Brilliant colors glimmer in carved hardwood doors, variegated tile floors, brown and green pottery and rugs affixed to walls, and snatches of bougainvillea rushing down the sides of buildings.

But for all of Yucatán's fine attributes, the peninsula faces grave danger, especially in the state of Quintana Roo. Coastlines are being polluted, coral reefs destroyed, tropical rain forests razed to make way for farms and ranches. Public services for the state's booming population, which—at 16%—has the highest growth rate in the country, have become woefully inadequate. The gap between rich and poor is widening, and as the laws governing foreign ownership of coastal lands are eased, time-share condominium developers are making more and more of the peninsula's land off-limits to its Mexican residents. On the up side, however, the government is beginning to realize that in the long run unbridled development can only hurt the country. Consequently, hotel construction in both Cancún and Cozumel has been slowed. The biggest area of growth at present is the so-called Cancún–Tulum Corridor.

Yucatán's color extends beyond the physical to the historical. From the conquistadores' first landfall off Cape Catoche in 1517 to the bloody skirmishes that wiped out most of the Indians to the razing of Mayan temples and burning of their sacred books, the peninsula was a battlefield. Pirates wreaked havoc off the coast of Campeche for centuries. Half the Indian population was killed during the 19th-century uprising known as the War of the Castes, when the enslaved indigenous population rose up and massacred thousands of Europeans; Yucatán was attempting to secede from Mexico, and dictator Porfirio Díaz sent in his troops. These events, like the towering Mayan civilization, have left their mark throughout the peninsula: in its archaeological museums, its colonial monuments, and the opulent mansions of the hacienda owners who enslaved the natives to cultivate their henequen.

But years after all the violent conflicts with foreigners, the people of Yucatán treat today's visitors with genuine hospitality and friendliness. Once you leave the beach resorts, you are likely to enjoy spontaneous, honest interaction with the locals. They appreciate any attempts you make to communicate with them in Spanish, and if you learn a few words in their native tongue you will be rewarded with an even warmer greeting.

1 Essential Information

Before You Go

Government Tourist Offices

In the United States 405 Park Ave., Suite 1402, New York, NY 10022, tel. 212/755–8233, fax 212/753–2874; 1911 Pennsylvania Ave. NW, Washington, DC 20006, tel. 202/728–1750, fax 202/728–1758; 70 E. Lake St., Suite 1413, Chicago, IL 60601, tel. 312/565–2778, fax 312/606–9012; 10100 Santa Monica Blvd., Los Angeles, CA 90067, tel. 310/203–8191, fax 310/203–8316; 2707 North Loop W, Suite 450, Houston, TX 77008, tel. 713/880–5153, fax 713/880–1833; 11522 S.W. 81st St., Miami, FL 33156, tel. 305/252–1440, fax 305/443–1186. All offices can be reached toll-free at 800/262–8900.

The Department of State's **Citizens Emergency Center** issues Consular Information Sheets, which cover crime, security, and health risks as well as embassy locations, entry requirements, currency regulations, and other routine matters. (Travel Warnings, which counsel travelers to avoid a country entirely, are issued in extreme cases.) For the latest information, call the interactive hotline (tel. 202/647–5225); or, with your PC's modem, tap into the Bureau of Consular Affairs' computer bulletin board (tel. 202/647–9225).

In Canada 1 Place Ville Marie, Suite 2409, Montreal, Quebec H3B 3M9, tel. 514/871–1052, fax 514/871–3425; 2 Bloor St. W, Suite 18011, Toronto, Ontario M4W 3E2, tel. 416/925–0704, fax 416/925–6061.

Tours and Packages

Should you buy your Cancún travel arrangements packaged or do it yourself? There are advantages either way. Buying packaged arrangements, you save money, particularly if you find a program that includes exactly the features you want. You also get a pretty good idea of what your trip will cost from the outset. Independent packages allow plenty of flexibility. They generally include airline travel and hotels, with certain options available, such as sightseeing, car rental, and excursions. Escorted tours, usually via motorcoach with a tour director in charge, don't make much sense here and are not widely available.

Travel agents are your best source of recommendations for both tours and packages. They can sell any of the packages offered by operators listed below, and the cost to you is the same as buying direct. Whatever program you ultimately choose, be sure to find out exactly what is included: taxes, tips, transfers, meals, baggage handling, ground transportation, entertainment, excursions, sports or recreation (and rental equipment if necessary). Ask about the level of hotel used, its location, the size of its rooms, the kind of beds, and its amenities, such as pool, room service, or programs for children, if they're important to you. Another important point: If the beach is the centerpiece of your vacation, ask exactly where your hotel is located with respect to the nearest one: The words "beach nearby" can have a disturbing number of meanings.

Find out the operator's cancellation penalties. Nearly everyone charges them, and the only way to avoid them is to buy trip-cancellation insurance (*see* Trip Insurance, *below*). Also ask about the single supplement, a surcharge assessed to solo travelers. Some operators do not make you pay it if you agree to be matched up with a roommate of the same sex, even if one is not found by departure time. Remember that a program that has features you won't use, whether for rental sporting equipment or discounted museum admissions, may not be the most cost-wise choice for you.

Packages from U.S.-based Operators Independent packages are offered by airlines, tour operators who may also do escorted programs, and any number of other companies from large, established firms to small, new entrepreneurs. Among the many airline-sponsored packages are **American Airlines Fly AAway Vacations** (tel. 800/321–2121), **Continental's Grand Destinations** (tel. 800/634–5555), and **Delta Dream Vacations** (tel. 800/872–7786). Other operators with a large selection of resort packages (mostly roundtrip airfare plus three to seven days with extra nights available) are **American Express Vacations** (300 Pinnacle Way, Norcross, GA 30093, tel. 800/241–1700); **American Leisure** (9800 Centre Parkway, Suite 800, Houston TX 77036, tel. 800/777–1980); **Asti Tours** (21 E. 40th St., New York, NY 10016, tel. 800/327–4390 outside NY, 800/535–3711 within New York State); **Friendly Holidays** (1983 Marcus Ave., Suite C130, Lake Success, NY 11042, tel. 800/221–9748); **Globetrotters** (139 Main St., Cambridge, MA 02142, tel. 617/621–9911 or 800/999–9696); **Travel Impressions/Cavalcade** (465 Smith St., Farmingdale, NY 11735, tel. 800/284–0044 from the eastern U.S., 800/284–0077 in the West), with a low-priced charter program to Cancún out of New York's JFK and Stewart airports, and Newark, New Jersey; **Magnatours** (325 E. 75th St., New York, NY 10021, tel. 212/517–7770 or 800/223–0476), with over 50 resorts; **Mexico Travel Advisors**, with offices in Los Angeles, San Francisco, and Chicago (tel. 800/876–4MTA), with round-trip airfare from Houston on Aeromexico; and **Mexico Travel Consultants** (246 S. Robertson Blvd., Beverly Hills, CA 90211, tel 800/252–0100). In addition, **Club Med** sells packages to its resort in Cancún, which features tennis, most water sports, optional deep-sea fishing, and excursions to the ruins.

Special-interest Programs from U.S.-based Operators Yucatán travelers come not only for sand and sun but also for the area's archaeology, ecology, and natural history. Special-interest programs may be fully escorted or independent. Some require a certain amount of expertise, but most are for the average traveler with an interest and are usually hosted by experts in the subject matter. When the program is escorted, it enjoys the advantages and disadvantages of all escorted programs (your baggage is handled, your time rigorously scheduled, and most meals planned); because your fellow travelers are apt to be passionate or knowledgeable about the subject, they can prove as enjoyable a part of your travel experience as the destination itself. The price range is wide, but the cost is usually higher—sometimes a lot higher—than for ordinary escorted tours and packages, because of the expert guiding and special activities. Here is a sampling of what is available for Cancún.

Archaeology and Nature Look into programs from **Forum Travel International** (91 Gregory La., #21, Pleasant Hill, CA 94523, tel. 415/671–2900, fax

415/946–1500) and **Tropical Travel** (5 Grogans Park, Suite 102, Woodlands, TX 77380-2190, tel. 713/688–1985 or 800/451–8017), which highlights ruins and wildlife. **M.I.L.A./Peru Tours** (100 S. Greenleaf Ave., Gurnee, IL 60031, tel. 800/367–7378) has archaeological programs to the Yucatán and other points in Mexico.

Custom Tours **Maya-Caribe Tours** (87 Wolfs La., Pelham, NY 10803, tel. 914/738–8254 or 800/223–4084) does custom tours that include lodging, airport transfers, ground transportation, and a guide.

Cruises **Special Expeditions** (720 Fifth Ave., New York, NY 10019, tel. 800/762–0003) cruises are escorted by historians, naturalists, and geologists.

Scuba **Rothschild Travel Consultants** (900 West End Ave., Suite 1B, New York, NY 10025, tel. 212/662–4858 or 800/359–0747) offers eight-day packages that include hotel, two dives daily, and rental car.

Packages from U.K.-based Operators Many organizations offer packages in the area, including **British Airways Holidays** (Atlantic House, Hazelwick Ave., Three Bridges, Crawley, W. Sussex RH10 1NP, tel. 0293/611611); **Club Med** (110 Brompton Rd., London SW# 1JJ, tel. 071/581–1161), for its Cancún resort; **Kuoni Travel** (Kuoni House, Dorking, Surrey RH5 4AZ, tel. 0306/740–888, fax 0306/740–328); and **Sunset Travel Ltd.** (306 Clapham Rd., London SW9 9AE, tel. 071/622–5466).

Special-interest Programs from U.K.-based Operators **Journey Latin America** (14-16 Devonshire Rd., Chiswick, London W4 2HD, tel. 081/747–8315, fax 081/742–1312) has special-interest packages to Cancún and the Mayan ruins. **Mexican Tours** (61 High St., Barnet, Herts. EN5 5UR, tel. 081/440–7830), which specializes in the Cancún area and the archaeological sites of the Yucatán, will prepare individualized tours, including flights, accommodations, and all ground arrangements. **Steamond International** (23 Eccleston St., London SW1W 9LX, tel. 071/730–8640, fax 071/730–3024) can customize any itinerary to any part of Mexico.

When to Go

High season along the Mexican Caribbean runs from mid-December through Easter week. Seasonal price changes are less pronounced in Mérida and other inland regions than at the beach resorts, but it still may be difficult to find a room during Christmas and Easter, as well as the last week of July and first three weeks of August, when Mexicans are traveling.

Climate Spring and summer are usually pleasant along the coast, although you may experience some afternoon rain and evening breezes; in autumn, storms are common. The steamiest time of year inland is late spring, just before the May–October rainy season. What follows are the average daily maximum and minimum temperatures for Mérida. The rest of Yucatán follows the same general pattern.

Mérida	**Jan.**	83F	28C	**May**	94F	40C	**Sept.**	90F	32C
		62	17		72	22		73	23
	Feb.	85F	29C	**June**	92F	33C	**Oct.**	87F	31C
		63	17		73	23		71	22
	Mar.	89F	37C	**July**	92F	33C	**Nov.**	85F	29C
		66	19		73	23		67	19

Apr.	92F	41C	**Aug.**	91F	33C	**Dec.**	82F	28C
	69	21		73	23		64	18

Information For current weather conditions for cities in the United States
Sources and abroad, plus the local time and helpful travel tips, call the
Weather Channel Connection (tel. 900/WEATHER; 95c per
minute) from a touch-tone phone.

Festivals and Seasonal Events

Traditional religious and patriotic festivals rank among Yucatán's most memorable activities. Towns throughout the region host a number of additional annual fairs, shows, and local
celebrations.
Jan. 1: New Year's Day is celebrated throughout the region.
Feb.–Mar.: Carnaval (Mardi Gras) festivities take place the
week before Lent, with parades, floats, outdoor dancing, music,
and fireworks, and are especially spirited in Mérida, Cozumel,
Isla Mujeres, Campeche, and Chetumal.
Mar. 21 and Sept. 21: At the **Equinoxes** Kukulcán, the plumed
serpent deity, appears to emerge from his temple atop El Castillo Pyramid at Chichén Itzá and slither down to earth. The phe-
nomenon happens through a fascinating interplay of light and
shadow (sunshine is necessary, however). It attracts large
crowds; be sure to make hotel reservations well in advance.
Apr.–May: The **Sol a Sol International Regatta,** launched from
St. Petersburg, Florida, arrives in Isla Mujeres and Cozumel,
sparking regional dances and a general air of festivity.
Late Apr.–early June: Isla Mujeres Regattas bring a fleet of sail-
boats from Florida and Texas for a series of races.
Late Apr.–June: Billfish Tournaments take place in Cozumel
and Cancún.
Apr. 28–May 3: Holy Cross Fiestas in Chumayel, Celestún,
Hopelchén—all in Yucatán state—include cockfights, dances,
and fireworks.
Memorial Day Weekend: The Cancún Jazz Festival, an annual
event as of 1991, has featured top musicians, such as Wynton
Marsalis and Gato Barbieri.
Last week in May: Hammock Festival, hailing the furnishing
that originated here, is held in Tecoh, on the southern outskirts
of Mérida.
Last week of July: Fiesta de San Ignacio takes place in Chetu-
mal and features reggae and calypso rhythms and traditional
Mexican music.
Sept. 14: *Vaquerías* (traditional cattle-branding feasts) attract
pilgrims who gather for bullfights, fireworks, and music.
Sept. 14–28: Fiesta of San Román attracts 50,000 people to
Campeche to view the procession carrying the Black Christ of
San Román—the city's most sacred patron saint—through the
streets.
Sept. 15–16: Independence Day is celebrated throughout Mexico
with fireworks and parties.
Sept. 27: Fiesta of Our Lord of the Blisters (El Señor de las
Ampollas), Mérida's biggest festival, begins two weeks or more
of processions, dances, bullfights, and fireworks.
Oct. 18–25: Fiesta of the Christ of Sitilpech in Izamal, near
Mérida, begins a week of daily processions in which the image
of Christ is carried from Sitilpech village to Izamal; dances and
fireworks accompany the processions.

Oct. 23–Nov. 2: Cancún Fair serves as a nostalgia trip for provincials who now live along the Caribbean shore but still remember the small-town fiestas back home.

Nov. 1–2: Day of the Dead, or All Saints' Day, is celebrated throughout the peninsula with graveside picnics. Bakers herald the annual return of the departed from the spirit world with pastry skulls and candy.

Nov. 13–20: Fiesta de Santiago, in Tekax, Yucatán, features a week of bullfights, cockfights, dancing, and fireworks.

Nov. 31–Dec. 8: Fiesta of the Virgin of the Conception is held each year in Champotón, Campeche.

Dec. 1–8: Fiesta of Isla Mujeres honors the island's patron saint, as members of various guilds stage processions, dances, and bullfights.

Dec. 3–9: Day of the Immaculate Conception, celebrated for six days in the village of Kantunilkin, Quintana Roo, with processions, folkloric dances, fireworks, and bullfights.

Dec. 8: The **Aquatic Procession** highlights festivities at the fishing village of Celestún, west of Mérida.

Dec. 16–25: Christmas is celebrated in the Yucatán villages of Espita and Temax with processions culminating in the breaking of candy-filled piñatas.

National Holidays Banks, government offices, and many businesses close on these days, so plan your trip accordingly: January 1, New Year's Day; February 5, Constitution Day; March 21, Benito Juárez's birthday; May 1, Labor Day; September 16, Independence Day; November 20, Revolution Day; December 25, Christmas Day.

Banks and government offices close during Holy Week, especially the Thursday and Friday before Easter; on May 5, anniversary of the Battle of Puebla; May 10, Mother's Day; September 1, opening of Congress; October 12, Día de la Raza; November 2, Day of the Dead; December 12, Feast of the Virgin of Guadalupe; December 25–January 2, Christmas week.

What to Pack

Pack light, because you may want to save space for purchases: Yucatán is filled with bargains on clothing, leather goods, jewelry, pottery, and other crafts.

Clothing Resort wear is all you will need for the Caribbean beach towns: Bring lightweight sports clothes, sundresses, bathing suits, sun visors, and cover-ups for the beach and a jacket or sweater to wear in the chilly, air-conditioned restaurants. If you plan to visit any ruins, bring comfortable walking shoes with rubber soles. Lightweight rain gear is a good idea during the rainy season. Cancún is the dressiest spot on the peninsula, but even fancy restaurants don't require men to wear jackets. Women may wear shorts at the ruins, on the beaches, and in the beach towns, but should not do so in the cities.

Miscellaneous Insect repellent, sunscreen, and umbrellas are a must for Yucatán. A spare pair of eyeglasses and sunglasses and an adequate supply of prescription drugs are essentials on any trip. You can probably find over-the-counter drugs in pharmacies, but in some cases a local doctor's prescription is required. Other handy items—especially if you will be traveling on your own or camping—include toilet paper, facial tissues, and a flashlight (for occasional power outages or use at campsites).

If you have a health problem that may require you to purchase a prescription drug, take enough to last the duration of the trip. And don't forget to pack a list of the addresses of offices that supply refunds for lost or stolen traveler's checks. Snorkelers should consider bringing their own equipment unless traveling light is a priority; shoes with rubber soles for rocky underwater surfaces are also advised. For long-term stays in remote rural areas, *see* Staying Healthy, *below.*

Customs will allow you to bring one still and one movie or video camera, with 12 rolls of film for each; bring the limit, because film is expensive in Mexico.

Luggage Regulations Free baggage allowances on an airline depend on the airline, the route, and the class of your ticket. In general, on domestic flights and on international flights between the United States and foreign destinations, you are entitled to check two bags—neither exceeding 62 inches, or 158 centimeters (length + width + height), or weighing more than 70 pounds (32 kilograms). A third piece may be brought aboard as a carryon; its total dimensions are generally limited to less than 45 inches (114 centimeters), so it will fit easily under the seat in front of you or in the overhead compartment. There are variations, so ask in advance. The single rule, a Federal Aviation Administration safety regulation that pertains to carry-on baggage on U.S. airlines, requires only that carryons be properly stowed and allows the airline to limit allowances and tailor them to different aircraft and operational conditions. Charges for excess, oversize, or overweight pieces vary, so inquire before you pack. If you are flying between two foreign destinations, note that baggage allowances may be determined not by the piece method but by the weight method, which generally allows 88 pounds (40 kilograms) of luggage in first class, 66 pounds (30 kilograms) in business class, and 44 pounds (20 kilograms) in economy. If your flight between two cities abroad *connects* with your transatlantic or transpacific flight, the piece method still applies.

Safeguarding Your Luggage Before leaving home, itemize your bags' contents and their worth; this list will help you estimate the extent of your loss if your bags go astray. To minimize that risk, tag them inside and out with your name, address, and phone number. (If you use your home address, cover it so that potential thieves can't see it.) At check-in, make sure that the tag attached by baggage handlers bears the correct three-letter code for your destination. If your bags do not arrive with you, or if you detect damage, do not leave the airport until you've filed a written report with the airline.

Insurance In the event of loss, damage, or theft on domestic flights, airlines limit their liability to $20 per kilogram for checked baggage (roughly about $640 per 70-pound bag) and $400 per passenger for unchecked baggage. On domestic flights, the ceiling is $1,250 per passenger. Excess-valuation insurance can be bought directly from the airline at check-in but leaves your bags vulnerable on the ground. Your own homeowner's policy may fill the gap; or you may want special luggage insurance. Sources include **The Travelers Companies** (1 Tower Sq., Hartford, CT 06183, tel. 203/277–0111 or 800/243–3174) and **Wallach and Company, Inc.** (107 W. Federal St., Box 480, Middleburg, VA 22117, tel. 703/687–3166 or 800/237–6615), underwritten by Lloyds, London.

Electricity   Electrical converters are not necessary, because the country operates on the 60-cycle, 120-volt system; however, most Mexican outlets have not been updated to accommodate three-prong and polarized plugs (those with one larger prong), so you may need an adapter.

Taking Money Abroad

Traveler's checks and major U.S. credit cards are accepted in larger cities and resorts, although American Express is accepted somewhat less often than MasterCard and Visa. Many stores will take your credit cards but tack on a surcharge of about 6%, claiming that this is what they will have to pay the credit card companies. Whether or not this is true, or even legal, is a moot point in Mexico. The general rule is that you get a better deal with cash or traveler's checks. However, there is some risk involved in carrying cash, and even traveler's checks are not always that convenient to replace, so you will have to weigh the trade-off yourself.

Traveler's Checks   Although you will want plenty of cash when visiting small cities or rural areas, traveler's checks are generally preferable. The most widely recognized are **American Express, Barclay's, Thomas Cook,** and those issued by major commercial banks such as **Citibank** and **Bank of America.** American Express also issues *Traveler's Cheques for Two,* which can be signed and used by you or your traveling companion. Although some checks are free, you will usually pay 1% of the checks' face value as a fee. Be sure to buy a few checks in small denominations to cash toward the end of your trip, when you don't want to be left with more foreign currency than you can spend. (There is no limit on the amount of pesos that can be changed back into dollars; however, coins are not accepted.) Always record the numbers of checks as you spend them, and keep this list separate from the checks.

Currency   Banks charge the lowest commissions on currency exchange,
Exchange   but their hours (weekdays 9–1:30, in most cases) may not suit you; you should also avoid the 15th and 30th of the month, when Mexicans are paid. Next best are probably the exchange houses (*casas de cambio*), and your last resort should be the hotel cashier's desk. Changing money on the street is not a good idea.

Though you won't get as good an exchange rate at home as abroad, it's wise to change a small amount of money into pesos before you go: Lines at airport currency-exchange booths can be very long, and in any event they are not always open when flights arrive late at night or on Sundays. **Thomas Cook Currency Services** (630 5th Ave., New York, NY 10111, tel. 212/757–6915) supplies foreign currency by mail.

Getting Money from Home

Cash Machines   Automated-teller machines (ATMs) are proliferating; many are affiliated with international networks such as **Cirrus,** which has 60,000 machines worldwide, and **Plus,** which has 80,000. Thanks to such networks, you can use your bank card away from home to withdraw money from an account and to get cash advances on a credit-card account (providing your card has been programmed with a personal identification number, or

PIN). Check in advance on limits on withdrawals and cash advances within specified periods. Ask whether your PIN number will need to be reprogrammed for use in the area you'll be visiting—a possibility if the number has more than four digits.

For specific foreign Cirrus locations, call 800/424–7787; for foreign Plus locations, consult the Plus directory at your local bank.

Withdrawals　Although transaction fees for ATM withdrawals abroad will probably be higher than fees for withdrawals at home, Cirrus and Plus exchange rates tend to be good. But plan ahead: Obtain ATM locations and the names of affiliated cash-machine networks before departure.

Cash Advances　Remember that finance charges apply on credit-card cash advances and you are charged interest from the day you get the money from ATMs as well as from tellers.

American Express Cardholder Services　The company's **Express Cash** system lets you withdraw cash and/or traveler's checks from a worldwide network of 57,000 American Express dispensers and participating bank ATMs. You must *enroll first* (call 800/227–4669 for a form and allow two weeks for processing). Withdrawals are charged not to your card but to a designated bank account. You can withdraw up to $1,000 per seven-day period on the basic card, more if your card is gold or platinum. There is a 2% fee (minimum $2.50, maximum $10) for each cash transaction, and a 1% fee for traveler's checks (except for the platinum card), which are available only from American Express dispensers.

At AmEx offices, cardholders can also cash personal checks for up to $1,000 in any 21-day period; of this $200 can be in cash, more if available, with the balance paid in traveler's checks, for which all but platinum cardholders pay a 1% fee. Higher limits apply to gold and platinum cards.

Wiring Money　You don't have to be a cardholder to send or receive an **American Express MoneyGram** for up to $10,000. To send one, go to an American Express MoneyGram agent, pay up to $1,000 with a credit card and anything over that in cash, and phone a transaction reference number to your intended recipient, who needs only present identification and the reference number to the nearest MoneyGram agent to pick up the cash. There are MoneyGram agents in more than 60 countries (call 800/543–4080 for locations); there are agents in Mérida and Cozumel, through Banamex, and three offices in Cancún. Fees range from 5% to 10%, depending on the amount and how you pay. You can't use American Express, which is really a convenience card—only Discover, MasterCard, and Visa credit cards.

You can also use **Western Union.** To wire money, take either cash or a check to the nearest office. (Or you can call and use a credit card.) Fees are roughly 5%–10%. Money sent from the United States or Canada will be available for pickup at agent locations in Mexico within minutes. (Note that once the money is in the system it can be picked up at *any* location. You don't have to miss your train waiting for it to arrive in City A, because if there's an agent in City B, where you're headed, you can pick it up there, too.) There are approximately 20,000 agents worldwide (call 800/325–6000 for locations).

Currency

As of January 1, 1993 the new unit of currency in Mexico is the *nuevo peso,* or new peso, which is subdivided into 100 centavos. At press time (March 1993) one U.S. dollar was equal to three nuevo pesos, one Canadian dollar was equal to 2.3 pesos, and a pound sterling equaled 4.11 pesos. The old peso, which had a cumbersome exchange of 3,000 to one U.S. dollar, is suppose to be completely phased out by January 1994, but at press time there was still a lot of old currency in circulation, and many public phones and vending machines still accepted only the old coins. The new paper currency is the same color as the old and comes in denominations of 10, 20, 50, and 100, equal to the old 10,000, 20,000, 50,000, and 100,000 notes, respectively. Newly introduced are the 2-, 5-, and 10-peso coins, which replace the 2,000, 5,000, and 10,000 notes. The 1,000-, 500-, 200-, 100-, and 50-peso coins have been replaced by the smaller, newly designed 1-peso and 50-, 20-, 10-, and 5-centavo coins. Needless to say, it is somewhat confusing. Travelers should examine coins carefully before paying and when receiving change.

Dollars are widely accepted in many parts of Mexico, particularly near the border and in Cozumel. Many tourist shops and market vendors, as well as virtually all hotel service personnel, take them, too.

What It Will Cost

Mexico has a reputation for being inexpensive, particularly compared with other North American vacation spots such as the Caribbean. Cancún, however, is probably the most expensive destination in Mexico, with Cozumel running a close second. In Mérida and the other cities in Yucatán, which are considerably less expensive, you will find the best value for your money. For obvious reasons, if you stay at international chain hotels and eat at restaurants geared to tourists (especially hotel restaurants), you may not find Yucatán such a bargain.

Rates in Yucatán decrease in the off-season by as much as 30%. Speaking Spanish is helpful in bargaining and when asking for dining recommendations. As a general rule, the less that English is spoken in a region, the cheaper things will be (*see also* Language, *below*).

Sample costs are as follows: cup of coffee, NP$3; bottle of beer, NP$5; plate of tacos, NP$5 or, with rice and beans, NP$10–12; 2-km taxi ride, NP$5.

Off-season, Cancún hotels cost one-third to one-half what they cost during the peak season. Cozumel is less costly than Cancún, and Isla Mujeres is slightly less costly than Cozumel.

Taxes Mexico has a value-added tax, or I.V.A. (*impuesto de valor agregado*) of 10%, which is occasionally (and illegally) waived for cash purchases. Other taxes and charges apply for phone calls, dining, and lodging. An air departure tax of US$12 or the peso equivalent must be paid at the airport for international flights from Mexico, and there is a domestic air departure tax of US$4.86. Traveler's checks and credit cards are not accepted as payment for these taxes.

Passports and Visas

If your passport is lost or stolen abroad, report it immediately to the nearest embassy or consulate and to the local police. If you can provide the consular officer with the information contained in the passport, they will usually be able to issue you a new passport. For this reason, it is a good idea to keep a copy of the data page of your passport in a separate place, or to leave the passport number, date, and place of issuance with a relative or friend at home.

U.S. Citizens   U.S. citizens can enter Mexico with a tourist card and proof of citizenship. The only acceptable proof of citizenship is either a valid passport or a certified birth certificate plus a photo ID. Tourist cards are available from any Mexican consulate or tourism office and from most airlines serving Mexico. They are valid for a single entry for up to six months. For more information, contact the **Mexican Consulate** (2827 16th St. NW, Washington, DC 20009, tel. 202/736–1000, and at 39 other U.S. locations).

You can pick up new and renewal application forms at any of the 13 U.S. Passport Agency offices and at some post offices and courthouses. Although passports are usually mailed within two weeks of your application's receipt, it's best to allow three weeks for delivery in low season, five weeks or more from April through summer. Call the Department of State Office of Passport Services' information line (1425 K St. NW, Washington, DC 20522, tel. 202/647–0518) for details.

Canadian Citizens   Canadian citizens also need a tourist card and proof of citizenship to enter Mexico. Application forms are available at 23 regional passport offices as well as post offices and travel agencies. Passports are valid for five years and are usually mailed within two weeks of an application's receipt. For fees, documentation requirements, and other information in English or French, call the Passport Office (tel. 514/283–2152).

U.K. Citizens   Applications are available from six passport offices and main post offices. You may apply in person at any passport office or by mail to all except the London office. Children under 16 may travel on a parent's passport when accompanying them. All passports are valid for 10 years. Allow a month for processing.

Customs and Duties

On Arrival   Entering Mexico, you may bring in (1) 200 cigarettes or 50 cigars or 250 grams of tobacco, (2) up to 3 liters of wine and spirits, (3) one photographic camera and one 18mm film or video camera and 12 rolls of film for each, and (4) gift items not exceeding a combined value of $300. You are not allowed to bring meat, vegetables, plants, fruit, or flowers into the country.

On Departure   Provided you've been out of the country for at least 48 hours
U.S. Customs   and haven't already used the exemption, or any part of it, in the past 30 days, you may bring home $400 worth of foreign goods duty-free. So can each member of your family, regardless of age; and your exemptions may be pooled, so that one of you can bring in more if another brings in less. A flat 10% duty applies to the next $1,000 of goods; above $1,400, the rate varies with the merchandise. (If the 48-hour or 30-day limits apply,

your duty-free allowance drops to $25, which may *not* be pooled.) Because Mexico is considered a developing country, many arts and handicrafts may be brought back into the United States duty-free as part of the U.S. Generalized System of Preferences (GSP) program. Though these allowances are in addition to the $400 limit, you will still need to declare the items and state their value and purpose.

Travelers 21 or older may bring back one liter of alcohol duty-free, provided the beverage laws of the state through which they reenter the U.S. allow it. In addition, 100 non-Cuban cigars and 200 cigarettes are allowed, regardless of age. Antiques and works of art over 100 years old are duty-free.

Gifts under $50 may be mailed duty-free to stateside friends and relatives, with a limit of one package per day per addressee (do not send alcohol or tobacco products, nor perfume valued at over $5). These gifts do not count as part of your exemption, although if you bring them home with you, they do. Mark the package "Unsolicited Gift" and include the nature of the gift and its retail value.

For a copy of "Know Before You Go," a free brochure detailing what you may and may not bring back to the United States, rates of duty, and other pointers, contact the **U.S. Customs Service** (Box 7407, Washington, DC 20044, tel. 202/927–6724). A copy of "GSP and the Traveler" is available from the same source.

Canadian Customs Once per calendar year, when you've been out of Canada for at least seven days, you may bring in $300 worth of goods duty-free. If you've been away less than seven days but more than 48 hours, the duty-free exemption drops to $100 but can be claimed any number of times (as can a $20 duty-free exemption for absences of 24 hours or more). You cannot combine the yearly and 48-hour exemptions, use the $300 exemption only partially (to save the balance for a later trip), or pool exemptions with family members. Goods claimed under the $300 exemption may follow you by mail; those claimed under the lesser exemptions must accompany you on your return.

Alcohol and tobacco products may be included in the yearly and 48-hour exemptions but not in the 24-hour exemption. If you meet the age requirements of the province through which you reenter Canada, you may bring in, duty-free, 1.14 liters (40 imperial ounces) of wine or liquor *or* two dozen 12-ounce cans or bottles of beer or ale. If you are 16 or older, you may bring in, duty-free, 200 cigarettes, 50 cigars or cigarillos, and 400 tobacco sticks or 400 grams of manufactured tobacco. Alcohol and tobacco must accompany you on your return.

Gifts may be mailed to friends in Canada duty-free. These do not count as part of your exemption. Each gift may be worth up to $60—label the package "Unsolicited Gift—Value under $60." There are no limits on the number of gifts that may be sent per day or per addressee, but you can't mail alcohol or tobacco.

For more information, including details of duties on items that exceed your duty-free limit, ask the Revenue Canada Customs and Excise Department (Connaught Bldg., MacKenzie Ave., Ottawa, Ont., K1A OL5, tel. 613/957–0275) for a copy of the free brochure "I Declare/Je Déclare."

U.K. Customs From countries outside the EC, such as Mexico, you may import duty-free 200 cigarettes, 100 cigarillos, 50 cigars or 250 grams of tobacco; 1 liter of spirits or 2 liters of fortified or sparkling wine; 2 liters of still table wine; 60 milliliters of perfume; 250 milliliters of toilet water; plus £36 worth of other goods, including gifts and souvenirs.

For further information or a copy of "A Guide for Travellers," which details standard customs procedures as well as what you may bring into the United Kingdom from abroad, contact HM Customs and Excise (New King's Beam House, 22 Upper Ground, London SE1 9PJ, tel. 071/620–1313).

Traveling with Cameras and Camcorders

About Film and Cameras If your camera is new or if you haven't used it for a while, shoot and develop a few rolls of film before leaving home. Pack some lens tissue and an extra battery for your built-in light meter, and invest in an inexpensive skylight filter, to both protect your lens and provide some definition in hazy shots. Store film in a cool, dry place—never in the car's glove compartment or on the shelf under the rear window.

Films above ISO 400 are more sensitive to damage from airport security X-rays than others; very high speed films, ISO 1,000 and above, are exceedingly vulnerable. To protect your film, don't put it in checked luggage; carry it with you in a plastic bag and ask for a hand inspection. Such requests are honored at American airports, up to the inspector elsewhere. Don't depend on a lead-lined bag to protect film in checked luggage—the airline may very well turn up the dosage of radiation to see what you've got in there. Airport metal detectors do not harm film, although you'll set off the alarm if you walk through one with a roll in your pocket. Call the Kodak Information Center (tel. 800/242–2424) for details.

About Camcorders Before your trip, put new or long-unused camcorders through their paces, and practice panning and zooming. Invest in a skylight filter to protect the lens, and check the lithium battery that lights up the LCD (liquid crystal display) modes. As for the rechargeable nickel-cadmium batteries that are the camera's power source, take along an extra pair, so while you're using your camcorder you'll have one battery ready and another recharging. Most newer camcorders are equipped with the battery (which generally slides or clicks onto the camera body) and, to recharge it, with what's known as a universal or worldwide AC adapter charger (or multivoltage converter) that can be used whether the voltage is 110 or 220. All that's needed then is the appropriate plug.

About Videotape Unlike still-camera film, videotape is not damaged by X-rays. However, it may well be harmed by the magnetic field of a walk-through metal detector. Airport security personnel may want you to turn the camcorder on to prove that that's what it is, so make sure the battery is charged when you get to the airport. Bring plenty of blank tapes, since they cost more in Mexico.

Language

Spanish is the official language of Mexico, although Indian languages are spoken by approximately 20% of the population, many of whom speak no Spanish at all. This is the case in

Mérida and much of the State of Yucatán, where Mayan dialects are spoken. In the beach resorts of Cancún and Cozumel, English is understood by most people employed in tourism; at the very least, shopkeepers will know the numbers for bargaining purposes. Mexicans welcome even the most halting attempts to use their language, and if you are in Mérida, you may even be introduced to a few Mayan words and phrases. For a rudimentary vocabulary of terms that travelers are likely to encounter in Yucatán, *see* the Spanish Vocabulary and Menu at the end of this book.

The Spanish most North Americans learn in high school is based on Castilian Spanish, which is different from Latin American Spanish. In terms of grammar, Mexican Spanish ignores the *vosotros* form of the second person. As for pronunciation, the lisped Castilian "c" or "z" is dismissed in Mexico as a sign of affectation. The most obvious differences are in vocabulary: Mexican Spanish has thousands of Indian words, and the use of *¿mande?* instead of *¿cómo?* (excuse me?) is a dead giveaway that one's Spanish was acquired in Mexico. Words or phrases that are harmless or commonplace in one Spanish-speaking country can take on salacious or otherwise offensive meanings in another. Unless you are lucky enough to be briefed on these nuances by a native coach, the only way to learn is by trial and error.

Staying Healthy

Shots and Medications The major health risk in Yucatán, as elsewhere in Mexico, is posed by the contamination of drinking water and fresh fruit and vegetables by fecal matter, which causes the intestinal ailment known facetiously as Montezuma's Revenge and more mundanely as traveler's diarrhea. It usually lasts only a day or two. A good antidiarrheal agent is paregoric, which dulls or eliminates abdominal cramps, but you will need a doctor's prescription to get it in Mexico. Two drugs recommended by the National Institutes of Health for mild cases of diarrhea can, however, be purchased over the counter: Pepto-Bismol and loperamide (Imodium). If you come down with the malady, rest as much as possible and drink lots of fluids (such as tea without milk—chamomile is quite common in Mexico, and a good folk remedy for diarrhea). In severe cases, rehydrate yourself with a salt-sugar mixture added to purified water. The best defense against food- and water-borne diseases is a careful diet. Stay away from unbottled or unboiled water, ice, raw food, and unpasteurized milk and milk products.

According to the Centers for Disease Control (CDC), there is a limited risk of malaria, hepatitis B, dengue, and rabies in certain rural areas of Mexico. Travelers to the beach resorts need have no worries. However, if you plan to visit remote regions or stay for more than six weeks, check with the CDC's **International Travelers Information Hotline** (Center for Preventive Services, Division of Quarantine, Traveler's Health section, 1600 Clifton Rd., MSE03, Atlanta, GA 30333, tel. 404/332–4559). The hot line recommends chloroquine (Analen) as an antimalarial agent. Malaria-bearing mosquitoes bite at night, so travelers to susceptible regions should take mosquito nets, wear clothing that covers the body, and carry repellent containing Deet and a spray against flying insects for living and sleeping areas. There is currently no vaccine against dengue, so travelers should use aerosol insecticides indoors as well as repellents against the mosquito, which bites in daytime.

Scuba divers take note: PADI recommends that you not scuba dive and fly within a 24-hour period.

Finding a Doctor The **International Association for Medical Assistance to Travellers** (IAMAT, 417 Center St., Lewiston, NY 14092, tel. 716/754–4883; 40 Regal Rd., Guelph, Ontario N1K 1B5; 57 Voirets, 1212 Grand-Lancy, Geneva, Switzerland) publishes a worldwide directory of English-speaking physicians whose qualifications meet IAMAT standards and who have agreed to treat members for a set fee. Membership is free.

Insurance

For U.S. Residents Most tour operators, travel agents, and insurance agents sell specialized health-and-accident, flight, trip-cancellation, and luggage insurance as well as comprehensive policies with some or all of these features. But before you make any purchase, review your existing health and homeowner policies to find out whether they cover expenses incurred while traveling.

Car Rentals

Most major car-rental companies are represented in Cancún, including **Avis** (tel. 800/331–1212, 800/879–2847 in Canada); **Budget** (tel. 800/527–0700); **Dollar** (tel. 800/800–4000); **Hertz** (tel. 800/654–3131, 800/263-0600 in Canada); **National** (tel. 800/227–7368), known internationally as InterRent and Europcar. Daily car-rental rates vary from about $20 to $120. Not included in the daily rate are a per-kilometer charge and insurance and tax, which on car rentals in Cancún is 10%. Weekly package rates including unlimited free mileage cost about $150–$700.

Requirements You'll need a driver's license from your home country and a major credit card. Note that without a credit card, you may not be able to rent a car in Cancún.

When you drive in Cancún or anywhere in the Yucatán area, it is necessary to carry at all times proof of Mexican auto insurance, which is usually provided by car rental agencies and included in the cost of the rental. If you don't carry proof of insurance and happen to injure someone—whether it's your fault or not—you stand the risk of being jailed.

Extra Charges Picking up the car in one city or country and leaving it in another may entail drop-off charges or one-way service fees, which can be substantial (up to 33¢ per kilometer). The cost of a collision or loss-damage waiver (*see below*) can be high, also. Automatic transmissions and air-conditioning are not universally available; ask for them when you book if you want them, and check the cost before you commit yourself to the rental.

Cutting Costs If you know you will want a car for more than a day or two, you can save by planning ahead. Major international companies have programs that discount their standard rates by 15%–30% if you make the reservation before departure (anywhere from two to 14 days), rent for a minimum number of days (typically three or four), and prepay the rental. Ask about these advance-purchase schemes when you call for information. More economical rentals are those that come as part of fly/drive or other packages, even those as bare-bones as the rental plus an airline ticket (*see* Tours and Packages, *above*).

One last tip: Remember to fill the tank when you turn in the vehicle, to avoid being charged for refueling at what you'll swear is the most expensive pump in town.

Insurance and Collision Damage Waiver The standard rental contract includes liability coverage (for damage to public property, injury to pedestrians, etc.) and coverage for the car against fire, theft (not included in certain countries), and collision damage with a deductible—most commonly $2,000–$3,000, occasionally more. In the case of an accident, you are responsible for the deductible amount unless you've purchased the collision damage waiver (CDW), which costs an average $12 a day, although this varies depending on what you've rented, where, and from whom.

Because this adds up quickly, you may be inclined to say "no thanks"—and that's certainly your option, although the rental agent may not tell you so. Planning ahead will help you make the right decision. By all means, find out if your own insurance covers damage to a rental car while traveling (not simply a car to drive when yours is in for repairs). And check whether charging car rentals to any of your credit cards will get you a CDW at no charge. Note before you decline that deductibles are occasionally high enough that totaling a car would make you responsible for its full value.

Student and Youth Travel

Travel Agencies The foremost U.S. student travel agency is **Council Travel,** a subsidiary of the nonprofit Council on International Educational Exchange. It specializes in low-cost travel arrangements, is the exclusive U.S. agent for several discount cards, and, with its sister CIEE subsidiary, **Council Charter,** is a source of airfare bargains. The Council Charter brochure and CIEE's twice-yearly *Student Travels* magazine, which details its programs, are available at the Council Travel office at CIEE headquarters (205 E. 42nd Street, New York, NY 10017, tel. 212/661–1450) and at 37 branches in college towns nationwide (free in person, $1 by mail). The **Educational Travel Center** (ETC, 438 N. Francis St., Madison, WI 53703, tel. 608/256–5551) also offers low-cost rail passes, domestic and international airline tickets (mostly for flights departing from Chicago), and other budgetwise travel arrangements. Other travel agencies catering to students include **Travel Management International** (TMI, 18 Prescott St., Suite 4, Cambridge, MA 02138, tel. 617/661–8187) and **Travel Cuts** (187 College St., Toronto, Ont. M5T 1P7, tel. 416/979–2406).

Discount Cards For discounts on transportation and on museum and attractions admissions, buy the **International Student Identity Card** (ISIC) if you're a bona fide student, or the **International Youth Card** (IYC) if you're under 26. In the United States the ISIC and IYC cards cost $15 each and include basic travel accident and sickness coverage. Apply to **CIEE** (*see* address *above,* tel. 212/661–1414; the application is in *Student Travels*). In Canada the cards are available for $15 each from **Travel Cuts** (*see above*). In the United Kingdom they cost £5 and £4, respectively, at student unions and student travel companies, including Council Travel's London office (28A Poland St., London W1V 3DB, tel. 071/437–7767).

Hosteling An **International Youth Hostel Federation** (IYHF) membership card is the key to more than 5,300 hostel locations in 59 countries; the sex-segregated, dormitory-style sleeping quarters, including some for families, go for $7–$20 a night per person. Membership is available in the United States through **American Youth Hostels** (AYH, 733 15th St. NW, Washington, DC 20005, tel. 202/783–6161), the American link in the worldwide chain, and costs $25 for adults 18–54, $10 for those under 18, $15 for those 55 and over, and $35 for families. *Hostelling North America*, a guide to hostels in North America, is free to members ($8 to nonmembers, postage included). IYHF membership is available in Canada through the **Canadian Hostelling Association** (CHA, 1600 James Naismith Dr., Suite 608, Gloucester, Ont. K1B 5N4, tel. 613/748–5638) for $26.75, and in the United Kingdom through the **Youth Hostel Association of England and Wales** (Trevelyan House, 8 St. Stephen's Hill, St. Albans, Herts. AL1 2DY, tel. 0727/55215) for £9.

Traveling with Children

The advisability of traveling with children in Yucatán will depend on the age and maturity of your child. Infants may be bothered by the heat, and finding pure water or fresh milk may be a problem. Since children are especially prone to diarrhea, special care must be taken with regard to food. If they enjoy travel in general, children will probably do well in Yucatán, where they can clamber over ruins and frolic on beaches.

Getting There On international flights, the fare for infants under 2 not occu-
Airfares pying a seat is generally 10% of the accompanying adult's fare; children ages 2–11 usually pay half to two-thirds of the adult fare. On domestic flights, children under 2 not occupying a seat travel free, and older children currently travel on the "lowest applicable" adult fare. Other routes are considered neither international nor domestic and have still other rules.

Baggage In general, infants paying 10% of the adult fare are allowed one carry-on bag, not to exceed 70 pounds or 45 inches (length + width + height). The adult baggage allowance applies for children paying half or more of the adult fare. Check with the airline for particulars.

Safety Seats The FAA recommends the use of safety seats aloft and details approved models in the free leaflet "**Child/Infant Safety Seats Recommended for Use in Aircraft**" (available from the Federal Aviation Administration, APA–200, 800 Independence Ave. SW, Washington, DC 20591, tel. 202/267–3479). Airline policy varies. U.S. carriers must allow FAA-approved models, but because these seats are strapped into a regular passenger seat, they may require that parents buy a ticket even for an infant under 2 who would otherwise ride free. Foreign carriers may not allow infant seats, may charge the child's rather than the infant's fare for their use, or may require you to hold your baby during takeoff and landing, thus defeating the seat's purpose.

Lodging Several hotel chains provide services that make it easier to travel with children. The **Westin Camino Real Hotel** (tel. 800/228–3000) in Cancún offers free summer activities for children and a comprehensive recreational and sports program for teenagers. The **Cancún Sheraton Hotel** (tel. 800/334–8484) provides connecting "family rooms" at regular rates. **Club Med**

(tel. 800/CLUB–MED) offers special programs for children and teenagers, including visits to Cancún's attractions.

Baby-sitting English-speaking baby-sitters are available through a number
Services of Cancún's large hotels and resorts. Ask the concierge at your hotel or the local tourist office for further information.

Publications *Family Travel Times,* published 10 times a year by **Travel With**
Newsletter **Your Children** (TWYCH, 45 W. 18th St., 7th Floor Tower, New York, NY 10011, tel. 212/206–0688; annual subscription $55), covers destinations, types of vacations, and modes of travel; an airline issue comes out every other year (the last one, February/March 1993, is sold to nonsubscribers for $10). On Wednesday, the staff answers subscribers' questions on specific destinations.

Books *Great Vacations with Your Kids,* by Dorothy Jordan and Marjorie Cohen ($13; Penguin USA, 120 Woodbine St., Bergenfield, NJ 07621, tel. 800/253–6476) and *Traveling with Children— And Enjoying It,* by Arlene K. Butler ($11.95 plus $3 shipping per book; Globe Pequot Press, Box 833, Old Saybrook, CT 06475, tel. 800/243–0495 or 800/962–0973), help you plan your trip with children, from toddlers to teens. Also from Globe Pequot is *Recommended Family Resorts in the United States, Canada, and the Caribbean,* by Jane Wilford with Janet Tice ($12.95), which describes 100 resorts at length and includes a "Children's World" section describing activities and facilities as part of each entry.

Tour Operators **GrandTravel** (6900 Wisconsin Ave., Suite 706, Chevy Chase, MD 20815, tel. 301/986–0790 or 800/247–7651) offers tours for grandparents traveling with their grandchildren. The catalogue, as charmingly written and illustrated as a children's book, positively invites armchair traveling with lap-sitters aboard. **Rascals in Paradise** (650 5th St., Suite 505, San Francisco, CA 94107, tel. 415/978–9800 or 800/872–7225) specializes in programs for families.

Hints for Travelers with Disabilities

For people with disabilities, traveling in the Yucatán can be both challenging and rewarding. Mobility impaired travelers used to venturing on their own in the United States should not be surprised if locals try to prevent them from doing things. This is mainly out of concern; most Mexican families take complete care of wheelchair-bound relatives, so the general public is not accustomed to interacting with them. Additionally, very few places in the Yucatán have handrails, let alone special facilities and means of access. Knowing how to ask for assistance is extremely important. If you are not fluent in Spanish, be sure to take along a pocket dictionary. Visually impaired travelers with no knowledge of Spanish will probably need a translator; the hearing impaired who are comfortable using body language usually get along very well.

Lodging Many chain hotels are wheelchair-accessible, including the **Radisson Paraiso Cancún** (tel. 800/333–3333), the **Hyatt Cancún Caribe** (tel. 800/228–9000), and the **Hyatt Regency** (tel. 800/228–9000).

Organizations Several organizations provide travel information for people with disabilities, usually for a membership fee, and some publish newsletters and bulletins. Among them are the **Informa-**

tion Center for Individuals with Disabilities (Fort Point Pl., 27–43 Wormwood St., Boston, MA 02210, tel. 617/727–5540 or 800/462–5015 in MA between 11 and 4, or leave message; TDD/TTY tel. 617/345–9743); **Mobility International USA** (Box 3551, Eugene, OR 97403, voice and TDD tel. 503/343–1284), the U.S. branch of an international organization based in Britain and present in 30 countries; **MossRehab Hospital Travel Information Service** (1200 W. Tabor Rd., Philadelphia, PA 19141, tel. 215/456–9603, TDD tel. 215/456– 9602); The **Society for the Advancement of Travel for the Handicapped** (SATH, 347 5th Ave., Suite 610, New York, NY 10016, tel. 212/447–7284, fax 212/725–8253); **Travel Industry and Disabled Exchange** (TIDE, 5435 Donna Ave., Tarzana, CA 91356, tel. 818/368–5648); and **Travelin' Talk** (Box 3534, Clarksville, TN 37043, tel. 615/552–6670).

Travel Agencies and Tour Operators **Directions Unlimited** (720 N. Bedford Rd., Bedford Hills, NY 10507, tel. 914/241–1700), a travel agency, has expertise in tours and cruises for the disabled. **Evergreen Travel Service** (4114 198th St. SW, Suite 13, Lynnwood, WA 98036, tel. 206/776–1184 or 800/435–2288) operates Wings on Wheels Tours for those in wheelchairs, White Cane Tours for the blind, and tours for the deaf, and makes group and independent arrangements for travelers with any disability. **Flying Wheels Travel** (143 W. Bridge St., Box 382, Owatonna, MN 55060, tel. 800/535–6790 or 800/722–9351 in MN), a tour operator and travel agency, arranges international tours, cruises, and independent travel itineraries for people with mobility disabilities. **Nautilus**, at the same address as TIDE (*see above*), packages tours for the disabled internationally.

In the United Kingdom Main sources include the **Royal Association for Disability and Rehabilitation** (RADAR, 25 Mortimer St., London W1N 8AB, tel. 071/637–5400), which publishes travel information for the disabled in Britain, and **Mobility International** (228 Borough High St., London SE1 1JX, tel. 071/403–5688), the headquarters of an international membership organization that serves as a clearinghouse of travel information for people with disabilities.

Publications In addition to the fact sheets, newsletters, and books mentioned above are several free publications available from the Consumer Information Center (Pueblo, CO 81009): "New Horizons for the Air Traveler with a Disability," a U.S. Department of Transportation booklet describing changes resulting from the 1986 Air Carrier Access Act and those still to come from the 1990 Americans with Disabilities Act (include Department 608Y in the address), and the Airport Operators Council's *Access Travel: Airports* (Dept. 5804), which describes facilities and services for the disabled at more than 500 airports worldwide.

Twin Peaks Press (Box 129, Vancouver, WA 98666, tel. 206/694–2462 or 800/637–2256) publishes the *Directory of Travel Agencies for the Disabled* ($19.95), listing more than 370 agencies worldwide; *Travel for the Disabled* ($19.95), listing some 500 access guides and accessible places worldwide; the *Directory of Accessible Van Rentals* ($9.95) for campers and RV travelers worldwide; and *Wheelchair Vagabond* ($14.95), a collection of personal travel tips. Add $2 per book for shipping.

Hints for Older Travelers

Active older travelers who enjoy outdoor attractions, especially water-related activities, will enjoy Yucatán. Being in good physical shape is a definite advantage. If proximity to medical services is a major concern, travelers of all ages should keep to the major resorts and cities.

Organizations The **American Association of Retired Persons** (AARP, 601 E St. NW, Washington, DC 20049, tel. 202/434–2277) provides independent travelers the Purchase Privilege Program, which offers discounts on hotels, car rentals, and sightseeing, and the AARP Motoring Plan, provided by Amoco, which furnishes domestic trip-routing information and emergency road-service aid for an annual fee of $39.95 per person or couple ($59.95 for a premium version). AARP also arranges group tours, cruises, and apartment living through AARP Travel Experience from American Express (400 Pinnacle Way, Suite 450, Norcross, GA 30071, tel. 800/927–0111); these can be booked through travel agents, except for the cruises, which must be booked directly (tel. 800/745–4567). AARP membership is open to those 50 and over; annual dues are $8 per person or couple.

Two other membership organizations offer discounts on lodgings, car rentals, and other travel products, along with such nontravel perks as magazines and newsletters. The **National Council of Senior Citizens** (1331 F St. NW, Washington, DC 20004, tel. 202/347–8800) is a nonprofit advocacy group with some 5,000 local clubs across the United States; membership costs $12 per person or couple annually. **Mature Outlook** (6001 N. Clark St., Chicago, IL 60660, tel. 800/336–6330), a Sears Roebuck & Co. subsidiary with 800,000 members, charges $9.95 for an annual membership.

Note: When using any senior-citizen identification card for reduced hotel rates, mention it when booking, not when checking out. At restaurants, show your card before you're seated; discounts may be limited to certain menus, days, or hours. If you are renting a car, ask about promotional rates that might improve on your senior-citizen discount.

Educational Travel **Elderhostel** (75 Federal St., 3rd floor, Boston, MA 02110, tel. 617/426–7788) is a nonprofit organization that has run inexpensive study programs for people 60 and older since 1975. Programs take place at more than 1,800 educational institutions in the United States, Canada, and 45 countries overseas, and courses cover everything from marine science to Greek myths and cowboy poetry. Participants generally attend lectures in the morning and spend the afternoon sightseeing or on field trips; they live in dorms on the host campuses. Unique homestay programs are offered in a few countries. Fees for the two- to three-week international trips—including room, board, tuition, and transportation from the United States—range from $1,800 to $4,500.

Tour Operators **Saga International Holidays** (222 Berkeley St., Boston, MA 02116, tel. 800/343–0273), which specializes in group travel for people over 60, offers a selection of variously priced tours and cruises covering five continents. If you want to take your grandchildren, look into **GrandTravel** (*see* Traveling with Children, *above*).

Further Reading

Most English-language books about Yucatán focus on the ancient Maya and the archaeological sites. Popularized scholarly descriptions of Mayan history, architecture, religion, astronomy, and culture include *The Maya*, by Michael D. Coe; *Maya*, by Charles Gallenkamp; *The Ancient Maya*, by Sylvanus G. Morley; *The Rise and Fall of Maya Civilization*, by J. Eric S. Thompson; and *World of the Maya*, by Victor Von Hagen. *The Maya World*, by Demetrio Sodi Morales, weaves information on the modern-day Mayan region into a discussion of architecture and history, but the book is sold only in Mexico. For a more contemporary overview of the ground-breaking work that has revolutionized our understanding of the Maya, see the handsome coffee-table book entitled *The Blood of Kings: Dynasty & Ritual in Maya Art*, by Linda Schele and Mary Ellen Miller. Also by Linda Schele, with David Freidel, is the newer *A Forest of Kings: The Untold Story of the Ancient Maya*. For a scholarly overview of the region's history, people, politics, and literature, try *Yucatán: A World Apart*, edited by E. H. Moseley and E. D. Terry.

Some older but still enlightening books include *Incidents of Travel in Central America, Chiapas, and Yucatán* (1841), which contains the vivid impressions of John Lloyd Stephens, one of the first white men to explore and chart the Mayan ruins; *The Caste War of Yucatán*, by Nelson Reed, an unusually detailed account of the massacre that enveloped the peninsula in the 1840s; and Robert Redfield's *The Folk Culture of Yucatán*, an anthropological classic. Frans Blom, archaeologist and explorer extraordinaire, wrote a colorful account of *The Conquest of Yucatán* in 1936. A translation of one of the earliest Spanish chronicles is to be found in *The Discovery of Yucatán*, by Francisco Hernández de Córdoba. Many of these older books are now out of print and available only in libraries.

One of the few recent pieces of fiction to focus on Yucatán is *Gringos*, by Charles Portis, which uses the peninsula as a backdrop for the antics of a motley group of North Americans. Mary Morris has written *Nothing to Declare*, her memoirs of a Mexican sojourn that encompassed parts of Yucatán and Central America. *Time Among the Maya: Travels in Belize, Guatemala, and Mexico*, by Ronald Wright, is another recent travelogue/ethnographic book. But it is Kate Simon's exquisitely written *Mexico: Places and Pleasures* (1962), with its timeless descriptions of Isla del Carmen, Campeche, Cozumel, and Mérida, that reigns supreme on the Mexico travel-writing shelf.

Arriving and Departing

From the United States by Plane

Flights are either nonstop, direct, or connecting. A **nonstop** flight requires no change of plane and makes no stops. A **direct** flight stops at least once and can involve a change of plane, although the flight number remains the same; if the first leg is late, the second waits. This is not the case with a **connecting** flight, which involves a different plane and a different flight number.

Airports and Airlines Airports in Cancún, Cozumel, and Mérida receive nonstop flights from the United States and Canada. Campeche, Chetumal, and Playa del Carmen have smaller airports served primarily by domestic carriers. Some of the ruins have airstrips that can handle small planes.

The number of airlines serving Mexico from the United States changes frequently with revisions of bilateral agreements. At press time, scheduled airlines with nonstop and/or direct service to Cancún, Cozumel, and Mérida included **Aeromexico** (tel. 800/237–6639), from Houston, Miami, and New York to Cancún, and from Cancún, Mexico City, Miami, and Villahermosa to Mérida; **American** (tel. 800/433–7300), from Dallas, Miami, and Raleigh/Durham to Cancún and Cozumel; **Continental** (tel. 800/231–0856), from Houston to Cancún and Cozumel; **Mexicana** (tel. 800/531–7921), from Chicago, Los Angeles, Miami, New York, and San Francisco to Cancún, and from Miami to Cozumel; **Northwest** (tel. 800/447–4747), from Tampa to Cancún; and **United** (tel. 800/538–2929), from Chicago and Washington, DC, to Cancún.

In addition, since 1986 more charter carriers, along with several smaller domestic Mexican airlines, have been providing service. Among them is **Aerocancún** (tel. 212/679–0360). **LACSA** (tel. 800/225–2272), the national airline of Costa Rica, has nonstop charter service from New York to Cancún and continuing service to Guatemala, Honduras, and Costa Rica. **American** and **Transair** also charter from New York to Cancún. **Aviateca** (tel. 800/327–9832), a Guatemalan carrier, has connecting service from Houston to Mérida.

Flying Time Flight times to Cancún are: from Los Angeles, 5 hours; from New York, 4 hours; from Chicago, 3½ hours; from Dallas, 2½ hours; from Houston, 2 hours; from Miami, 2 hours. Flights to Cozumel and Mérida are comparable in length.

Cutting Flight Costs The Sunday travel section of most newspapers is a good source of deals. When booking, particularly through an unfamiliar company, call the Better Business Bureau to find out whether any complaints have been registered against the company, pay with a credit card if you can, and consider trip-cancellation and default insurance.

Promotional Airfares Most scheduled airlines offer three classes of service: first class, business class, and economy or coach. To ride in the first-class or business-class sections, you pay a first-class or business-class fare. To ride in the economy or coach section—the remainder of the plane—you pay a confusing variety of fares. Most expensive is full-fare economy or unrestricted coach, which can be bought one-way or round-trip and can be changed or turned in for a refund.

All the less expensive fares, called promotional or discount fares, are round-trip and involve restrictions. The exact nature of the restrictions depends on the airline, the route, and the season, and on whether travel is domestic or international, but you must usually buy the ticket—commonly called an APEX (advance purchase excursion) when it's for international travel—in advance (7, 14, or 21 days are usual). You must also respect certain minimum- and maximum-stay requirements (for instance, over a Saturday night or at least seven and no more than 30, 45, or 90 days), and you must be willing to pay penalties for changes. Airlines generally allow some changes for a fee. But the cheaper the fare, the more likely the ticket is nonrefundable; it would take a death in the family for the airline to give you any of your money back if you had to cancel. The cheapest fares are also subject to availability; because only a certain percentage of the plane's total seats will be sold at that price, they may go quickly.

Consolidators   Consolidators or bulk-fare operators—also known as bucket shops—buy blocks of seats on scheduled flights that airlines anticipate they won't be able to sell. They pay wholesale prices, add a markup, and resell the seats to travel agents or directly to the public at prices that still undercut the airline's promotional or discount fares. You pay more than on a charter but ordinarily less than for an APEX ticket, and, even when there is not much of a price difference, the ticket usually comes without the advance-purchase restriction. Moreover, although tickets are marked nonrefundable so you can't turn them in to the airline for a full-fare refund, some consolidators sometimes give you your money back. Carefully read the fine print detailing penalties for changes and cancellations. If you doubt the reliability of a company, call the airline once you've made your booking and confirm that you do, indeed, have a reservation on the flight.

The biggest U.S. consolidator, C.L. Thomson Express, sells only to travel agents. Well-established consolidators selling to the public include **UniTravel** (Box 12485, St. Louis, MO 63132, tel. 314/569–0900 or 800/325–2222); **Council Charter** (205 E. 42nd St., New York, NY 10017, tel. 212/661–0311 or 800/800–8222), a division of the Council on International Educational Exchange and a longtime charter operator now functioning more as a consolidator; and **Travac** (989 6th Ave., New York, NY 10018, tel. 212/563–3303 or 800/872–8800), also a former charterer.

Charter Flights   Charters usually have the lowest fares and the most restrictions. Departures are limited and seldom on time, and you can lose all or most of your money if you cancel. (Generally, the closer to departure you cancel, the more you lose, although sometimes you will be charged only a small fee if you supply a substitute passenger.) The charterer, on the other hand, may legally cancel the flight for any reason up to 10 days before departure; within 10 days of departure, the flight may be canceled only if it becomes physically impossible to operate it. The charterer may also revise the itinerary or increase the price after you have bought the ticket, but if the new arrangement constitutes a "major change," you have the right to a refund. Before buying a charter ticket, read the fine print for the company's refund policy and details on major changes. Money for charter flights is usually paid into a bank escrow account, the name of which should be on the contract. If you don't pay by credit card, make your check payable to the escrow account (unless you're dealing with a travel agent, in which case, his or her check should be payable to the escrow account). The Department of Transportation's Consumer Affairs Office (I–25, Washington, DC 20590, tel. 202/366–2220) can answer questions on charters and send you its "Plane Talk: Public Charter Flights" information sheet.

Charter operators may offer flights alone or with ground arrangements that constitute a charter package. Well-established charter operators include **Council Charter** (205 E. 42nd St., New York, NY 10017, tel. 212/661–0311 or 800/800–8222), now largely a consolidator, despite its name, and **Travel Charter** (1120 E. Long Lake Rd., Troy, MI 48098, tel. 313/528–3570 or 800/521–5267), with Midwestern departures. **DER Tours** (Box 1606, Des Plains, IL 60017, tel. 800/782–2424), a charterer and consolidator, sells through travel agents.

Enjoying the Flight Unless you're flying from Europe, jet lag won't be a problem, since the time difference between most points in the United States and Yucatán is relatively small. Because the air aloft is dry, drink plenty of beverages while on board; remember that drinking alcohol contributes to jet lag, as do heavy meals. Sleepers usually prefer window seats to curl up against; restless passengers ask to be on the aisle. Bulkhead seats, in the front row of each cabin, have more legroom, but since there's no seat ahead, trays attach awkwardly to the arms of your seat, and you must stow all possessions overhead. Bulkhead seats are usually reserved for the disabled, the elderly, and people traveling with babies. PADI recommends that you not scuba dive and fly within a 24-hour period.

Smoking Since February 1990, smoking has been banned on all domestic flights of less than six hours duration; the ban also applies to domestic segments of international flights aboard U.S. and foreign carriers. On U.S. carriers flying overseas, a seat in a no-smoking section must be provided for every passenger who requests one, and the section must be enlarged to accommodate such passengers if necessary as long as they have complied with the airline's deadline for check-in and seat assignment. If smoking bothers you, request a seat far from the smoking section.

Foreign airlines are exempt from these rules but do provide no-smoking sections, and some nations, including Canada as of July 1, 1993, have gone as far as to ban smoking on all domestic flights; other countries may ban smoking on flights of less than a specified duration. The International Civil Aviation Organization has set July 1, 1996, as the date to ban smoking aboard airlines worldwide, but the body has no power to enforce its decisions.

From the United States by Ship

Cozumel and Playa del Carmen have become increasingly popular ports for Caribbean cruises. Cruise lines that depart from Miami include **Carnival** (tel. 800/327–9501), **Celebrity Cruises** (tel. 800/437–3111), **Dolphin** (tel. 800/222–1003), **Norwegian** (tel. 800/327–7030), and **Royal Caribbean** (tel. 800/327–2055). From other Florida ports, including Fort Lauderdale, Port Everglades, Palm Beach, Tampa, and St. Petersburg: **Costa Cruises** (tel. 800/327–2537), **Crown** (tel. 800/841–7447), **Holland America** (tel. 800/426–0327), **Ocean Quest** (tel. 800/554–2784), and **Princess Cruises** (tel. 800/446–6690). From New Orleans: **Commodore** (tel. 800/327–5617). From New York: **Regency** (tel. 800/457–5566).

Discount Cruises Usually, the best deals on Cruise bookings can be found by consulting a cruise-only travel agency. Contact the **National Association of Cruise Only Travel Agencies (NACOA)** (Box 7209,

Freeport, NY 11520) for a listing of member firms in a particular state. Enclose a self-addressed stamped envelope.

Specialty Cruises A diverse selection of upscale, special-interest cruises on small, luxury ships is available through **Classical Cruises** (132 E. 70th St., New York, NY 10021, tel. 212/794–3200 or 800/252–7745, 800/252–7746 in Canada, fax 212/517–0077). Participants join sails designed for museums and university groups. Arts, culture, and natural history programs include renowned personalities and scholarly lectures.

Staying in Cancún and Yucatán

Getting Around

By Plane **Aerocaribe** (tel. 800/531–7921 in the United States, 800/531–7923 in Canada) makes stops in Cancún, Cozumel, Mérida, and Veracruz. **Aerocozumel** (tel. 52/988–48103) provides service from Cancún and Mérida to Chetumal, Chichén Itzá, Ciudad del Carmen, Cozumel, Huatulco, Minatitlán, Playa del Carmen, Veracruz, Villahermosa, and Belize.

By Bus Bus travel in Yucatán, as throughout Mexico, is very inexpensive by North American standards, with rates averaging about $1 per hour. While there is not much difference in price between first- and second-class fares, there is a great difference in service. **ADO** (Autobuses del Oriente) is the principal first-class bus company serving the peninsula. First-class buses make fewer stops, travel faster, run more frequently, and are far more modern and comfortable.

By Car The road system in the Yucatán peninsula is extensive and generally in good repair. **Route 307** parallels most of the Caribbean Coast from Punta Sam, north of Cancún, to Tulum; there it turns inward to Chetumal and the Belize border. **Route 180** runs west from Cancún to Valladolid, Chichén Itzá, and Mérida, then turns southwest to Campeche, Isla del Carmen, and on to Villahermosa. From Mérida, there is also **Route 261** south to Campeche and Francisco Escárcega, where it joins Route 186 going east to Chetumal. These highways are two-lane roads. **Route 295** (from the north coast to Valladolid and Felipe Carrillo Puerto) and **Route 134** (which crosses the peninsula from Felipe Carrillo Puerto until it meets **Route 261** in central Yucatán) are also good two-lane roads.

Once off the main highways, however, motorists will find the roads in varying conditions. Some roads are unmarked, which makes it confusing to reach a given destination. Many are unpaved and full of potholes. If you must take one of the smaller roads, the best course is to allow plenty of daylight hours and never to travel at night. Always slow down when approaching towns and villages—which you are forced to do by the ubiquitous *topes* (speed bumps)—because you will find small children and animals in abundance. Resist the temptation to buy oranges or nuts from the children who approach your car; if they can make money this way, they don't go to school.

Always park your car in a parking lot, or at least in a populated area. Never leave anything of value in an unattended car.

Make sure there is proof of Mexican insurance in your rental car; if you're driving your own car be sure to purchase Mexican insurance at the border. Do not rely on credit card companies' assurances that you do not have to purchase auto insurance in Mexico unless you are ready to fork over large sums and be reimbursed later. If you are involved in an accident, Mexican authorities will demand that damage be paid for on the spot, in cash. (*See* Car Rentals, *above.*)

Speed Limits Mileage and speed limits are given in kilometers. In small towns, observe the posted speed limits, which can be as low as 30 kph (18 mph).

Fuel PEMEX franchises all gas stations, so prices throughout Yucatán will be the same. Prices tend to be comparable to those in the United States; stations in Mexico, however, do not accept credit cards or dollars. Unleaded fuel is not widely available. When filling your tank, ask for a specific peso amount of gas rather than for a number of liters. Keep the tank full, because gas stations are not plentiful.

National Road Emergency Services The Mexican Tourism Ministry operates a fleet of some 250 pickup trucks, known as the *Angeles Verdes*, or Green Angels, to render assistance to motorists on the major highways. The bilingual drivers provide mechanical help, first aid, radio-telephone communication, basic supplies and small parts, towing, and tourist information. Services are free, and spare parts, fuel, and lubricants are provided at cost. Tips are always appreciated.

The Green Angels patrol fixed sections of the major highways twice daily from 8 AM to 8 PM. If your car breaks down, pull as far as possible off the road, lift the hood, hail a passing vehicle, and ask the driver to notify the patrol. Most bus and truck drivers will be quite helpful. The Green Angels' 24-hour nationwide hot-line number is 250–4817.

If you witness an accident, do not stop to help, but instead locate the nearest official.

By Ferry Yucatán is served by a number of ferries and boats, ranging from the spiffy, usually efficient jetfoils (motorized catamarans) between Playa del Carmen and Cozumel to the more modest launches plying the waters from Puerto Juárez and Cancún to Isla Mujeres, and the tiny craft and catamarans heading out to the smaller offshore islands (Isla Holbox, Isla del Carmen, the Alacranes Reef).

Schedules are approximate and often vary with the weather and the number of passengers. Prices are quite reasonable.

Car ferries are also available from Punta Sam (north of Cancún) to Isla Mujeres and from Puerto Morelos to Cozumel. This service is slow but reliable.

Telephones

The country code for Mexico is 52.

International phone calls can be made from many hotels, but excessive taxes and surcharges—on the order of 60%—usually apply. Cancún, Cozumel, and Mérida are putting up more and more "Ladatel" phone booths on streets and in hotel lobbies; these phones accept pre-paid Ladatel cards, which are inserted into the phone and debited for the cost of the call. Throughout Mexico you dial 09 to place an international call; 02 for long-distance calls; 04 for local information; and 01 for international information. AT&T operators can be accessed in Cancún by dialing **01 or 95800–462–4240; you can charge calls to your AT&T credit card or call collect.

Time Zone

The Yucatán Peninsula remains on central standard time year-round.

Mail

Postal Rates Postcards to the United States cost NP$1; to Great Britain, NP$1.2. Letters to the United States cost NP$1.5; to Great Britain, NP$1.7.

Receiving Mail Mail can be sent either to your hotel or to the post office. In the latter case, have it addressed to your name, "LISTA DE CORREOS," followed by the city, state, postal code, and country. A list of names for which mail has been received is posted and updated daily by the central post office in each location. American Express cardholders can have mail sent to them at the local American Express office. In Yucatán, these are **American Express Travel Service** (Avs. Tulum and Agua, Suite A, Cancún, QR 77500); **Fiesta Cozumel** (Av. Rafael Melgar 27, Cozumel, QR 77600); **Turismo Bahamita** (Calle 41-A No. 3-E, Plaza Carmel, Cd. del Carmen, CAMP 24140); and **Viajes Programados** (Prolongacíon Calle 56, Edif. Belmar Depto. 5, Campeche, CAMP 24000).

Be forewarned, however, that mail service to and within Mexico is notoriously slow and can take anywhere from 10 days to three weeks. Never send anything of value to Mexico through the mails.

Tipping

It is not necessary to add a tip to your restaurant bill unless you feel the service was exceptional. Bellhops and porters should be given around NP$2 per bag, or NP$4 at deluxe hotels; hotel maids, NP$3 per day. Tour guides warrant the equivalent of $2 for a half-day tour, $3 for a full day, and $20 to $25 per person for a week. Tour bus drivers should receive $1 per person per day. Car watchers and windshield wipers (usually young boys), as well as gas station attendants and theater ushers, should be satisfied with the equivalent of 50¢. Taxi drivers appreciate a 10% tip, but shoe shiners do not expect tips.

Shopping

Throughout Yucatán, you'll find original Mexican handicrafts, including basketry, gold and silver filigree jewelry, leather goods, *huipiles* (embroidered cotton dresses), *hamacas* (hammocks), *huaraches* (leather sandals), and *jipis* (Panama hats). Prices will vary depending on where you purchase these items. Shopping is convenient in such resort areas as Cancún and Cozumel, but often you'll be paying top peso for items that you can find in smaller towns for less money. As for bargaining, it is widely accepted in the markets, but you should understand that in many small towns the locals earn their livelihoods from the tourist trade. Start off by offering no more than half the asking price and then slowly come up, but never pay more than 70% of the original price. Bargaining is not accepted in most shops except when you are paying cash.

Sports and Outdoor Activities

Archaeology Major Mayan ruins at such sites as Cobá and Tulum (*see* Chapter 6, Mexico's Caribbean Coast), Chichén Itzá and Uxmal (*see* Chapter 8, Mérida and the State of Yucatán), and Campeche (*see* Chapter 7, Campeche) continue to attract professional and amateur archaeologists as well as historians interested in ancient culture.

Bird-watching The Yucatán peninsula is one of the finest areas for birding in Mexico. Habitats range from wildlife and bird sanctuaries to unmarked lagoons, estuaries, and mangrove swamps. Frigates, tanagers, warblers, and macaws inhabit Isla Contoy and the Laguna Colombia on Cozumel; more than 350 bird species, including sparrow hawks and woodpeckers, are to be found in the Sian Ka'an biosphere reserve on the Boca Paila peninsula south of Tulum. Along the north and west coasts of Yucatán—at Río Lagartos, Laguna Rosada, and Celestún—flamingos, herons, ibis, cormorants, pelicans, and peregrine falcons thrive.

Fishing Sportfishing is popular in Cozumel and throughout the Caribbean Coast. The rich waters of the Caribbean and the Gulf of Mexico support hundreds of species of tropical fish, making the entire Yucatán coastline and the outlying islands a paradise for deep-sea fishing, sportfishing, fly-fishing, flatfishing, and bonefishing. Particularly between the months of April and July, the waters off Cancún, Cozumel, and Isla Mujeres teem with sailfish, marlin, red snapper, tuna, barracuda, and wahoo, among other fish. Billfishing is so rich around Cozumel that a tournament is held here each year.

Farther south, along the Boca Paila peninsula, banana fish, bonefish, mojarra, shad, permit, and sea bass provide great sport for flatfishing and fly-fishing, while oysters, shrimp, and conch lie on the bottom of the Gulf of Mexico near Campeche and Isla del Carmen. At Progreso, on the north coast, sportfishing for grouper, dogfish, and pompano is quite popular.

Hunting Hunting, although increasingly frowned upon as a result of Mexico's heightened ecological awareness, is good along the northwestern side of the peninsula and around Mérida and Campeche. Game includes waterfowl, deer, quail, and wild boar.

Water Sports All manner of water sports—jetskiing, Hobie Catting, sailboarding, waterskiing, sailing, and parasailing—are practiced along the Caribbean Coast, which has numerous marinas and well-equipped water-sports centers.

Scuba Diving and Snorkeling Divers and snorkelers come to Cozumel and Akumal and other parts of Mexico's Caribbean Coast for the clear turquoise waters, the colorful and assorted tropical fish, and the exquisite coral formations along the Belize reef system. Currents allow for drift diving, and both reefs and offshore wrecks lend themselves to dives, many of which are safe enough for neophytes. The peninsula's cenotes, or natural sinkholes, provide an unusual dive experience. Individual chapters will direct you to the dive sites that will best suit you.

Beaches

Cancún and the Yucatán area provide beach goers with a variety of options from which to choose. Cancún and Yucatán offer a stunning variety of beaches: There are white sand, rocky coves and promontories, curvaceous bays, and murky lagoons. Those who thrive on the resort atmosphere will probably enjoy Playa Chac Mool and Playa Tortugas on the windward side of Cancún, which is calmer if less beautiful than the leeward side. On the north end of Isla Mujeres, Playa Cocoteros and Playa Norte offer handsome sunset vistas. Beaches on the east coast of Cozumel—once frequented by buccaneers—are rocky, and the swimming is treacherous, but they are deserted and powdery. On the relatively sheltered leeward side are the widest and best sand beaches.

The Caribbean Coast abounds with tiny, hidden beaches (at Xcaret, Paamul, Chemuyil, Xcacel, Punta Bete, south of Tulum, and along the Boca Paila peninsula), but there are also long stretches of white sand, usually filled with sunbathers, at Puerto Morelos, Playa del Carmen, and especially Akumal.

Travelers to Campeche and Progreso will find the waters of the Gulf of Mexico deep green, shallow, and tranquil. Such beaches as Payucán, Sabancuy, Isla del Carmen, and Yucalpetén are less visited by North Americans; facilities are minimal, but some prefer it that way.

Dining

The mystique of Yucatecan cooking has a lot to do with the generous doses of local spices and herbs, although generally the food tends not to be too spicy. Among the specialties are *cochinita píbil* and *pollo píbil* (succulent pork or chicken baked in banana leaves with a tangy sour-orange sauce); *poc chuc* (Yucatecan pork marinated in the same sour-orange sauce with pickled onions); *panuchos* (fried tortillas covered with turkey, pickled onions, and avocado, with fried beans on the side); *papadzules* (tortillas piled high with hard-boiled eggs and drenched in a sauce of pumpkin seed and fried tomato); and *codzitos* (rolled tortillas in pumpkin-seed sauce). *Achiote* (annatto), cilantro (coriander), and the fiery *chile habanero* are heavily favored condiments.

Yucatecans are renowned for—among other things—their love of idiosyncratic beverages. *Iztabentún*, a liqueur made of fermented honey and anise, dates back to ancient Mayan times; like straight tequila, it's best drunk in small sips between bites of fresh lime. Local brews, such as the dark bock León Negra and the light Carta Clara and Montejo, are excellent but hard to find in peninsular restaurants. Yucatecan *horchata*, a favorite all over Mexico, is made from milled rice and water flavored with vanilla. Also try the *licuados*, either milk- or water-based, made from the tropical fruits of the region. For more Mexican specialties and translations, see the Menu Guide at the back of this book.

The rule of thumb in such areas as Cancún, Isla Mujeres, and Cozumel is to stay away from restaurants in the large chain hotels because prices there tend to be exorbitant. Also, when buying fish from beachside and roadside palapas, make sure the facilities are sanitary so you don't get food poisoning. Be especially careful with shellfish and anything to which mayonnaise may have been added.

Restaurants in Yucatán, including those in hotels, are for the most part very casual. The exceptions will be noted within reviews.

Lodging

If you plan to stay in Cancún or Cozumel, you'll have a variety of accommodations to choose from. There are luxurious and expensive internationally affiliated properties with numerous food and beverage outlets, the latest room amenities, boutiques, and sports facilities. These beach resorts also have more modest hostelries—usually a short walk from the water. As you get into the less populated and less visited areas of Yucatán, particularly the cities, accommodations tend to be simpler and more "typically Mexican." The hotels discussed in this book all meet a minimum standard of cleanliness, and most have a certain rustic charm. Inexpensive bungalows, campsites, and places to hang a hammock along many of the beaches are other options.

Apartment and Villa Rentals If you want a home base that's roomy enough for a family and comes with cooking facilities, a furnished rental may be the solution. It's generally cost-wise, too, although not always—some rentals are luxury properties (economical only when your party is large). Home-exchange directories do list rentals—often second homes owned by prospective house swappers—and there are services that can not only look for a house or apartment for you (even a castle if that's your fancy) but also handle the paperwork. Some send an illustrated catalogue and others send photographs of specific properties, sometimes at a charge; up-front registration fees may apply.

Among the companies are **At Home Abroad** (405 E. 56th St., Suite 6H, New York, NY 10022, tel. 212/421–9165); **Overseas Connection** (31 North Harbor Dr., Sag Harbor, NY 11963, tel. 516/725–9308); **Rent a Home International** (7200 34th Ave. NW, Seattle, WA 98117, tel. 206/789–9377 or 800/488–7368); **Vacation Home Rentals Worldwide** (235 Kensington Ave., Norwood, NJ 07648, tel. 201/767–9393 or 800/633–3284); **Villa Leisure** (Box 209, Westport, CT 06881, tel. 407/624–9000 or 800/526–4244), specializing in the Caribbean, with a few properties elsewhere; **Villas and Apartments Abroad** (420 Madison Ave., Suite 1105, New York, NY 10017, tel. 212/759–1025 or 800/433–3020); and **Villas International** (605 Market St., Suite 510, San Francisco, CA 94105, tel. 415/281–0910 or 800/221–2260). **Hideaways International** (767 Islington St., Box 4433, Portsmouth, NH 03802, tel. 603/430–4433 or 800/843–4433) functions as a travel club. Membership ($79 yearly per person or family at the same address) includes two annual guides plus quarterly newsletters; rentals are arranged directly between members, not by the club staff.

Home Exchange This is obviously an inexpensive solution to the lodging problem, because house-swapping means living rent-free. You find a house, apartment, or other vacation property to exchange for your own by becoming a member of a home-exchange organization, which then sends you its annual directories listing available exchanges and includes your own listing in at least one of them. Arrangements for the actual exchange are made by the two parties to it, not by the organization. Principal clearinghouses include **Intervac U.S./International Home Exchange** (Box 590504, San Francisco, CA 94159, tel. 415/435–3497), the oldest, with thousands of foreign and domestic homes for exchange in its three annual directories; membership is $62, or $72 if you want to receive the directories but remain unlisted. The **Vacation Exchange Club** (Box 650, Key West, FL 33041, tel. 800/638–3841), also with thousands of foreign and domestic listings, publishes four annual directories plus updates; the $50 membership includes your listing in one book. **Loan-a-Home** (2 Park La., Apt. 6E, Mount Vernon, NY 10552, tel. 914/664–7640) specializes in long-term exchanges; there is no charge to list your home, but the directories cost $35 or $45 depending on the number you receive.

Credit Cards

The following credit-card abbreviations are used throughout this book, particularly in the Dining and Lodging sections: AE, American Express; DC, Diners Club; MC, MasterCard; V, Visa.

Personal Security

When visiting Yucatán, even in such resort areas as Cancún and Cozumel, use common sense. Wear a money belt, make use of hotel safes when available, and carry your own baggage whenever possible. Reporting a crime to the police is often a frustrating experience unless you speak excellent Spanish and have a great deal of patience.

Women traveling alone are likely to be subjected to catcalls, although this is less true of Yucatán than of other parts of Mexico. Avoid direct eye contact with men on the streets—it invites further acquaintance. Don't wear tight clothes if you don't want to call attention to yourself. If you speak Spanish and are being harassed, pretend you don't understand and ignore would-be suitors or say "no" to whatever they say. Don't enter street bars or cantinas alone.

2 Portraits of the Yucatán Peninsula

Chronology of the Maya and History of Yucatán

11,000 BC Hunters and gatherers settle in Yucatán.

Preclassical Period: 1500 BC–AD 200

1500–900 BC The emergence and expansion of early civilizations, including the powerful and sophisticated Olmec Gulf of Mexico in the present-day states of Veracruz and Tabasco. Primitive farming communities develop in Yucatán.

900–300 BC The rise of the Olmecs, whose iconography and social institutions strongly influence the rapidly expanding Mayan population. The Maya adopt the Olmecs' concepts of tribal confederacies and small kingships as they move across the lowlands.

600 BC Tikal and Edzná are settled.

300 BC–AD 200 The emergence of large population centers and city-states (Tikal, El Mirador, Kaminaljuyú, Izapa) in highlands and on Pacific Coast of Guatemala, Honduras, and El Salvador. New architectural elements include the corbeled arch and roofcomb.

400 BC–AD 100 Dzibilchaltún had an important center, in a sector west of Progreso–Mérida highway known as Komchen. By this time Becán and Uaxactún (as well as Dzibilchaltún) were settled.

300 BC–AD 900 Florescence of Edzná.

AD 200 Cancún is settled.

Classical Period: 200–900

A formative stage for lowland Mayan culture, marked by the emergence of the calendar and the written word. Architectural highlight of the period is stepped platforms topped by limestone and masonry superstructures (temple-pyramids with frontal stairways), arranged around plazas and decorated with stelae, bas-reliefs, and frescoes.

200–600 Economy and trade flourish. Mayan culture becomes increasingly secular and warlike.

Development of Petén architectural style (polychrome modeled-stucco decoration and uniform room size and construction) in the Petén lowlands and along Usamacinta River at Palenque, Bonampak, Yaxchilán, Piedras Niegras, Tikal, Uaxactún.

250–300 Fortification ditch and earthworks built at Becán.

300 San Gervasio is built on Cozumel.

300–600 Florescence of Kohunlich.

400–1100 Florescence of Cobá.

431–799 The Palenque dynasty is founded.

432 The first settlement is established at Chichén Itzá.

6th Century Major Mayan centers in Petén, Tabasco, southern Campeche, Belize, parts of Guatemala and western Honduras strongly influenced by Teotihuacán. Larger, more elaborate palaces, temples, ballcourts, roads, and fortifications evident.

500–700 Florescence of Becán, Xpuhil, Chicanná.

600–900 Northern Yucatán ceremonial centers become increasingly important as centers farther south reach and pass developmental climax; the influence of Teotihuacán wanes. Three new Mayan architectural styles develop: Puuc (exemplified by Chichén Itzá and Edzná and used at the "Route of the Convents" sites, including Uxmal, Kabah, Sayil, and Labná) is the dominant style; Chenes (in northern Campeche, between the Puuc hills and the Río Bec area) is characterized by ornamental facades with serpent masks; and Río Bec (at Río Bec and Becán) features small palaces with high towers exuberantly decorated with serpent masks.

600–900 Florescence of Jainá.

700–1000 First florescence of Tulum.

9th Century Putún (Chontal) Maya from Tabasco and southern Campeche occupy southern Petén and possibly Cozumel.

Postclassical Period: 900–1541

900–1050 Classical Mayan centers of Petén and southern lowlands are abandoned, probably through a combination of overpopulation, weather calamities, and misuse of land.

ca. 920 Itzá, a branch of Putún Maya, establish themselves at Champotón and then at Chichén Itzá.

987 Toltecs, a Nahua-speaking tribe from central Mexico, leave their capital at Tula for Yucatán, under the leadership of Quetzalcoatl or Kukulcán, the "feathered serpent."

987–1185 Toltec/Itzá rule at Chichén Itzá, a cosmopolitan city in which architecture and sculpture can be seen alongside forms more like those of Central Mexico.

987–1007 The Xiu settle near ruins of Uxmal.

1200–1250 Decline and overthrow of Chichén Itzá.

1200 The Itzá abandon Chichén Itzá for Lake Petén Itzá.

1224–1244 The Itzá return to the abandoned Chichén Itzá as squatters.

1224 The Cocomes, an Itzá dynasty that emerged as a dominant group in Mayapán, force Itzá out of Chichén Itzá and rule northern Yucatán until mid-15th century.

1250–1450 The League of Mayapán—including the key cities of Uxmal, Izamal, Chichén Itzá, Mayapán—is formed in northern Yucatán.

15th Century By this time most of the coastal cities had been founded and were developing.

1263–1283 Mayapán, under rule of Cocomes aided by Canul (Tabascan mercenaries), becomes most powerful city-state in Yucatán.

1441 Mayan cities under Xiu rulers sack Mayapán, ending centralized rule of peninsula. Yucatán henceforth is governed as 18 petty provinces, with constant internecine strife. The Itzá return to Lake Petén Itzá and establish their capital at Tayasal (modern-day Flores).

ca. 1443 Ah-Canul chieftainship is founded at Calkiní.

15th Century Cancún is abandoned.

1502 A Mayan canoe is spotted during Columbus's fourth voyage.

1511 Aguilar and Guerrero, Spanish sailors, are shipwrecked off Yucatán.

1517 Fernández de Córdoba discovers Isla Mujeres.

1517 Córdoba lands at Campeche, marking first Spanish landfall on mainland. He is defeated by the Maya at Champotón.

1518 Juan de Grijalva reaches Cozumel.

1519 Hernán Cortés lands at Cozumel.

1527, 1531, 1541 Unsuccessful Spanish attempts to conquer Yucatán.

1540 Montejo founds Campeche, the first Spanish settlement in Yucatán.

Colonial Period: 1541–1821

1542 Mayan chieftains surrender to Montejo at T'Ho; 500,000 Indians are killed during the conquest of Yucatán. Indians are forced into labor under the *encomienda* system, by which conquistadores are charged with their subjugation and Christianization. The Franciscans contribute to this process.

1542 Mérida is founded on the ruins of T'Ho.

1543 Valladolid is founded on the ruins of Zací.

1546 A Mayan group attacks Mérida, resulting in five-month-long rebellion.

1549 The Indian population of Yucatán numbers 235,000.

1562 Bishop Diego de Landa burns Mayan codices at Maní.

1600 Cozumel is abandoned after smallpox decimates population.

1639 The Indian population of Yucatán falls to 210,000.

1624 The Spanish captain sent to subdue the Maya at Tayasal has his heart torn out.

1686 Campeche's walls are built, ending the pirates' reign of terror.

1697 The last independent Mayan kingdom, at Tayasal, is destroyed.

1700 182,500 Indians account for 98% of Yucatán's population.

1712 The Tzeltal uprising in Chiapas.

1736 Indian population of Yucatán declines to 127,000.

1761 The Cocom uprising near Sotuta leads to death of 600 Maya.

1794 Indian Population of Yucatán: 254,000.

1810 Port of Sisal opens, ending Campeche's ancient monopoly on peninsular trade and its economic prosperity.

Post-Colonial/Modern Period: 1821 – present

1823 Yucatán achieves statehood.

1840s Tulum serves as outpost of Chan Santa Cruz Indians; Chan Santa Cruz is modern-day Felipe Carrillo Puerto.

1847 Mexico City, in the struggle to regain Texas, imposes heavy taxes and forced military service on Yucatán's resentful Creole population, which arms and recruits Maya to fight the capital. Following years of oppression, the Indians attack Valladolid, launching War of the Castes, which continues fitfully until 1901.

1846–1850 The Indian population of Yucatán is nearly halved during Caste War.

1848 Indians occupy four-fifths of the peninsula but abandon their arms during corn-planting season.

ca. 1848 Twenty refugee families from the Caste War settle in Cozumel, which has been almost uninhabited for centuries. By 1890, Cozumel's population numbers 500.

1863 Campeche achieves statehood.

1869 The Chamula, a Tzotzil-speaking Mayan group in Chiapas, rise up against San Cristóbal de las Casas.

1872 The founding of Progreso.

1898 Mexican forces capture Chan Santa Cruz, the last stronghold of the Maya rebels.

1898 The founding of Payo Obispo (present-day Chetumal).

1880–1914 Yucatán's monopoly on henequen, enhanced by plantation owner's exploitation of Mayan peasants, leads to its Golden Age as one of the wealthiest states in Mexico.

1890–1910 Waves of Middle Eastern immigrants arrive in Yucatán and become successful in commerce, restaurants, cattle ranching, and tourism.

1901 The Caste War virtually ends with Porfirio Díaz's defeat of most Maya.

1902 Díaz creates the Territory of Quintana Roo to isolate rebellious pockets of Indians and increase his hold on regional resources.

1915–1924 Felipe Carrillo Puerto, Socialist governor of Yucatán, institutes major reforms in land distribution, labor, women's rights, and education during Mexican Revolution.

1934–1940 President Lázaro Cárdenas implements significant agrarian reforms in Yucatán.

1935 Chan Santa Cruz rebels in Quintana Roo relinquish Tulum and sign a peace treaty.

1930–1980 With collapse of the world henequen markets, Yucatán gradually becomes one of the poorest states in Mexico.

1974 Quintana Roo achieves statehood; development of Cancún tourism begins.

Magnífico Mexico

By Susan Farewell

Cancún is vacationland with a capital V: A place where *reality* is a dirty word, where you might end up showing your taxi driver Polaroids of your wedding, and where trying to decide how to have your eggs cooked is the most difficult decision of the day.

Plop down in a chaise lounge on the beach, and you'll see the surf full of deliriously happy body surfers, water-treaders, and dog paddlers. Sure, every now and then some show-off swims seriously by, but the real appeal here is to simply soak in the bathtub-warm water, which comes in every imaginable hue of blue. When lunch time comes around, you can head for a beach-side *palapa* (thatched umbrella) restaurant filled with sun-worshippers, who divide their time between quenching swigs of chilled Montejo (a local beer made in Mérida) and lemon-doused piles of fresh shrimp or *langosta* (lobster). At night, walk into a restaurant and you'll inevitably see a table full of tanned—or should-have-put-on-number-15—revelers singing, posing for pictures, or trying to keep straight faces as a quartet of mariachis dressed in the traditional Mexican cowboy, or *charro*, outfits serenades them with songs of passion and lost love.

There are three main tourist areas in this part of the Mexican Caribbean—Cancún, Cozumel, and Isla Mujeres—and all have a different appeal. But the common denominators here are beaches that rival the beauty of any beach in the world, translucent waters teeming with reef life, and easy access to Mayan ruins, some which date as far back as 2500 BC.

With blindingly white sands lapped by tepid Caribbean waters, the beaches alone are enough to let your hopes soar. They come in all sizes, shapes, and styles, from the isolated, no-sign-of-other-people type to the let's party, spirited Rio variety backed by bars and restaurants. The most populated strands are those facing the Caribbean along the Zona Hotelera (Hotel Zone) in Cancún. In fact, many visitors spend their days "hotel-beach hopping," since the beaches are all public. You can walk between them or grab a bus marked "Hotel Zone." These buses stop wherever you happen to flag them down. Taxis are also plentiful. The hotel-zone beaches are best for sun bathers, swimmers, and snorkelers. Water-skiers, windsurfers, kayakers, jet-skiers, and other water-sport gadget enthusiasts congregate on the lagoon side of the strip. Equipment and instruction are available at centers along Avenida Kukulcán, the road that links all the resorts. Those wanting to see the underwater world without getting wet can step aboard the Nautibus and observe the seascapes and phosphorescent fish through glass.

When not soaking up rays on the *playa* (beach), there's some shopping to do in Cancún, especially for handicrafts and duty-free items. Look for baskets, coral jewelry, animals made of papier-mâché, leather bags, *huaraches* (sandals), pottery, and hand-blown glass. The temptation to buy can be great, and you should go ahead and have some fun— just remember to bargain a bit and check carefully for quality.

If your idea of a great gift comes complete with a worm, tequila is the answer, and this is just the place to buy some. Sauza, Cuervo, and Herradura are three of the best brands. The word *añejo* on the bottle means it has aged a bit and is quite smooth; *hurnitos* indicates that it is well aged; and *commemorative* signifies that it is over six or seven years old. Once you've bought the clear, burning liquid, you'll have to learn the proper way to drink it: Sprinkle grains of salt onto the crook of the thumb of your non-drinking hand, lick them off, then suck a lime wedge, and take a swig (a guzzle, a sip, whichever you prefer) out of the *fajo*, the traditional tequila drinking cup. Follow that with another lip-smacking nip of the lime.

Other diversions in Cancún include a combination platter of landlubber sports. There are plenty of tennis courts to go around (most of the big resort hotels have their own) and a couple of golf courses. The Pok-Ta-Pok Golf Course, which is open to the public, has a Mayan ruin at its 12th hole (many say you should drive around it, so not to disturb the gods). You can rent bikes and cycle along a 6-mile bike path on the northern side of the island all the way to downtown. Mopeds—or *motos*—are also available at some of the resort hotels.

Perhaps the most Mexican of experiences to be had in Cancún is attending a bullfight. At the Cancún bullring (on Av. Bonampak, across from Los Almendros restaurant), every Wednesday, at 3:30 PM, cape-waving matadors, resplendent in suits of silk and gold embroidery, skillfully attempt to outsmart raging, snorting bulls. Almost always, they end with a triumphant thrust of the sword. The fiesta brava, a sport that can be traced back to the 5th century BC in Greece and later was known as the sport of nobles in the Middle Ages, is still very much alive in Mexico. Although not recommended for animal lovers or the faint at heart, it is a thrilling spectacle. Olé!

Dining out in Cancún goes hand in hand with partying. In fact, many people book a table for dinner and stay for the duration of the evening. Often the evening kicks off with a "hotel hop," taking in the numerous happy hours that precede dinners and Vegas-style floor shows. The big party dinner spots (especially for college age and those in their twenties) include Carlos 'n Charlie's (it's part of a nationwide chain, often referred to as C 'n C's), Cancún's very own Hard Rock Cafe, and the Bombay Bicycle Club, where you can feast on heaps of ribs.

There are several very good restaurants to try both in Cancún City and the hotel zone, the latter tending to be more expensive. Along with Yucatecan and Mayan dishes such as *sopa de lima* (lime soup) and *poc chuc* (pork broiled with sour oranges, onions, and spices), you'll find all the customary Mexican favorites (enchiladas, tortillas, guacamole) as well as other cuisines, including French, Tex-Mex, Italian, and Asian.

After-dark hours in Cancún are fun and potentially exhausting. You can take your pick of night clubs and discos that psychedelically throb till ungodly hours. Topping the disco list these days are Dady'O (with a laser mover), La Boom (its moving dance floor is a real hit), and Christine (video screens, lasers, and rolling spotlights). Most charge a cover, anywhere from $5 to $15 per person. While disco hopping, you'll surely want to sample some tequila, and try out your newly learned tequila-drinking technique.

As much fun as the Cancún disco-hopping scene is, do set aside an evening for the Ballet Folklórico, a regional song-and-dance extravaganza held at the Convention Center. The performance is preceded by a Mexican buffet. Another night, join in on one of the dinner cruises.

Easy Excursions

The last thing you want to do on a honeymoon or vacation is have a list of things to do. Nevertheless, Cancún is within easy reach of quite a few worthwhile attractions—and some neighboring islands with more beaches, more snorkeling, and more shops—that you can see in a day trip or by taking an overnight excursion.

To begin with, some of Mexico's most prized Mayan ruins are nearby. You can set out to see these on your own in a rented Jeep (or car) or sign up for an escorted bus tour. One of the most impressive sites is Chichén Itzá, about 75 miles (47 kilometers) east of the Colonial town of Mérida, or three driving hours from Cancún. It's a sprawling Mayan center (7 square miles of temples, carvings, and statues) with a 75-foot- (23-meter-) high pyramid (worth the climb to see the throne at the top), a ball court that's bordered by intricately carved walls, and a Sacred Cenote (a sacred well that was used for sacrifices).

Uxmal, south of Mérida, is known for its Palace of the Governor and Pyramid of the Magician—both of which should not be missed if you're in this part of the world. They are truly magnificent and comparable to the ancient cities of the Greek and Roman empires.

Tulum, which is south of Cancún in Quintano Roo, was the first Mayan city Spanish conquistadors visited in 1518. It's spectacularly situated on top of a cliff overlooking the Caribbean Sea.

From Cancún, there are several "party" cruises daily to nearby Isla Mujeres, which is right off the northeastern tip of the Yucatán Peninsula. These short trips are fun in themselves complete with live music, open bar, lunch, and snorkeling stops. Isla Mujeres is a tiny island (a mere 5 miles long and half a mile wide) offering all the simple pleasures of an island retreat. There are thatched-hut restaurants, a handful of shops, and beaches washed by water so blue it looks dyed. Favorite swimming beaches on Isla Mujeres include Playa Los Cocos near the northern tip of the island and Playa Lancheros, by the southern end of the island. The latter has the added attraction of shark pens that were once used for the now-endangered sea turtles. El Garrafón, an underwater national park just beyond Lancheros, is a popular snorkeling spot. So much so, that you might want to go early in the morning to avoid the crowds (it opens at 8 AM).

From Isla Mujeres, you can charter a boat to visit nearby Isla Contoy, a national park and bird sanctuary. Here, you can spend hours watching flamingos, herons, red-pouched frigates, and pelicans doing their jet-like take-offs and dive-bomb fishing routines. En route and just off Contoy, there's some good snorkeling. (Note: At press time Isla Contoy was temporarily closed to tourists, but it should reopen by 1994.)

Nights on Isla Mujeres are highlighted by seafood dinners (next to tourism, fishing is the second-largest local industry). Many restaurants specialize in Yucatecan specialties. Later on, there's serious partying and dancing at Calipso Disco and Tequila.

Cozumel, Cancún's sister island, can easily be reached by plane (a 30-minute flight) or ferry (about an hour's ride from the mainland port, Playa del Carmen). This island is not as glitzy and developed as Cancún but does get many tourists because it is a cruise ship port of call. Hand in hand with cruise ships, go shops, of which there are many. However, the geared-for-cruise-ship-passenger prices are not always the best. For local handicrafts, take a look around the crafts market behind the San Miguel plaza, where vendors sell everything from carved wooden figurines to outrageously huge sombreros.

But the biggest draw of Cozumel is the Palancar Reef, which was made famous by Jacques Cousteau. It attracts divers and snorkelers from around the globe who slowly move along in the dense silence, mercurylike bubbles rising to the surface, seascapes that resemble Disney's Magic Kingdom wobbling like the air above a hot runway all around. Equipment, instruction, and boat reservations can be made at the numerous dive shops along San Miguel's waterfront.

Nonsnorkelers and divers can view Cozumel's hauntingly beautiful submarine world in glass-bottom boats, which leave from the docks throughout the day. If you prefer to lounge around on the island's beaches, make your way to Playa San Francisco, the island's most social beach, or Punta Chiquero, a less populated spot.

On land, there are hundreds of birds to keep an eye out for, including parrots, macaws, and hummingbirds. If you want to really escape reality, sign aboard a Robinson Crusoe cruise to Isla Passion, off the north shore. Here, in addition to a bit of history to see (the remains of ceremonial centers and temples dot the island), there are a wealth of talcum-soft strands for all-out sunning.

Cozumel is home to several good restaurants, including everything from Ernesto's Fajitas Factory (a big roadside palapa where everyone goes for fajitas) to Pepe's Grill, which serves the kind of dishes you'd expect to see on the cover of *Gourmet* magazine.

Whether visiting on a honeymoon, fleeing winter doldrums, or just seeking an island vacation, you'll find that this part of the world always has a tipsy air of carnival. After a week or so, you might have to face the "R" word—reality. Of course, you could always put it off for *mañana*.

Yucatán's Great Archaeology

By Kate Simon

Although they seem to lie very near one another, the going among Mayan sites can be rough. Some of the edifices are still shrouded in heavy jungle, others were too thoroughly destroyed by time and warfare to make much structural or aesthetic sense. For the visitor who comes equipped with a normal amount of time (five to seven days in Yucatán) and interest, the twin splendors of Uxmal and Chichén, both easily accessible, plus the less-known Kabah, Labná, and Sayil, should suffice for a good view of "Mayan" architecture and art. (Keep in mind that Uxmal and Kabah can be visited on your way from Campeche to Mérida—and possibly the others as well—particularly easy if you are driving.)

One doesn't necessarily have to be taken by the hand to Uxmal and Chichén. They have been described and photographed almost as much as the splendors of Egypt and their looks have become familiar to most of the civilized world. Pamphlet in hand—available in town and at the sites—one can wander through the ruins on a do-it-yourself basis. Buses run to both cities frequently; the trip to Chichén takes about three hours, to Uxmal it is about an hour and a half. A taxi needn't be wildly expensive and the drivers are usually well informed or will put you in the hands of a local guide if you like. *His* fee will be little but he may suffer from a common form of Mayaphilia: he may insist that everything you look at is "pure" Mayan, whatever that may mean.

Like Uxmal, Kabah sits close to the road, but the wait for a bus to take you there from Uxmal or back may be hot and time-consuming. Guide services usually make Uxmal-Kabah one trip and Sayil-Labná another. For those with prodigious stamina, Uxmal, Kabah, and Sayil can be arranged as a long one-day trip.

Kabah is a bitter structure, with the inelegant proportions of a squat fortress. It sits on a height of terraces and platforms as befits a fortress but its most imposing building has been given a singularly nonbelligerent name, the Palace of the Rolled Mat (Codz-Pop). This refers to the "nose" of the stylized masks of the rain god, Chac, a characteristic of local ornamentation valued by adherents of the trans-Pacific theory of Mayan origin as proof that the migrants brought with them a memory of the elephant's trunk. Opponents consider it phallic, or an ornamental step device which facilitated scrambling up and down the building.

Tour cars or jeeps continue on to Sayil; check at Uxmal or Kabah to find out if the road is ready for your car. The Palacio at Sayil (the guides like to expound on it salaciously as a fertility center) is, next to Palenque, the most dramatically placed of the structures now visible. High and alone, long, horizontal planes surrounded by a silent, motionless sea of green, it echoes the isolated Greek temple at Segesta in Sicily. The three-layered building bears a section of Mayan frieze, including the mask motif, and a preponderance of small columns as architectural and ornamental elements. Tight clusters of columns like pipers of Pan (Puuc style) flank the doorways, then change to sets of thicker, peculiarly shaped columns; one of each pair is straight, the other softly indented—rather like a waist—suggesting a primitive female figure. Other than these details, there is not much on or in the Palacio to surprise or enchant: it is the total effect—the ride through the brush, the stillness, the sudden sight of the isolated, regal building. There are ruined buildings of which one says, "I would love to have seen it before it fell apart," but not of Sayil. Like the Greek temples, it must have been covered with much more ornament and brilliant color and, like the Greek temples now, has achieved a new beauty in decay.

One of the best places from which to get a distant view of the building in its setting is at the "observatory," a few minutes away by car. From here one walks a short distance to suggestions of other buildings, and on to a grove in which lies a huge figure of a priapic god who may have fallen from a set of columns nearby. In another direction from the Palacio, a short ride and short walk again, there is a cave on which is clearly carved a figure of a woman in a froglike squatting position, and just below her, on a ledge farther back in the curve of the wall, the figure of what might be another woman, or more possibly, a baby; it has no breasts, its shape is rounder and less clearly defined than the other figure—more evidence of fertility rites, the guide eagerly points out.

The road to Labná should be usable in dry weather. Labná, again judging from jungle-choked mounds, must have been a very large city, and to judge from what is left, an ornately beautiful one. It has some of the clustered, banded columns of Sayil, the elaborated rain-god masks of the whole area, the open work, and the geometric ornaments of stone mosaic which adorn Uxmal. The famous arch of Labná, of itself strikingly large and tall, offers a clear demonstration of how near the Mayans were to the keystone arch, and also how much they could do without it—as they did without the wheel and without metal until late in their history.

With more time and the proper passion for Mayan, you might investigate (always checking the condition of roads) the Cave of Balancanche, less than three miles from

Chichén, which revealed, some years ago, a good number of pottery objects still to be dated. Chacmultun gives evidences of once having been a large center and its frescoes are not altogether gone. It is reached via Muna and Ticul, a town which embroiders *ipiles* and whose inhabitants are purportedly the descendants of the Xius, kings of Uxmal.

Or try either the ruins of Dzibalchen or Xtampak (savoring the pleasure of rolling these names out when you get home).

Much less demanding is Dzibilchultun, off the Progreso road, now being excavated and potentially an enormous, important site. At the present writing it shows a few structures, including remains of an ancient church, one tall pyramid, and a platform holding a plump column. The rest is a small museum, the first stirrings of a university, and a few distinguished statuettes that were found in the Temple of the Seven Dolls (now in the museum). One wonders how long it will take Tulane University and the national Geographic Society to rebuild the large city, which was, it is said, in continuous use from 1000 BC until the arrival of the Spaniards. It is not a particularly rewarding site at present except for the young picnickers who play their portable phonographs and swim at the edge of the cenote. Or go by bus to Progreso, an unprepossessing port town whose beaches are steadily coming out of a long slump. At the end of a road shortly before one reaches Progreso, there are two beaches equipped with cabins and snack bars and numerous of the local young: Chelen and Yucapeten. From Progreso one turns left for the white sands of Sisal, and right to Chixulub, whose fine sand holds interesting shells and a respected seafood restaurant. Should you be in Mérida in mid-August—a daring time—find out the precise dates of the Chixulub fiesta, which includes regional dancing, lots of seafood, and often a bullfight. If you have the energy, take a walk along the avenue which parallels the beachfront for a glimpse of some of the wildest domestic architecture extant, and some very good modern. On your return, get to the bus station early. For one thing, this obviates waiting through the filling and departure of two buses before you get a seat, but more important, the bus station is the pulse of the town and to sit on one of its benches is to be the spectator of an eloquent pageant. A bus from Mérida delivers a covey of old ladies in white, their thin hair pulled back tightly into the clublike knot which has been the fashion for centuries; a few wear shoes. Two younger women glowing in white rayon heavy with bright embroidery and lace, hung with gold chains and earrings, with stiff new sandals on their feet, step down solemnly, like young priestesses. The general factotum of the bus—not yet of the aristocracy of drivers—helps an old man lift down a cake of ice wrapped in cloth and rope which, somehow, survived the hour's trip of many stops. A sack of dried kernels of corn to be soaked and made into tortilla mash is the next bundle down, and the assistant arranges it as a great deep hat on the head of a Mayan woman who is also carrying a large, ugly doll dressed in a man's hat and a cloth whose embroidered banner names it Saint Michael.

At the entrance to the station, a timeless tableau goes on: A young man, red-eyed, weaving, his gestures watery, is trying to placate a girl of 15, an unkempt, savage little beauty, who answers him in snarls and grunts. He had taken her to the beach for the night, rather than the hotel room he had promised, and drank up the fare money which was to take them back to Mérida. They approach the factotum-collector of the bus, who assures them in a reasonable manner that he cannot take them to Mérida without fares. They start to walk down the dusty road, separate and morose.

An insistent drunk who has been gently urged off two buses now boards yours. The man of all work of the bus, resigned to his company, helps him curl up under some seats and at each stop, when the bewildered head rises to look around blindly, pats him back to sleep in a mixture of Spanish and Mayan. When his charge is asleep and all the fares collected, the young man fixes a doll, adjusts a slipping bundle, and dandles one of a pair of babies while the mother attends to the second.

The return from this second-class bus ride might be just the time to leave Yucatán, carrying the savor of its pretty, generous people whose sophisticated lineage shows in their profiles, in their open, trusting manner, their easy smiling, and complete lack of xenophobia. You interest them, they assume they interest you, and they make it clear that the encounter is a mutual pleasure.

3 Cancún

Updated by Edie
Jarolim

Flying into Cancún, Mexico's most popular destination, all you see are green treetops for miles. It's clear from the air that this resort was literally carved out of the jungle. When development began here in 1974, the beaches were deserted except for their iguana inhabitants. Now, luxury hotels line the oceanfront, and nearly 2 million foreign visitors a year come for the white sand beaches and crystalline Caribbean waters. They also come for the sizzling nightlife and, in some cases, for proximity to the Yucatán ruins. Although the resort is too glitzy and tourist-oriented for some, it draws thousands of repeat visitors.

Cancún City is on the mainland, but the hotel zone is on a 22½-kilometer (14-mile) barrier island off the Yucatán peninsula. The resort is designed to please American tastes; most people speak English, and devotees of cable TV and Pizza Hut will not be disappointed. Dedicated beach bums will cherish the cool, white, porous limestone sand and clear blue waters here, and the sun shines an average of 240 days a year, reputedly more than at almost any other Caribbean spot. Temperatures linger appealingly at about 80°F. You can sample Yucatecan foods and watch folkloric dance demonstrations as well as knock back tequila slammers at the myriad night spots.

But there can be more to the resort than plopping down under a *palapa* (pre-Hispanic thatched roof). For divers and snorkelers, the surrounding reefs and other islands—Isla Mujeres and Cozumel—are among the best in the world. Cancún also provides a relaxing home base for visiting the stupendous ruins of Chichén Itzá, Tulum, and Cobá on the mainland—remnants of the area's rich Mayan heritage—as well as the Yucatán coast and its lagoons.

The most important buildings in Cancún, however, are modern hotels. The resort's architecture tends to be a cross between Mediterranean and Mayan. In many cases the combination yields an appealing, if sometimes kitschy, style. Typical Mediterranean structures—low, solid, rectangular, with flat, red-tile roofs and white stucco walls covered with exuberantly pink bougainvillea—acquire palapas and such ornamental devices as colonnettes, latticework, and beveled cornices.

Cancún has gone through the life cycle typical of any tourist destination. At its inception, the resort drew the jet set; lately, it has attracted increasing numbers of less affluent tourists, primarily package-tour takers and college students, particularly during spring break when hordes of flawless, tanned young bodies people the beaches and restaurants.

As for the island's history, not much was written about it before its birth as a resort almost 20 years ago. The island does not appear on the early navigators' maps and little is known about the Mayans who lived here; apparently Cancún's marshy terrain discouraged development. It is recorded that Mayans settled the area during the preclassical era, in about AD 200, and remained until about the 14th or 15th century. In the mid-19th century minor Mayan ruins were sighted; however, they were not studied by archaeologists until the 1950s and mid-1970s. In 1970 then-President Luis Echeverría first visited the site that had been chosen to retrieve the state of Quintana Roo from obscurity and abject poverty.

Cancún's natural environment has paid a price. Its lagoons and mangrove swamps have become polluted, and a number of species, like conch and lobster, are dwindling. Although the beaches still appear pristine for the most part, an increased effort will have to be made in order to preserve the physical beauty that is the resort's prime appeal.

Essential Information

Important Addresses and Numbers

Tourist Information The **state tourist office** (Av. Tulum 29, S.M. 5, tel. 98/848073), located next to Multibanco Comermex, is open daily 9–9. At this office, at the airport, and at many hotels, you can pick up a copy of *Cancún Tips,* a free pocket-size guide to hotels, restaurants, shopping, and recreation that usually contains a discount card for use at various establishments. Although it's loaded with advertising, the booklet, published twice a year in English and Spanish editions, has useful maps and up-to-date information. The magazine staff also runs a number of information centers around town, including one at Plaza Caracol (tel. 98/832745) that is open daily 10–10. Several similar publications, among them *Cancún Scene, Cancún Inside,* and *Passport Cancún,* are also available.

The Mexican Ministry of Tourism recently established a 24-hour English-language help line for tourists; it's toll free, 800/90392.

Consulates **U.S. Consulate** (Av. Nader 40, S.M. 2A, Edificio Marruecos 31, tel. 98/842411 or 98/846399) is open daily 9–2 and 3–6.

Canadian Consulate (Plaza México Local 312, upper floor, tel. 98/843716) is open daily 11 AM–1 PM. For emergencies outside office hours, call the Canadian Embassy in Mexico City (tel. 5/254–3288).

Emergencies **Police** (tel. 98/841913); **Red Cross** (Av. Xcaret and Labná, S.M. 21, tel. 98/841616); **Highway Patrol** (tel. 98/840710).

Medical Clinics **Hospital Americano** (Calle Viento 15, S.M. 4) and **Total Assist** (Claveles 5, tel. 98/841092 or 98/848116), both with English-speakers on staff, provide emergency medical care.

Late-night Pharmacies **Farmacia Turística** (Plaza Caracol, tel. 98/831894) and **Farmacia Extra** (Plaza Caracol, tel. 98/832827) deliver to hotels 9 AM–10 PM. **Farmacia Paris** (Av. Yaxchilán, in the Marrufo Bldg., tel. 98/840164) also fills prescriptions.

Banks Generally, banks in Cancún are open weekdays 9–5, with money-exchange desks open 9–1. To exchange or wire money try one of the locations of **Banamex** (Av. Tulum, next to City Hall, tel. 98/845411; and Av. Chichén Itzá 24, tel. 98/847226). Other centrally located banks downtown include **Banco del Atlantico** (Av. Tulum 15, tel. 98/841095) and **Bancomer** (Av. Tulum, tel. 98/843508, or Plaza Kabah, tel. 98/849234).

English-language Bookstores **Fama** (Av. Tulum, tel. 98/846586) specializes in books on the Yucatán and offers a large selection of English-language magazines. **La Surtidora** (Av. Tulum 17, tel. 98/841103) sells a variety of English- and Spanish-language books.

Travel Agencies and Tour Operators Cancún-based agencies include **Intermar Caribe** (Calle Cereza 37 at Av. Bonampak, S.M. 2A, tel. 98/844266), **Turismo Aviomar** (Calle Venado 30, S.M. 20, tel. 98/846742 and 98/846433), and **Visa Tours** (Plaza Quetzal 15, tel. 98/831800 and 98/831091).

Arriving and Departing by Plane

Airport and Airlines **Cancún International Airport** is 16 kilometers (9 miles) southwest of the heart of Cancún City, 10 kilometers (6 miles) from the southernmost point of the hotel zone. **Aeromexico** (tel. 800/237–6639, tel. 98/860079 in Cancún) flies nonstop from Houston and New York. **American** (tel. 800/433–7300, tel. 98/860055 in Cancún) has nonstop service from its hub in Dallas and from Miami. **Continental** (tel. 800/231–0856, tel. 98/860040 in Cancún) offers daily direct service from Houston and Newark, NJ. **Mexicana** (tel. 800/531–7921, tel. 98/860120 in Cancún) nonstops depart from Chicago, Los Angeles, Miami, and New York. **Northwest** (tel. 800/225–2525, tel. 98/860046 in Cancún) flies direct from Tampa. From mid-December through April, **United** (tel. 800/538– 2929, tel. 98/860025 in Cancún) flies from Chicago via Washington, D.C. In Cancún, Mexicana subsidiaries **Aerocaribe** (tel. 98/842000 [downtown], 98/860083 [airport]) and **Aerocozumel** (tel. 98/842000 [downtown], 98/860162 [airport]) offer flights to Cozumel, the ruins at Chichén Itzá, Mérida, and other Mexican destinations.

Between the Airport and Hotels A counter at the airport exit sells tickets for buses (called *colectivos*) and for taxis; prices for the latter range from $15 to $20, depending on the exact destination. Buses, which cost about $6, are air-conditioned and vend soft drinks and beer on board, but may be slow if they're carrying a lot of passengers and need to stop at many hotels.

Arriving and Departing by Car or Bus

By Car Cancún is at the end of Route 180, which goes from Matamoros on the Texas border to Campeche, Mérida, and Valladolid. The road trip from Texas to Cancún can take up to three days. Cancún can also be reached from the south via Route 307, which passes through Chetumal and Belize. Gas stations on these roads are few in number, so try to keep your tank filled.

By Bus The bus terminal (Av. Tulum and Av. Uxmal, tel. 98/841378 or 98/843948) downtown serves first-class buses making the trip from Mexico City and first- and second-class buses arriving in Cancún from Puerto Morelos, Playa del Carmen, Tulum, Chetumal, Cobá, Valladolid, Chichén Itzá, and Mérida. Public buses (Route 8) make the trip out to Puerto Juárez and Punta Sam for the ferries to Isla Mujeres.

Getting Around

Motorized transport of some sort is necessary, since the island is somewhat spread out. Public bus service is good and taxis are relatively inexpensive.

When you first visit Cancún City (downtown), you may be confused by the layout. There are four principal avenues: Tulum and Yaxchilán, which run north–south; and Uxmal and Cobá, running east–west. Streets bounded by those avenues and running perpendicular to them are actually horseshoe-shaped, so you will find two parallel streets named *Tulipanes,* for instance. However, street numbers or even street names are not of much use in Cancún; the proximity to landmarks, such as specific hotels, is the preferred way of giving directions.

By Bus Public buses run between the hotel zone and downtown from 6 AM to midnight; the cost is NP$2. There are designated bus stops, but drivers can also be flagged down along Paseo Kukulcán. The service is a bit erratic, but buses run frequently and can save you considerable money on taxis, especially if you're staying at the southern end of the hotel zone.

By Car and Moped Renting a car for your stay in Cancún is probably an unnecessary expense, entailing tips for valet parking, as well as gasoline and rather costly rental rates (on a par with those in any major resort area around the world). What's more, driving here can be harrowing when you don't know your way around. However, if you plan to do some exploring, using Cancún as a base, the roads are excellent within a 100-kilometer (62-mile) radius.

Car Rentals Rental cars are available at the airport or from any of a dozen agencies in town, and most are standard-shift subcompacts and jeeps; air-conditioned cars with automatic transmissions should be reserved in advance. Rental agencies include **Avis** (tel. 98/860222 at the airport, 98/830800 at Hotel Calinda Viva, or 98/830803 at Galería Mayfair); **Budget** (tel. 98/840730 or 98/840204 [reservations], with offices at the airport, downtown, and at the Galería Mayfair); **Econo-Rent** (tel. 98/842147 at the airport, 98/841826 or 98/841435 at Calle Tulipanes 16); **National** (tel. 98/864492 or 98/860152 on Av. Uxmal 12); or **Hertz** (9 locations, tel. 98/841326 or 98/876604 at Reno 35). The **Car Rental Association** (tel. 98/842039) can help you arrange a rental as well.

Moped Rentals Mopeds and scooters are also available throughout the island. While fun, they are risky, and there is no insurance available for the driver or the vehicle. The accident rate is high, especially downtown, which is considered too congested for novice moped users.

By Taxi Taxis to the ferries at Punta Sam or Puerto Juárez cost $5–$16 or more; between the hotel zone and downtown, $6 and up; and within the hotel zone, $2–$4. All prices depend on the distance, your negotiating skills, and whether you pick up the taxi in front of the hotel or go onto the avenue to hail a green city taxi (the latter will be cheaper). Since taxi rates fluctuate according to gasoline taxes and the drivers' whims, check with your hotel. Most list rates at the door; confirm the price with your driver before you set out. If you lose something in a taxi or have a complaint, call the **Sindicato de Taxistas** (tel. 98/886992 or 98/886990).

By Ship Boats leave Puerto Juárez and Punta Sam (both north of Cancún City) for Isla Mujeres every half hour or so; *see* Chapter 4 for details.

Telephones

The local telephone prefix is 98. Ladatel (the Mexican long-distance phone service) phones, which enable you to pay for calls by credit card, are now located in many hotels and on downtown streets. From these phones, you can also dial **01 and reach an AT&T operator in the states, allowing you to charge calls to an AT&T card or call collect. The operator can connect you to any 800 number, a useful service if you must report lost or stolen credit cards. Direct-dial international calls can be made through AT&T operators from most of the hotels on Paseo Kukulcán, but the hotels also charge $3–$5 per call extra for this service. Bypassing the Mexican phone system is worthwhile, however, even if it means calling collect, because of the 60% tax on overseas calls.

Mail

The **post office** (Av. Sunyaxchén at Xel-ha, tel. 98/841418) is open weekdays 8–5, Saturday 9–1; there's also a **Western Union** office (tel. 98/841529) in the building. Mail can be received here if marked "Lista de Correos, Cancún, QR 77500, México." Bear in mind, however, that postal service to and from Mexico is extremely slow and may take two weeks or more. If you have an American Express card, you can have mail sent to you at the **American Express Cancún Office** (Av. Tulum, corner Agua, tel. 98/841999); the office is open weekdays 9–6, Saturday 9–1.

Guided Tours

There are few guided tours of Cancún per se, because other than several tiny Mayan ruins, there is virtually no sightseeing on the island. **Tranviás Turísticos** (tel. 98/844055), which has booths at Ki Huic Market, downtown, and Nautilus Shopping Center and Gypsy's restaurant in the hotel zone, runs sightseeing trolleys around the island. More popular are tours to the surrounding islands, the beaches along the Cancún–Tulum corridor (Akumal is the best known), or the Mayan ruins on the mainland—Chichén Itzá, Cobá, and Tulum (these trips usually include a stop at the lagoons at Xel-Ha (pronounced *shell-HA*) or Xcaret (pronounced *SHAR-et*).

Cruises A lobster-dinner cruise on board the 62-foot vessel *Columbus* (tel. 98/831488 or 98/831021) includes a full lobster or steak dinner, open bar, and dancing for $54; the boat departs the Royal Mayan Yacht Club Monday–Saturday, and sails from 4 to 7. The "Sun Tour" run by **Turismo Aviomar** (tel. 98/848944) to Isla Mujeres departs the Playa Linda dock daily at 10 AM and returns at 6 PM; the $48 price (half that for kids) includes a Continental breakfast, buffet lunch on a private beach, open bar, and live music. The outfit also offers "Pancho's Night," an Isla Mujeres beach-party excursion aboard a triple-decker boat that sails from Playa Linda Pier. Trips last from 6 to 11 PM, cost $50, and include a buffet dinner, open bar, live music, and Mexican comedy show. **Nautibus** (tel. 98/831004 or 98/832119), or the "floating submarine," has a 1½-hour Caribbean-reef cruise that departs the Playa Linda marina four times daily; during high season, boats sail at 10, 12, 2, and 4. The $28 price ($15 for children) includes music and drinks.

Air Tours A 15-minute, $50-per-person seaplane ride over the lagoons and Caribbean reefs departs from **Pelican Pier** (Paseo Kukulcán, Km 5.5, tel. 98/830315 or 98/831935), across from the Casa Maya; a 35-minute ride, covering the whole island, costs $90. Cessna 206 air taxis are also available for charters; the cost is $360 per hour (a maximum of five passengers can split the price).

Special-Interest **Aeroquetzal** (Plaza México, Av. Tulum 200, tel. 98/871353 or 98/843938), a small Guatemalan carrier, flies between Cancún and Guatemala City, continuing on to Flores and the ruins at Tikal, for $270 round-trip.

Intermar Caribe (tel. 98/844266) leads daily jeep tours through the jungle to unexcavated ruins. The $50 price includes lunch.

Exploring

The island of Cancún, which is shaped roughly like the numeral 7, is divided into two zones, with the hotel zone constituting the much larger of the two and occupying both legs of the 7. Picture the horizontal leg as extending east from the mainland into the Caribbean; Punta Cancún is where the vertical leg takes over, going north–south. Hotel development began at the north end (close to the mainland), headed east toward Punta Cancún, and is moving south to Punta Nizuc, where the tip of the seven almost joins up again with the mainland. The other zone—Cancún City or downtown Cancún, known as *el centro*—is actually 4 kilometers (2½ miles) west of the hotel zone on the mainland. The 7 is separated from the mainland by a system of four lagoons: Nichupté, the largest (about 29 sq. km, or 18 sq. mi), containing both fresh and salt water; Bojórquez, at the juncture of the two legs of the 7; del Amor; and Río Inglés. North of the horizontal leg lies Bahía de Mujeres, the 9-kilometer- (5½-mile-) wide bay that separates Cancún from Isla Mujeres. Regularly placed kilometer markers on the roadside help indicate where you are; they go from Km 1 on the mainland, near downtown, to Km 20 at Punta Nizuc.

Paseo Kukulcán is the main drag in the hotel zone, and because most of the 7 is less than a kilometer wide, both the Caribbean and the lagoons can be seen from either side of it. The hotel zone consists entirely of hotels, restaurants and shopping complexes, marinas, and time-share condominiums; there are no residential areas as such. It's not the sort of place you can get to know by walking. Paseo Kukulcán is punctuated by driveways with steep inclines turning into the hotels, most of which are set at least 100 yards from the road. The lagoon side of the boulevard consists of scrubby stretches of land, many of them covered with construction cranes, alternating with marinas, shopping centers, and restaurants. What is most scenic about Cancún is the dramatic contrast between the vivid turquoise-and-violet sea and the blinding alabaster-white sands.

Numbers in the margin correspond to points of interest on the Cancún map.

Cancún's scenery consists mostly of its beautiful beaches and crystal-clear waters. There are also a few intriguing sites tucked away among the modern hotels. Heading north from Punta Nizuc and keeping your eye on the seaside, as many as eight hotels are situated within the space of 1 kilometer, one right after the next, with barely any distance between them.

❶ The small **Ruinas del Rey** are located on the lagoon side at Km 17, roughly opposite Days Inn and Playa de Oro. Large signs point out the site, which is being incorporated into a complex that will include a hotel, golf course, shops, and residential units. At this writing, because of the construction, the ruins are

Cancún

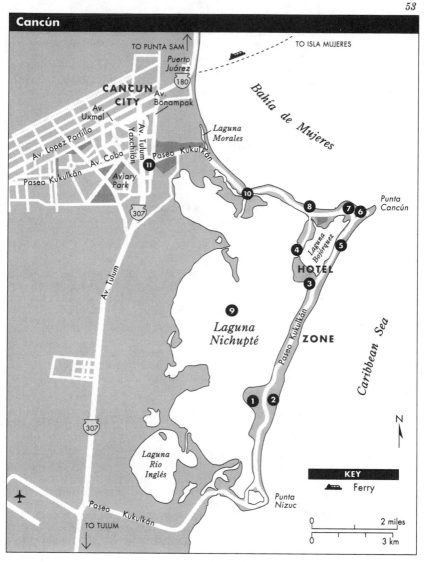

Bullring, **11**
Cancún Convention Center, **6**
Laguna Nichupté, **9**
Playa Chac Mool, **5**
Playa Linda, **10**
Playa Tortugas, **8**
Pok-Ta-Pok, **4**

Ruinas del Rey, **1**
San Miguelito, **2**
Shopping malls, **7**
Yamil Lu'um, **3**

closed to public access, and no one seems to know when they will open again. First mentioned in a 16th-century travelogue and then, in 1842 when they were sighted by American explorer John Lloyd Stephens and his draftsman, Frederick Catherwood, the ruins were finally explored by archaeologists in 1910, though excavations did notbegin until 1954. In 1975 archaeologists, along with the Mexican government, began the restoration of El Rey and San Miguelito (*see below*).

Although El Rey is not particularly impressive, it is worth a look. The ruin is notable for its unusual architecture: two main plazas bounded by two streets. Most of the other Mayan cities, which were not in any sense planned but had developed over centuries, contained one plaza with a number of ceremonial satellites and few streets. The pyramid here is topped by a platform, and inside its vault are stucco paintings. Skeletons found buried both at the apex and at the base indicate that the site may have been a royal burial ground. Originally named Kin Ich Ahau Bonil, Maya for "King of the Solar Countenance," the 2nd–3rd-century BC site was linked to astronomical practices in the ancient Mayan culture.

About half a kilometer away from El Rey—between Km 16 and 17—but on the east side of Kukulcán, is another Mayan site: **San Miguelito,** a very small stone building (about the size of a shack) with a number of columns about 4 feet high. There is no signage, so if you take a taxi, make sure the driver knows how to reach the site.

Another ruin, **Yamil Lu'um** (meaning "hilly land"), stands on the highest point of Cancún and is situated at Km 12, to the left of the Sheraton. A small sign at the hotel will direct you to the dirt path leading to the site. Although it's composed of two structures—one probably a temple, the other probably a lighthouse—this is the smallest of Cancún's ruins. Discovered in 1842 by John Lloyd Stephens, the remains date from the late 13th or early 14th century.

Just after Km 12, near the Melia Turquesa, Sheraton, and Radisson hotels, you'll come in sight of Laguna Bojórquez on your left; buildings span nearly the entire length of the spit of land that encloses the lagoon. On the far side of that spit, along the road that forks to the left (between Km 6 and Km 7), is **Pok-Ta-Pok** golf course, whose Mayan name means "ball game." Situated on the 12th hole is yet another Mayan ruin, consisting of two platforms and vestiges of other buildings.

Approaching the northern tip of the vertical leg of the 7—Punta Cancún—you'll pass **Playa Chac Mool** at Km 10, one of the few public beaches on Cancún, with restaurants and changing areas. Leaving the beach, you'll round the corner to the bay side (Bahía de Mujeres). Calmer waters prevail here, as opposed to the sea side, where you can also swim, and which has the more beautiful beaches. On the sea side of the tip of Punta Cancún, look for the fourth Mayan ruin, a tiny shrine that is fairly insignificant except that it's been cleverly incorporated into the architecture of the **Hotel Camino Real.**

After the beach, you'll come upon a traffic circle at Km 9, where the **Cancún Convention Center,** a large venue for cultural events, is located. At press time, the convention center, damaged by Hurricane Gilbert, was in the process of being rebuilt.

It is scheduled to reopen in March 1993, but that date is probably optimistic.

Between the convention center and the Stouffer Presidente is a ½-mile-long string of **shopping malls,** including Plaza Caracol, La Mansión–Costa Blanca, Plaza Lagunas, Plaza Terramar, and Galería Mayfair.

Right beyond the Stouffer Presidente, at Km 7, is **Playa Tortugas,** the other beach where those staying at the beachless downtown hotels are welcome. To the south, on your left, you'll reach **Laguna Nichupté,** the center for most of the watersports activities. Also in the lagoon are swampy areas that host mangrove trees and more than 200 species of birds. Ask your hotel to arrange for a boat and guide.

Continue along Paseo Kukulcán past the numerous hotels. Just before you cross the causeway onto the mainland, at the Hotel Calinda, you'll come to **Playa Linda,** from which ferries depart for Isla Mujeres. The less expensive public ferries leave for the island from Puerto Juárez, about 9 kilometers (6 miles) farther north.

As you enter downtown Cancún, Paseo Kukulcán turns into Avenida Cobá at the spot where it meets **Avenida Tulum,** the main thoroughfare and the location of many restaurants and shops. Life-size reproductions of ancient Mexican art, including the Aztec calendar stone, giant Olmec head, the Atlantids of Tula, and the Mayan Chac Mool (reclining rain god), line the grassy strip dividing Tulum's northbound and southbound lanes. Visitors looking for shopping bargains, however, generally find better prices if they stick to the parallel Avenida Yaxchilán.

The Cancún **bullring,** a block south of the Pemex station, hosts year-round bullfights. *Paseo Kukulcán at Av. Bonampak, tel. 98/845465 or 98/848248. Admission: $33, Wed. 3:30 PM.*

Shopping

Resort wear and handicrafts are the most popular purchases in Cancún, but the prices are high and the selection standard; if you're traveling elsewhere in Mexico, it's best to postpone your shopping spree until you reach another town. Still, you can find a respectable variety of Mexican handicrafts ranging from blown glass and hand-woven textiles to leather to jewelry made from local coral and tortoiseshell. (Don't be tempted by the tortoiseshell products: The turtles they come from are endangered species, and it is illegal to bring tortoiseshell into the United States and several other countries.)

Caveat emptor applies as much to Cancún as it does to the "bargain" electronics stores on Fifth Avenue in New York City or in Hong Kong. Throughout Mexico you will often get better prices by paying with cash (pesos or dollars) or traveler's checks. This is because Mexican merchants are averse to the commissions charged by credit-card companies, and frequently tack that commission—6% or more—onto your bill. If you can do without the plastic, you may even get the 10% sales tax lopped off.

Bargaining is expected in Cancún, but mostly in the market. Suggest half the asking price and slowly come up, but do not pay more than 70% of the quoted price. Shopping around is a good idea, too, because the crafts market is very competitive. But closely examine the merchandise you are purchasing: Some "authentic" items—particularly jewelry—may actually be shoddy imitations.

In Cancún, shopping hours are generally weekdays 10–1 and 4–7, although more and more stores are staying open throughout the day rather than closing for siesta between 1 and 4 PM. Many shops keep Saturday morning hours, and some are now open on Sunday until 1 PM. Shops in the malls tend to be open weekdays from 9–10 AM to 8–10 PM.

Shopping Districts, Streets, Malls

Shopping can be roughly categorized by location: In the malls and in-house boutiques in the hotel zone, prices are generally—but not always—higher than in the shops and markets downtown. However, at the latter you'll have to sift through lots of overpriced junk and haggle a bit in order to land some good deals in silver or handicrafts.

Downtown The wide variety of shops downtown along Avenida Tulum (between Avenidas Cobá and Uxmal) and Avenida Cobá (between Avenidas Bonampak and Tulum) includes the **Plaza México** (Av. Tulum 200, tel. 98/843506), a cluster of 50 handicrafts shops. Next door, visit **Pama** (Av. Tulum and Calle Lluvia, tel. 98/841839), a department store offering clothing, beachwear, sports gear, toiletries, liquor, and *latería* (crafts made of tin). Also on Tulum is the oldest and largest of the crafts markets, **Ki Huic** (Av. Tulum, between Bancomer and Banco Atlantico, no phone), which is open daily from 9 AM to 10 PM and houses about 100 vendors. Nearby is **Margarita's** (Av. Tulum 10, tel. 98/842359), one of the better silver shops.

Hotel Zone Fully air-conditioned malls (known as *centros comerciales*), as streamlined and well kept as any in the United States or Canada, sell everything from fashion clothing, beachwear, and sportswear to jewelry, household items, video games, and leather goods.

Flamingo Plaza (Paseo Kukulcán, Km 11, across from the Hotel Flamingo, tel. 98/832855), the latest addition, includes a full-service gym, exchange booth, some designer emporiums and duty-free stores, several sportswear shops, two boutiques selling Guatemalan imports, and a new Planet Hollywood boutique. At the food court, in addition to the usual McDonald's and fried chicken concessions, you'll find **Chicádole,** offering what might be the only fast-food molé enchiladas around.

Just across from the convention center site at Km 8.5 is **Plaza Caracol** (tel. 98/830905 or 98/831038), the largest and most contemporary mall in Cancún, with about 200 shops and boutiques, including two pharmacies, art galleries, and folk art and jewelry shops, as well as cafés and restaurants. Fashion boutiques include Benetton, Bally, Gucci, and Ralph Lauren; in all these stores, prices are less than those in their U.S. counterparts. One drawback: Aside from formal restaurants, there are no places here for shoppers to rest their feet.

To the back of—and virtually connected to—Plaza Caracol are two outdoor shopping complexes: the pink stucco **La Mansíon–Costa Blanca** (tel. 98/844261), which specializes in designer clothing and has several restaurants, a bank, and a liquor store; and **Plaza Lagunas** (tel. 98/831266), dedicated primarily to sportswear shops, such as Ellesse and Ocean Pacific. Also nearby, **Plaza Terramar** (tel. 98/831588, opposite the Hotel Fiesta Americana) sells beachwear, souvenirs, and folk art, and has a restaurant and a pharmacy.

Plaza Nautilus (Km 3.5, lagoon side, tel. 98/831903), the mall closest to downtown and a favorite of American shoppers, has a bookstore, liquor store, art gallery, perfumery, folk art shop, and Super Deli, as well as about 65 other shops.

Specialty Shops

Galleries **Orbe** (tel. 98/831333), in the Plaza Caracol mall, specializes in sculptures and paintings by contemporary Mexican artists; **La Galería** (no phone), in the La Mansíon–Costa Blanca mall, is both the showroom and studio of Gilberto Silva, a sculptor who employs Mayan techniques on local limestone; **Las Palmeras** (tel. 98/831415), also at Costa Blanca, and **Akakena** (tel. 98/830539), by the convention center, display replicas of Mayan art, temple rubbings, and contemporary painting and sculpture. Temporary exhibits are also displayed and sold in the **Galerie du Mexique** (tel. 98/830448) on Paseo Kukulcán at Avenida Bonampak, downtown. The **Galería de Sergio Bustamante** (tel. 98/830044), in the Hyatt Cancún Caribe, displays and sells the work of this popular Mexican ceramist.

Grocery Stores Major supermarkets include **Comercial Mexicano** (Av. López Portillo at Libramiento Kabah, tel. 98/871202 or 98/871303); **San Francisco de Asís** (Av. Tulum, S.M. 5, at Av. Xel Há, tel. 98/842812); **Super Deli** (Av. Tulum at Xcaret, tel. 98/841122, ext. 149; Plaza Nautilus, tel. 98/831984); and **Comercial Mexicana de la Glorieta** (Av. Tulum, S.M. 2, where it crosses Av. Uxmal, tel. 98/871303).

Sports and Fitness

Golf The main course is at **Pok-Ta-Pok** (Paseo Kukulcán between Km 6 and Km 7, tel. 98/830871), a club with fine views of both sea and lagoon, whose 18 holes were designed by Robert Trent Jones, Sr. The club also has a practice green, swimming pool, tennis courts, and restaurant. The greens fees are $50; electric cart, $30; clubs, $15; caddies, $15; and golf clinics, $25 per hour. Playing hours are 6 AM–6 PM (last tee-off is at 4:30). There are also 18- and 5-hole golf courses at the **Hotel Melia Cancún** (Paseo Kukulcan, Km 12, tel. 98/851160) and a 9-hole course at the **Oasis Hotel** (Paseo Kukulcán Km 20, tel. 98/850867).

Health Clubs Most of the deluxe hotels have their own health clubs, although few of them are very large. There are, however, two gyms in Cancún: Both **Gold's Gym** (Plaza Flamingo, tel. 98/832933 or 98/832966) and **Michel's Gym** (Av. Sayil 66, S.M. 4, tel. 98/842394 or 98/842550) feature modern equipment and exercise facilities.

Jogging Although to some people the idea of jogging in the intense heat of Cancún sounds like a form of masochism, fanatics should know that there is a 14-kilometer (9-mile) track extending along half the island, running parallel to Paseo Kukulcán from the Punta Cancún area into Cancún City.

Water Sports Water sports—particularly snorkeling, scuba diving, and deep-sea fishing—are popular pastimes in Cancún, because some 500 species of tropical fish, including sailfish, bluefin, marlin, barracuda, and red snapper, live in the adjacent waters. Sports centers and marinas (which provide gear and charters) are scattered around the island, both at hotels and on the lagoon side, where many water-related activities take place. Other popular activities include parasailing, sailboarding, waterskiing, sailing, and jetskiing.

Snorkeling gear can be rented for $10 per day. Sailboards are available for about $50 an hour; classes go for about $35 an hour. Parasailing costs $35 for eight minutes; waterskiing, $60–$65 per hour; jetskiing, $50–$55 per hour.

Fishing Deep-sea fishing boats and other gear may be chartered from outfitters for about $320 for four hours, $420 for six hours, and $520 for eight hours. Charters generally include a captain, a first mate, gear, bait, and beverages. **Tiki Island** (tel. 98/833481) and **Marina Aqua Ray** (tel. 98/853007) are just a couple of the companies that operate large fishing fleets.

The newest and most ambitious marina, **San Buenaventura,** between Bahía de Mujeres and Laguna Nichupté, is scheduled to open in late 1993 and will be located in downtown Cancún, near the bullring. Other marinas include **Aqua Tours Dive Center and Marina** (tel. 98/830400 or 98/831137), **Aqua-quin** (tel. 98/830100 or 98/831883), **Club Lagoon** (tel. 98/831111), and **Playa Blanca** (tel. 98/830344).

Sailboarding Although some people sailboard on the ocean side in the summer, activity is limited primarily to the bay between Cancún and Isla Mujeres. If you visit the island in July, don't miss the National Windsurfing Tournament (tel. 98/843212), in which athletes test their mettle. The **International Windsurfer Sailing School** (tel. 98/842023), located at Playa Tortugas, rents equipment and gives lessons.

Snorkeling and Snorkeling is best at Punta Nizuc, Punta Cancún, and Playa
Scuba Diving Tortugas, although you should be especially careful of the strong currents at the latter. Some charter-fishing companies offer a two-tank scuba dive for about $100. As the name implies, **Scuba Cancún** (tel. 98/831011) specializes in diving trips and offers NAUI, CMAS, and PADI instruction. **Aqua Tours Dive Center and Marina** (tel. 98/830400 or 98/830227) offers scuba tours and a resort course, as well as snorkeling trips. If you've brought your own snorkeling gear and want to save money, just take a city bus down to Club Med and walk along the resort's beach for about a mile until you get to Punta Nizuc.

Beaches

Cancún Island is one long, continuous beach, although about 7 kilometers (4 miles) of beachfront were eroded by Hurricane Gilbert in 1988. Some stretches lost as much as 40 meters (131 feet) to the storm. However, if you've never been here, you won't know the difference.

By law the entire coast of Mexico is federal property and open to the public; in practice, however, hotel security guards keep peddlers off the beaches, and hotel guests are easily identified by the color of the towels they place on their beach lounge chairs. Most hotel beaches have lifeguards, but as with all ocean swimming, use common sense—even the calmest-looking waters can have currents and riptides. Overall, the beaches on the windward stretch of the island—those closest to the city, facing the Bahía de Mujeres—are best for swimming; farther out, the undertow can be tricky. Swim with caution when the red danger flags fly; yellow flags indicate that you should proceed with caution; green or blue means waters are calm. On shore, be sure to protect yourself from the searing tropical sun, an obvious precaution once you feel the heat or see the scorched bodies here. Avoid prolonged exposure during peak sunlight hours (11–3) and always use sunscreen or sunblock.

Two popular areas, **Playa Tortugas** (Km 7) and **Chac Mool** (Km 10), have restaurants and changing areas, making them especially appealing for vacationers who are staying at the beachless downtown hotels. Be careful of strong waves at Chac Mool, where it's tempting to walk far out into the shallow water.

Dining

By Judith Glynn

At last count, there were more than 1,200 restaurants in Cancún, but—according to one profiting restaurateur—only about 100 are worth their salt, so to speak. Finding the right restaurant in Cancún is not easy. The downtown restaurants that line the noisy Avenida Tulum often have tables spilling onto pedestrian-laden sidewalks; however, gas fumes and gawking tourists tend to detract from the romantic outdoor-café ambience. Many of the hotel-zone restaurants, on the other hand, cater to what they assume is a tourist preference for bland, not-too-foreign-tasting food.

One key to good dining in Cancún is to find the haunts—mostly located in the downtown area—where locals go for Yucatán-style food prepared by the experts. Many menus are highlighted by seafood made with fresh lime juice and other authentic Mexican specialties, but it takes more to make a Cancún dining experience: Look for a place where the waiters artistically prepare meals at tableside or where cocktails are served flaming. Fish caught from the waters around the island, then grilled and seasoned with lime juice, is a sure bet. Grilled pork and chicken prepared with spices used in Mayan cooking, such as *achiote*, are other local specialties. Service at most Cancún restaurants is attentive and friendly. A cheap and filling trend in Cancún's dining scene is the sumptuous buffet breakfasts offered by an increasing number of restaurants and hotels on the island. These are especially pleasant when served at palapa restaurants on the beach. At about $12, the brunches are a good value—eat on the late side and you won't be hungry until dinner. Another hint: Many Very Expensive and Expensive restaurants feature floor shows during peak months (mid-December–late March). Usually there are two seatings nightly, each including entertainment and dinner; reservations are advised, since the shows draw crowds. Note, too, that although the great majority of restaurants fall into the Moderate price category, if you order lobster at any of the places serving seafood, you're in for a considerably more expensive meal.

Generally speaking, dress is casual here, but many restaurants will not admit diners with bare feet, short shorts, or no shirts. The "casual but neat" code implies that a restaurant is a bit upscale and that slightly fancier attire is appropriate.

When reviewing Cancún's restaurants, we looked for places where your money will best be spent and your meal most enjoyed. It's important to note that although hotels make strong efforts to keep guests on the premises, you'll be paying high prices for what may well be an average meal. Therefore, only the truly exceptional hotel restaurants are listed, allowing for more comprehensive coverage of independently operated cafés. Unless otherwise stated, restaurants serve lunch and dinner daily.

Highly recommended restaurants are indicated by a star ★.

Category	Cost*
Very Expensive	over $35
Expensive	$25–$35
Moderate	$15–$25
Inexpensive	under $15

per person, excluding drinks and service

Hotel Zone

Hotel Zone restaurants are located on the Cancún Hotel Zone Dining and Lodging map.

Very Expensive **Blue Bayou.** Six levels of snug dining areas, decorated in wood, rattan, bamboo, and flourishing greens, create the atmosphere for a memorable evening. Sounds from the cascading waterfall and waiters dressed in white pants and blue blazers further accent the sophisticated tone, set off by jazz that drifts in from the adjoining bar. Blackened meat, fish, and lobster—Cajun and Creole style—are featured on the menu, which is nicely balanced by a number of Mexican specialties. *Hyatt Cancún Caribe, Paseo Kukulcán, tel. 98/830044. Reservations advised. Dress: casual but neat. AE, MC, V. No lunch.*

Bogart's. Whether you consider it amusingly elaborate or merely pretentious, it's hard to be neutral about Bogart's, probably the most expensive and talked-about restaurant in town. Taking off from the film *Casablanca,* the place is decorated with Persian rugs, fans, velvet-cushioned banquettes, and fountains; waiters wear fezzes and white suits. A menu as eclectic as the patrons of Rick's Cafe features many seafood and Mediterranean dishes. The food is good, but don't expect large portions; servings are nouvelle style. *Paseo Kukulcán, Hotel Krystal, tel. 98/831133. Reservations required; seatings at 7 and 9:30. Dress: casual but neat. AE, MC, V. No lunch.*

Grimond's Mansion. Although the management has changed— this restaurant was formerly called Maxime's—the French chef and 19th-century French-country decor, with its ornate furnishings, remain. The outside terrace, with lush greenery and a fountain, is a relaxing spot for lunch; in the evening, you'll dine to the strains of a piano and classical guitar. An upstairs

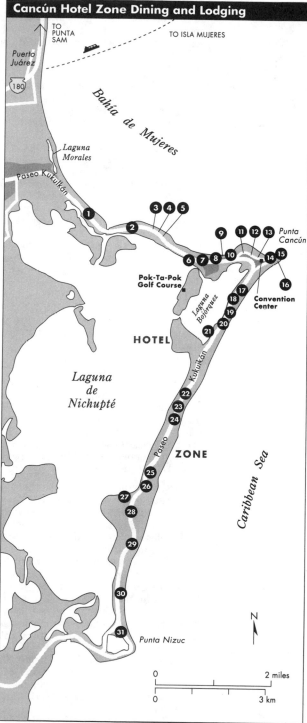

Cancún Hotel Zone Dining and Lodging

Dining

Augustus Caesar, **11**

Blue Bayou, **19**

Bogart's, **14**

Captain's Cove, **2, 27**

Carlos 'n Charlie's, **5**

Casa Rolandi, **12**

Chac Mool, **17**

El Mexicano, **11**

Grimond's Mansion, **4**

Gypsy's, **20**

Hacienda El Mortero, **14**

Jalapeños, **7**

Karl's Keller, **12**

Lorenzillos, **21**

Savios, **12**

Splash, **6**

Lodging

Albergue CREA, **1**

Calinda Viva Cancún, **9**

Camino Real, **15**

Cancún Playa, **28**

Conrad Cancún, **31**

Fiesta Americana Cancún, **10**

Fiesta Americana Condesa, **24**

Fiesta Americana Coral Beach Cancún, **13**

Hyatt Cancún Caribe Villas & Resort, **19**

Hyatt Regency Cancún, **16**

Krystal Cancún, **14**

Marriott Casamagna, **22**

Meliá Cancún, **23**

Oasis, **25**

Omni Cancún, **26**

Puerta al Sol, **30**

Radisson Sierra Plaza, **18**

Royal Solaris Caribe, **29**

Stouffer Presidente, **8**

Villas Tacul, **3**

bar features a billiard table. Although there are many standard French dishes, the menu bears a decided Mexican influence; specialties include a filet of beef served with *cuitlacoche*, an Aztec sauce made with corn and mushrooms. *Calle Pez Volador 8, tel. 98/830438. Reservations suggested during high season. Dress: casual but neat. AE, MC, V.*

Expensive **Chac Mool.** One of the few beachfront restaurants in the Hotel Zone, this establishment takes full advantage of the setting. Though the wrought-iron furniture is not particularly comfortable, the piped-in classical music, complemented by the sound of the surf, attracts the repeat clientele. The food is Continental—pasta, seafood, and beef dishes. Homemade rolls shaped as treble clefs emphasize the musical theme, while a sculpture of Chac Mool, the Mayan god of rain and plenty, decorates the front lawn. *Paseo Kukulcán, next to the Aristos Hotel, tel. 98/831107. Reservations suggested. Dress: casual but neat. MC, V. No lunch.*

El Mexicano. One of Cancún's largest restaurants seats 320 for a folkloric dinner show in a room resembling the patio of a hacienda. Details such as elaborately hand-carved chairs created by Indians from central Mexico and numerous regional Mexican dishes convey a feeling of authenticity. Be forewarned, however: Though indisputably popular, this is a touristy spot, and the dancing-girl show is not a window into Yucatecan culture. Granted that, try the *empanxonostle* (steamed lobster, shrimp, fish, and herbs); it promises to be as extravagant as El Mexicano's surroundings. When the final show ends, you're invited to dance until midnight. *La Mansión-Costa Blanca Shopping Center, tel. 98/832220 (restaurant), 98/844261 (reservations). Reservations required; show begins at 7:30. Dress: casual but neat. AE, MC, V.*

Hacienda El Mortero. Pampering waiters, strolling mariachi, lush hanging plants, fig trees, and candlelight make this reproduction plantation home a very popular spot to dine. The menu offers a selection of country cooking, and the steaks and ribs are first class. *Paseo Kukulcán, Hotel Krystal, tel. 98/831133. Reservations required for 7 and 9:30 seatings. Dress: casual but neat. AE, MC, V. No lunch.*

Moderate **Augustus Caesar.** In spite of the shopping-center location and the constant stream of shoppers passing by, this restaurant produces classic Italian specialties with an emphasis on seafood in a sophisticated, impressive setting. The gray, pink, and white color scheme, enhanced by white stucco columns, potted palms, tile floors, and soft jazz, creates a romantic ambience at night. *La Mansión–Costa Blanca Shopping Center, tel. 98/833384. Reservations suggested. Dress: casual. AE, MC, V.*

Captain's Cove. Both waterfront locations feature popular breakfast buffets served under palapa roofs. The decor is decidedly nautical, with rigging draped on the walls and chandeliers in the shape of ships' steering wheels. The restaurant near the Casa Maya Hotel overlooks the Caribbean Sea toward Isla Mujeres; the other is situated beside the Nichupté Lagoon. Both present lunch and dinner menus filled with seafood dishes and charbroiled steak and chicken. Parents appreciate the lower-priced children's menu, an unusual feature in Cancún. *Lagoonside, across from the Royal Mayan Hotel, tel. 98/850016; beachside, next to Casa Maya Hotel, tel. 98/830669. No reservations. Dress: casual. MC, V.*

★ **Carlos 'n Charlie's.** A lively atmosphere, a terrific view overlooking the lagoon, and good food make this restaurant—part of the popular Anderson chain—Cancún's best-known hot spot. You'll never run out of bric-a-brac to look at: The walls are catchalls, with tons of photos; sombreros, bird cages, and wooden birds and animals hang from the ceilings. For dinner you may be tempted by the barbecued ribs sizzling on the open grill, or one of the steak or seafood specials. After your meal, dance off the calories under the stars at the Pier Dance Club. *Paseo Kukulcán, Km 5.5, tel. 98/830846. No reservations. Dress: casual. AE, MC, V.*

Casa Rolandi. Authentic northern Italian and Swiss dishes are skillfully prepared by the Italian owner-chef, who grew up near the Swiss border. Homemade lasagna, baked in the large stucco oven, and an ample salad bar make for a satisfying dinner. Many fish and beef dishes are also on the menu. The decor is appropriately Mediterranean—white walls, lots of plants, and copper plates decorating the tables—and the back room offers a view of the beach. *Plaza Caracol, tel. 98/831817. Reservations suggested during high season. Dress: casual. AE, MC, V.*

★ **Gypsy's.** This all-time favorite restaurant sits upon stilts and overlooks an illuminated lagoon where crocodiles and fish can be seen. The decor hints at Spain, and the two dinner shows (7:30 and 9:30) with flamenco dancers convey the message loud and clear. Don't pass up the paella prepared by a Spanish chef from León. *Paseo Kukulcán, Km 10.5, tel. 98/832015. Reservations suggested. Dress: casual. AE, MC, V. Buffet brunch served 7:30 AM–noon.*

Jalapeños. Folks crowd this place in the morning for its inexpensive breakfast buffet and in the evening for the dancing under the stars to reggae music. Seven TV screens broadcast major sports events, while bartenders whip up tropical fruit drinks and margaritas to go along with jalapeños stuffed with shrimp or grouper prepared with wine, cilantro, and garlic. *Paseo Kukulcán, Km 7, tel. 98/832896. No reservations. Dress: casual but neat. MC, V.*

Karl's Keller. The Bavarian atmosphere here offers a refreshing change of pace from the many seafood and Mexican restaurants on the island, and for breakfast this place really serves up a hearty meal. The German owner whips up a mean sauerbraten as well as other Old World specialties. Don't leave without trying the sausage. *Plaza Caracol, tel. 98/831104. No reservations. Dress: casual. MC, V.*

Lorenzillos. Perched on its own peninsula in the lagoon, this nautical spot provides a pleasant spot to watch the sunset, sip a drink on the outdoor patio, or sample excellent seafood. Specialties include grilled or broiled lobster (you can pick your own) and whole fish Veracruz-style. The seafaring theme extends to the names of both the dishes (like Jean Lafitte beef) and the restaurant itself (Lorenzillo was a 17th-century pirate). *Paseo Kukulkán Km 10.5, tel. 98/831254. Reservations advised. Dress: casual. AE, MC, V.*

Savio's. The sea-green, white, and peach decor, a central staircase, floor-to-ceiling windows, and a sleek design with lots of greenery make this mall restaurant a fresh, lively spot for lunch. For dinner, candlelight and guitar and flute music create a romantic setting. Filling out the menu are homemade pastas and seafood. *Plaza Caracol, tel. 98/832085. No reservations ac-*

cepted. *Dress: casual for lunch; casual but neat for dinner. AE, MC, V. Closed New Year's Day.*

Splash. Good-quality Art Deco furnishings set amid a purple-and-aqua color scheme and neon lights add to the sleek design of this restaurant. During high season, go upstairs to the large bar and terrace, where in the distance you can see the water. Downstairs offers a more intimate dining experience. You can't go wrong with any of the homemade pastas or the grilled bora-bora fish with mango slices. *Paseo Kukulcán, no phone. No reservations. Dress: casual. MC, V. No lunch.*

Downtown

Downtown restaurants are located on the Downtown Cancún Dining and Lodging map.

Expensive **du Mexique.** The combination of an upstairs art gallery and a restaurant that serves Mexican fare with a nouvelle twist presents a creative alternative for diners who are looking for something new. The decor features dark-wood floors, a vaulted white stucco ceiling, and sleek contemporary design. *Av. Cobá 44, tel. 98/841077. Reservations suggested. Dress: casual but neat. AE, MC, V. No lunch.*

Moderate **Bucanero.** Quiet dining in a candlelit marine atmosphere is the drawing card for this seafood restaurant, and the seafood—especially lobster specialties—is tops. For starters, try the lobster bisque or black bean soup, and round the meal out with the seafood combination, which includes lobster in garlic sauce, shrimp and squid brochette, and a fish fillet. Piano music played throughout the evening and waiters dressed as pirates add character to the place. *Av. Nader, tel. 98/842280. Reservations accepted. Dress: casual but neat. MC, V. No lunch.*

★ **Café Amsterdam.** The Dutch wife–British husband team brings lots of flavor to this combination bakery, salad bar, and bistro. Visitors and locals find Amsterdam a bright and cheery lunch spot that serves a hearty meal at a low fixed price. Candles and flowers are brought out in the evenings for an intimate bistro effect. This café opens at 7AM, so it is also a good meeting place for breakfast. *Av. Yaxchilán 70, tel. 98/844098. No reservations. Dress: casual. AE, MC, V. Closed Mon.*

Carrillo's. This cheerful restaurant, with a large, sweeping veranda and pink-and-purple palm trees, features lobster specials—brochette, thermidor, and Mexican-style. Other house favorites include broiled red snapper smothered with ham, cheese, bacon, shrimp, and a red sauce, and one of the four ceviches. Carrillo's also provides lots of entertainment and festivities, beginning with happy hour from noon to 2, and the musical trio that plays nightly. *Claveles 12, tel. 98/841227. No reservations. Dress: casual. AE, MC, V.*

★ **El Pescador.** It's first-come, first-served, with long lines, especially during high season. But people still flood into this rustic Mexican-style restaurant with nautical touches; the open-air patio is particularly popular. Heavy hitters on the menu include red snapper broiled with garlic and freshly caught lobster specials. For dessert consider sharing the cake filled with ice cream and covered with peaches and strawberry marmalade. *Tulipanes 28, tel. 98/842673. No reservations. Dress: casual. MC, V.*

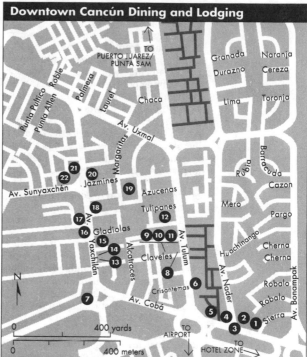

Downtown Cancún Dining and Lodging

La Fonda Del Angel. This unpretentious restaurant in a Mexican colonial–style setting has walls that are painted pink, lemon, and aqua; wood beams and wrought-iron details add a bit more pizzazz. The menu, which includes a variety of Mexican dishes, features the special Fillet Angel (beef covered with melted cheese and mushroom sauce). During high season, the outside patio offers a quiet alternative. Live music is played nightly. *Av. Cobá 32, tel. 98/843393. Reservations suggested. Dress: casual. AE, MC, V.*

★ **La Habichuela.** This charmer—once an elegant home—is perfect for hand-holding romantics or anyone looking for a relaxed, private atmosphere. The candlelit garden, with white, wrought-iron chairs, pebbled ground, and thick, tropical greenery, exudes peacefulness, while a statue of Pakal, the Mayan god of astronomy and culture, surveys all. Try the *cocobichuela*—lobster and shrimp in a light Indian sauce served on a bed of rice inside a coconut—a specialty of the house. *Margaritas 25, tel. 98/843158. Reservations suggested. Dress: casual but neat. MC, V.*

★ **La Parrilla.** If you're looking for the place where local Mexicans—young and old—hang out, you've found it in this popular downtown spot, an old classic by Cancún standards (it opened in 1975). Everything from the food to the bougainvillea and palapa roof is authentic. Popular dishes include the grilled beef with garlic sauce and the *tacos al pastor* (tacos with pork, pineapple, coriander, onion, and salsa). *Av. Yaxchilán 51, tel. 98/845398. No reservations. Dress: casual. AE, MC, V. No lunch; closed Christmas.*

Mi Ranchito. Don't come looking for privacy at this lively spot situated along a busy sidewalk, but come here for fun and you're guaranteed to find it. Serapes, piñatas, and straw sombreros hang from the ceiling, and a Mexican party every Saturday night provides a festive atmosphere. Meals are prepared by Mayan chefs who cook up a banana flambé crepe covered with flaming peaches and tequila tableside while dancing waiters balance trays of 20 drinks on their heads. *Av. Tulum 15, tel. 98/847814. Reservations accepted. Dress: casual. MC, V.*

Perico's. Find the antique car perched atop the palapa roof and you've found this zany, eclectic restaurant and bar. Saddles top bar stools, caricature busts of political figures from Castro to Queen Elizabeth line the walls, and waiters in firemen's uniforms serve flaming desserts. The Mexican menu, including Pancho Villa (grilled beef with Mexican side dishes), is reliable, but the real reason to come here is the party atmosphere that begins nightly at 7 when the mariachi and marimba bands play. *Av. Yaxchilán 71, tel. 98/843152. No reservations. Dress: casual. MC, V.*

Pizza Rolandi. Bright red-and-yellow decor, plants, wood beams, ceiling fans, and visible wood-burning ovens have turned this otherwise simple sidewalk pizza place into a quick-dining treat. Ten homemade pasta dishes and 15 different pizzas—some with chicken or fish—make up a large part of the huge wooden menu that's slid across the floor from table to table. *Av. Cobá 12, tel. 98/844047. No reservations. Dress: casual. MC, V.*

★ **Rosa Mexicano.** One of Cancún's prettiest Mexican colonial–style restaurants presents waiters dressed as *charros* (Mexican cowboys), pottery and embroidered wall hangings, floor tiles with floral designs, and a cozy, softly lighted atmosphere. For extra romance, make a reservation for the candlelit patio. Savory appetizers include *nopalitos* (a tamale-type treat with cactus, corn, cilantro, and cheese). Specialties are *filete Rosa* (beef and onions in a tequila-orange sauce) and *camarones al ajillo* (shrimp sautéed in olive oil and garlic, with chili peppers). *Calle Claveles 4, tel. 98/846313. Reservations advised. Dress: casual. MC, V. No lunch.*

Inexpensive **El Tacolote.** Only tacos are served here, and the standard order includes three. Mix-and-match fillings, but don't overlook the filet mignon taco. Bowls of sliced limes and salsa come with your order, in keeping with the very casual tone of this brightly tiled and comfortable place. *Av. Cobá, tel. 98/844453. No reservations. Dress: casual. MC, V.*

Lodging

The most important buildings in Cancún are its hotels, which presently number more than 100 (the number of new hotels is increasing by 5–10 per year). Choosing from this variety can be bewildering, because most hotel brochures sound—and look—alike. Many properties were built in the mid-1970s by international hotel chains known for their streamlined, standardized versions of hospitality, and some were substantially renovated following the damage wrought by Hurricane Gilbert in 1988. Hotels here tend to favor "neo-Mayan" architecture (palapa roofs, massive pyramidal stone structures, and stucco walls interspersed with red tile roofs and quasi-Mediterranean

Moorish arches), bland contemporary-style furniture, and pastel hues. As for the amenities—particularly in luxury hotels—expect minibars, cable TV, and laundry and room service. Almost every major hotel has an in-house travel agency and a car-rental concession.

Hotels that are affiliated with international chains tend to be large in terms of both the number of rooms (averaging more than 200) and the size of individual rooms (averaging about 538 square feet). Properties in the hotel zone offer rooms with both sea and lagoon views unless otherwise noted.

If proximity to downtown is a priority, then staying at one of the hotel zone properties at the island's northern end is advantageous; many of the malls are within walking distance, and taxis to downtown and to the ferries at Puerto Juárez cost less than from hotels farther south. If, however, you seek something more secluded, there is less development at the southern end.

For the most part, the hotels located in the downtown area don't offer anything near the luxury or amenities of the hotel zone properties. They do, however, afford visitors the opportunity to stay in a popular resort without paying resort prices, and many offer free shuttle service to the beach. In addition, a downtown location has the advantage of proximity to restaurants that are far more authentic—and less expensive—than those you'll find in the hotel zone.

All hotels have air-conditioning and private bathrooms unless otherwise noted. In addition, all properties in the Very Expensive and Expensive categories have water-sports facilities and parking unless otherwise noted. All Cancún hotels are within the 77500 postal code. Rates quoted refer to the peak winter season, mid-November–March. For more information, but *not* for reservations, contact the **Cancún Hotel Association** (Box 1339, Cancún, QR 77500, tel. 98/842853 or 98/845895, fax 98/847115).

Note: At press time the Ritz Carlton Cancún (tel. 800/241–3333) had recently opened. Although we were unable to visit the property, all reports have been glowing.

Highly recommended hotels are indicated by a star ★.

Category	Cost*
Very Expensive	over $160
Expensive	$90–$160
Moderate	$40–$90
Inexpensive	under $40

All prices are for a standard double room, excluding the 10% tax.

Hotel Zone

Hotel Zone properties are located on the Cancún Hotel Zone Dining and Lodging map.

Very Expensive **Camino Real.** This Westin resort, situated at the tip of Punta
★ Cancún, was selected as one of the Leading Hotels of the World because of its luxury accommodations and excellent manage-

ment, staff, housekeeping, and maintenance. The hotel comprises two very different structures—a four-story building incorporating a small Mayan ruin and a newer high rise—that are strikingly coordinated in design. Rooms in both units are unusually attractive. In the tower, the 85 Royal Beach Club accommodations, with pink and turquoise color schemes and well-wrought rattan furniture, capture the spirit of Cancún; a number have Jacuzzis, and each has its own balcony. Rooms in the older building were recently redone in a similar style. In the evening, guests can dance to live salsa at the hotel's popular Azucar disco (*see* Nightlife, *below*). *Punta Cancún (Box 14), tel. 98/830100 or 800/228–3000, fax 98/831730. 381 rooms. Facilities: 5 restaurants, 4 bars, 3 lighted tennis courts, disco, pool, 2 beaches, water sports, shopping arcade. AE, DC, MC, V.*

★ **Fiesta Americana Cancún.** The first of three Fiestas in Cancún, this intimate-feeling hotel is a perennial favorite among Europeans and Mexicans as well as Americans. A warm atmosphere and charming design—painted villas in rose, yellow, and sand—make it a standout. The lobby, with its palm trees, ceiling fans, bright prints, and rattan furniture, is a lovely, eclectic mix of Mexican, the South Seas, and Mediterranean designs. Eat lunch at the poolside Bikini Bar or slumber by the calm Northern waters of Bahía de Mujeres on this palapa-dotted beach. Rooms, which all have balconies, are spacious; brightly furnished with rattan, white wood, and smoky glass; and decorated with white, cobalt-blue, and coral hues. Suites are available. *Paseo Kukulcán, Km 9.5 (Box 696), tel. 98/831400 or 800/FIESTA–1, fax 98/832502. 281 rooms. Facilities: 3 restaurants, 4 bars, pool. AE, DC, MC, V.*

Fiesta Americana Condesa. This sprawling, friendly hotel has the same casual elegance and luxurious amenities of its older sister, the Fiesta Americana Cancún. Situated toward the southern end of the hotel zone, the Condesa has a Mediterranean-style facade featuring balconies, rounded arches, and alternating ocher, salmon, and sand-colored walls. But it's the huge palapa fronting the structure that makes it hard to miss. An attractive and spacious lobby bar has Tiffany-style stained-glass awnings, tall palms, and ceiling fans. Three seven-story towers overlook a tranquil inner courtyard with hanging plants and falling water. The rooms, highlighted by dusty-pink stucco walls and gray-blue carpets, offer the same tranquillity. Balconies are shared by three standard rooms; costlier rooms have their own balconies. Suites are available. *Paseo Kukulcán (Box 5478), tel. 98/851000 or 800/FIESTA–1, fax 98/851800. 502 rooms. Facilities: 4 restaurants, 2 bars, health club, 3 indoor tennis courts, 15 meeting rooms, beauty parlor, boutiques, in-room safes. AE, DC, MC, V.*

Fiesta Americana Coral Beach Cancún. Opened in late 1990, this all-suite hotel lies just in front of the convention center and shopping malls at the rotary opposite the Hyatt Regency. The large salmon-colored structure—built in Mediterranean style with blue wrought-iron balconies—houses a lobby with marble-tiled floors, potted palms, and a stained-glass skylight. All rooms are ample in size, with oceanfront balconies, marble floors, rounded doorways, and stained-glass windows; slate-blue, lavender, and beige tones create a soothing, pleasant mood. As for outdoor activities, choose between the 1,000-foot beach and the 660-foot pool. This is Cancún's largest convention hotel; expect the clientele to match. *Paseo Kukulcán, Lote*

6 (Box 14), tel. 98/832900 or 800/FIESTA–1, fax 98/832502. 602 suites. Facilities: 3 restaurants, 3 bars, pool, health club, 3 indoor tennis courts, shopping arcade. AE, MC, V.

Hyatt Cancún Caribe Villas & Resort. Intimate yet endowed with modern conveniences, this semicircular property was one of the first hotels in Cancún, but it was remodeled after suffering damage from Hurricane Gilbert. An attractive, contemporary room decor with Mexican accents now predominates: colorful stenciled borders on the walls near the ceilings, tile floors, curtains and bedspreads in dusty pinks and pale green prints, and light wood furniture. Beach-level rooms have gardens, and all rooms in the main tower have ocean views. *Paseo Kukulcán (Box 353), tel. 98/830044 or 800/228–9000, fax 98/831514. 198 rooms, including 62 beachfront villas. Facilities: 4 restaurants, 2 bars, 3 tennis courts, 3 pools, marina, 2 Jacuzzis, putting green, jogging path, car rental, travel agency, beauty salon. AE, DC, MC, V.*

Hyatt Regency Cancún. A cylindrical 14-story tower with the Hyatt trademark—a striking central atrium filled with tropical greenery and topped by a skylit dome—affords a 360° view of the sea and the lagoon. Plants spill over the inner core of the cylinder, at the base of which is a bar. Pink and purple tones prevail in the rooms, which also feature glossy gray-marble floors and warm hardwood furniture. This hotel, much larger and livelier than its sister property, boasts an enormous two-level pool with a waterfall. The Punta Cancún location is convenient to the convention center and several shopping malls. Suites are available. *Paseo Kukulcán (Box 1201), tel. 98/830966, 98/831566, or 800/228–9000, fax 98/831349. 300 rooms; rooms for disabled people available. Facilities: 2 restaurants, 4 bars, shops, car rental, travel agency, game room, pool, fitness center. AE, DC, MC, V.*

Krystal Cancún. Its rooms, done in nondescript contemporary style, are nothing to write home about, and its lobby can be rather hectic; but the location of this hotel, part of a Mexican chain, can't be beat. At the tip of Punta Cancún, within walking distance of three major shopping malls and across the street from the convention center, the Krystal affords spectacular views of the entire ocean coast of the island, the lagoon, and parts of downtown. The property also hosts Bogart's and Hacienda El Mortero, two of the best-known restaurants in town (*see* Dining, *above*), as well as the popular Christine disco (*see* Nightlife, *below*). *Paseo Kukulcán, Lote 9, tel. 988/31133 or 800/231-9860. 330 rooms. Facilities: 5 restaurants, 3 bars, pool, tennis and racquetball courts, weight room, Jacuzzi, sauna, shops. AE, DC, MC, V.*

Marriott Casamagna. One of Cancún's newest luxury properties, the six-story Marriott is rather eclectically designed: In the lobby modern furnishings are set in an atrium with Mediterranean-style arches, crystal chandeliers, and hanging vines. Three restaurants overlook the handsome pool area and the ocean. The rooms, decorated in contemporary Mexican style, have tile floors and ceiling fans and follow a soft rose, mauve, and earth-tone color scheme. Suites are available. *Paseo Kukulcán (Retorno Chac L-41), tel. 98/85200 or 800/228–9290, fax 98/851385. 450 rooms, including 38 suites. Facilities: 4 restaurants, bar, nightclub, whirlpool, in-room safes, 2 lighted tennis courts, health club, shops, car rental, beauty salon, parking. AE, DC, MC, V.*

★ **Meliá Cancún.** The stunning new Meliá Cancún is a boldly modern version of a Mayan temple, fronted by a sheer black marble wall and a sleek waterfall. The spacious, airy atrium, filled with lush tropical flora, is dappled with sunlight flooding in from corner windows and from the steel-and-glass pyramid skylight overhead. Public spaces, displaying loving attention to detail, exude elegance; the boutiques could not be more chic. Ivory, dusty-pink, and light-blue hues softly brighten rooms (all with private balconies); white-lacquered furniture and wall-to-wall carpeting create a luxurious ambience. The long two-level pool is deliciously unobstructed; service is unusually courteous and fast. Suites are available. *Paseo Kukulcán, Km 16, tel. 98/851160 or 800/336–3542, fax 98/851263. 450 rooms. Facilities: 5 restaurants, 4 bars, 2 pools, in-room safes, shopping arcade, beauty salon, car rental, travel agency, 18-hole golf course, health center, 3 tennis courts. AE, DC, MC, V.*

Omni Cancún. This 10-story pink hotel is topped off by a Spanish-style orange tile roof. The small lobby conveys the same elegant but comfortable feel as the guest rooms, which feature marble floors, sea-green and pink color schemes, and tasteful wood furniture. Some rooms have balconies; all have either ocean or lagoon views (the former are more expensive). Ranking as a primary attraction is the three-level pool, divided by a bar. Suites are available. *Paseo Kukulcán L–48 (Box 127), tel. 98/850226 or 800/THE–OMNI, fax 98/850059. 329 rooms, including 11 villas. Facilities: 3 restaurants, bars, hair dryers, gym, pool, 2 tennis courts, marina, shops, travel agency. AE, DC, MC, V.*

★ **Puerta al Sol.** The water pressure in the showerheads is fantastic, and in case you have trouble figuring out how to turn on the Jacuzzi, it's the little white button behind you in the bathtub. Puerta al Sol opened its restorative doors in 1990. Its marble-floored suites, delicate desert pastel appointments, and the spare, cool furnishings are a virtual massage to the senses the minute you unload your bags and get used to the idea that you've really jumped the rat-race-ridden mean streets back home. Every suite overlooks the Caribbean's sparkling, aquamarine water. All-inclusive means convenience—what with unlimited food and beverages, day-and-night activities and entertainments, tours to Mayan ruins and Isla Mujeres—but why does it mean the food just doesn't cut it? *Paseo Kukulcán, Km 20, tel. 98/851555 or 800/346–8225. 146 suites. Facilities: 3 restaurants, above-ground diving tank, outdoor whirlpool, indoor pool, outdoor pool, tennis, fitness center, game room with Ping-Pong and billiard tables, video theater. AE, DC, MC, V.*

Royal Solaris Caribe. Now an all-inclusive property, the former Aston Solaris recently took over the hotel next door and more than doubled its guest capacity. The grounds, which boast what's billed as the largest pool in Cancún, feature Japanese-style bridges and lush tropical foliage. A number of the units are time-share apartment suites, with large living rooms, kitchenettes, and bathtubs (as opposed to the shower stalls in the smallish standard rooms). Studio rooms, which also have kitchenettes, offer twice the space of superior rooms. *Paseo Kukulcán, Km 20, tel. 98/850600 or 98/850100, fax 98/850975. 450 rooms. Facilities: 3 restaurants, 2 bars, small grocery store, pool, tennis court, car rental, travel agency. AE, DC, MC, V.*

Stouffer Presidente. Located five minutes from Plaza Caracol, this hotel has a striking Mexican-pink facade. One of the first to open in Cancún, but extensively remodeled in 1988, it boasts a quiet beach and a waterfall in the shape of a Mayan pyramid by the pool. Well-appointed, larger-than-average-size rooms offer either one king-size or two queen-size beds, and are decorated in blue, cream, and pink pastels with light wood furnishings and tile floors. The property prides itself on its superior service. *Paseo Kukulcán, Km 7.5, tel. 98/830200, or 800/HO-TELS–1, fax 98/832602 or 98/832515. 294 rooms; rooms for disabled people and no-smoking rooms available. Facilities: 4 restaurants, bar, in-room safes, fitness center, 2 pools, 5 Jacuzzis, lighted tennis court, travel agency, car rental, beauty parlor, shops. AE, DC, MC, V.*

Villas Tacul. The accommodations in this large complex, set on its own stretch of beach en route to downtown, are appointed with red-tile floors and authentic Mexican colonial–style furniture, wagon-wheel chandeliers, and tin-work mirrors. Each villa has a kitchen and from two to five bedrooms, making this a good place for families and couples traveling together. An individual housekeeper keeps each unit spotless and serves private breakfasts for an extra charge. The grounds are beautifully landscaped, with well-trimmed lawns and palm trees surrounding the pool. *Paseo Kukulcán, Km 5.5, tel. 98/830000, 98/830080, or 800/842–0193, fax 98/830349. 23 villas. Facilities: restaurant, bar, pool, 2 tennis courts. AE, DC, MC, V.*

Expensive **Cancún Playa.** This hotel's airy lobby, with plenty of marble and cozy sunken sofas, is a popular gathering spot: You can get a quick breakfast of good coffee and pastries here in the morning; make arrangements for car rentals and tours during the day; and enjoy a drink to the strains of a piano player in the evening. Smartly modern, the property has white facades and royal blue canvas-topped lean-tos at the pool area, which is nicely divided by lawns. The rooms are equally spiffy, with lovely pine furniture, and corner suites are equipped with private hot tubs and large terraces. *Paseo Kukulcán, Km 19.5, tel. 98/851111, 98/851115, or 800/44–OASIS, fax 98/851151 or 713/622–5955 (Houston). 388 rooms. Facilities: 3 restaurants, 3 bars, 3 pools, car rental, travel agency. AE, MC, V.*

Conrad Cancún. Opened in 1991, this luxury property stands at the southern end of the island, on Punta Nizuc. It is one of the few hotels with direct access to both a 1,600-foot beach and Laguna Nichupté, which it shares with Club Med. The hotel comprises four nondescript low- rise concrete blocks, and the reception area is post-modern almost to the point of austerity, with scattered pieces of art posed against large, empty areas. In contrast, the restaurant set dramatically below the lobby floor is cheerfully decorated and has stunning beach views. Understated beige guest rooms are enhanced by handsome rustic furnishings. Concierge towers and suites are available. *Paseo Kukulcán, Km 20 (Box 1808), tel. 98/850086, 98/850537, or 800/445–8667, fax 98/850074. 391 rooms. Facilities: 2 restaurants, 3 bars, 5 pools, fitness center, 2 lighted tennis courts, 7 whirlpools, in-room safes, hair dryers. AE, DC, MC, V.*

Oasis. The modern tone of this hotel—one of the largest in Mexico—is enhanced by the twin waterfalls and black-gray marble floors in the lobbies. A seemingly endless arrangement of pools allows for unobstructed swimming, while a great lawn, wood walkways (easy on bare feet in the hot sun), and Japanese-style wood bridges provide pedestrian access. Inside, beige rooms with light blue drapes, dusty-blue bedspreads, and dark wood furniture provide a subdued but stylish ambience. Though not yet completed, the Oasis complex will eventually comprise four four-story buildings grouped around a taller trapezoid structure, which will contain 200 suites. Guests should be advised that our readership has informed us that service at this establishment is not equal to its impressive appearance. *Paseo Kukulcán, Lote 42, tel. 98/850867 or 800/44–OASIS, fax 98/850131. 960 rooms. Facilities: 5 restaurants, 6 bars, gym, pool, 2 tennis courts, 9-hole golf course, disco. AE, DC, MC, V.*

Radisson Sierra Plaza. The former Inter-Continental has the advantage of being closer to town than the hotels on the southern end, while still seeming to be away from it all. Pastel-decorated rooms with light wood furnishings and tile floors are airy and comfortable. All rooms have a sunken lanai or private balcony. The poolside palapa restaurant is a serene spot for lunch. At press time, the spacious lobby was undergoing renovation. *Paseo Kukulcán, Km 10, tel. 98/832444 or 800/333–3333, fax 98/833486. 261 rooms. Facilities: 3 restaurants, 3 bars, tennis courts, gym, beauty salon, travel agency, shopping, car rental, doctor on premises. AE, DC, MC, V.*

Moderate **Calinda Viva Cancún.** This white stucco 10-story building—part of a Mexican chain—is not one of the most attractive in town, but it makes a reliable standby and is in a good location, on the north beach near many malls. The rooms have marble floors; some have private balconies, ocean views, and kitchenettes. The property also features a small garden, a beach, and Mexican-theme restaurants. *Paseo Kukulcán, Km 8.5 (Box 673), tel. 98/830800. 216 rooms. Facilities: 2 restaurants, bar, pool, 2 lighted tennis courts, boutique. AE, DC, MC, V.*

Inexpensive **Albergue CREA.** This modern, government-run youth hostel on the beach has glass walls, cable TV, a pool, and dormitory beds (separate rooms for men and women). A cafeteria and lounge on the ground floor lend themselves to the sort of congenial mingling one expects of a youth hostel. *Paseo Kukulcán, Km 3, tel. 98/831337. 33 rooms (350 beds) with shared baths. Facilities: cafeteria, basketball, volleyball, Ping-Pong. No credit cards.*

Downtown

Downtown properties are located on the Downtown Cancún Dining and Lodging map.

Expensive **Holiday Inn Centro Cancún.** The place to stay if you want to be downtown and have all the amenities, this is the newest (built 1990) and most upscale hotel in the area. It's less expensive than similar properties in the hotel zone and provides free transportation to the beach of the Holiday Inn Crowne Plaza. The attractive pink four-story structure, with a Spanish tile roof, affords easy access to restaurants and shops. Although rooms are somewhat generic motel modern, with mauve and blue color schemes, they have appealing Mexican touches. *Av. Nader 1, S.M. 2, tel. 98/87455, fax 98/847954. 190 rooms. Facilities: restaurant, 2 bars, nightclub, pool, shops, beauty salon, travel agency, car rental agency, conference rooms. AE, DC, MC, V.*

Moderate **Antillano.** This old but prettily appointed property features
★ wood furnishings, a cozy little lobby bar, and a tiny pool. Extras

such as tiled bathroom sinks and air-conditioning in the halls and rooms make this hotel stand out a bit from the others in its league. Suites with kitchenettes are available. *Av. Tulum at Calle Claveles, tel. 98/841532 or 98/841132, fax 98/841878. 48 rooms. Facilities: pool, bar, travel agency, shop. AE, DC, MC, V.*

Caribe Internacional. Located on a major traffic circle downtown, this relatively modern hotel can be somewhat noisy. The gray concrete exterior is matched by big stucco walls and ceilings, and the rooms—though on the small side and sparsely furnished—are pleasant enough and have brightly colored walls. The small pool in a garden at the back adds a bit to this otherwise average property. *Yaxchilán 36 at Sunyaxchén, tel. 98/843999 or 800/223–6510, fax 98/841992. 80 rooms. Facilities: restaurant, cafeteria, pool, travel agency, parking. AE, MC, V.*

Margarita Cancún. This five-story property, situated just across from the Caribe Internacional, is Mission-style white stucco with yellow-tile trim. The rooms are done in a tasteful beige and white color scheme and have tiled floors. Ask for a room with a view of the pool. *Av. Yaxchilán 41, S.M. 22, tel. 98/849333 or 98/841324. 100 rooms. Facilities: restaurant, snack bar, lounge, pool, shops, travel agency, parking. DC, MC, V.*

★ **Plaza del Sol.** Popular with students, Europeans, and Canadians, this three-story Spanish colonial-style hotel is situated on one of the less-trafficked main streets downtown. Inside the large lobby is a pleasant bar. Rooms feature above-average (for this price category) carved furnishings but tend to be somewhat dark; bathrooms are large. *Av. Yaxchilán 31, tel. 98/843888. 86 rooms. Facilities: 2 bars, restaurant, pool, laundry service, car rental, free shuttle to beach, travel agency, parking. AE, DC, MC, V.*

Inexpensive **Hacienda Amigotel.** Part of a local Yucatán hotel chain, this property next door to the Caribe Internacional features a Spanish colonial-style lobby, an inner courtyard with a small pool, and a palapa-covered restaurant/bar. The rooms were originally decorated in a faintly colonial manner but have long since faded into what can best be termed "Mexican generic." Those with a pool view are slightly larger. *Av. Sunyaxchén, Lote 39-40, S.M. 24, tel. 98/843672 or 800/458–6888, fax 98/841208. 36 rooms. Facilities: cafeteria, bar, pool. V.*

María del Lourdes. The María del Lourdes has some nice touches throughout, such as the colonial-style restaurant with rust-and-white stucco walls and the garden surrounding a small pool in the back. The rooms are bright, with sparse, functional decor. *Av. Yaxchilán 80, tel. 98/844744, fax 98/841242. 51 rooms. Facilities: restaurant, pool. AE, MC, V.*

★ **Plaza Carrillo's.** One of the first hotels to be built in Cancún City, this one is conveniently located in the heart of the downtown area next to the Plaza Carrillo shopping arcade and Carillo's restaurant (*see* Dining, *above*), which are under the same ownership. The rooms are simply furnished but clean and well maintained and are equipped with small refrigerators. *Calle Claveles 35, tel. 98/841227 or 98/844833. 43 rooms. Facilities: restaurant, pool. AE, MC, V.*

Posada Lucy. This place isn't much to look at, but its location, on a quiet side street, is good. The cheerful blue-and-white rooms in the main building are small, with no views, but some include kitchenettes; there are another 12 rooms in an adjacent building behind Restaurant Pericos, under separate owner-

ship. Not all of the desk staff speak English. *Gladiolas 25, S.M.
22, tel. 98/844165. 25 rooms. MC, V.*

The Arts and Nightlife

The Arts

Film Local movie theaters showing American and Mexican films include **Espectáculos del Caribe** (Av. Tulum 44, tel. 98/840449) and
Cines Cancún 1 and 2 (Av. Cobá 112, tel. 98/841646).

Performances The **ballet folklórico** dinner show consists of stylized performances of regional Mexican dances including the hat dance and
la bamba. By comparison with the far superior Ballet Nacional
Folklórico of Mexico City, this troupe suffers, but if it's all you'll
get to see of the brilliant Mexican dance traditions, which blend
pre-Hispanic and Iberian motifs, then go for it. Admission includes the buffet—a sampling of regional Mexican cooking—
the show, and one drink. *Hotel Continental Villas Plaza, Paseo
Kukulkán, Km 11, tel. 98/821583. Admission: about $40. Per-
formances Tues.–Sun.; dinner 7 PM, show 8:30 PM.*

Cancún's **Jazz Festival** (tel. 800/542–8953) premiered in May of
1991 and featured Wynton Marsalis and Gato Barbieri. Spon-
sored by the Cancún Office of Special Events, the jazz fest is
scheduled to continue as an annual event and is being included
in tour packages from the U.S. At press time, the 1994 schedule
was not yet available.

Nightlife

Mexican **fiestas,** including dinner and folkloric dance performances, are staged at several of the large chain hotels.

A Mexican *charreada,* or rodeo show, is performed Monday-
Saturday at 7 PM at El Corral de JF (Km 6, Prolongación Av.
López Portillo). In addition to the show you get dinner and do-
mestic drinks.

Discos Cancún wouldn't be Cancún without its glittering discos and
hotel-lobby bars. Generally discos start jumping about 10:30.
Dady'O (Paseo Kukulcán, Km 9.5, tel. 98/833184 or 98/833333)
is presently a very "in" place. **Christine** (Krystal Cancún hotel,
tel. 98/831133) is among the most spectacular and popular
joints in town. **La Boom** (Paseo Kukulcán, Km 3.5, tel.
98/831458; closed Sun.) includes a video bar with a light show
and is not always crowded, although it can squeeze in 1,200
people. Visit the **Hard Rock Café** (Plaza Lagunas, Paseo Kukulcán, tel. 98/832024) for nostalgic rock music. The new **Azucar**
disco in the Camino Real hotel (tel. 98/830100, ext. 8037) sizzles
to a salsa beat from 8 PM to 4 AM daily.

Music **Cat's Reggae Bar** (Av. Yaxchilán 12, tel. 98/840407) plays island
music starting at 9 PM. You can also hear live reggae at **Jalapeños** (Paseo Kukulkan, Km 7, tel. 98/8328960) and **Tequila
Boom** (Paseo Kukulcán, Km 3.5, tel. 98/831458 or 98/831641)
nightly from 8. **Batacha** (Hotel Miramar Misión, tel. 98/831755)
is a piano bar with a small dance floor. **La Palapa** (Club Lagoon
Hotel, tel. 98/831111), offering dancing on a pier over the lagoon, inspires romance. **Reflejos** (Hyatt Regency, tel.
98/830966) has a chic lounge with a small dance floor.

4 Isla Mujeres

Updated by
Edie Jarolim

A tiny fish-shaped island just five miles off Cancún, Isla Mujeres (*IS-lah moo-HAIR-es*) is a tranquil alternative to its bustling western neighbor. Only about five miles long by a half-mile wide, Isla has flat sandy beaches on its northern end and steep rocky bluffs to the south. Because of its proximity to Cancún, it has turned into a small-scale tourist destination, but it is still a peaceful island retreat with a rich history and culture centered on the sea.

Part of that history is blessed by the presence of Isla's first known inhabitants, the ancient Mayas. Their legacy lies in the names, features, and language of their descendants here, but not, unfortunately, in the observatory they built on the Southern tip (Hurricane Gilbert obliterated the well-preserved ruin in '88; restoration efforts are ongoing).

The Spanish conquistadores followed: After setting sail from Cuba in 1517, Hernández de Córdoba's ship blew here accidentally in a storm. Credited with "discovering" the island, he and his crew dubbed their find "Isle of Women." One explanation of the name's origins is that Córdoba and company came upon wooden idols of Mayan goddesses. Another theory claims the Spaniards found only women when they arrived—the men were out fishing.

For the next several centuries, Isla, like many Caribbean islands, became a haven for pirates and smugglers, then settled into life as a quiet fishing village. In this century, it started out as a vacation destination for Mexicans; the '60s witnessed a hippie influx; since the late '70s, day-trippers from Cancún increasingly disembark here, and Isla's hotel, restaurant, and shop owners are seeing more activity than ever.

Most important, the laid-back island life attracts a crowd that prefers beach pleasures to nightlife—scuba diving, snorkeling, and relaxation to the cable TV and rollicking discos of Cancún. Thanks to concerned locals like Ramon Bravo, a renowned expert on sharks, underwater filmmaker, and author, Isleños themselves are working to preserve the island's ecology and tranquillity so that those arriving here for the first time will still find an unusually peaceful, authentically Mexican retreat.

As part of this effort, plans are currently afoot to have the Mexican government declare Isla Mujeres a national park. A fee would be levied on tourists who visit the island—money that would be used, it is argued, to keep the island's fragile ecology intact and to provide better services for visitors without damaging the site's unique character.

Essential Information

Important Addresses and Numbers

Tourist Information The **tourist office** (Calle Hidalgo 6, behind the basketball court, tel. 987/70316), located on the main square, two blocks from the ferry, is open weekdays 9–2 and 6–8. There, or at your hotel, you can pick up a copy of the monthly *Islander* magazine, which has most of the tourist information you'll need for your stay.

Emergencies **Medical Service** (tel. 987/70195); **Health Center** (tel. 987/70117); **Police** (tel. 987/70082).

Late-night **Farmacia Isla Mujeres** (Av. Juárez, next to the Caribbean
Pharmacies Tropic Boutique, no phone) and **Farmacia Lily** (Avs. Madero
and Hidalgo, no phone) are open Monday–Saturday 9 AM–9 PM.

Banks Banks are open weekdays 9–1:30 and exchange money from 10
to noon. They include **Banco del Atlántico** (Av. Rueda Medina
3, tel. 987/70104 or 987/70005) and **Banco Serfín** (Calle Juárez
3, tel. 987/70051 or 987/70083).

Arriving and Departing by Boat

Arriving Passenger ferries leave from Puerto Juárez, on the mainland,
for the main ferry dock in Isla Mujeres at approximately 6,
8:30, 9:30, 10, 10:30, and 11:30 AM, and at 12:30, 1:30, 2:30, 3:30,
4:30, 5:30, 6:30, 7:30, and 8:30 PM; the schedule varies depending
on the season, so check the times posted at the dock. The one-
way fare is only about $1.50 and the trip takes 45 minutes, but
delays and crowding are frequent. Preferable is the private
lancha, or motorboat, which makes the crossing from Punta
Sam, 5 kilometers (3 miles) north of Punta Juárez, in about 15
minutes. The fare is usually about $4 per person but varies:
Water taxis charge a flat fee, about $20, divided by the number
of passengers; a full load keeps the price low. Another convenient, more expensive service, the **Shuttle** (tel. 98/846433, in
Cancún), runs directly from the Playa Linda dock in Cancún's
hotel zone and costs $12 round-trip. Cars are unnecessary on
Isla (*see* Getting Around, *below*), but **municipal ferries** that accommodate passengers and vehicles leave from Punta Sam and
take about 45 minutes. Check departure times posted at the
pier, but you can count on the schedule running from about 7
AM to 9 PM, and until 11 PM in the summer. The fare is under
$1.50 per person. In addition, a number of tour companies offer
day trips to Isla Mujeres from Cancún; *see* Chapter 3 for some
possibilities.

Departing The passenger ferry departs from the main dock at Isla Mujeres to Puerto Juárez at approximately 5, 6:30, 7:30, 8:15, 8:45,
9:30, 10:30, and 11:30 AM, and at 12:30, 1:30, 2:30, 3:30, 4:30, 5,
5:30, and 6:30 PM. The first car ferry from Isla Mujeres to Punta
Sam leaves at about 6 AM and the last departs at about 7:15 PM.
The 91-foot *Caribbean Queen* (tel. 987/70254 or 987/70088, fax
987/70253), an air-conditioned ship with a bar, makes one or two
30-minute crossings daily; the fare is under $3 per person.
Again, schedules vary, so you should call ahead or check the
boat schedule posted at the pier.

Getting Around

For orientation purposes, think of Isla Mujeres as an elongated
fish: The southern tip is the head and the northern prong the
tail. The minute you step off the boat, it's clear how small Isla
is. The town, simply known as *el pueblo*, is seven blocks long by
five blocks wide and is centered around the dock and main
square, two blocks inland. Street names and addresses don't
matter much here (islanders have been known to look up their
own addresses, and signage is virtually nonexistent). At the
northern tip, the lovely Playa Cocoteros, also called Playa
Norte but more often "Cocos," is within easy walking distance
from town. One main paved road, Avenida Rueda Medina, runs
the length of the island.

By Bus **Municipal buses** run at 20- to 30-minute intervals daily between 6 AM and 10 PM from the Posada del Mar hotel on Avenida Rueda Medina out to Colonia Salinas on the windward side. There is also service from the dock to Playa Lancheros on the leeward side, toward the south end of the island. As you might expect, however, the service is slow, because the buses make frequent stops.

By Car There is little reason for tourists to bring cars to Isla Mujeres, because there are plenty of other forms of transportation that cost far less than renting and transporting your own private vehicle. Moreover, though the main road is paved, speed bumps abound and some areas are poorly lighted.

By Taxi If your time is limited you can hire a taxi (Av. Rueda Medina, tel. 987/70066) for a private island tour at about $8 an hour. Fares run $1–$2 from the ferry or downtown to the hotels on the north end, at Playa Cocoteros. Taxis line up right by the ferry dock between 5 AM and well past midnight.

By Moped The island is full of moped rental shops. **Motorent Kankin** (Calle Abasolo 15, tel. 987/70071) rents two-seater, three-speed Hondas for about $5 per hour or $20 per day ($35 for 24 hours); a $20 deposit— or a credit card or passport left behind—is required. **Pepe's Motorenta** (Calle Hidalgo 19, tel. 987/70019) offers two-seater Honda Aero-C50s, Aero-C90s, and fully automatic Aeros, starting at $5 per hour, for a minimum of two hours. **Ciro's Motorent** (Calle Guerrero N 11 at Calle Matamoros, tel. 987/70351) also has two-seater Elite-80 and Tact 50-80 mopeds.

By Bicycle Bicycles are available for hardy cyclists, but don't underestimate the hot sun and the tricky road conditions. **Rent Me Sport Bike** (Calles Juárez and Morelos, 1 block from the main pier, no phone), offers five-speed cycles starting at less than $2 for an hour; a full day costs about $5. You can leave your driver's license in lieu of a deposit, and it's open daily 8–6.

Moped and bicycle riders should watch for the many speed bumps, which can give you an unexpected jolt. Avoid riding at night; some roads have no street lights.

Mail The **post office** (tel. 987/70085), open weekdays 8–7:30 and Saturday 9–1, is located on Calle Guerrero, half a block from the market.

Telephones Ladatel phones allow you to reach an AT&T operator in the U.S. by dialing 01 or to charge calls using major credit cards. They may be found at various places around the island, including Av. Rueda, across from the ferry; outside Bucanero's restaurant (*see* Dining, *below*); across from the taxi stand; and outside the post office. In addition, long-distance phone service is available in the lobby of the **Hotel María José** (Calle Madero 21) or at **Club de Yates** (Calle Guerrero 8).

Guided Tours

Tour Operators Local agencies include **Club de Yates de Isla Mujeres** (Av. Rueda Medina, tel. 987/70211 or 987/70086), open daily 9–noon; and **La Isleña** (Calles Morelos and Juárez, tel. 987/70578), half a block from the pier, open daily 7–6. **Intermar Caribe** (Calle Morelos 3, tel. and fax 987/70102), with headquarters in Cancún, is the only full-service travel agency, and is open daily, except

Sunday; hours are erratic, however, and the Isla Mujeres office is frequently unattended.

Boat Tours **Cooperativa Lanchera** (waterfront, near the dock, no phone) offers four-hour launch trips to the Virgin, the lighthouse, the turtles at Playa Lancheros, the coral reefs at Los Manchones, and El Garrafón, for $35. **Cooperativa Isla Mujeres** (Av. Rueda Medina, tel. 987/70274), next to Mexico Divers, rents out boats at $120 for a maximum of four hours and six people, and $15 per person for an island tour with lunch (minimum six people). A trip to **Isla Contoy** (45 minutes to the north), with a minimum of 10 people, costs $30 per person and includes a light breakfast, snorkeling, lunch, and drinks; it departs at 8 AM and returns at 4 or 5 (*see* Excursion to Isla Contoy, *below*).

Exploring

Numbers in the margin correspond to points of interest on the Isla Mujeres map.

We start our itinerary in the island's only town, known simply as *el pueblo,* which extends the full width of Isla's northern "tail." The village is sandwiched between sand and sea to the north, south, and east; no high rises block the view. Activity **①** centers around the waterfront **piers** and on the coastal main drag, Avenida Rueda Medina. Two blocks inland you'll find the **②** other spot where everyone gathers—the **main square,** *la placita* or *el parque,* bounded by Calle Morelos, Avenida Bravo, and Calles Guerrero and Hidalgo. This is an ideal place to take in the life of the town. Daily scenes include basketball games on the permanent courts, children playing in the playground, and locals gathered to chat in front of the Government Palace. On holidays and weekends the square gets set up for dances, concerts, and fiestas.

③ Follow any of the north–south streets out to **Playa Cocoteros,** one of the finest beaches on the island, where you can wade far out in the placid waters. Hurricane Gilbert's only good deed, according to isleños, was to widen this and other leeward-side beaches by blowing sand over from Cancún. Along the way sit congenial palapa bars for drinks and snacks, and stands where you can rent snorkel gear, jet-skis, floats, sailboards, and sometimes parasails. At the northernmost end of Cocos, you'll find Punta Norte and come upon a hotel on its own private islet. A wood-planked bridge leads to the property, which has changed hands several times and is suppose to open by 1994 as an all-**④** inclusive resort called **Costa Club.** (The other building you'll see jutting out on a rocky point is a private home.)

Time Out Try to get to Cocos in the late afternoon, just before sunset, and stop in for a beer at **Rutilio's y Chimbo's,** twin palapa restaurant-bars right on the beach, where locals come to drink beer, play dice, and chat. You can sit on the high stools and watch sailboarders or children playing until the sun sinks below the horizon. A glorious setting at the end of the day, Cocos is a great place to talk to isleños, who are clearly happy to share the beauty of this place.

⑤ On the road parallel to Playa Cocos (Lopez Mateos), you'll find Isla's **cemetery,** with its hundred-year-old gravestones. Among

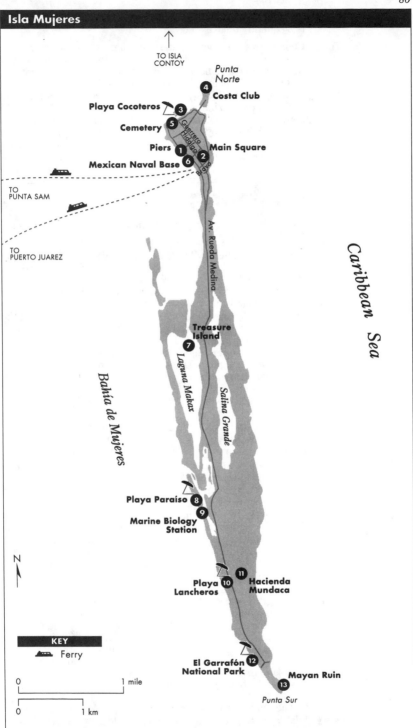

Isla Mujeres

TO ISLA CONTOY

Punta Norte

4 **Costa Club**

Playa Cocoteros **3**

Cemetery **5**

Piers **1** **2** **Main Square**

Mexican Naval Base **6**

Guerrero Hidalgo

Brava

TO PUNTA SAM

TO PUERTO JUAREZ

Av. Rueda Medina

Caribbean Sea

Treasure Island **7**

Laguna Makax

Salina Grande

Bahía de Mujeres

Playa Paraíso **8**

9

Marine Biology Station

N

Playa Lancheros **10** **11** **Hacienda Mundaca**

El Garrafón National Park **12**

Mayan Ruin **13**

Punta Sur

KEY

⛴ Ferry

0 _____ 1 mile

0 _____ 1 km

the lovingly decorated tombs, many in memory of children, is that of Fermín Mundaca (*see* Hacienda Mundaca, *below*). A notorious 19th-century slave trader (often billed more glamorously as a pirate), Mundaca is said to have carved his own tombstone with a skull and crossbones. On one side of the tomb an inscription reads in Spanish: "As You Are, I Once Was;" the other side warns, "As I Am, So Shall You Be." Mundaca's grave is empty, however; no one knows exactly where his remains lie. The monument is not easy to find—ask a local to point out the unidentified marker.

To explore the rest of the island, you'll need to take a moped or taxi south along the Avenida Rueda Medina, which leads out of
6 town. The first landmark you'll pass after the piers is the **Mexican naval base,** which is closed to the public. From the road, however, you can see (but don't photograph) the modest flag-raising and -lowering ceremonies at sunrise and sunset. Continuing southward, the *salinas* (salt marshes) will be on your left, and on your right you'll see the **Laguna Makax,** where pirates are said to have anchored their ships as they lay in wait for the hapless vessels plying Spanish Main (the geographical area in which Spanish treasure ships trafficked).

Follow the road until you come to an unmarked turnoff that
7 leads to a bridge across the lagoon and out to **Treasure Island,** where there's **Pirates Cove,** a small theme park visited mostly by Cancún day-trippers. Though few overnighters take an interest in this attraction, families who stop in enjoy the model shipwreck, open-air theater, shops, restaurant, and some caged birds and animals.

Head back to the main road and travel south for about 4 kilo-
8 meters (2½ miles); take the right turnoff at the sign to **Playa Paraíso.** The lovely beach is fronted by Hacienda Gomar, a good restaurant featuring a buffet lunch and marimba music. If you'd rather not put your shoes back on, try the barbecued grouper, snapper, or barracuda at Blacky's open grill on the beach. Also in the area you'll find boutiques and a beach bar with small palapas.

Walk about ½ kilometer south, either along the beach or on the soon-to-be-paved dirt road, until you come to the sign that says "Pesca." This signals the entrance to the government-run
9 **marine biology station,** which is devoted primarily to the study and preservation of the sea turtle, the lobster, and coral reefs. Technically the station is not open to the public, but during working hours visitors can examine various species and talk to the biologists about their work. The budget is small, but because the turtle population in the Mexican Caribbean continues to dwindle toward extinction, these dedicated ecologists have taken it upon themselves to care for young hatchlings until they are big enough to be let out to sea. Recent efforts have resulted in successful hatchings, and there is heightened awareness on the island concerning the preservation of vanishing species.

10 Just south of Paraíso lies **Playa Lancheros,** where you can eat lunch in the modest restaurant or shop for handicrafts, souvenirs, and T-shirts at the small stands. Also housed here, in a sea pen, are some pet sea turtles and harmless *tiburón gato* (nurse sharks). On the ocean side live the carnivorous *tintorera* (female sharks), which have seven rows of teeth and weigh as much as 500 kilograms (1,100 pounds). There is a small entrance fee to the beach, and you can buy refreshments and souvenirs. Live music is played on certain afternoons.

Off the main road, across from the entrance to Playa Lancheros, a tiny footpath cut through the brush leads to the ⑪ remains of the **Hacienda Mundaca,** built by Fermín Mundaca de Marechaja, the 19th-century slave-trader-cum-pirate mentioned above. When the British navy began cracking down on slavers, he settled on the island and built an ambitious estate with resplendent tropical gardens. The story goes that he constructed it to woo a certain island woman who, in the end, chose another man.

What little remained of the hacienda—something was left even after the 1988 hurricane—has mysteriously vanished, except for a sorry excuse of a guardhouse, an arch, a pediment, and a well. Locals say that the government tore down the mansion, or at least neglected its upkeep. (Purportedly, the government will soon rebuild the site for the cause of tourism.) If you push your way through the jungle—the mosquitoes are fierce—you'll eventually come to the ruined stone archway and triangular pediment, carved with the following inscription: *Huerta de la Hacienda de Vista Alegre MDCCCLXXVI* (Orchard of the Happy View Hacienda, 1876).

⑫ The next major site along the main road is **El Garrafón National Park,** the much-hyped, overvisited snorkeling mecca for thousands of day-trippers from Cancún. Although still beautiful, Garrafón—which lies at the bottom of a bluff—was once almost magical in its beauty. Now, as a result of the hands and fins of eager divers, Hurricane Gilbert, and anchors cast from the fleets of tourist boats continually arriving from Cancún, the coral reef here is virtually dead. There has been talk of closing the park to give the coral time to grow back (coral grows at the rate of 1 centimeter every 10 years), but too many locals make their living off it for this solution to be feasible. Still, visitors will be impressed by the scenery—parrotfish, angelfish, and the rich blue-greens of the water. Arriving early is essential if you wish to avoid the hordes that begin arriving around 10 AM. Snorkeling is much more pleasant when you aren't dodging the stray fin-kicks and churning waters caused by scores of enthusiasts. There are food stands and souvenir shops galore, as well as palapas, lockers, equipment rental, and a small aquarium. *No phone. Admission: $5. Open daily 9–5.*

Continuing around the southern tip of Isla Mujeres, about 1 kilometer (⅗ mile) from Garrafón, you'll come to the sad ves- ⑬ tiges of a **Mayan ruin,** formerly a temple dedicated to Ixchel, the goddess of fertility. Though Hurricane Gilbert whalloped the ruin and succeeded in blowing most of it away, restoration efforts are underway. The adjacent **lighthouse** still stands, and the keeper sometimes allows visitors to go up. Just past that point, on the windward side, is one of the island's most scenic patches of coastline, from which you can also make out the skyline (and lights, if it's dark) of Cancún. From here, follow the road into town; it's about an hour's walk. Flag a cab on the road if you wish.

Shopping

Shopping on Isla Mujeres used to be limited to basic resort wear, suntan lotions, and groceries. Now, more Mexican crafts shops offering good deals on silver, fabric bags, and handcrafted objects are opening here. Even the smaller shops often accept credit cards. Shopping hours are generally daily 10–1 and 4–7, although many stores now stay open through siesta and after 7.

Local Crafts **La Loma** (Calle Guerrero 6, 2nd floor, on the east side of the main square, tel. 987/70446) has a selection of exquisite crafts from all over Mexico and Guatemala, including amber, silver, black jade, leather jewelry, and masks, pottery, and textile bags. Although the shop is not inexpensive, La Loma offers the biggest and best collection on the island. Owner Judith Fernández does the buying herself and is a good source of information about the island.

Tienda Paulita (Calles Morelos and Hidalgo, tel. 987/70014) features a standard selection of folk art and handmade clothing in a fairly large space.

Rachat & Rome (Av. Rueda Medina, tel. 987/70250), housed in the pink building by the dock, sells gold, silver, and gemstones. In 1991, the same owners opened **Van Cleef,** with a similarly impressive jewelry selection in a large corner shop (Av. Juarez and Calle Morelos, tel. 987/70499).

Casa del Arte Mexica (Calle Hidalgo 6, no phone) has a good choice of clay reproductions, silver jewelry, batiks, rubbings, wood carvings, leather, and hammocks.

Grocery Stores There are two fair-size groceries: **Super Betino** (Calle Morelos 3) and **Super Mirtita** (Calle Juárez and Av. Bravo). Food, including fresh fruit, can also be purchased in the municipal market on Calle Guerrero Norte.

Sports and Fitness

Water Sports

Fishing Billfish are a popular catch in spring and early summer; the rest of the year, you can fish for barracuda and tuna, as well as for shad, sailfish, grouper, and red snapper.

Bahía Dive Shop (Av. Rueda Medina, across from the pier, tel. and fax 987/70340) charges $250 for a day of deep-sea fishing, $200 a day for cast fishing (tarpon, snook, and bonefish), and $20 an hour for offshore fishing (barracuda, snapper, and smaller fish).

Snorkeling and Scuba Diving Even though there is widespread concern over loss of reef, ocean lovers will still be impressed by the underwater spectacle here. From the surface and below, plenty of fascinating sea life can be observed. The best time to snorkel is during summer months between 8 AM and 3 PM, when the water is warm and calm. Not only will more fish be attracted by the mild temperature, but the placid conditions also increase visibility.

The famous coral reefs at **El Garrafón** (*see* Exploring, *above*) have suffered tremendously from negligent tourists, Hurricane Gilbert, and the constant dropping of anchors. Though still a beautiful sight (you can spot parrotfish, angelfish, and schools of sargeant majors), the reef is far from its past splendor. Get there early; Cancún day-trippers start churning up the waters at around 10. Good snorkeling continues at the **lighthouse** (*el farito*) near Playa Cocos on the north end, and up the beach near the Costa Club. Underneath is a partially buried but still visible statue of the Virgin.

Offshore, there's excellent diving and snorkeling at **Xlaches** (Isla Che) reef, due north on the way to Isla Contoy (*see* Excursion to Isla Contoy, *below*). Another one of the island's most alluring diving attractions is the **Cave of the Sleeping Sharks,** east of the northern tip. The caves were discovered by an islander and extensively explored by Ramon Bravo, a local diver, cinematographer, and Mexico's foremost expert on sharks. *National Geographic* and Jacques Cousteau have also studied the curious phenomena of the snoozing *tiburones* (sharks)—it's a fascinating site for experienced divers.

At the extreme southern end of the island on the leeward side lies **Los Manchones.** At 30–40 feet deep and 3,300 feet off the southwestern coast, this coral reef makes a good dive site. **Los Cuevones,** to the southwest near La Bandera, reaches a depth of 65 feet. Another site, complete with two shipwrecked galleons, is on the windward side of the islet north of Mujeres. Dive shops will be able to direct you.

Bahía Dive Shop (Av. Rueda Medina 166, across from the pier, tel. and fax 987/70340) rents snorkeling and scuba equipment and runs three-hour boat and dive trips to the reefs and the Cave of the Sleeping Sharks. Snorkel gear goes for $4 a day; tanks, $40–$55, depending on the length of the dive. **Mexico Divers** (Av. Rueda Medina and Av. Medero, 1 block from the ferry, tel. 987/70131 or 987/70274), also called **Buzos de México,** runs three-hour snorkeling tours for $15; trips for certified divers start at $40 per tank. Dive master Carlos Gutiérrez also gives a resort course for $80 and open-water PADI certification for $350.

Beaches

For any water sport, beaches on the north and west sides are the calmest. For more detailed descriptions of the following beaches, *see* Exploring, *above*. At the northern tip of the island, **Playa Cocos** is a tranquil white-sand beach. Locals come here to drink beer and watch the sunset, but you can also rent sailboards or meander into a palapa-covered restaurant. Both the eastern side, by the Costa Club, and the western side, at Nautibeach, have superb views and fine white sand. **El Garrafón,** on the opposite (southern) tip of the island, has a coral reef 6 feet from shore, but it's been eroded by tourists and environmental conditions. On the western side of Isla, you'll find **Playa Paraíso** and **Playa Lancheros.**

Dining

Dining on Isla Mujeres offers what you would expect on a small island: plenty of fresh-grilled seafood—lobster, shrimp, conch, and fish. You can also try Mexican and Yucatecan specialties like *carne asada* (broiled beef), *mole poblano* (a spicy sauce of chile, chocolate, sesame, and almonds), *pollo píbil* (chicken baked in banana leaves in a tangy sour orange sauce), and *poc chuc* (pork marinated in sour orange sauce with pickled onions). Those who crave more familiar fare can opt for pizza, steak, or shish-kebob.

Generally, restaurants on the island are informal (shirts and shoes required). Most of these have outdoor facilities or palapas, and the only dress requirement here is that swimsuits and feet should be covered. As in the rest of Mexico, locals eat their main meal during siesta hours, between 1 and 4, and a light dinner in the evening. Unless otherwise stated, restaurants are open daily for lunch and dinner.

Highly recommended restaurants are indicated by a star ★.

Category	Cost*
Very Expensive	over $20
Expensive	$15–$20
Moderate	$8–$15
Inexpensive	under $8

*per person, excluding drinks and service

Expensive **Chez Magaly.** A very elegant establishment on the grounds of
★ the Nautibeach Condo-hotel, this mostly French restaurant is tastefully furnished with wood floors, plants, leather chairs, Chinese blinds, and handsome place settings. Seafood grills, lobster quiche, jambalaya (Caribbean paella), and tequila-flambéed mangos are among the specialties. To complement the meal, choose from an extensive wine list. *Av. Rueda Medina, Playa Norte, tel. 987/70259. Reservations advised. MC, V. Closed 2 weeks in June.*

Maria's Kan Kin. Near El Garaffón, at the southern end of the island, this beach restaurant features gourmet seafood. Choose a live lobster or try one of the specialties, which tend to be prepared with a French twist, like lobster bisque and chocolate mousse. It's the perfect spot for a long lunch that extends to sunset. *On the main road to Garaffón, tel. 987/70015. MC, V.*

Moderate **Bucanero.** With a prime location, near the *parque* on one of the main pedestrian drags, this appealing restaurant has attractive wood tables with blue-and-white inset tiles and terra-cotta floors. For breakfast, the *huevos motuleños* (fried eggs served on a corn tortilla heaped with beans, ham, cheese, peas, marinated red onions, all drenched in tomato sauce) are excellent and cheap; lunch and dinner specialties include avocado stuffed with shrimp and *mar y cielo* (fish fillet and chicken breast with french fries and onions). The palapa-roofed section is a good choice by day, but the mosquitos will eat you alive there at night. *Av. Hidalgo 11, tel. 987/70236. No reservations. AE, MC, V.*

Cafécito. This airy café is a popular hangout for locals and Europeans who come for coffee, ice cream, crepes, and waffles. Artfully decorated with glass-topped turquoise wood tables, shells, and mobiles, Cafécito serves full dinners during high season. *Corner of Avs. Juarez and Matamoros. No phone. No* *reservations. AE. Open 9 AM–noon and 6 PM–10 PM. Closed Thurs.*

El Limbo. This restaurant—housed in the Hotel Roca Mar, which has been carved into the side of a cliff—offers a sensational view of the sea, which laps up to the lower level windows. The decor remains typical for the island: Nets, seashells, and tortoiseshells adorn the walls, while rustic wood furniture fills the dining area. Included on the menu are pollo píbil, pork chops, and steak, as well as many seafood specials. You have the choice of fish or shellfish broiled, breaded, fried, or in garlic, all served with rice or french fries and salad. *Av. Bravo and Calle Guerrero, at Hotel Roca Mar, tel. 987/70101. No reservations. MC, V.*

★ **Pizza Rolandi.** Red tables, yellow director's chairs, green walls and window trim, and dark wood beams set the cozy tone at this very "in" chain restaurant. Select from a broad variety of Italian food: lobster pizzas, calzones, and pastas. Grilled fresh fish and shrimp are highly recommended, and salads are excellent. Or just stop in for a drink at one of the outside tables; the margaritas are the best in town. *Calle Hidalgo (between Calles Madero and Abasolo), tel. 987/70430. No reservations. MC, V.*

Inexpensive **Cocos Fríos.** With nightly live music and tables on the sidewalk, this is a hopping place for people-watching. The rough-cut pine tables, chairs, and bar add character to an otherwise modest establishment. Choose from such specialties as beef shish kebab, carne asada, cheese fondue, chicken with french fries, or fried fish. *Calle Hidalgo 4, no phone. No reservations. No credit cards.*

Lonchería Poc Chuc. This tiny restaurant is named for the famous Yucatán dish of pork marinated in sour orange, which is a house specialty. The no-frills Mexican eatery has a decent breakfast, too. *Calle Juárez (between Calles Madero and Morelos), no phone. No reservations. No credit cards.*

Mirtita's, Tropicana, and **Villa del Mar.** Next to each other on Av. Rueda Medina across from the ferry dock, these are favorite local hangouts. All serve fresh seafood and Yucatecan specialties. *Av. Rueda Medina. No phone. No credit cards.*

Lodging

The approximately 25 hotels (about 600 rooms) on Isla Mujeres generally fall into one of two categories: The older, more modest places are situated right in town, and the newer, more expensive properties tend to have beachfront locations around Punta Norte and, increasingly, on the peninsula near the lagoon. Most hotels have ceiling fans and air-conditioning. Luxurious, self-contained time-share condominiums are another option, which you can learn more about from the tourist office (tel. 987/70316). All hotels share the 77400 postal code.

Highly recommended hotels are indicated by a star ★.

Category	Cost*
Very Expensive	over $90
Expensive	$60–$90

Category	Cost*
Moderate	$25–$60
Inexpensive	under $25

*All prices are for a standard double room, excluding the 10% tax.

Expensive **Cristalmar.** Although the location of this condo-hotel (a five-minute drive from town) is inconvenient for those without their own transportation, the property—situated on a peninsula by the lagoon—boasts a stunning sea view. Other pluses include the spacious suites, from which you can choose one-, two-, or three-bedroom units, and the spanking modernity of the property overall. All rooms open to the courtyard, which has a pool and a palapa bar. Local artwork adorns the walls of this property and dark brown wicker furnishings and glass-top tables decorate the rooms. *Paraíso Laguna Mar, Lot 16, tel. 987/70007 or 800/622–3838. 37 suites. Facilities: small pool, beach, sauna, bar, kitchenettes. MC, V.*

★ **Na-Balam.** This intimate, informal hostelry set on Playa Cocos will fulfill all your tropical-paradise fantasies. Three corner suites with balconies affording outstanding views of sea and sand are well worth $75. The simple, attractive rooms have turquoise-tiled floors, carved wood furniture, dining areas, and patios facing the beach; photos of Mexico in its bygone days and Mexican carvings grace the walls. Breakfast at the hotel's restaurant is a delightful way to kick off the day. *Calle Zazil Ha 118, tel. 987/70279, fax 987/70446. 12 suites. Facilities: air-conditioning, restaurant, bar, beach. AE, MC, V.*

Perla del Caribe. On the eastern edge of town, the three-story Perla has rooms that face either the open sea or town, priced accordingly. Rooms are comfortable and functional, but not palatial. You can listen to music in the restaurant/bar most evenings. *Av. Madero 2, tel. 987/70444 or 800/258–6454, fax 987/70011. 130 rooms. Facilities: restaurant/bar, pool, beach, laundry. AE, MC, V.*

Moderate **Belmar.** Right in the heart of town, above Pizza Rolandi, this small hotel shares a charming plant-filled inner courtyard with the restaurant, which means it can be noisy here until 11 PM. Standard rooms are pretty, with tiled baths and light-wood furniture. One enormous suite features a private Jacuzzi on a patio, a tiled kitchenette, and a sitting area. All rooms have cable TV and air-conditioning. *Calle Hidalgo 110 (between Calles Madero and Abasolo), tel. 987/70430. 11 rooms. AE, DC, MC, V.*

★ **Cabañas María del Mar.** A rather mind-boggling assortment of rooms are available in this unusual beachfront hotel, but all have a great deal of character, and the place as a whole has a unique Mexican atmosphere. There are hand-carved wood furnishings by local artisans in a combination of Spanish and Mayan styles, folk art, tiled baths, hand-painted sinks, and, for Yucatecan visitors who don't like beds, some rooms even have hammock rings. The hotel has a prime location on Playa Cocos, next to Na-Balam, and its reasonable room rates include Continental breakfast. *Av. Carlos Lazos 1, tel. 987/70213, 987/70179, or 800/826–6842, fax 305/531–7616 or 987/70173. 51 rooms, including 12 cabanas. Facilities: air-conditioning, pool, moped rental, restaurant/bar, travel agency, car and boat service. MC, V.*

Mesón del Bucanero. In the midst of an expansion that will add eight suites, this new (1990) Spanish colonial–style hotel features attractive contemporary wood furnishings in bright rooms. Reasonably priced suites have small sitting areas and balconies, and large closets. Standard rooms are unusually diminutive, however, and the baths have a strong antiseptic odor. *Calle Hidalgo 11, tel. 987/70126 or 987/70210. 6 rooms and 4 suites. Facilities: restaurant. AE, MC, V.*

Posada del Mar. This hotel's assets include its prime location between town and Playa Cocos and its reasonable prices. Rooms have balconies overlooking a main road and beyond to the waterfront. The simple wood furnishings appear somewhat worse for wear, although baths are clean, with cheerful sea green tiles. Inexpensive private bungalows are also available. A new bar, in the process of construction, promises to be as popular as the current palapa-roofed local hangout. *Av. Rueda Medina 15, tel. 987/70300, 987/70044, fax 987/70266. 42 rooms. Facilities: 2 restaurants, bar, pool. AE, MC, V.*

Inexpensive **Poc-Na.** The island's youth hostel, located at the eastern end of town, rents bunks or hammocks (which cost less), but it requires a deposit that's almost twice the cost of the accommodations. One bonus is its proximity to the beach. *Calle Matamoros 15, tel. 987/70090 or 987/70059. Facilities: dining room, lockers, showers. No credit cards.*

Private Bungalows Several pretty, small bungalows near Garrafón are rented for the long term by the owner, Tino. Inquire at **Mexico Divers** (tel. 987/70131) at the main pier in town.

The Arts and Nightlife

The Arts

Festivals and cultural events occur on many weekends, with live entertainment on the outdoor stage in the main square. The whole island celebrates events like the spring regattas and the Caribbean music festivals. (For annual celebrations, *see* Festivals and Seasonal Events in the Before You Go section of Chapter 1, Essential Information.) **Casa de la Cultura,** near the youth hostel, offers folkloric dance and aerobics classes year-round. The center also operates a small public library and book exchange. *Av. Guerrero, tel. 987/70307. Open Mon.–Sat. 9–1, 4–8.*

For English-language films visit **Cine Blanquita** (Calle Morelos, between Calles Guerrero and Hidalgo, no phone).

Nightlife

Most restaurant bars feature a happy hour from 5 to 7; the palapa bars at Playa Cocos are an excellent place to watch the sunset. The bar at the **Posada del Mar** (Av. Rueda Medina 15, tel. 987/70300) can be subdued or hopping, depending on what's going on in town. **Buho's,** the bar/restaurant at Cabañas María del Mar (Calle Carlos Lazo 1, tel. 987/70213), serves food and is another good choice for a relaxing drink at sunset or later at night. **Restaurante La Peña** (Calle Guerrero 5, tel. 987/70321) has music and dancing on its open-air terrace overlooking the sea. Locals swear by the down-home ambience at **Calypso** (Av. Rueda Medina, near the lighthouse and Playa Cocos, no phone). Go watch music videos or sports events at **Tequila** (Calle Hidalgo 19, tel. 987/70019), which also hosts a disco in high season. Hours vary, but you will find it open weekend nights. Head for the main square if you're in the mood for Caribbean, salsa, or other live music.

Excursion to Isla Contoy

Isla Contoy (Isle of Birds) is a national wildlife park and bird sanctuary and a perfect getaway, even from Isla Mujeres. Birders, snorkelers, and fishing aficionados come here to enjoy the setting and the numerous varieties of animal life.

Important Addresses and Numbers

Government Office SEDESOL (tel. 98/845955 in Cancún), the national ecology and urban-development ministry, can provide information about the island.

Getting There Only 6.5 kilometers (4 miles) long and less than a kilometer (about ⅗ mile) wide, Contoy is 30 kilometers (19 miles) from Isla Mujeres and 12 kilometers (8 miles) from the coast of Yucatán. The island can also be reached by boat from Cancún.

Guided Tours At least two of Isla Mujeres's boating cooperatives sell day
From Isla Mujeres tours to Contoy for $35–$40. Ricardo Gaitán Puerto's **Sociedad Cooperativa "Isla Mujeres"** (at the pier, tel. 987/70274) and **La Isleña** (½ block from the pier, at the corner of Calles Morelos and Juárez, tel. 987/70036) launch boats daily at 8:30 AM; they return at 4 PM. Trip operators provide a fruit breakfast on the boat and gear for snorkeling, plus a stop at Xlaches reef. On the way, your crew fishes for the lunch they'll cook on the beach at Contoy—you may easily be in for anything from barracuda to lobster (unlimited beer and soda are also included). The tour of Contoy's leeward side includes visits to Bird Beach and Puerto Viejo Lagoon. Explore the island, snorkel, check out the museum, or just laze under a palapa. The size of the group depends on the boat, but it's usually a minimum of 6 and a maximum of 25. Overnight excursions can be arranged.

From Cancún The **Contoy II** (tel. 98/871909 or 98/871862, fax 98/841254) departs from Playa Linda dock Tuesday through Saturday at 8:30 AM and returns at 5 PM. The package includes swimming, snorkeling, and an open-bar lunch.

Exploring Isla Contoy

About 45 minutes north of Isla (depending on the boat), the sanctuary—a place of sand dunes, mangroves, and coconuts—remains beautiful and unspoiled. People come for the birds, the small museum, and the healthy waters on the leeward side. Seventy species of bird life—including gulls, pelicans, petrels, cormorants, cranes, ducks, flamingos, herons, frigates, sea swallows, doves, quail, spoonbills, and hawks—fly this way in late fall, some of them to breed and make their nests. Although the number of species is diminishing, Contoy is still a rare treat for bird-watchers.

Anyone with an interest in nature will be fascinated by the sea life around this nearly deserted island. For snorkelers, the coral and fish are dazzling. Immense rays, occasionally visible in the shallows, average about five feet across and can sometimes be seen jumping out of the water. The island's waters also abound with mackerel, barracuda, flying fish, trumpetfish, and shrimp; in December, lobsters pass through in great numbers as their southerly migration route takes them past.

Black rocks and coral reefs fringe the island's east coast, which drops off abruptly 15 feet into the sea; at the west are sand, shrubs, and coconut palms. At the north and the south you find nothing but trees and small pools of water. The sand dunes inland on the east coast rise as high as 70 feet above sea level. Other than the birds and the dozen or so park rangers who make their home on Contoy, the only denizens are iguanas, lizards, turtles, hermit crabs, and boa constrictors.

Visit the outdoor museum, which displays about 50 photographs depicting the island, with captions in English, French, and Spanish. An observation tower offers a superb view of the surroundings. Wildlife lovers can even spend the night camping (bring a sleeping bag and insect repellent), but should contact SEDESOL (*see* Important Addresses and Numbers, *above*) for information first.

Note: At press time Isla Contoy was temporarily off-limits to tourists, but it should reopen by 1994.

5 Cozumel

Updated by
Edie Jarolim

Cozumel provides a balance between Cancún and Isla Mujeres: Though attuned to North American tourism, the island has managed to keep development to a minimum. Its expansive beaches, superb coral reefs, and copious wildlife—in the sea, on the land, and in the air—attract an active, athletic crowd. Rated one of the top destinations in the world among underwater enthusiasts, Cozumel is encircled by a garland of reefs entrancing divers and snorkelers alike. Despite the inevitable effects of docking cruise ships (shops and restaurants actively recruit customers on an increasingly populous main drag), the island's earthy charm and tranquillity remain intact. The relaxing atmosphere here is typically Mexican—friendly and unpretentious. Cozumel's rich Mayan heritage is reflected in the faces of 60,000 or so isleños; you'll see people who look like ancient statues come to life, and occasionally hear Mayan spoken.

A 490-square-kilometer (189-square-mile) island 19 kilometers (12 miles) to the east of Yucatán, Cozumel is mostly flat, its interior covered by parched scrub, dense jungle, and marshy lagoons. White sandy beaches with calm waters line the island's leeward (western) side, which is fringed by a spectacular reef system, while the powerful surf and rocky strands on the windward (eastern) side, facing the Caribbean, are broken up here and there by calm bays and hidden coves. Most of Cozumel is undeveloped, with a good deal of the land and the shores set aside as national parks; a few Mayan ruins provide what limited sightseeing there is aside from the island's glorious natural attractions. San Miguel is the only established town.

Before Cozumel was rediscovered by oceanographic explorer Jacques Cousteau in the early 1960s, it was just another backwater, where locals hunted alligators and iguanas and worked on coconut plantations to produce copra (dried kernels from which coconut oil is extracted). Zapote trees were cultivated for chicle, once prized as the source of chewing gum, and Cozumeleños subsisted largely on the fruits of the sea, including lobster, conch, sea turtles, and fish, which remain staples of the economy.

Although the island was first inhabited by distant cousins of the Maya, it was the Maya who transformed it into a key center of trade and navigation as well as the destination for pilgrimages honoring Ixchel, the goddess of fertility, childbirth, and the moon; it is said that every Mayan woman was required to visit the site at least once in her lifetime. The Maya called the island *Ah-Cuzamil-Peten*, "place of the swallows."

In 1518, Spanish explorer Juan de Grijalva arrived on Cozumel in search of slaves. His tales of gold and other treasures inspired the most famous Spanish explorer Hernán Cortés—to come to Mexico—to visit the island the following year and, shortly thereafter, to settle two missionaries there to convert the Indians. Although the Spaniards never succeeded in colonizing Cozumel, disease eventually wiped out much of the native population that had not already been massacred. By 1600 the island was abandoned.

During the 17th and 18th centuries Cozumel became a hideout for famous pirates and buccaneers, including Jean Laffite and Henry Morgan, who found the catacombs and tunnels dug by the Indians useful for burying their treasure. These corsairs also laid siege to numerous cargo ships, many of which still lie at the bottom of the surrounding waters. In the 19th century Cozumel was primarily a fishing village and supply port for shipping routes to Central America. At the start of this century, the island began to capitalize on the chewing-gum industry; forays into the jungle in search of chicle led to interest in the archaeological remains. Many of the ruins still stand, but Cozumel's importance as a seaport and a chicle-producing region diminished with the advent of the airplane and the invention of synthetic chewing gum. In the 1950s the island eked out an existence as a health resort for wealthy Yucatecans, and with the arrival of Cousteau—who had learned of the magnificent diving opportunities—Cozumel began its climb out of oblivion.

Cozumel's prolific wildlife has made this an island for exploring: Brilliantly feathered tropical birds, lizards, armadillos, coati, deer, and small foxes populate the undergrowth and the swamps, and you can even rescue turtle eggs as part of a nationwide campaign. Teeming ocean life, particularly at the Palancar reef, makes the island a mecca for experienced divers but even a first-time snorkeler can take in the spectacular underwater scenery since the reefs are close to shore. Billfishing, deep-seafishing, and bottom fishing are other popular pursuits, as are glass-bottom-boat trips to the reefs or lagoons. If you're planning to stay on Cozumel for three or more days, you may want to consider excursions to the mainland beaches around Akumal and to the ruined, walled city of Tulum. You can ferry over to Cancún for a day or fly to Chichén Itzá to spend the night, then come back to explore more of Cozumel's unique habitat.

Essential Information

Important Addresses and Numbers

Tourist Information The **state tourism office** (tel. 987/20218 or tel. and fax 987/23318) is located upstairs in the Plaza del Sol mall, at the east end of the main square, or *la plaza,* and is open weekdays 8:30–3. Here you can pick up the *Blue Guide* and *Cozumel in One Day,* designed for cruise ship passengers. At the **Cozumel Tips** office across the patio from the tourism office, you can get a copy of the magazine bearing that name. These publications, all free, tend to be heavily advertiser-driven, but they are helpful all the same. The "Brown Map" is the best available on the island and can be purchased in local shops. A good source of information on lodgings (as well as of general information) is the **Cozumel Island Hotel Association** (Calle 2 N at 15a, tel. 987/23132, fax 987/22809), open weekdays 8–2 and 4–7. But *avoid* the "tourist information" booths on the main square: they're actually trying to sell time-share tours.

Emergencies **Police** (Anexo del Palacio Municipal, tel. 987/20092); **Red Cross** (Av. Rosada Salas at Av. 20a S, tel. 987/21058); **Air Ambulance** (tel. 987/20912); **Port Captain** (tel. 987/20169); **Recompression Chamber** (Calle 5 S 21-B, between Av. Rafael Melgar and Av. 5a S, tel. 987/22387).

Medical Clinics The **Centro de Salud clinic** (Av. Circunvalación, tel. 987/20140) and the **IMSS hospital** (Av. 30a at Calle 11 S, tel. 987/23797) provide 24-hour emergency care, and the new **CEM hospital/clinic** (Av. 20 N 425, tel. 987/21419 or 987/22919) offers 24-hour air ambulance service and a 24-hour pharmacy.

Late-night Pharmacies **Farmacia Joaquín** (plaza, tel. 987/20125) is open Monday–Saturday 8 AM–10 PM and Sunday 9–1 and 5–9.

Banks Banks are open weekdays 9–1:30. Hours for foreign currency exchange vary; your best bet is between 10 AM and noon. Banks include **Banpaís** (across from the main pier, tel. 987/21682); **Bancomer** (Av. 5a at the plaza, tel. 987/20550); **Banco del Atlántico** (Av. 5a S at Calle 1, tel. 987/20142 or 987/20182); and **Banco Serfín** (Calle 1 S between Avs. 5a and 10a, tel. 987/20930).

Money Exchange If you need to exchange money after banking hours, go to **Promotora Cambiaria del Centro** (Av. 5a S at Calle 1), which provides service Monday–Saturday 8–8.

English-language Bookstores **Zodiaco** (east side of the plaza, tel. 987/20031) carries a limited selection of guidebooks and English-language publications and is open weekdays 8–2 and 4–10, Saturday 9–2 and 5:30–9, and Sunday 9–1 and 6–9. There's no name on the awning, but the store is right next door to Farmacia Joaquin.

Travel Agencies and Tour Operators Agencies with branches in Cozumel include **Intermar Caribe** (Calle 2 N 101-B between Avs. 5a and 10a, tel. 987/21535 or 987/21098, fax 987/20895), **Fiesta Cozumel/American Express** (Calle 11 S, between Av. 25 and Av. 30, tel. 987/20974 or 987/20831), and **Turismo Aviomar** (Av. 5a N 8a between Calles 2 and 4, tel. 987/20477 or 987/20588).

Arriving and Departing by Plane

Airport and Airlines The **Cozumel Airport** is 3 kilometers (2 miles) north of town. **Continental** (tel. 800/231–0856, tel. 987/20847 in Cozumel) provides nonstop service from Houston. **Mexicana** (tel. 800/531–7921, 987/22945 in Cozumel) flies nonstop from Dallas/Fort Worth, Miami, and San Francisco; **Aerocaribe** and **Aerocozumel** (tel. 987/20877 or 987/20928), both Mexicana subsidiaries, fly to Cancún (12 round-trip flights daily) and other destinations in Mexico, including Chichén Itzá, Chetumal, Mérida, and Playa del Carmen.

Between the Airport and Hotels Because of an agreement between the taxi drivers' and the bus drivers' unions, there is no taxi service from the airport; taxi service is available to the airport, however. Arriving passengers reach their hotels via the *colectivo*, a van with a maximum capacity of eight. Buy a ticket at the airport exit: the charge is $5 per passenger to the hotel zones, a little under $3 into town. If you want to get to your hotel without waiting for the van to fill and for other passengers to be dropped off, you can hire an "especial"—an individual van costing a little under $20 to the hotel zones, about $8 to the city. Taxis to the airport cost about $8 from the hotel zones and approximately $5 from downtown. Most car rental agencies (*see* Getting Around, *below*) maintain offices in the terminal.

Arriving and Departing by Ferry, Jetfoil, and Cruise Ship

By Ferry Passenger-only ferries depart from the **Playa del Carmen dock** (no phone) for the 40-minute trip to the main pier in Cozumel. They leave approximately every hour between 5:30 AM and 9

PM and cost about $7. Return service to Playa operates from roughly 4 AM to 10 PM. Verify the regularly changing schedule. A new 320-passenger boat, *La Vikinga,* now provides fast service between Cozumel, Cancún, and Isla Mujeres; departures for Cancún from Cozumel are at 10:45 AM and 6:30 PM, and the cost is $27 one way. Call 987/20477 or 987/21588 for more information. The older car ferry from **Puerto Morelos** (tel. 987/21722) is not recommended unless you *must* bring your car. The three- to four-hour trip costs about $30 depending on the size of the car or $4.50 per passenger. Again, schedules change frequently, so we advise you to call ahead. Tickets can be bought up to a day in advance.

By Jetfoil Two waterjet catamarans make the trip between Cozumel (downtown pier, at the zócalo) and Playa del Carmen. This service, operated by **Aviomar** (tel. 987/20588 or 987/20477), costs the same as the ferry and takes as much time, but the vessel is considerably more comfortable and offers on-board videos and refreshments. The boats make at least eight crossings a day, leaving Playa del Carmen approximately every two hours between 7:30 AM and 9:30 PM and returning from Cozumel between 6:30 AM and 8 PM. Tickets are sold at the piers in both ports one hour before departure, but call to confirm the schedule.

By Cruise Ship At least a dozen cruise lines call at Cozumel and/or Playa del Carmen, including, from Fort Lauderdale, **Costa Cruises** (tel. 800/327–2537); from Miami, **Carnival** (tel. 800/327–9501), **Chandris** (tel. 305/576–9900), **Dolphin** (tel. 800/222–1003), **Norwegian** (tel. 800/327–7030), and **Royal Caribbean** (tel. 800/327–2055); from New Orleans, **Commodore** (tel. 800/327–5617) and **Regency** (tel. 800/338–5500); from Tampa, **Holland America** (tel. 800/426–0327) and **Princess Cruises** (tel. 800/568–3262). **Special Expeditions** (tel. 212/765–7740) offers 15-day sailings between the Panama Canal and the "Maya Coast," with passengers disembarking in Cozumel.

Getting Around

By Bus Because of a union agreement with taxi drivers, no public buses operate in the north and south hotel zones; local bus service runs mainly within the town of San Miguel, although there is a route from town to the airport. Service is irregular but inexpensive (under NP$1).

By Car Open-air Jeeps and other rental cars, especially those with four-wheel drive, are a good way of getting down dirt roads leading to secluded beaches and small Mayan ruins (although the rental insurance policy may not always cover these jaunts). The only gas station on Cozumel, at the corner of Avenida Juárez and Avenida 30a, is open daily 7 AM–midnight.

Car Rentals Following is a list of rental firms that handle two- and four-wheel-drive vehicles (all the major hotels have rental offices): **Avis** (Calle 20 between Calle Rosada Salas and Calle 3 S, tel. 987/21923; at Hotel Stouffer Presidente, tel. 987/20322), **Budget** (Av. 5a, between Calle 2 N and Calle 4 N, tel. 987/20903; at the cruise-ship terminal, tel. 987/21732; and at the airport, tel. 987/21742), **Fiesta Cozumel** (Hotel Mesón San Miguel, tel. 987/21389), and **Hertz** (Av. Juárez and Calle 10, tel. 987/22136). Car rates start at $50 a day.

Mopeds and Motorcycles Mopeds and motorcycles are very popular here, but also extremely dangerous because of heavy traffic, potholes, and hidden stop signs; accidents happen all too frequently. Mexican law now requires all passengers to wear helmets. For mopeds, go to **Fiesta Cozumel, Rentadora Caribe** (Calle Rosada Salas 3, tel. 987/20955), or **Rentadora Cozumel** (Calle Rosada Salas 3 B, tel. 987/21429, and Av. 10a S at Calle 1, tel. 987/21120). Mopeds rent for $25 per day.

By Taxi **Taxi service** is available 24 hours a day, with a 25% surcharge between midnight and 6 AM, at the main location (2 Calle N, tel. 987/20041 or 987/20236) or at the *malecón*, as the oceanside walkway is called, at the main pier in town. You can also hail taxis on the street, and there are taxis waiting at all the major hotels. Fixed rates of about $3 are charged to go between town and either hotel zone, about $8 from most hotels to the airport, and about $10 from the northern hotels or town to Chankanaab park or San Francisco beach. However, cruise-ship passengers taking taxis to or from the international terminal are often charged about twice as much as tourists staying on the island.

Mail

The local **post office** (Calle 7 S at Av. Rafael Melgar, tel. 987/20106), six blocks south of the square, is open weekdays 9–1 and 3–6 and Saturday 9–1. If you are an American Express cardholder, you can receive mail at **Fiesta Cozumel/American Express** (Calle 11 S, between Av. 25 and Av. 30, tel. 987/20522 or 987/20831) weekdays 8–1 and 5–8 and Saturday 8–5.

Telephones

Long-distance calls can be placed from the designated **booths** on Av. 5a N at Calle 2, next to Budget Rent-a-Car, and on Calle 1 S at the main square, daily 8–1 and 4–9.

Guided Tours

Orientation Island tours are offered for about $30 by at least two of Cozumel's leading travel agencies. The **Intermar Caribe** (tel. 987/21535) version includes swimming at a beach on the windward side, a visit to a "coral factory" in town, and snorkeling and lunch at Chankanaab. **Turismo Aviomar** (tel. 987/20588) sells the same tour and a variation: the Mayan ruins at San Gervasio, swimming, beach games, and jetskiing at Playa del Sol (near Palancar Beach, on the leeward side). Another option is to take a private taxi tour of the island; they range from $30 to $50 per day depending on which parts of the island you wish to visit.

Air Tours **Turismo Aviomar** offers a plane trip to Chichén Itzá; the price of $109 includes the flight, transfers to the ruins, and a guide.

Specialty Tours **Snorkeling tours** go for anywhere from $18 to $35, depending on the length, and take in the shallow reefs off Palancar or the Colombia lagoon. Lunch on a beach and equipment are usually included. A tour by **Turismo Aviomar** departs from Playa del Sol and caters particularly to cruise-ship passengers, who are taken directly from the ship to the beach. **Fiesta Cozumel** runs snorkeling tours from its 45-foot catamaran, the *Zorro*. **Diving tour** rates begin at about $56 per day; snorkelers wishing to accompany dive boats may do so for about $25, but it is much less expensive—under $10 a day—to rent your own equipment at one of the dive shops in town or out at the beaches (*see* Sports and Fitness, *below*).

Strictly for professional divers is the all-inclusive scuba trip to **Banco Chinchorro,** a ship graveyard 16 kilometers (10 miles) off the coast of southern Quintana Roo, almost due east of Chetumal. This unusual excursion, offering 100-foot dives, reef dives, and night dives, takes place aboard the luxurious 100-foot MV *Oceanus,* which houses guests for a minimum of three nights (cost: $600). **Barbachano Tours** (1570 Madruga Ave., Ph. #1, Coral Gables, FL 33146, tel. 305/662–5971) sponsors the trip.

Glass-bottom-boat trips provided by **Turismo Aviomar** (tel. 87/20588) appeal to people who don't want to get wet but do want to see the brilliant underwater life around the island. Four times a week, the air-conditioned semi-submarine *Mermaid* glides over a number of reefs that host a dazzling array of fish; the tour, which costs $30, lasts 1 hour and 45 minutes and includes soft drinks and beer.

Off-island tours to Tulum and Xel-Há, run by **Intermar Caribe** and **Turismo Aviomar,** cost about $54 and include the 30-minute ferry trip to Playa del Carmen, the 45-minute ride to Tulum, 1½–2 hours at the ruins, entrance fees, guides, lunch, and sometimes a stop for snorkeling at Xel-Há lagoon.

The Cozumel Museum offers evening **turtle-watching tours** during which visitors aid in the preservation of the endangered turtle species. The tours run between May and September, when the babies hatch. After a slide show, a guide takes participants to the eastern shore of the island, where they seek out and mark nests and collect the eggs, which are the size of Ping-Pong balls. The expedition ends, following a lecture by biologists at the hatchery, at midnight. Tours are offered several days a week, for a minimum of six people. *Av. Rafael Melgar, between Calles 4 and 6 N, tel. 987/21545. Suggested donation: $10. May–Sept., check museum for weekly tour schedules.*

Exploring

Cozumel is about 53 kilometers (33 miles) long and 15 kilometers (9 miles) wide, but only a small percentage of its roads—primarily those in the southern half—are paved. Dirt roads can be explored, with care, in a four-wheel-drive vehicle. Aside from the 3% of the island that has been developed, Cozumel is made up of vast expanses of sandy or rocky beaches, quiet little coves, palm groves, scrubby jungles, lagoons and swamps, and a few low hills (the maximum elevation is 45 feet).

San Miguel, Cozumel's hub, is simply laid out in characteristically Mexican grid fashion. Avenida Benito Juárez stretches east from the pier for 16 kilometers (10 miles) across the island, dividing north from south. Running perpendicular is Avenida Rafael Melgar, the coastal road on the island's leeward side (the walkway across the street, on the ocean side, is known as the malecón). Avenues, which are labeled "norte" or "sur" depending on where they fall in relation to Juárez, parallel Melgar and are numbered in multiples of five. This means that the avenue after Avenida 5a Sur is Avenida 10a Sur, but if you were to cross Juárez on Avenida 5a Sur it would turn into Avenida 5a Norte. The side streets are even-numbered north of Avenida Juarez (2, 4, 6, etc.) and odd south of the avenue (3, 5, 7 ...), only confusing until you've walked around town.

Numbers in the margin correspond to points of interest on the Cozumel map.

❶ Cozumel's principal town, **San Miguel,** serves as the hub of the island; its Avenida Rafael Melgar, along the waterfront, is the main strip of shops and restaurants. The **Plaza del Sol** is the main square, most often simply called *la plaza* or *el parque.* Directly across from the docks, it's hard to miss. A number of government buildings are here, including the large and modern convention center (used more for local functions than for formal conferences) and the **state tourist office** (tel. 987/20218 or 987/23318). The square is the heart of the town, where everyone congregates in the evenings. Heading inland (east) from the malecón takes you away from the touristy zone and toward the residential sections. The commercial district is concentrated in the 10 blocks between Calle 10 N and Calle 7 S. North of that point, you find almost no development until you reach the stretch of hotels beyond the airport; south of town, development continues almost uninterrupted as far as the Stouffer Presidente.

The **Museo de la Isla de Cozumel** is a good place to begin orienting yourself. Housed on two floors of what was once the island's first luxury hotel are four permanent exhibit halls of dioramas, sculptures, charts, and explanations of the island's history and ecosystem. Displays, which are well laid out and labeled, cover Mayan, colonial, and modern times and detail the local geology, flora, and fauna. A charming reproduction of a Mayan house is a highlight. The museum also presents temporary exhibits, guided tours, and workshops. *Av. Rafael Melgar between Calles 4 and 6 N, tel. 987/21545 or 987/21475. Admission: $3. Open Sun.–Fri. 10–6; closed Sat.*

Time Out On the terrace off the second floor of the museum, the **Restaurante del Museo** (Av. Rafael Melgar, between Calle 4 and 6 N, tel. 987/20838) offers breakfast, drinks, or a full meal of *fajitas* or grilled red snapper, all enhanced by a great waterfront view.

Heading south of town, divers and snorkelers may want to take **❷** a plunge off the pier at **La Ceiba:** About 100 yards offshore lie the remains of a small airplane that was placed there in 1977 during the making of a Mexican movie. An underwater trail marks various types of sea life, including sponges and enormous coral formations; visibility is excellent to about 30 meters (about 98 feet). La Ceiba, which is part of the second cluster of hotels and shops south of town, lies adjacent to the international passenger terminal for cruise ships.

About a 10-minute drive south of San Miguel you will find **❸** **Chankanaab Nature Park** (the name means "small sea"), a lovely saltwater lagoon that the government has made into a wildlife sanctuary and botanical garden. Underwater caves, offshore reefs, a protected bay, and a sunken ship attract droves of snorkelers and scuba divers. The botanical garden boasts about 350 varieties of plant life from more than 20 coun-

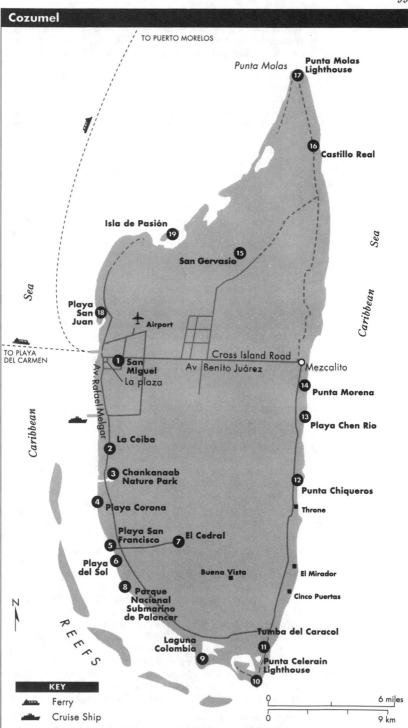

Cozumel

TO PUERTO MORELOS

Punta Molas · **Punta Molas Lighthouse** 17

16 **Castillo Real**

Sea

Isla de Pasión 19

San Gervasio 15

Caribbean

Playa San Juan 18

Airport

Sea

TO PLAYA DEL CARMEN

1 **San Miguel** · La plaza

Cross Island Road

Av Benito Juárez · Mezcalito

14 **Punta Morena**

Caribbean

13 **Playa Chen Río**

La Ceiba 2

3 **Chankanaab Nature Park**

12 **Punta Chiqueros**

4 **Playa Corona**

■ Throne

Playa San Francisco 5 · 7 **El Cedral**

Playa del Sol 6

■ Buena Vista

■ **El Mirador**

8 **Parque Nacional Submarino de Palancar**

■ Cinco Puertas

Tumba del Caracol

Laguna Colombia

11

9

Punta Celerain Lighthouse

10

Av. Rafael Melgar

R E E F S

N

KEY

⛴ Ferry

⛴ Cruise Ship

0 ———— 6 miles

0 ———— 9 km

tries; if mosquitoes are particularly attracted to you, consider buying insect repellent at one of the park's shops before you venture on the nature walk into the jungle. Some 60-odd species of marine life, including fish, coral, turtles, and various crustaceans, reside in the lagoon. Sadly, swimming through the underwater tunnels from the lagoon to the bay is now forbidden, but visitors may walk through the shallow lagoon. Be warned, however, that the bottom is rocky, so wear shoes with rubber soles. As to the bay and its contents, the beach is excellent, and the waters hide crusty old cannons and anchors as well as statues of Jesus Christ and Chac Mool. Four dive shops, a restaurant, four gift shops, a snack stand, and a dressing room with lockers and showers are on the premises. *Carretera Sur, Km 9, no phone. Admission: $4. Open daily 9–5.*

4 Just south of Chankanaab, **Playa Corona** offers the same brilliant marine life as the park by sharing access to the Yucab reef. Snorkeling equipment is available for rent, and the restaurant here serves conch and shrimp ceviche, *fajitas,* and more. The crowds that visit Chankanaab haven't yet discovered this tranquil neighbor.

5 More southerly still lies **Playa San Francisco,** an inviting 5-kilometer (3-mile) stretch of sandy beach that's considered one of the longest and finest on Cozumel. Comprising the beaches known as Playa Maya and Santa Rosa, San Francisco gets especially crowded during high season, on weekends (with cruise-ship passengers), and on Sunday (when locals come to eat fresh fish and hear live music). Environmental concerns have halted plans to build five new luxury hotels here. In the meantime, however, the beach has everything beach-goers need (though costs run higher here than on other, less frequented beaches): two outdoor restaurants, a bar, dressing rooms, gift shops, volleyball nets, beach chairs, and snorkeling equipment. Divers also use this beach as their jumping-off point for dives to the San Francisco reef and the Santa Rosa **6** wall. Just past San Francisco is **Playa del Sol.** Now open to the public, this beach was once privately owned by the tour operator Aviomar; it has complete facilities, including a restaurant-bar, shops, and snorkeling and jetskiing equipment; you can also rent horses and trot down the beach.

A turnoff at Km 17.5 leads about 3 kilometers (2 miles) inland **7** to the village and ruins of **El Cedral,** once the largest Mayan site on Cozumel and the temple sighted by the original Spanish explorers in 1518. (To explore the areas off the paved road, a four-wheel-drive vehicle is strongly recommended. Beware of flash flooding during the rainy season: a number of the dirt roads can become difficult to navigate in minutes.) The first Mass in Mexico was reportedly celebrated at this temple, most of which was torn down by the conquistadores. The site was uninhabited at the turn of the century, and the ruined temple was used as a jail. The U.S. Army Corps of Engineers destroyed most of the ruin during World War II to make way for the island's first airport, and now all that remains is a small structure capped by a Mayan arch and covered by faint traces of paint and stucco. A defiant tree grows from its roof. Every May a fair, with dancing, music, and a cattle show, is held here.

More interesting than the ruin is the small green contemporary church housing 92 crosses shrouded in embroidered lace mantles. The crosses, which were thought to have oracular qualities, testify to the cult of the "Speaking Cross," which inspired the rebellious Mayas during the War of the Castes in the mid-1800s. In this war, the Indians vainly attempted to win back the land that had been wrested from them three centuries before. Families fleeing the mainland settled in San Miguel and made their living off the Colombia hacienda south of San Francisco Beach.

Backtrack to the coast and continue south, and you'll come to **⑧ Parque Nacíonal Submarino de Palancar,** whose beach, with a gently sloping shore enlivened by palm trees, is far more deserted than San Francisco. Offshore lies the famous **Palancar Reef,** which is practically Cozumel's raison d'être. Because of the diversity of coral formations and the dramatic underwater peaks and valleys, divers rank this reef among the top five in the world.

At the island's southern tip and most commonly reached by **⑨** boat (although there is a trail) is the **Laguna Colombia,** a prime site for jungle aficionados. Fish migrate here to lay their eggs, and barracuda, baby fish, and birds show up in great numbers in season. Popular diving and snorkeling spots can be found offshore in the reefs of **Tunich, Colombia,** and **Maracaibo.**

If you continue east on the paved road, you'll reach the Caribbean coast. Make a right turn off the paved road onto a dirt road and follow it for 4 kilometers (3 miles) south to get to the **⑩ Punta Celerain Lighthouse,** surrounded by sand dunes at the narrowest point of land. The lighthouse affords a misty, mesmerizing view of pounding waves, swamps, and scraggly jungle. Alligators were once hunted nearby; nowadays you may spot a soldier or two from the adjacent army base catching an iguana. On Sunday at noon, the point comes to life when Primo the lighthouse keeper serves fried fish and beer, and locals and tourists gather to chat. A number of secluded beaches trail off to the left.

After visting the lighthouse, backtrack on the dirt road north. **⑪** You will first pass the **Tumba del Caracol,** another Mayan ruin that may have served as a lighthouse. The east coast of Cozumel, at which you have now arrived, presents a splendid succession of mostly deserted rocky coves and narrow, powdery beaches—sadly garbage-strewn in spots—posed dramatically against astoundingly turquoise water. Swimming can be treacherous here, but there is nothing (except perhaps the lack of changing facilities, since most of the beaches can be seen from the road) to prevent solitary sunbathing on any of the several beaches. A few other minuscule ruins are in the area—**Buenavista, Cinco Puertas,** and the **Throne.**

⑫ Punta Chiqueros, a moon-shaped cove sheltered from the sea by an offshore reef, is the next attraction en route; you'll be back on the paved road by the time you get to this point. Part of a longer stretch of beach that most locals call **Playa Bonita**— it's also known as Playa San Martin or *Tortuga Desnuda* (Naked Turtle)—it has fine sand, clear water, and moderate waves. You can swim and camp here, watch the sun set and the moon rise, and dine at the Playa Bonita restaurant. A little less **⑬** than 5 kilometers (3 miles) away, is **Playa Chen Río,** another good spot for camping or exploring, where the waters are clear and the surf is not too strong.

Nearly 1 kilometer (½ mile) north of Chen Río along the main
(14) road is **Punta Morena,** where waves crash on the rocky beach
and, on June nights when the moon is full, turtles come to lay
their eggs. If you're on the beach then, you may be stopped by
soldiers who are stationed here to control poaching. This is also
the site of the eastern coast's only hotel, also called Punta
Morena, which has a restaurant and bar.

The cross-island road meets the east coast at **Mezcalito Café;**
here you can turn back to town or continue north. If you choose
the latter, you'll have to travel along a dead-end dirt road; eventually you'll have to turn around.

At this point you may decide to detour inland to the jungle, and
(15) view the ruins of **San Gervasio,** the largest extant Mayan site
on Cozumel. To get there, take the cross-island road west to
the army airfield and turn right; follow this road north for 10
kilometers (6 miles). San Gervasio was once the island's capital
and probably its ceremonial center, dedicated to the fertility
goddess Ix-Chel. The classical- and postclassical-style site was
continuously occupied from AD 300 to AD 1500. Typical architectural features from the era include limestone plazas and masonry superstructures atop stepped platforms; stelae,
bas-reliefs, and frescoes. What remains today are several small
mounds scattered around a plaza and several broken columns
and lintels that were once part of the main building or observatory. Unless you hire one of the English-speaking guides who
wait at the entry to the site (there's a minimum charge of $12,
which covers groups as large as six; try to join with other visitors to share a guide), you won't get much out of the unlabeled
ruins. There are a snack bar and some gift shops at the entrance. *Admission: $1 for access to the road, $3.50 for access to
the ruins; $1 for use of a video camera. Open daily 8–5.*

The road to the ruins is a good one, but a nearly unmaneuver-
able dirt road leads northeast of San Gervasio back to the unpaved coast road. At the junction is a marvelously deserted
beach where you can camp. At the northern end of the beach
(16) you'll find **Castillo Real,** another Mayan site comprising a look-
out tower, the base of a pyramid, and a temple with two chambers capped by a false arch. The waters here harbor several
shipwrecks, remnants from the days when buccaneers lay in
wait for richly cargoed galleons en route to Europe. It's a fine
spot for snorkeling because there are few visitors to disturb
the fish.

A number of other minor ruins are spread across the northern
(17) tip of Cozumel, which terminates at the **Punta Molas Lighthouse,** an excellent spot for sunbathing, birding, and camping.
This entire area is accessible only by four-wheel-drive vehicles
(or by boat), but the jagged shoreline and the open sea offers
magnificent views, making it well worth the trip.

Back on the leeward side of the island, north of town, is a long
(18) expanse of sandy beach known as **Playa San Juan,** which cul-
minates in Punta Norte. The island's northern cluster of hotels
occupies the sea side of the highway here; across the way are
several restaurants. Just beyond Punta Norte, smack in the
(19) middle of Abrigo Bay, you'll find **Isla de Pasión.** The secluded
beaches of this tiny island are now part of a state reserve, and
fishing is permitted. Backtrack along the coast road to return
to San Miguel.

Cozumel as a Port of Call

In 1991 Cozumel, Mexico's largest cruise-ship port, hosted more than 400 ships unloading almost 500,000 passengers, many of whom claim that Cozumel is their favorite destination. Generally, boats arrive around 7 AM and depart at 5 PM, though some spend as many as 18 hours in port. Because of the limited amount of time on shore, most cruise visitors opt for shore excursions sold on board and operated exclusively by Aviomar. These packages are specially designed to coincide with the ship's itinerary. Going off on one's own may entice the adventurer, but it also may entail greater expense and risk. For example, if taxi drivers become aware that they are your only means of transportation, they may try to take advantage of you; they will sometimes charge cruise-ship passengers as much as twice the rate they charge on-island visitors. Similarly, a tour operator who knows you won't be around long enough to file a complaint for unprofessional service may sign you up for some dubious, overpriced tour or snorkeling trip.

The island tours and diving packages sold to ship passengers by Aviomar or Intermar Caribe (*see* Guided Tours, *above*) survey Cozumel's lagoons, parks, and beaches. Another, considerably cheaper option is to take a taxi to the pier at La Ceiba, Playa San Francisco, or some other beach on the west coast and rent your own snorkeling equipment. You might decide to spend all your time shopping, possibly taking a break for a margarita at Carlos 'n Charlie's, or seeing the museum. You could hire a taxi for a quick tour around the island's southern point, taking in one of the small ruins or finding a quiet beach on the windward side (ask the driver to wait for you—you don't want to get stranded). Experienced riders may wish to rent a moped for a spin around the island, but bear in mind that accidents are frequent; check with your activities director about liability.

What to See and Do with Children

Chankanaab Nature Park (*see* Exploring, *above*).
Museo de la Isla de Cozumel (*see* Exploring, *above*).

Shopping

Shopping is an even bigger industry for Cozumel than diving, principally because of the lucrative trade with cruise-ship passengers. Thousands disembark each year in San Miguel, and consequently prices are relatively high compared to, say, Mérida. The variety of folk art ranges from downright schlocky curios to some excellent silver jewelry, pottery, painted balsawood animals, blown glass, and *huipiles* (embroidered cotton dresses).

As in other Mexican resort destinations, Cozumel's shops accept dollars as readily as pesos, and many goods are priced in dollars. You'll get a better price everywhere on Cozumel if you pay with cash or traveler's checks, although credit cards—MasterCard and Visa more often than American Express or Diners Club—are widely accepted. If you use plastic, however, you may be asked to pay a surcharge. Authorities and experienced travelers alike warn against buying from street vendors, because the quality of their merchandise leaves much to be desired, although this may not be apparent until it's too late.

Cruise ships traditionally dock at Cozumel on Monday, but there is traffic here almost every weekday, and the shops are fullest from 10 to 11 and 1 to 2. Generally, stores are open 9–1 and 5–9, but a number of them disregard siesta hours and open even on weekends, particularly during high season. Don't pay much attention to written or verbal offers of "20% discounts, today only" or "only for cruise-ship passengers," because they're nothing but bait to get you inside. Similarly, many of the larger stores advertise "duty-free" wares, but these are of greater interest to Mexicans from the mainland than to North Americans since the prices tend to be higher than retail prices in the United States.

A last word of caution: Cruise-ship activities directors tend to push the black coral "factories." These should be avoided, not only because they are usually overpriced but also because coral is an endangered species.

Shopping Districts/Streets/Malls

Cozumel has three main shopping areas: **downtown** along the waterfront, on Avenida Rafael Melgar, and on some of the side streets around the plaza (there are more than 150 shops in this area alone); at the **crafts market** (Calle 1 S, behind the plaza) in town, which sells a respectable assortment of Mexican wares; and at the cruise-ship **passenger terminal** south of town, near the Casa Del Mar, La Ceiba, and Sol Caribe hotels. There are also small clusters of shops at **Plaza del Sol** (on the east side of the main plaza), **Plaza de las Garzas** (Av. Rafael Melgar at Calle 8), and **Plaza Maya 2000** (across from the Sol Caribe). As a general rule, the newer, trendier shops line the waterfront, while the area around Avenida 5a houses the better crafts shops. The **town market** (Calle Rosada Salas, between Avs. 20a and 25a) sells fresh produce and other essentials.

Department Stores Relatively small and more like U.S. variety stores than department stores, the following nevertheless carry a relatively wide array of goods, from the useful to the frivolous: **Orbi** (Av. Rafael Melgar S 27, tel. 987/20685) sells everything from liquor and perfume to snorkeling gear and luggage; **Pama** (Av. Rafael Melgar S 9, tel. 987/20090), near the pier, features imported food, luggage, snorkeling gear, jewelry, and crystal; and **Prococo** (Av. Rafael Melgar N 99, tel. 987/28113) offers a good selection of liquor, jewelry, and gift items.

Specialty Stores Several trendy sportswear stores line Avenida Rafael Melgar
Clothing (between Calles 2 and 6), including **Aca Joe, Bye-Bye Cozumel,** and **Explora.** Although prices tend to be a bit cheaper here than in the United States, the quality of the merchandise may be inferior.

La Fiesta Cotton Country (Av. Rafael Melgar N 164-B, tel. 987/22032), a large store catering to the cruise ships, sells a variety of T-shirts as well as souvenirs.

Jewelry Jewelry on Cozumel is pricey, but it tends to be of higher quality than the jewelry you'll find in many of the other Yucatán towns. **Van Cleef** (Av. Rafael Melgar N 54, tel. 987/21143) offers a good collection of silver jewelry and gemstone rings.

Another good jeweler, down the block from Van Cleef, is **Casablanca** (Av. Rafael Melgar N 33, tel. 987/21177), which specializes in gold, silver, and gemstones, as well as expensive crafts.

La Fiesta Silver Country (Av. Rafael Melgar N 164-A, tel. 987/22143 or 987/22054) offers silver, much of it of the cheap, junky variety, but with some nice-looking pieces.

Nothing but fine silver, gold, and coral jewelry—particularly silver bracelets and earrings—is sold at **Joyería Palancar** (Av. Rafael Melgar N 15, tel. 987/21468).

Mexican Crafts **La Concha** (at the corner of Rafael Melgar and Calle 2a N, tel. 987/20571) offers a selection of good, if somewhat pricey, Mexican and Guatemalan folk art, jewelry, and clothing.

Na Balam (Av. 5a N 14, no phone) sells high-quality Mayan reproductions, batik clothing, and jewelry.

Xaman-Ek: The Bird Sanctuary (Av. Rafael Melgar, tel. 987/20940), specializes, as its name implies, in all manner of artificial birds, made of papier-mâché, ceramics, and other materials.

Your best bet for one-stop shopping, the nearly block-long **Los Cinco Soles** (Av. Rafael Melgar N 27, tel. 987/20132), features an excellent variety of well-priced, well-displayed items, including blue-rim glassware, brass and tin animals from Jalisco, tablecloths and place mats, cotton gauze and embroidered clothing, onyx, T-shirts, papier-mâché fruit, reproduction Mayan art, Mexican fashions, silver jewelry, soapstone earrings and beads, and other Mexican wares.

Talavera (Av. 5a S 349, tel. 987/20171) sells beautiful ceramics from all over Mexico—including tiles from the Yucatán—as well as masks and brightly painted wooden animals from Oaxaca and carved chests from Guadalajara.

Unicornio (Av. 5a S 1, tel. 987/20171) specializes in Mexican folk art, including calcedonia stone picture frames and jewelry boxes. Though you'll find a lot of junk, some pretty *talavera* (blue-and-white pottery from Pueblo) ceramic notions are on sale.

Gordon Gilchrist (Studio I, Av. 25a S at Calle 15, tel. 987/26159), a local artist, displays—by appointment—his etchings of local Mayan sites.

Hammocks (Av. 5a N and Calle 4, no phone) are made and sold by Manuel Azueta from his front porch.

Sports and Fitness

Most people come to Cozumel to take advantage of the island's water-related sports—particularly scuba diving, snorkeling, and fishing (*see below*), but jetskiing, sailboarding, waterskiing, and sailing remain popular as well. You will find services and rentals throughout the island, especially through major hotels and water-sports centers such as **Del Mar Aquatic** (Carretera a Chankanaab, Km 4, tel. 987/21665 or 987/21833) and **Agua Safari** (Av. Rafael Melgar 39A, tel. 987/20101 or 987/20892).

Fishing

The waters off Cozumel swarm with more than 230 species of fish, the numbers upholding the island's reputation as one of the world's best locations for trolling, deep-sea fishing, and bottom fishing. Beaky jawed billfish—including swordfish, blue marlin, white marlin, and sailfish—are plentiful here in late April through June, their migration season. World records for catches are frequently set on the island in these months. For the past 22 years, the annual **International Billfish Tournament,** held in May, has drawn anglers from around the world to Cozumel; for more information, contact The International Billfish Tournament, Box 442, Cozumel 77600; tel. 800/253–2701, fax 987/20999.

Deep-sea fishing for tuna, barracuda, wahoo, and kingfish is productive year-round. Aficionados also enjoy Cozumel's bottom fishing (grouper, yellowtail, and snapper) on the shallow sand flats at the northern end of the island, which also harbor bonefish, tarpon, snook, cubera, and small sharks. The best times to fish are sunrise and sunset, just before a full moon.

Please obey regulations forbidding commercial fishing, sportfishing, spearfishing, and the collection of any marine life between the shore and El Cantil Reef and between the cruise-ship dock and Punta Celerain. As part of a growing conservation movement, it's forbidden to kill certain species, including billfish, so be prepared to return prize catches to the sea. (Regular participants in the annual billfish tournament have seen some of the same fish—notched by successful anglers—caught over and over again.) U.S. Customs allows you to bring up to 30 pounds of fish back into the country.

Charters High-speed fishing boats can be chartered for $350 for a halfday or $400 for a full day, for a maximum of six people, from the **Club Náutico de Cozumel** (Puerto de Abrigo, Av. Rafael Melgar, Box 341, tel. 987/20118 or 800/253–9701), the island's headquarters for game fishing. Full-day rates include the boat and crew, tackle and bait, and lunch with beer and soda (lunch isn't included on half days). You can also book three- and fourday trips from the U.S. at discounted rates. Daily charters are easily arranged from the dock or at your hotel, but you might also try **Aquarius Fishing and Tours** (Calle 3 S, tel. 987/21092) for a 4½-hour fishing trip ($125; maximum 3 people) or **Yucab Reef Diving & Fishing** (Av. Rosado Salas between Rafael Melgar and 5a, tel. 987/24110 or tel. and fax 987/21842); the latter's general manager, Mariano Miguel Mendoza, is the head of the Cozumel Association of Dive Operators (*see below*) and a font of knowledge about fishing and diving on the island. All rates vary with the season.

Scuba Diving

With more than 30 charted reefs whose average depths range from 15 to 24 meters (50 to 80 feet) and a water temperature that hits about 75–80°F during peak diving season (June–August, when hotel rates are coincidentally at their lowest), Cozumel is far and away Mexico's number-one diving destination. Sixty thousand divers come here each year to explore the underwater coral formations, caves, sponges, sea fans, and tropical fish. The diversity of options includes deep dives, drift dives, shore dives, wall dives, and night dives, as well as theme dives focusing on ecology, archaeology, sunken ships, and photography. With all the shops to choose from, divers, especially those with less experience or who don't bring their own equipment, should look for high safety standards and documented credentials. Members of CADO, the **Cozumel Association of Dive Operators** (at Yucab Reef Fishing and Diving, Av. Rafael Salas between Av. Rafael Melgar and Av. 5 S, Box 450, Cozumel, 77600, tel. 987/24110, tel. and fax 987/21842), are required to meet a number of safety standards. Make sure your instructor has PADI certification (or FMAS, the Mexican equivalent) and is one of the 25 or so shops affiliated with the **SSS recompression chamber** (Calle 5 S 21B, between Av. Rafael Melgar and Av. 5a S, next to Discover Cozumel, tel. 987/22387) or the new recompression chamber recently set up at the **Hospital Civil** (Av. 11 S, between calles 10 and 15, tel. 987/20140 or 987/20525). These chambers, which boast a 35-minute response time from reef to chamber, treat decompression sickness, commonly known as "the bends," by giving patients oxygen. The sickness occurs when divers surface too quickly and nitrogen is absorbed into the bloodstream. Other injuries treated here include nitrogen narcosis, collapsed lungs, and overexposure to the cold.

Diving requires that you be reasonably fit. It should also go without saying that—particularly if you are new to diving—you should find a qualified instructor. Another caveat: Always stay at least 3 feet above the reef, not just because the coral can sting or cut you, but also because coral is easily damaged and grows very slowly: It's taken 2,000 years for it to reach its present size.

Dive Shops and Tour Operators Most dive shops can provide you with all the incidentals you'll need, as well as with guides and transportation. You can choose from a variety of two-tank boat trips and specialty dives ranging from $46 to $56; three-hour resort courses cost about $60, and 1½-hour night dives, $35. Certification courses are available from $300 to $350, while dive-master courses cost as much as $700. Equipment rental is relatively inexpensive, ranging from $6 for tanks or a lamp to about $8 for a regulator or jacket; underwater cameras can cost as much as $35, and videos of your own dive, about $75.

Because dive shops tend to be competitive, it is well worth your while to shop around when choosing a dive operator. In addition to the dive shops in town, many hotels have their own operations and offer dive and hotel packages starting at about $350 for three nights, double occupancy, and two days of diving. For an unusual live-aboard scuba experience, *see* Guided Tours, *above.* You can also pick up a copy of the *Chart of the Reefs of Cozumel* in any dive shop. Here's a list to get you started on your search: Before choosing a shop among the many choices, check credentials, look over the boats and equipment, and consult experienced divers who are familiar with the operators here. **Aqua Safari** (Av. Rafael Melgar 39a, tel. 987/20101); **Blue Angel** (next to Hotel Villablanca, tel. 987/21631), for PADI certification; **Blue Bubble** (Av. 5a S at Calle 3 S, tel. 987/21865), for PADI instruction; **Dive House** (Av. 1a, no. 6, tel. 987/21953, fax 987/23068); **Dive Paradise** (Av. Rafael Melgar 601 at Calle 3 S, tel. 987/21007, fax 987/21061); **Fantasia Divers** (Av. 25, enter at Adolfo Rosado Salas and Av. 35, tel. 987/22840, fax 987/21210);

Marine Sports (Hotel Fiesta Inn, tel. 987/22900); **Pro Dive** (Av. Rosado Salas at 5a, downtown and at the Holiday Inn Cozumel Reef, tel. 987/20816 or 987/20700); **Scuba Shack** (next to Hotel Sol Caribe, tel. 987/20145, 987/20145, or 800/445–4716); **Yucab Reef** (Av. Rosado Salas 11, between Rafael Melgar and 5a, tel. 987/24110, tel. and fax 987/21842).

Reef Dives The reefs stretch for 32 kilometers (20 miles), beginning at the international pier and continuing on to Punta Celerain at the southernmost tip of the island. The following is a rundown of Cozumel's main dive destinations.

Colombia Reef This reef—reaching 25–30 meters (82–98 feet)—is excellent for experienced divers who want to take some deep dives. Its underwater structures are as labyrinthine and varied as those of Palancar (*see below*); large groupers, jacks, eagle rays, and even an occasional sea turtle cluster at the mouths of caves and near the overhangs.

Maracaibo Reef Generally considered the most difficult of all the Cozumel reefs for divers, this one—located off the southern end of the island—lends itself to drift dives because of its length. You don't even see the ledge of the reef until you go 37 meters (121 feet) below the surface. Although there are shallow areas, only expert divers who can cope with the strong current should attempt Maracaibo.

Palancar Reef This reef system, situated nearly 2 kilometers (1 mile) offshore, offers about 40 dive locations. Black and red coral and huge elephant-ear sponges and barrel sponges are among the attractions at the bottom. The reef, which begins at about 25 meters (75 feet) below the surface, is particularly suitable for drift dives. A favorite of divers is the section called **Horseshoe,** comprising several coral heads at the top of the drop-off. Towering coral columns and deep ravines and canyons make for some of the most sensational dives in the Caribbean.

Paraíso Reef Just north of the cruise-ship pier, about 200 meters (656 feet) offshore and up to 13 meters (40 feet) deep, Paraíso provides a practice spot for divers before they head to deeper drop-offs. Also a wonderful site for night diving, this reef is inhabited by star coral, brain coral, sea fans and other gorgonians, and sponges. From Paraíso you can swim out to the drop-offs called La Ceiba and Villa Blanca.

Plane Wreck This airplane was taken about 91 meters (about 300 feet) off the La Ceiba pier and sunk during a 1977 Mexican motion picture production. Because of its reassuring proximity to the shore and because the average depth of the water is only 3 to 9 meters (9 to 30 feet), it has been a favorite training ground for neophyte divers ever since. Enormous coral structures and colorful sponges surround the reef, while an underwater trail guides divers by the marine life.

Santa Rosa Wall Also a renowned spot for deep dives and drift dives, this wall—just north of Palancar—drops off abruptly at 18 meters (60 feet) to enormous coral overhangs and caves below. Sponges are especially populous here, as are angelfish, groupers, and eagle rays—along with a shark or two.

Tormentos Reef Sea fans and other gorgonians and sponges live on this variegated reef, where the maximum depth reaches about 21 meters (70 feet). Tormentos, one of the best locations for underwater photography, hosts sea cucumbers, arrow crabs, and other marine life, which provide a terrifically colorful backdrop.

Yucab Reef About 121 meters (400 feet) long and 17 meters (55 feet) deep, this reef is located less than a mile from shore, near Chankanaab. Coral, sponge, sea whips, and angelfish swim in these waters, where the currents can reach 2 or 3 knots.

Snorkeling

Snorkeling ranks just after diving among the island's popular sports. There is good snorkeling in the morning off the piers at the Stouffer Presidente and La Ceiba, where fish are fed. The shallow reefs in Chankanaab Bay, Playa San Francisco, and the northern beach at the Club Cozumel Caribe also provide clear views of brilliantly colored fish and sea creatures, among them fingerlings, parrot fish, sergeant majors, angelfish, and squirrel fish, along with elk coral, conch, and sand dollars.

Tour operators that specialize in snorkeling include **Fiesta Cozumel** (tel. 987/22935 or 987/20974) and **Turismo Aviomar** (tel. 987/20477 or 987/20588). As its name suggests, **Snorkozumel** (Calle 5 S 11A, between Av. Rafael Melgar and Av. 5, tel. 987/24166) is devoted to running snorkeling excursions. Locals say that the best snorkeling trips are aboard the *Zorro* (*see* Guided Tours, *above*), a 35-passenger, 45-foot catamaran with a huge sun deck, operated by Fiesta Cozumel. Directly off the beach, excellent snorkeling is to be had near the Stouffer Presidente and the Holiday Inn Cozumel Reef, as well as at Chankanaab and Playa Corona; snorkeling equipment is available for less than $10 a day at these locations.

Beaches

Cozumel's beaches vary from long, treeless, sandy stretches to isolated coves and rocky shores. Virtually all development remains on the leeward (western) side, where the coast is relatively sheltered by the proximity of the mainland 19 kilometers (12 miles) to the west. Reaching beaches on the windward (eastern) side is more difficult and requires transportation, but you'll be rewarded if you are looking for solitude. For descriptions of individual beaches, *see* Exploring, *above*.

Leeward Beaches The best sand beaches lie along the northern half of Cozumel's leeward side, some 5 kilometers (3 miles) long; names have been given to several stretches, including **San Francisco, Santa Rosa, Palancar,** and **Punta Sur.**

The southwestern beaches are the widest and among the most beautiful. One favorite is **Playa del Sol,** 2 kilometers (1 mile) south of Playa San Francisco. One drawback, however, is Playa del Sol's popularity with cruise-ship passengers. Also lovely and marvelously secluded are the beaches around Punta Celerain, near the lighthouse at the southern point. **Santa Pilar** and **San Juan** beaches, which run along the northern hotel strip, sell soft drinks and rent water-sports equipment.

Windward Beaches On this side you'll find dramatic and solitary, but somewhat narrow beaches, including **Punta Morena, Chen Río, San Martín, Punta Chiqueros,** and **Playa Encantada.** A couple of them have small snack bars. Swimming on this side is dangerous only if you go out too far or on those rare occasions when a southwestern wind blows. There is a string of nameless beaches on the dirt road leading to **Punta Molas** at the northern tip, which can be reached by Jeep, but you should allow plenty of time for the trip.

Dining

Dining options on Cozumel reflect the nature of the place as a whole, with some harmless pretension at times but mainly the insouciant, natural style of the tropical island. More than 80 restaurants in the downtown area alone offer a broad choice, from air-conditioned, Americanized places serving Continental fare and seafood in semiformal "nautical" settings to sensible, simple outdoor eateries that specialize in fish. For the most part, the more established restaurants accept credit cards, while the café-type places accept only cash. Resort hotels offering buffet breakfasts and dinners are good values for bottomless appetites. Casual dress and no reservations is the rule in most Moderate and Inexpensive Cozumel restaurants. In Expensive restaurants, you would not be out of place if you dressed up, and reservations are advised.

Highly recommended restaurants are indicated by a star ★.

Category	Cost*
Expensive	$25–$35
Moderate	$15–25
Inexpensive	under $15

per person, excluding drinks and service

Expensive **Arrecife.** A well-trained staff and impeccably prepared seafood
★ and Continental fare put this hotel restaurant in a class by itself. Tall windows and excellent views of the sea complement the stylish decor—potted palms, white wicker furniture, pink walls— while jazz quartets, which play regularly, further enhance the romantic mood. *Hotel Stouffer Presidente, tel. 987/20322. AE, DC, MC, V. Closed Sept.–Nov. 15.*

Café del Puerto. The eclectic decor, including wood furniture, wood-paneled walls, and wood palm trees, contributes to the appealing tropical ambience of this second-floor restaurant overlooking the pier. Nightly specials may include oysters or a grilled seafood platter, and the regular menu features prime rib, ham, and lobster and other seafood, along with a multi-item salad bar. Live piano music accompanies your meal. *Av. Rafael Melgar, across from the main pier, tel. 987/20316. AE, MC, V. No lunch.*

Donatello's. Pale pink walls, pink marble floors, and dim lighting lend a certain elegance to this place. Although not yet world-class, Donatello's ranks as the most sophisticated restaurant in town; it offers less formal dining in the back garden. Italian accents enhance the menu, which includes such specialties as scampi, lobster, veal, and pasta (including macaroni with salmon). A pianist and mariachis entertain nightly. Exquisite desserts, including coconut ice cream and bananas flambées, nicely round out the meal. *Av. Rafael Melgar S 131, tel. 987/20090 or 987/22586. AE, MC, V. No lunch.*

★ **La Cabaña del Pescador.** To get to this rustic palapa-covered hut, you've got to cross a gangplank, but it'll be worth it if you're looking for well-prepared fresh lobster. The tails are sold by weight, and the rest—including a delicious eggnog-type drink served at the end of the meal—is on the house. Seashells and nets hang from the walls of this small, dimly lit room and geese stroll outside, hoping to be fed by diners seated next to the windows. *Across the street from Playa Azul Hotel, north of town, no phone. No credit cards. No lunch.*

Pepe's Grill. This large, bustling restaurant follows the nautical mode, from the fishnets and ship wheels to the wind vanes covering the walls. Tall windows provide exceptional views of the malecón. You can choose between the quiet air-conditioned setting upstairs and the livelier atmosphere in the open-air dining room downstairs. This restaurant caters to the cruise-ship clientele, so most North Americans will feel right at home, but with the comforts of home come long lines and high prices. Caribbean seafood dishes—lobster, shrimp flambée, shellfish grill, and King Crab—are featured as specials, but the steaks—particularly the chateaubriand in béarnaise sauce, from the state of Chihuahua—are superb. The dolphin fish is fresh and good, as are the Caesar salad and the salad bar. Live music is played daily. *Av. Rafael Melgar S at Calle Rosada Salas, tel. 987/20213. AE, V.*

Moderate **Carlos 'n' Charlie's & Jimmy's Kitchen.** Rock 'n' roll, a Ping-Pong table, and drinking contests are the status quo here. American-style ribs, chicken, and beef selections taste good, but the drinks are better. You can recognize this place by the red wall just north of the ferry pier. *Av. Rafael Melgar between Calles 2 and 4 N, tel. 987/20191. MC, V.*

★ **El Capi Navegante.** Locals say you'll find the best seafood in town here: The captain's motto is: "The fish we serve today slept in the sea last night." Specialties like whole red snapper and stuffed squid are skillfully prepared and sometimes flambéed at your table. Highly recommended dishes include conch ceviche and deep-fried whole snapper. Nautical blue-and-white decor, accented by the life preservers on the walls, adds personality to this place. *Av. 10a S 312 at Calle 3, tel. 987/21730. AE, MC, V.*

El Portal. Smack on the waterfront main drag, this is an airy, comfortable place to sit and watch the action go by at breakfast, lunch, or dinner. The cheery decor—red chairs, pink tablecloths, and lanterns—also makes it a great place to spend margarita hour. Entrées include ceviche, *pescado veracruzano* (fish served in a sauce of tomatoes, onions, and green peppers), *sopa de lima* (lime soup), enchiladas, and Yucatecan specialties. *Av. Rafael Melgar, tel. 987/20316. AE, MC, V.*

★ **La Choza.** Home-cooked Mexican food—primarily from the capital and among the best in town—is the order of the day at this family-run establishment. Dona Elisa Espinosa's specialties include chicken mole, red snapper in mustard sauce, and grilled lobster; meals come with soup and fresh tortillas. The informal palapa-covered patio is furnished with simple wood tables and chairs, oilcloth table coverings, and hand-painted pottery dishes—all in keeping with La Choza's down-home atmosphere. *Calle Rosada Salas 198 at Av. 10a S, tel. 987/20958. AE, MC, V.*

Las Palmeras. The redbrick patios with the requisite potted palms and ceiling fans set the mood at this unpretentious waterfront restaurant, where breakfast is a bargain. For lunch and dinner expect seafood specialties and some Mexican dishes. The restaurant also sells margaritas and piña coladas to go. *On Av. Rafael Melgar, just across from the pier; tel. 987/20532. AE, MC, V.*

Morgan's. No longer the big night out it used to be, this restaurant has managed to maintain impeccable service, a quiet atmosphere with the obligatory candlelight, and an international cuisine. Located in the former customs house and done up in honor of its namesake—the seafaring pirate Henry Morgan, who once plied these waters—the restaurant is decorated with ship paneling, portholes, and compasses. The menu offers such appetizers as avocado cocktail and ham with melon, in addition to a selection of steak and fish entrées. *South side of the plaza (Av. Benito Juarez and Calle 5a), tel. 987/20584. AE, DC, MC, V. Closed Sun. lunch.*

★ **Rincón Maya.** Spicy Yucatecan specialties are the order of the day in this festive, friendly eatery. Miguel Mena Mendosa serves up fresh seafood, beef, pork, and chicken prepared with *achiote* and other traditional herbs used in Mayan cooking. Lamps decorated in the colors of the Mexican flag, hats, and masks line the walls. *Av. 5a S between Calles 3 and 5, no phone. No credit cards. No lunch.*

Santiago's Grill. Beautiful American cuts of meat, including T-bones and sirloins, as well as beef brochettes and fresh shrimp, draw long lines nightly. Because this small outdoor restaurant, with only 10 tables, is included on a list given to cruise-ship passengers, it is particularly popular with these tourists. *Calle Rosada Salas 299 at Av. 15a S, tel. 987/20175. AE, MC, V. No lunch.*

Inexpensive **El Foco.** A *taqueria* serving pork, *chorizo* (spicy Mexican sausage), and cheese-soft tacos, this eatery also does ribs and steak. Graffitied walls and plain wood tables make it a casual, fun spot to grab a bite and a *cerveza. Av. 5 S and Calle 13, no phone. MC, V.*

★ **El Moro.** This family-run restaurant on the eastern edge of town specializes in low-priced local cuisine—seafood, chicken, and meat. Inside, the decor follows the regional theme, beginning with Yucatecan baskets hanging on the walls. Divers flock to this place, so you know portions are hearty and the food is delicious. Take a taxi; it's too far to walk. *Calle 70, no phone. No credit cards. Closed Thurs.*

La Cosa Nostra. This modestly decorated restaurant, with a long bar, wood tables, and white walls with paintings of Cozumel, attracts locals who gather here on the weekends to hear live organ music and meet with friends. The cooking's not bad, either: La Cosa Nostra excels in homemade Italian fare, from the fettuccine Giovanna (pasta with shrimp in a rich cream sauce) to pizza sold by the slice. It's open for breakfast and also has a happy hour from 6 to 7. *Av. 15a S 548, between Calles 5 and 7, tel.987/21275. AE, MC, V.*

Mr. Papa's. This place offers a dozen types of stuffed potatoes, as well as burgers, ribs, chicken, other North American dishes, and some standard Mexican fare such as guacamole, nachos, and tacos in a jovial air-conditioned setting with wood tables, green carpets, and poster-covered walls. Ask about the all-you-can-eat and all-you-can-drink specials. *Av. Rafael Malgar, near Calle 8, tel. 987/21882. MC, V.*

Plaza Leza. If you're craving the low-key, unpretentious atmosphere of a Mexican sidewalk café, stop here, where you can dawdle for hours over a cup of coffee or a beer. Choose a table on the plaza, or for more privacy, go indoors to the somewhat secluded, cozy inner patio. Plaza Leza serves everything from *poc chuc* (pork chops grilled Yucatán style), enchiladas, and lime soup to chicken sandwiches and coconut ice cream. *On the main plaza, south side, tel. 987/21041. AE, MC, V.*

Sports Page Video Bar and Restaurant. Signed team T-shirts and pennants line the walls and ceilings of this popular restaurant and watering hole. The main attraction is the sports coverage—large TVs simultaneously broadcast at least four athletic events—but the food's good too. Cheeseburgers are juicy and served with generous portions of crispy fries; Mexican specialties as well as seafood and steak dinners are offered. The place is open from 9 AM for breakfast, so you can have your eggs with ESPN. *Corner Av. 5a N and Calle 2 N, tel. 987/21199. MC, V.*

Lodging

Cozumel's hotels are located in three main areas, all on the island's western, or leeward, side: in town and north and south of town. Because of the proximity of the reefs, divers and snorkelers tend to congregate at the southern properties. Sailors and anglers, on the other hand, prefer the hotels to the north, where the beaches are better. Most budget hotels—with various architectural styles—are located in town.

Cozumel offers about 3,200 hotel rooms in more than 60 properties. Before booking you should call around, because you will find many bargains in the form of air, hotel, and dive packages, especially off-season; some packages offered combine Cozumel-Cancún stays, with free airfare between the two. Christmas reservations must be made at least three months ahead of time. The majority of the resort hotels (located north and south of town) are affiliated with international chains and offer all the usual amenities; they also generally rent watersports equipment and can arrange excursions. All hotels have air-conditioning unless otherwise noted, and all hotels share the 77600 postal code.

The **Cozumel Island Hotel Association** (Box 228, Cozumel, QR 77600 or Calle 2 N at 15a, tel. 987/23132; fax 987/22809), with 25 member-properties, functions unofficially as the island's tourist information bureau.

Highly recommended hotels are indicated by a star ★.

Category	Cost*
Very Expensive	over $160
Expensive	$90–$160
Moderate	$40–$90
Inexpensive	under $40

All prices are for a standard double room, excluding service charges and the 10% tax.

Very Expensive   **Diamond Hotel & Resort.** Completed in early 1993, this large, all-inclusive resort is the newest and the southernmost of the island's properties. The hotel is far from town, but lots of water-based activities—the Diamond's beach is close to Palancar and other reefs—as well as nightly entertainment keep guests occupied on the premises. Accommodations, set in small bi-level units spread across the grounds, are furnished in light wood and tropical pastels. Standard rooms are not very large, but duplex suites easily accommodate three or four people. *Carretera a Chankaanab, Km 16.5, tel. 987/23554. 296 rooms. Facilities: 2 restaurants, 3 bars, minibars, satellite TV, nightly entertainment, aerobics, volleyball, 2 pools, shops, water-sports center. AE, DC, MC, V.*

★ **Stouffer Presidente.** This hotel, dramatically refurbished since the 1988 hurricane, exudes luxury, from the courteous, prompt, and efficient service to the tastefully decorated interior. The Stouffer is famed not only for possessing one of the best restaurants on the island, Arrecife (*see* Dining, *above*), but also for its respectable and professional water-sports center. Located on its own beach near the end of the southern hotel zone, the property ranks among the best on the island for snorkeling; barracuda, angelfish, octopus, and more are visible in the waters a few feet off of the beach. All rooms are done in bright, contemporary colors with rich pine furnishings; deluxe rooms, with their own private terraces fronting the pool or beach, are huge. *Carretera a Chankanaab, Km 6.5, tel. 987/20322, 987/21520, or 800/HOTELS–1, fax 987/21360. 253 rooms. Facilities: nonsmoking rooms, 2 restaurants, coffee shop, 3 bars, pool, Jacuzzi, 2 lighted tennis courts, dive shop, water sports, boutiques, car and motorcycle rental, travel agency. AE, DC, MC, V.*

Expensive **Fiesta Americana Sol Caribe.** The largest hotel in Cozumel, the Sol Caribe is south of town, just across the street from its own small beach (accessible by underground footpath). The lobby in the 10-story main building is dramatically designed, with a high, wood-beamed palapa roof and waterfall. Rooms in the newer (1990) tower, all with balconies and considered deluxe, are slightly more expensive, but those in the main building—reached by a glass-encased elevator—are the same size and furnished in a lighter, more cheerful fashion. Nicely landscaped grounds and a large pool with a swim-up bar are among the hotel's pluses. *Box 259, Playa Paraíso, Km 3.5, tel. 987/20700 or 800/FIESTA–1, fax 987/21301. 321 rooms. Facilities: 3 restaurants, 4 bars, satellite TV, minibars, pool, dock, 3 tennis courts, water sports, travel agency, motorcycle and car rental, dive shop, boutiques, beauty salon. AE, DC, MC, V.*

★ **Fiesta Inn.** This three-story Spanish-roofed structure, south of town and across the street from the beach, has all the trademarks of the Fiesta brand name: a comfortable lobby with a fountain and garden, brightly decorated modern rooms with Moorish archways, a large pool, and an international dining facility. Fully carpeted rooms are painted light blue, with cream-color wicker furniture and private balconies; many have safes. The new sing-along Laser-Karaoke Bar draws exhibitionists from all over town. This property is less expensive than its larger sister property (*see above*). *Carretera a Chankanaab, Km 1.7, tel. 987/22811, 987/22900, or 800/FIESTA–1, fax 987/22154. 180 rooms. Facilities: nonsmoking rooms, restaurant, 2 bars, beach club, water sports, pool, Jacuzzi, tennis court. AE, DC, MC, V.*

Galápago Inn. This pretty white stucco hotel just south of town primarily accommodates divers; the attractive, brightly tiled rooms are not sold by the night but exclusively as part of dive packages—booked in Houston—that take full advantage of the hotel's expert diving staff and dive-master school. The central garden, with tiled benches and a small fountain, contributes to the inn's Mediterranean feel. *Carretera a Chankanaab, Km 1.5, tel. 987/20663 or 800/847–5708. 58 rooms. Facilities: restaurant, bar, pool, beach. AE, MC, V.*

★ **Holiday Inn Cozumel Reef.** Opened in the summer of 1991, this property is ideally situated for snorkeling and scuba diving. Located on the less developed southern end of the island, near the Stouffer Presidente and Chankanaab, the hotel's beach offers easy access to spectacular underwater scenery. The high-ceilinged lobby, with its rattan furniture and polished marble floors, hosts a glitzy silver shop featuring some unusual pieces. Standard rooms are large, with sea-green headboards and well-made light-wood furnishings; all have balconies looking out on the ocean as well as hair dryers and direct-dial phones. *Carretera a Chankanaab, Km 7.5, tel. 987/22622 or 800/HOLI-DAY, fax 987/22666. 162 rooms. Facilities: nonsmoking rooms, 3 restaurants, 3 bars, 2 lighted tennis courts, gym, 2 pools, dive shop, water sports. AE, MC, V.*

★ **Meliá Mayan Cozumel.** Lush tropical foliage and spectacular sunsets over the beach combine with modern architecture and amenities to make this hotel north of town a memorable place to stay. Large windows in the light, cheerful lobby look out onto a pool and swim-up palapa snack bar; windsurfing and other water sports are available at the beach. Standard rooms, some with small patios opening out onto the lawn, are attractively decorated with colorful tropical print bedspreads and light-wood furniture; larger superior rooms, somewhat more austere in decor, have balconies overlooking the water. *Box 9, Carretera a Sta. Pilar 6, tel. 987/20523, 987/20411, or 800/336–3542, fax 987/21599. 200 rooms. Facilities: 2 restaurants, 2 bars, beach, 2 pools, water-sports center, 2 tennis courts, minibars, travel agency, shop. AE, MC, V.*

Plaza Las Glorias. A Mediterranean atmosphere prevails inside and out here: This large, salmon-colored building features Mexican tiles, marble floors, and wrought-iron details in its public areas. The modern all-suites property, situated within walking distance of town, has private terraces and ocean views from each of its light, spacious units. *Box 435, Av. Rafael Melgar, Km 1.5, tel. 987/22000 or 800/342–AMIGO, fax 987/21937. 170 suites. Facilities: 2 restaurants, 2 bars, evening entertainment, minibar, in-room safe, hair dryers, dive center, water sports, pool, shopping arcade. AE, MC, V.*

Moderate **Bahía.** The lobby here is small but the hallways are pleasant enough, with white walls and red tile floors. The large rooms, decorated with the standard stucco, wood, and tile, come with sofabeds and kitchenettes. Ask for a room with a sea view; the balconies overlook the malecón and go for the same price as those facing town. Two penthouse suites are available. *Av. Rafael Melgar and Calle 3 S, tel. 987/21387, fax 987/20209. 27 rooms. Facilities: kitchenettes. AE, MC, V.*

★ **Casa del Mar.** Located south of town near several boutiques, sports shops, and restaurants, this three-story hotel is frequented by divers. An unpretentious but tasteful lobby, which has natural wood banisters and overlooks a small garden, exemplifies the overall simplicity of the place. Cheerful rooms feature yellow-tiled headboards, nightstands, and sinks; Mexican artwork; and small balconies with views of the pool or the sea. The bi-level suites, which sleep three or four, are a very good buy at $100. *Box 129, Carretera a Chankanaab, Km 4, tel. 987/21900 or 800/777–5873, fax 987/21855. 96 rooms, 8 cabanas. Facilities: 2 restaurants, 2 bars, pool, Jacuzzi, dive shop, car rental. AE, MC, V.*

Playa Azul. This Best Western–managed property north of town, just opposite the Cabaña del Pescador lobster house, is a nondescript pink-and-white low-rise that offers light-filled rooms and an attractive beach. Mexican families stay here, enjoying the garden and its coconut palms, which soften the effect of the boxy concrete structure. Choose between two types of suites—the master suites offer huge, if somewhat useless, sitting rooms—or bungalow-like villas near the pool (but without sea views or phones). *Box 31, Carretera San Juan, tel. 987/20033, 987/20043, or 800/528–1234, fax 987/21915. 64 rooms. Facilities: 2 restaurants, 2 bars, pool, boutique, water sports. AE, MC, V.*

★ **Villas Las Anclas.** Conveniently located parallel to the malecón and rated as a three-star hotel, these villas are actually furnished apartments for rent by the day, week, or month. The duplexes include a downstairs sitting room, dining area, and kitchenette, which is fully stocked with dishes, refrigerator, and hot plate; a spiral staircase leads up to a small bedroom with a large desk (but no phone) and inset shelves over the double bed. Rooms are extremely attractive, with tastefully bright patterns set off against white walls. You can buy fresh-ground coffee at the front desk, or head over to the nearby Café Caribe for a breakfast of cappuccino and croissants; the same friendly couple owns both properties. *Box 25, Av. 5a S 325 between Calles 3 and 5 S, tel. 987/21955, tel. and fax 987/21403. 7 units. Facilities: kitchenettes, garden in back. No credit cards.*

Inexpensive **Bazar Colonial.** This attractive modern three-story hotel, located over a small cluster of shops, has pretty red tile floors and bougainvillea, which add splashes of color. Natural wood furniture, kitchenettes, bookshelves, sofa beds, and an elevator make up for the lack of other amenities, such as a restaurant and a pool. *Av. 5a S 9, tel. 987/20506, fax 987/30309 or 987/21387. 28 rooms. Facilities: shops, kitchenettes. AE, MC, V.*

Mary Carmen. Functional and clean, this hotel offers rooms (but no phones) on the ground floor with both air-conditioning and ceiling fans; on the first floor, only air-conditioning is offered. Although the furniture and rugs are rather worn, the double bed and two chairs are adequate for the night. *Av. 5a S 4, tel. 987/20581. 27 rooms. No facilities. MC, V.*

★ **Mesón San Miguel.** Situated right on the square, this hotel sees a lot of action because of the accessibility of its large public bar and outdoor café, which are often filled with locals. The architecturally eclectic San Miguel, with four stories and an elevator, has a black-and-white–tiled lobby floor and a contemporary-style game room with a pool table. The remodeled rooms are clean and functional, with balconies overlooking the plaza—a good bet for your money. Sip a drink in the evenings at Cafe Alladino, the hotel's bar on the square. *Av. Juárez 2 bis, tel. 987/20323 or 987/20233, fax 987/21820. 100 rooms. Facilities: bar, café, small pool, game room. AE, MC, V.*

Suites Elizabeth. This basic and functional hotel offers rooms with fans and with air-conditioning. The latter include large balconies with a view of the rooftops, and many rooms come with refrigerators and hot plates (but no phones). The vintage '70s furnishings, including light-orange chenille bedspreads, look dated but are still functional. *Box 70, Calle Rosada Salas 44, tel. 987/20330. 19 rooms. No credit cards.*

The Arts and Nightlife

The Arts

Although Cozumel doesn't have much in the way of highbrow performing arts per se, it does offer the visitor an opportunity to attend performances that reflect the island's heritage, including Maya Night on Monday and Fiesta Mexicana on Thursday, both at 7 PM at the **Meliá Mayan Cozumel** (tel. 987/20411); Viva México, Wednesday (and Saturday during high season) at 6 PM at the **Fiesta Americana Sol Caribe** (tel. 987/20700); or Caribbean Night on Sunday at the **Stouffer Presidente** (tel. 987/20322). They all feature different variations on the theme of folkloric dances, mariachis, and dancing.

Nightlife

Cozumel offers enough daytime activities to make you want to retire early, but the young set keeps the island hopping late into the night. There is plenty of nightlife, but a word to the wise: Avoid the temptation to buy or use drugs here. A foreigner involved with drugs will have a particularly difficult time with the Mexican authorities.

Bars   For a quiet drink and good people-watching, try **Alladino** at the Mesón San Miguel, at the northern end of the plaza. Serious bar-hoppers like **Carlos 'n' Charlie's** (Av. Rafael Melgar, between Calles 2 and 4 N; tel. 987/20191) and **Chilly's** (Av. Rafael Melgan at Calle 2N, tel. 987/21832). You and your friends provide the entertainment at the **Laser-Karaoke Bar** (Fiesta Inn, tel. 987/22811); the more inhibited can play video games or check football scores at the **Sports Page Video Bar and Restaurant** (corner Av. 5 N and Calle 2 N, tel. 987/21199).

Discos   **Scaramouche** (Av. Rafael Melgar at Calle Rosada Salas, tel. 987/20213) features a fantastic laser show; and **Neptuno** (Av. Rafael Melgar at Calle 11 S, tel. 987/21537), preferred by the teenage set and locals, can be loud and fun.

Live Music   Sunday evenings bring locals to the zócalo to hear mariachis and island musicians playing tropical tunes. The piano bar in **La Gaviota** (Carretera a Sta. Pilar, tel. 987/20700, ext. 251), a restaurant at the Sol Caribe, is well attended, and trios and mariachis perform nightly in the lobby bar from 5 to 11.

Movies   **Cine Cozumel** (Av. Rafael Melgar between Calles 2 and 4 N, tel. 987/20766) and **Cine Cecillo Borgues** (Av. Juaréz s/n, at Av. 35, tel. 987/20402) both show films in English (generally with subtitles) and Spanish nightly at 9.

6 Mexico's Caribbean Coast

Updated by
Maribeth Mellin

Above all else, beaches are what define the eastern coast of the Yucatán peninsula. White, sandy strands with offshore coral reefs, oversize tropical foliage and jungle, Mayan ruins, and abundant wildlife make the coastline a marvelous destination for lovers of the outdoors. The scrubby limestone terrain is mostly flat and dry, punctuated only by sinkholes, while the shores are broken up by freshwater lagoons, underwater caves, and cliffs.

The coast consists of several destinations, each catering to different preferences. The lazy fishing village of Puerto Morelos so far has been only slightly altered to accommodate foreign tourists. Rustic fishing and scuba diving lodges on the even more secluded Boca Paila and Xcalak peninsulas are gaining a well-deserved reputation for fly-fishing and superb diving on virgin reefs. The beaches, from Punta Bete to Sian Ka'an, south of Tulum—beloved of scuba divers, snorkelers, birders, and beachcombers—offer accommodations to suit every budget, from campsites and bungalows to condos and luxury hotels. Ecotourism is on the rise, with special programs designed to involve visitors in preserving the threatened sea-turtle population. Then, too, there are the Mayan ruins at Tulum, superbly situated on a bluff overlooking the Caribbean, and Cobá—a short distance inland—whose towering pyramids evoke the magnificence of Tikal in Guatemala. At the Belizean border is Chetumal—a modern port and the capital of Quintana Roo—which, with its dilapidated clapboard houses and sultry sea air, is more Central American than Mexican. The waters up and down the coast, littered with shipwrecks and relics from the heyday of piracy, are dotted with mangrove swamps and minuscule islands where only the birds hold sway.

The wildlife on the Caribbean coast is unsurpassed in Mexico, except perhaps in Baja California. Along the more civilized stretches of road, wild pigs, turkeys, iguanas, lizards, and snakes appear in the clearings. Jaguars, monkeys, white-tail deer, armadillos, tapirs, wild boars, peccaries, ocelots, raccoons, and badgers all inhabit the tropical jungle's most isolated retreats. The reefs, lagoons, cenotes, and caves along the Caribbean and down the Hondo River—which runs along the borders between Mexico, Belize, and Guatemala—are filled with alligators, giant turtles, sharks, barracuda, and manatees. During July and August sea turtles throng the beaches, laying thousands of eggs. Birders come to stare into the jungle and seaside marshes for glimpses of parrots, toucans, terns, herons, ibis, and hundreds of nesting pink flamingos. Onlookers are entertained by yellow, blue, and scarlet butterflies, singing cicadas and orioles, sparkling dragonflies, kitelike frigates, and night owls nesting in the trees. Colorless crabs scuttle sideways toward the coconut groves—which are gradually recovering from a blight imported from Florida—over pale white limestone and sand that seldom burns the soles of your feet. Tiny mosquitoes and gnats, impervious to mild repellents, bore through the smallest rips in window screens, tents, and mosquito nets.

The music, food, and cultural traditions of the northern Caribbean coast are Yucatecan. Cancún's transformation into a world-class resort has brought an international flair to the region, where Continental restaurants and local handicraft boutiques flourish a short distance from small Mayan villages with their whitewashed huts covered with dried palm fronds (palapas). The Yucatán coastline south of Tulum is more purely Mayan: Seaside fishing collectives, jungles, and close-knit communities of Mexican Indians and Guatemalan refugees carry on ancient traditions. The far south, particularly Chetumal, is influenced by its status as a seaport and its proximity to Belize and Guatemala. The language spoken here is a blend of Spanish and a Caribbean patois, and most visitors to the area are either passing through to cross the border or shopping for foreign goods.

Quintana Roo entered the modern era in the 1970s, when Mexico City decided to develop the area for tourism (it did not become a state until 1974). With the advent of Cancún, huge resorts and time-share complexes began to appear, and now they are slowly spreading south. Thanks to the federal government's foresight in setting aside a 22-mile strip of coastline and jungle called Sian Ka'an Biosphere Preserve, wildlife and travelers who seek the Yucatán of old still have somewhere to go. The contrast of world-class resorts within a half-day's drive of wild beaches and tangled jungle is attracting more and more travelers who are eager to experience the Yucatán peninsula's tranquillity and beauty.

Essential Information

Important Addresses and Numbers

Tourist Information
Chetumal

The **main tourist office** (Palacio del Gobierno, 2nd floor, tel. 983/20266, fax 983/20855) is open weekdays 9–2:30 and 6:30–9:30. The **tourist information booth** (tel. 983/23663) on Avenida Héroes, just opposite Avenida Efraín Aguilar, will give you *Guía Turística Pasaporte*, the free monthly brochure you can also find at many hotels.

Playa del Carmen

The unreliable tourist information booth is located one block from the beach on Avenida 5 (no phone). It is supposed to be open Monday–Saturday 7–2 and 3–9 and Sunday 7–2, but it is often closed during these times.

Emergencies
Chetumal

Police (Av. Insurgentes and Av. Belice, tel. 983/21500); **Red Cross** (Av. Efraín Aguilar at Av. Madero, tel. 983/20571).

Playa del Carmen

Police (Av. Juárez between Av. 15a and Av. 20a, next to the post office, no phone); **Red Cross** (Av. Héroes de Chapultapec con Independencia, tel. 983/20571).

Medical Clinics
Chetumal

The **Hospital General** (tel. 983/21932) is on Avenida Andres Quintana Roo.

Playa del Carmen

Centro de Salud (Av. Juárez at Av. 15a, tel. 987/21230, ext. 147).

Pharmacies
Chetumal

Farmacia Social Mechaca (Av. Independencia 134C, tel. 983/20044).

Banks
Chetumal

Banco del Atlántico (Av. Héroes 37, tel. 983/22776 or 983/20631) and **Bancomer** (Av. Alvaro Obregón 222 at Av. Juárez, tel. 983/25300 or 983/25318) provide banking services, including foreign currency exchange.

Playa del Carmen

Banco del Atlántico (corner of Av. 10a and Av. Juárez, no phone) cashes traveler's checks weekdays 10–noon.

English-language In Playa del Carmen, a small selection of magazines and books,
Bookstores some of them in English, is sold at **Papaya Tropical** (Av. 5a at
Calle 6). Hours are daily 9:30–1 and 5–9. The gift shop at the-
Playacar hotel (tel. 987/21583) has a more up-to-date selection
of magazines and paperbacks.

Gas Stations There are gas stations in Puerto Juárez, Puerto Morelos,
Cancún, Playa del Carmen, Tulum, Felipe Carrillo Puerto, and
Chetumal.

Travel Agencies **Chetumal Caribe** (Hotel Del Prado, Av. Héroes 138, tel.
and Tour Operators 983/20544) and **Turistica Maya** (Hotel Continental Caribe, Av.
Chetumal Héroes 171, tel. 983/20555 or 983/21080) arrange tours
throughout the area.

Car Rental **Rent-a-Car** (Av. Juárez between Avs. 10a and 15a, no phone)
Playa del Carmen and **APSA** (Av. 5 between Av. Juárez and Playacar, 987/30033)
rent cars; if you want air-conditioning, reserve your car in advance. Some car rental operations in Cancún will deliver cars
to Playa.

Arriving and Departing by Plane, Ferry, Car, and Bus

By Plane The Chetumal airport is located on the southwestern edge of
Chetumal town, along Avenida Alvaro Obregón where it turns into Route
186. **Aerocaribe** (tel. 983/26675) has flights three times a week
to Mérida, Cozumel, Mexico City, Guatemala City, and Flores,
Guatemala (near the ruins at Tikal).

By Ferry Ferries and jetfoils—which can be picked up at the dock—run
between Playa del Carmen and Cozumel about every two hours
and take about 40 minutes on the old ferry, and 30 minutes on
the two enclosed hydrofoils. The fee varies depending on which
boat you choose, but the one-way trip costs approximately between $2 and $5.

By Car The entire coast, from Punta Sam to the main border crossing
to Belize at Chetumal, is traversable on Route 307. This
straight road is entirely paved and is gradually being widened
to four lanes from Cancún south. Gas stations are becoming
more prevalent, but it's still a good idea to fill the tank whenever you can. Good roads that run into Route 307 from the west
are Route 180 (from Mérida and Valladolid), Route 295 (from
Valladolid), Route 184 (from central Yucatán), and Route 186
(from Villahermosa and, via Route 261, from Mérida and Campeche). Approximate driving times are as follows: from Cancún
to Felipe Carrillo Puerto, three hours; from Cancún to Mérida,
4½ hours; from Carrillo Puerto to Chetumal, two hours; from
Carrillo Puerto to Mérida, about 4½ hours; from Chetumal to
Campeche, 6½ hours.

By Taxi Taxis can be hired in Cancún to go as far as Playa del Carmen,
Tulum, or Akumal, but the price is steep unless you have many
passengers. Fares run about $40 or more to Playa alone; be-
tween Playa and Tulum or Akumal, expect to pay at least $25.

By Bus There is first-class service on the **ADO** line (Av. Juárez, 4 blocks
Playa del Carmen from the beach, tel. 987/30141) between Playa and Cancún, Valladolid, Chichén Itzá, Chetumal, Tulum, Xel-Há, Mexico City,
and Mérida daily. **Autotransportes del Caribe** (Av. Juárez, no
phone) has second-class service to the above destinations, and
express service to Chetumal. **Autotransportes Oriente** (Av.

Juárez, no phone) has express service to Mérida twice daily, and three buses daily to Cobá. **Playa Express** (Av. Juárez at Av. 5, no phone) has express minibus service to Cancún every half hour 6 AM–9 PM, and to Tulum four times daily; the buses do not have space for luggage.

Chetumal The bus station (Av. Héroes at Av. Insurgentes) is served by ADO (tel. 983/20629) and other lines. Buses run regularly to Cancún, Villahermosa, Mexico City, Mérida, Campeche, and Veracruz.

Telephones

Electricity and telephones are the exception rather than the rule in this region, although most hotels have radio communication with the outside world.

Chetumal The government-run telephone office, **TELMEX,** is located at Avenida Juárez and Lázaro Cárdenas. For long-distance and international calls, you might also try the booths on Avenida Héroes: One is on the corner of Ignacio Zaragoza and the other is just opposite Avenida Efraín Aguilar, next to the tourist information booth.

Playa del Carmen Playa has finally received telephone service, after many years of having only one phone line. Hotels, restaurants, and shops were still in the process of getting phone numbers and fax machines at press time; numbers are included here where available. There are Ladatel long-distance phone booths in front of the post office on Av. Juárez and next to the Tourist Information booth on Av. 5.

Mail

Chetumal The post office (Plutarco Elias Calles, tel. 983/22578) is open Monday–Saturday 8–1 and 3–6.

Playa del Carmen The post office (Av. Juárez, next to the police station, no phone) is open weekdays 9–1 and 3–6, Saturday 9–1.

Guided Tours

There are few major travel agencies or tour operators up and down the coast, but the first-class hotels in Playa del Carmen and Puerto Aventuras can arrange day tours to Tulum, Chichén Itzá, and Cobá. Most of the sights you see along this stretch are natural, so there is little point in spending the money for a guided tour unless you don't want to drive. Naturalists may wish to engage a guided tour of the Sian Ka'an Reserve on the Boca Paila Peninsula. Tours can be arranged through the private, nonprofit Amigos de Sian Ka'an organization (Plaza América, Av. Cobá, No. 5, Suites 48–50, Cancún, QR 77500, tel. 98/849583). You can also hire guides at the ruins sites. The roads are generally quite good, so renting a car is probably the most efficient and enjoyable way of touring.

Exploring

Numbers in the margin correspond to points of interest on the Mexico's Caribbean Coast map.

Mexico's Caribbean Coast

Route 307 parallels the entire coastline for the 382 kilometers (233 miles) from Cancún to Chetumal. The highway is straight and flat, but since at most points it is 1 or 2 kilometers inland from the coast, there is little in sight but dense vegetation, an occasional hut, assorted billboards, roadside artisans' markets, and road signs marking the dirt-road entrances to the ruins, resorts, beaches, and campgrounds that are hidden off the road. It won't stay that way for long, however, because the Mexican government has already begun to develop the 130-kilometer (81-mile) stretch of coastline known as the **Cancún–Tulum Corridor.** Each year more picture-coded international tourist signs appear, pointing the way to restaurants, gas stations, and hotels. Though buses do traverse the region and are popular with backpackers, a rental car or four-wheel-drive vehicle allows you to explore more thoroughly and creatively without ending up alone in the jungle after dark or in the torrential rains that soak the coast from May to September. Huge tour buses from Cancún appear regularly at the ruins, parks, and beaches with their loads of sightseers.

Once you get beyond Tulum and detour inland to the ruins of Cobá, the landscape changes: The road becomes noticeably deserted, and the remaining traffic consists mostly of large, fume-ejecting trucks and an occasional passenger car speeding to Chichén Itzá or Mérida. Generally speaking, the only people who venture farther south on route 307 are en route to Belize, since otherwise there is little to entice them in the way of historic sites or beaches. On the highway south of Tulum, the scenery is monotonous until you reach the beautiful and enormous Laguna Bacalar just north of Chetumal. When you get there, you may wonder why the magnificence does not attract more visitors.

Our north–south exploration of the Caribbean coast takes you from Puerto Morelos to Chetumal, with brief detours inland to the ruins of Cobá and Kohunlich. **Puerto Morelos,** a small coastal town about 36 kilometers (22 miles) south of Cancún, is home to the car ferry that travels to Cozumel. The town has been left remarkably free of the large-scale development so common farther south, though each year more and more tourists stop here to take in its easygoing pace, cheap accommodations, and convenient oceanside location near a superb offshore coral reef. For obvious reasons, this place is particularly attractive to divers, snorkelers, and anglers. The reef at Morelos—about 550 meters (1,800 feet) offshore—has claimed many ships over the centuries, and nowadays divers visit the sunken wrecks. Snorkeling gear, fishing tackle, and boats can be rented from the **Ojo de Agua Dive Shop** (no phone) at the Ojo de Agua hotel, north of town.

Once the point of departure for Mayan women making pilgrimages by canoe to Cozumel, the sacred isle of the fertility goddess, today Morelos is not very different from many small towns in the Spanish-speaking Caribbean. There is not much to it beyond a gas station, a central square, and auto repair shops. If you wander down the dirt streets north and south of town, however, you will notice neighborhoods of new, Mediterranean-style houses and condos, home to part-time residents who enjoy the town's laid-back mode. Nature endowed Puerto Morelos with a fine deep-sea port (the principal port for the area until the road to Puerto Juárez was built), so today ferries and freight ships call regularly, and most of the action is centered on the long pier south of the square, where vehicles line up for hours waiting for the ferry to depart. Three lighthouses from different eras break up the long stretch of beach, and boats to take out to the surrounding reefs can be rented on the beach.

About 32 kilometers (20 miles) south of Puerto Morelos is **② Punta Bete,** a 6½-kilometer (4-mile) white sand beach between rocky lagoons. This point is the setting for several bungalow-style hotels that have almost become cult places for travelers who love being in or on the water. All the properties are set off from Route 307 at the end of a 2 ³⁄₁₀-kilometer (1⅖-mile) rutted road.

③ A 10-minute drive farther south will take you to **Playa del Carmen,** a once-deserted beach where only a few decades ago Indian families raised coconut palms to produce copra. Nowadays its alabaster-white beach and small offshore reefs lend themselves to excellent swimming, snorkeling, and turtle-watching, and the town has recently become the preferred destination of hip young Europeans who want to skip Cancún and go on to see the archaeological sights of Yucatán.

The 10-block-long, eight-block-wide village is not particularly charming, since it lacks scenery and its buildings have become somewhat shabby. Playa has a slew of inexpensive, funky bungalow-style hotels; equally eccentric, low-key restaurants; and all the basics for a short or extended stay, including an auto parts shop, a drugstore, a bank, fresh fruit and ice cream stands, liquor and food stores, and a travel agency, which also rents cars. A dive shop next to the pier rents snorkeling and scuba equipment, and plenty of young boys and men on the beach will gladly rent their boats for jaunts to the reefs and coves to the south.

The busiest parts of Playa are down by the **ferry pier** and at the **zócalo.** Take a stroll north from the pier along the beach and you'll see the essence of the town: simple restaurants roofed with palm fronds, where people sit around drinking beer for hours; two campgrounds; and lots of hammocks. Now head all the way south, along Avenida 5a (the first street in from the beach), a street lined with *tienditas* (little shops) selling crafts and groceries; the crafts stands are concentrated especially at the south end, where the street meets the ferry ramp. On the south side of the pier is **Playacar,** a first-class, lavish hotel that has brought a sense of luxury and style to Playa del Carmen. Playacar, which opened in 1991, has become a stunning success, particularly with European tour groups. A second hotel, the all-inclusive **Diamond Resort** has opened farther south along the beach. If you walk away from the beach, you'll come upon the affluent section: several condominium projects and well-tended gardens and lawns that can be seen from the street. From here, only the sandy streets, the small vestiges of Mayan structures, and the stunning turquoise sea on the horizon suggest you're in the tropics. The streets at both ends of town peter out into the jungle. Playa is slowly acquiring the confident veneer of an up-and-coming beach destination, which can be attributed, in part, to the amiability of the locals (including the growing number of expatriates who manage many of the hotels and restaurants). As always, however, popularity inevitably means that prices increase.

Six kilometers (4 miles) south of Playa is a paved road leading to **Xcaret,** which has been transformed from a tranquil cove into a waterside amusement park. A mind-boggling combination of construction and destruction has changed an idyllic hidden cove with a few small ruins into an expanse of winding jungle trails leading to man-made *caletas,* or inlets, with white sand beaches and waters that are still a bit clouded from the disturbances of bulldozers and trucks. The main feature at the new Xcaret park is an underground river ride, included in the admission price. Swimmers don life jackets (snorkels, masks, and fins come in handy as well) and float with the cool waters' currents through a series of caves. Holes were blasted and carved into the roofs of the caves to bring in sunlight and fresh air. Other attractions include a large palapa restaurant (expensive) overlooking the sea, horseback riding, several small saltwater ponds filled with tropical fish, and water-sports equipment on the beach. Lockers, showers, and changing rooms are available. *No phone. Admission: $17. Open daily 9–6.*

Time Out If you're hankering for fresh fish, you may want to go back to **Restaurant Xcaret** (no phone), just off the highway before the park. This small, casual palapa restaurant was around long before development hit Xcaret, and it continues to serve low-cost, high-quality grilled fish and tacos.

Beachcombers and snorkelers are fond of **Paamul** (10 kilometers/6 miles south of Xcaret), a crescent-shaped lagoon with clear, placid waters sheltered by the coral reef at the lagoon's mouth. Shells, sand dollars, and even glass beads—some from the sunken pirate ships at Akumal—wash onto the sandy parts of the beach. Trailer camps, cabañas, and tent camps are scattered along the beach; a restaurant sells cold beer and fresh fish; and in the summer visitors may view one of Paamul's chief attractions: sea turtle hatchlings on the beach. You can also take the jungle path to the north, which leads to a lagoon four times the size of the first and even more private.

Puerto Aventuras is a 900-acre self-contained resort, which will eventually include condominiums, a 250-slip marina, a tennis club, a beach club, a dive center, an 18-hole golf course, a shopping mall, a movie theater, and five deluxe hotels with a total of 2,000 rooms. At press time, facilities in operation included several restaurants and shops, nine holes of the golf course, an excellent dive shop, the marina, and the **CEDAM underwater archaeology museum** (open daily 9–6), where old ships, coins, and nautical devices are exhibited. Accommodations including two hotels and several condo and time-share units were also open. Puerto Aventuras includes a combination of Mediterranean, Caribbean, and Mexican architectural styles, and the buildings are spread apart along the golf course and marina. There is a dolphin show at the marina, and visitors may swim with the dolphins (who are kept in uncomfortably small pens) for $65.

Nine kilometers (5½ miles) south of Paamul along a narrow path is a little fishing community called **Xpuhá,** where residents weave hammocks and harvest coconuts. Some small, overgrown pre-Hispanic ruins in the area still bear traces of paint on the inside walls. A cluster of pastel-colored hotel buildings sit on the beach; inexpensive rooms are available on a first-come, first-served basis, although the smaller properties close for September and October.

⑧ **Akumal** lies about 35 kilometers (22 miles) south of Playa del Carmen and consists of three distinct areas. Half Moon Bay to the north is lined with private homes and condominiums and has some of the prettiest beaches and best snorkeling in the area. Akumal proper consists of a large resort and small Mayan community with a market, laundry facilities, and pharmacy. More condos and homes and an all-inclusive resort are located at Akumal Aventuras to the south. People come here to dive or simply to walk on the deliciously long beaches filled with shells, crabs, and migrant birds. The name, meaning "Place of the Turtle," recalls ancient Mayan times, when the beach was the nesting ground for thousands of turtles. It first attracted international attention in 1926, when explorers discovered the Mantanceros, a Spanish galleon that sank in 1741. Three decades later, Akumal became headquarters for the Mexican Underwater Explorers Club (CEDAM) and a resort for wealthy underwater adventurers who flew in on private planes and searched the waters for sunken treasures.

The long curved bay and beach are rarely empty now; but although Akumal can be crowded—especially at lunchtime, when tour buses stop here en route from Tulum—it is also expansive and generally much less developed than Cancún. Those who stay are seeking the comforts of an international resort without the high rises, and Europeans—who tend to gravitate toward Mexico's quieter side—are coming in ever-greater numbers.

First and foremost, however, Akumal is famous for its diving. Area dive shops sponsor resort courses and certification courses, and luxury hotels and condominiums offer year-round packages comprising airfare, accommodations, and diving (hotel rooms are at a premium during the high season, and reservations should be made well in advance). The reef, which is about 130 meters (425 feet) offshore, shelters the bay and its exceptional coral formations and sunken galleon; the sandy bottom invites snorkelers to wade out at the rocky north end, where they can view the diverse underwater topography. Deep-sea fishing for giant marlin, bonito, and sailfish is also popular.

⑨ Devoted snorkelers may want to walk to **Yalkú,** a practically unvisited lagoon just north of Akumal along an unmarked dirt road. Wending its way out to the sea, Yalkú hosts throngs of parrot fish in superbly clear water with visibility to 160 feet, but it has no facilities.

In stark contrast to the man-made finery of Akumal is the **⑩** beautiful little cove at **Chemuyil,** about 5 kilometers (3 miles) south, where you can stop for lunch and a swim. The crescent-shaped beach is small and secluded, but has been discovered by tour groups and is far less tranquil than it was in the past.

Time Out   In Chemuyil a circular, open-air bar and restaurant, **Marco**

Polo, is run by friendly owners who whip up excellent *limonada* and prepare shellfish as you sit on a bar stool or lounge in a Hammock cooled by ceiling fans.

Continue south for a couple of kilometers along Route 307 to
⑪ the **Laguna de Xcacel,** which sits on a sandy ridge overlooking yet another long white beach. The calm waters provide excellent swimming, snorkeling, diving, and fishing; birders and beachcombers like to stroll in the early morning. Camping is permitted, and a restaurant (closed on Sunday) is on the site. Tour buses full of cruise-ship passengers stop here for lunch, and the showers and dressing rooms get crowded at dusk.

A natural aquarium cut out of the limestone shoreline 6 kilo-
⑫ meters (4 miles) south of Akumal, **Xel-Há** (pronounced *shel-HA*) national park consists of several interconnected lagoons where countless species of tropical fish breed; the rocky coastline curves into bays and coves in which enormous parrotfish cluster around an underwater Mayan shrine. Several low wooden bridges over the lagoons have benches at regular points, so you can take in the sights at leisure. Though much of the fauna has been threatened by suntan oil and garbage, the waters are still remarkably clear and teem with brilliantly colored fish. Certain areas are off-limits to swimmers, but because the lagoons are quite large, in places you can swim fairly far out, or you can explore one of the underwater caves or the cenotes deep in the jungle. Glass-bottom boats travel to the far side of the lagoon, where stingrays and nurse sharks may be hovering beneath the surface. Lockers and dressing rooms are available, and you can rent snorkel gear ($10) and underwater cameras (the $18 fee includes a roll of film). Those who choose not to snorkel can rent chaise longues ($3) for sunbathing.

The park holds other attractions as well. A shrine stands at the entrance, and there are other small Mayan ruins throughout, including one named Na Balaam (Mayan for "tiger") for a yellow jaguar painted on one of its walls. There is also a huge but overpriced souvenir shop, food stands, and a small museum housing 10,000 artifacts from pre-Hispanic days, 16th- and 17th-century shipwrecks (including coins and cannons from the *Mantanceros*), and present-day displays. The enormous parking lot attests to the number of visitors who come here; you should plan to arrive in the early morning, before all the tour-bus traffic hits. For a pleasant breakfast or lunch, you may want to try the restaurant, which serves reasonably good ceviche, fresh fish, and drinks. *Admission: $5. Open daily 8–5.*

About 9½ kilometers (6 miles) south of Xel-Há, in the depths of the jungle, stands a small grouping of pre-Hispanic structures that cover 10 square kilometers (4 square miles) and once
⑬ served as a satellite city of Tulum. **Tan-kah,** as the place is known, has still not been fully explored, and while the buildings themselves may not warrant much attention, a curious bit of more recent history does. In the 1930s an airstrip was built here; Charles Lindbergh, who was making an aerial survey of the coast, was one of the first to land on it.

A couple of kilometers farther south lies one of the Caribbean
⑭ coast's biggest attractions: **Tulum.** The most visited Mayan ruin, it is the only Mayan city built on the coast, and the spectacle of those amber-gray stones etched against the fiercely blue-green Caribbean waters is nothing less than riveting. Al-

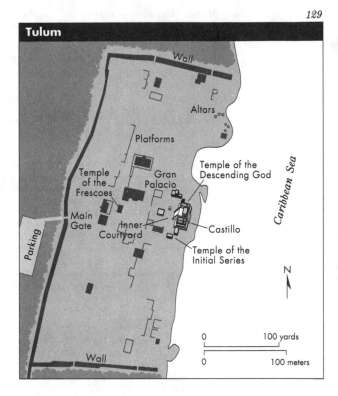

Tulum

most Grecian in its stark, low grayness, and vaguely medieval in the forbidding aspect of its walls, this site surpasses all others for the sheer majesty of its setting. Unfortunately, access to many of the most impressive structures is now limited; visitors can no longer climb or enter the buildings.

Resting about 130 kilometers (80 miles) south of Cancún, Tulum is comprised of 60-odd structures, most of which date from the 12th to the 15th centuries. Only about three structures merit visiting, so you can see the site in two hours, but you may wish to allow extra time for a swim or a stroll on the beach. A path leads from the cliff down to the sea, where it's likely that the ancient Maya beached their canoes.

Tulum—which means "City of the New Dawn," and which the ancient Maya called Zama ("sunrise")—is the only Mayan city known to have been inhabited when the conquistadores arrived. Juan de Grijalva and his men, who spotted it from their ships in 1518, were so intimidated by the enormity of its vivid 25-foot-high, blue, white, and red citadel (making Tulum the only walled Mayan site) that they were reluctant to land. What they had seen was four towns so close to one another as to appear to be one continuous metropolis. The Postclassical (AD 900–1541) architecture at Tulum evinces strong Toltec and Mixtec (a tribe from the Oaxacan Plateau) influences, because by the early 1500s the peninsular Maya had been absorbed into the empires of central and southern Mexico. Although artistic refinements found elsewhere in the Mayan world are missing here, the structure is extraordinarily well preserved. A 3,600-foot-long, 23-foot-thick wall—punctuated by five gateways and enclosing a dozen or so structures within 16 acres—surrounds Tulum on three sides.

Its largest building, the **Temple of the Descending God**—so called for the carving of a winged god plummeting to earth over the doorway—has skillfully rendered stucco masks in the corners. The deity they represent is thought either to be Ah Muzen Cab, the bee god, or to be associated with the planet Venus, guardian of the coast and of commerce. Visitors are no longer allowed to climb the temple's stairs for a closer view of the carvings.

The impressive **Castillo** (castle) looms over a 40-foot limestone cliff. Atop the castle, at the end of a broad stairway, sits a temple with stucco ornamentation on the outside and traces of fine frescoes inside the two chambers. Although you are not allowed to climb the stairs or enter the chambers, you can see the ornamentation from below. The front wall of the regal Castillo has faint carvings of the Descending God and columns depicting the plumed serpent god, Kukulcán, who was introduced to the Maya by the Toltecs. The Castillo overlooks an expanse of dense jungle and cactus to the west and the sea to the east. Until the 1940s, modern-day Maya from the Chan Santa Cruz group held an annual eight-day celebration honoring the sanctity of the place.

Tulum has long held special significance for the Indians. A key city in the League of Mayapán (987–1194), it was never conquered by the Spaniards, although it was abandoned about 75 years after the Conquest. For 300 years thereafter, it symbolized the defiance of an otherwise subjugated people; it was one of the last outposts of the Maya during the 1840s War of the Castes. Uprisings continued intermittently until 1935, when the Maya ceded Tulum to the government.

Most of the Chan Santa Cruz Indians are gone now, but some of their beliefs still prevail. For example, they thought that Tulum was connected to Cobá and other ruined cities by a living rope suspended in the sky and acting as a road. In fact, Tulum is linked to several other ancient Mayan sites by sacbeob, white stone causeways once used for ceremonial purposes and as trade arteries. One sacbe led from the northeast gateway to Xel-Há and then to Cobá, 42 kilometers (26 miles) west. Especially in its final days, Tulum functioned as a trading center, providing the much larger city of Cobá with an outlet to the sea and hence the control of commerce with Central America. Tulum's fortifications attest to its military importance. It may once have been home to 2,000 people living in houses set on man-made platforms along the main artery.

The blue-green frescoes outlined in black on the inner and outer walls of the two-story **Temple of the Frescoes** also refer to ancient Mayan beliefs. Reminiscent of the Mixtec style, the frescoes depict the three worlds of the Maya and their major deities, and are decorated with stellar and serpentine patterns, rosettes, and ears of maize and other offerings to the gods. One scene portrays the rain god seated on a four-legged animal- probably a reference to the Spaniards on their horses. *Admission: $4; free Sun. and holidays. Open daily 8–5.*

Entrances in Tulum are very low, even for the Maya, who are typically short of stature. Apparently the design forced those who entered to bow in deference to the divinities within.

Vaulted roofs and corbeled arches, such as the ones on the Temple of the Frescoes, are examples of Classical Mayan architecture. By contrast, flat roofs resting on wood beams and columns, the generally second-rate sculpture, and the urban layout of straight streets flanked by buildings on either side bear the mark of outside influence that typified the city's later years of decline.

Tourist services are clustered at the crossroads (El Crucero) between the highway and the turnoff to the ruins, marked by a bulky shopping center, which was under construction at press time. At the parking lot by the ruins, souvenirs, handicrafts, and snacks are sold from a semicircular row of stands, but prices tend to be excessive. You will also encounter unofficial guides who profess various degrees of expertise on Mayan archaeology. Using their services will help the local economy, but you should take their stories with a grain of salt. Tour buses arrive at the ruins by midmorning, so it is wise to get there early. There is also a present-day village of Tulum, just off Route 307 and about 4 kilometers (2½ miles) south of the ruins. This small community is undergoing changes as prosperity rises. Markets, taco stands, and other businesses line the highway close to town.

⓯ Beautiful but barely explored, **Cobá** is a 35-minute drive northwest of Tulum down a well-marked and well-paved road that leads straight through the jungle. Two tiny pueblos, Macario Gómez and Balché, with their clusters of thatched-roof white huts, are the only signs of habitation en route. Once one of the most important city-states in the entire Mayan domain, Cobá now stands in solitude; the spell this remoteness casts is intensified by the silence at the ruins, broken occasionally by the shriek of a spider monkey or the call of a bird. Processions of huge hunter ants cross the footpaths, and the sun penetrates the tall hardwood trees, ferns, and giant palms with fierce shafts of light. Cobá exudes the still, eerie ambience of a dead city.

Archaeologists estimate the presence of some 6,500 structures in the area, but only 5% have been uncovered, and it will take decades before the work is completed. Discovered by Teobert Maler in 1891, Cobá was subsequently explored in 1926 by the Carnegie Institute but not excavated until 1972, when the road from Tulum was built. At present there is no restoration work underway.

The city flourished from AD 400 to 1100, probably boasting a population of as many as 40,000 inhabitants. Situated on five lakes between coastal watchtowers and inland cities, its temple-pyramids towered over a vast jungle plain (one of them is 138 feet tall, the largest and highest in northern Yucatán). Cobá (meaning "ruffled waters") exercised economic control over the region through a network of at least 16 sacbeob, one of which, at 100 kilometers (62 miles), is the longest in the Mayan world. In the elegance of its massive, soaring structures and in its sheer size—the city once covered 210 square kilometers (81 square miles)—Cobá strongly resembles Tikal in northern Guatemala, to which it apparently had close cultural and commercial ties.

The main groupings are separated by several miles of intense tropical vegetation, so the only way to get a sense of the immensity of the city is to scale one of the pyramids. Maps and books about the ruins are sold at the makeshift restaurants and shops that line the parking lot. None of the maps are particularly accurate, and unmarked side trails lead temptingly into the jungle. Stay on the main, marked paths unless you have a guide; several men with guide licenses congregate by the entrance and offer their services. When you go, bring plenty of bug repellent, and if you plan to spend some time here, bring a canteen of water (you can also buy sodas and snacks at the entrance).

The first major grouping, off a path to your right as you enter the ruins, is the **Cobá Group,** whose pyramids are built around a sunken patio. At the near end of the group, facing a large plaza, you'll see the 79-foot-high Iglesia (church), where the Indians place offerings and light candles in hopes of improving their harvests. If you have strong legs and want a great view, scale this ruin—unless you want to to save your energy for the far taller Nohoch Mul (*see below*).

Farther along the main path to your left is the **Chumuc Mul Group,** little of which has been excavated. The principal pyramid here is covered with the stucco remains (*chumuc mul* means "stucco pyramid") of vibrantly painted motifs. A kilometer (3/10 mile) past this site is the **Nohoch Mul** (meaning "large hill") **Group,** the highlight of which is the pyramid of the same name, the tallest at Cobá. The pyramid has 120 steps— equivalent to 12 stories—and shares a plaza with Temple 10. The Descending God (also seen at Tulum) is depicted on a facade of the temple atop Nohoch Mul, from which the view is excellent; the temple seems to have been erected much later than the pyramid itself. It was from the base of this pyramid that the longest sacbe started; it extended all the way to Yaxuná, 20 kilometers (12 miles) southwest of Chichén Itzá. Sacbeob had widths of up to 33 feet, and there is considerable speculation about their function, since the Maya had no beasts of burden but carried all cargo on their own backs. The sacbeob's width, which may have been designed to allow people to walk abreast in processions, suggests that the roads played a role in religion as well as in trade. The unrestored **Crossroad Pyramid** opposite Nohoch Mul was the meeting point for three sacbeob.

Beyond the Nohoch Mul Group is the **Castillo** (castle); its nine chambers are reached by a stairway. To the south are the remains of a ball court, including the stone ring through which the ball was hurled. From the main route follow the sign to **Las Pinturas Group,** named for the still discernible polychromatic friezes on the inner and outer walls of its large, patioed pyramid. An enormous stela here depicts a man standing with his feet on two prone captives. Take the minor path for a kilometer (2/3 mile) to the **Macanxoc Group,** not far from the lake of the same name. The main pyramid at Macanxoc is accessible by a stairway. The portal of the temple at its summit is divided by a column; there are also a molded lintel and the remains of a stucco painting. Many of the stelae here are intricately carved with dates and other symbols of the history of Cobá.

Devotees of archaeology may wish to venture farther to the small **Kukulkán Group,** one of the larger satellites of Cobá, positioned just 5½ kilometers (3½ miles) south of the Cobá group. Only five structures remain, and they are among the more puzzling ruins in the Mayan world; their design and use have yet to be explained by archaeologists. The three-story temple is particularly intriguing because it is the only Mayan structure in which the top story does not rest on filled-in lower stories.

Cobá can be comfortably visited in a half-day, but if you want to spend the night, opt for the Villa Arqueólogica Cobá (*see* Lodging, *below*), operated by Club Med and only a three-minute walk from the site along the shores of Lake Cobá. Spending the night is highly advised—the nighttime jungle sounds will lull you to sleep, and you'll be able to visit the ruins in solitude when they open at 8 AM. Even on a day trip, consider taking time out for lunch and a swim at the Villa—an oasis of French civilization—after the intense heat and mosquito-ridden humidity of the ruins. *Buses depart Cobá for Playa del Carmen and Valladolid twice daily. Check with your hotel and the clerk at the ruins for the times, which may not be exact. Admission: $4; free on Sun. Open daily 8–5.*

Return to the coastal road heading south to Tulum and continue to the Boca Paila turnoff from Route 307. Several kilometers south, past a few bungalows and campsites, the paved road ends, and a rope over the sand marks the entrance to the **Sian Ka'an Biosphere Reserve.** The reserve includes the 1.3-million-acre **Boca Paila peninsula,** a secluded 35-kilometer (22-mile) strip of land established by the Mexican government in 1986 as one of UNESCO's internationally protected areas and named a World Heritage Site by UNESCO in 1987. The Man and the Biosphere program, of which this is part, was created to preserve threatened areas of the earth's surface and their natural resources. The reserves are particularly important in developing countries, where dwindling resources often represent the only form of subsistence for large segments of the population. Maintaining the ecological diversity of these areas while providing the local people with food and livelihoods is the challenge of the biosphere program, which has had great success at Sian Ka'an. Under the program, the land is divided for various purposes, including research, preservation, and economic activities in conjunction with conservation. Assisted by scientists, the local population lives off fishing, lobster harvests, coconuts, and small farming, and receives support from the low-impact tourism, biological research, and sustainable development programs under way.

The reserve constitutes 10% of the land in Quintana Roo and covers 100 kilometers (62 miles) of coast. Freshwater and coastal lagoons, mangrove swamps, watery cays, savannahs, tropical jungles, a barrier reef, hundreds of species of exotic migratory birds, fish, other animals and plants, and about 1,000 local residents—primarily Maya—share this area, one of the last undeveloped stretches of coastline in North America. About 20 ruined sites are scattered about; they are linked by a canal system—the only one of its kind in the Mayan world. Boca Paila is not easily reached, but those who take the time to get here feel rewarded.

Sian Ka'an, meaning "where the sky is born," was first settled by the Xiu tribe from Central America in the 5th century. The area once flourished with countless species of wildlife, many of which have fallen into the endangered category, but the waters here still teem with banana fish, bonefish, mojarra, snapper, shad, permit, sea bass, and alligator. Flat fishing and fly-fishing are especially popular, and the peninsula's few lodges run deep-sea fishing trips as far away as **Ascensión Bay**, two hours south of the lodges by boat. Birders take launches out to **Cajo Colibrí** (Hummingbird Cay) or to **Isla de Pájaros** to view the pelicans, frigate birds, woodpeckers, sparrow hawks, and some 350 other species of birds that roost on the mangrove roots or circle overhead. The beaches are wide and white, and although many of the palms have succumbed to the yellowing palm disease imported from Florida, graceful (but ecologically destructive) sea pines are growing up to take their place. The more adventuresome travelers can explore the caves with which the waterways are riddled or trek out to the tiny ruins of Chunyaxché (*see below*). For information and tours contact Amigos de Sian Ka'an (*see* Guided Tours, *above*).

The narrow, rough dirt road down the Boca Paila (meaning "mouth of the river") peninsula is dotted with campgrounds, fishing lodges, and deserted palapas and copra farms. It ends at **Punta Allen**, a fishing village whose main catch is the spiny lobster, and the site of a small guest house. In 1990 some muggings involving tourists took place on the Boca Paila road, but they seem to have been isolated events. In any case, you should travel by car or private plane, or charter a flight from Playa del Carmen or Cozumel.

Continue along the main route to the extensive archaeological site of **Chunyaxché**—known in ancient times as Muyil—which is currently under excavation by Tulane University and the Mexican government, with the help of local Maya and the latest laser and satellite technology. Dating from the Late Preclassical era (300 BC–AD 200), it was connected by road to the sea and served as a port between Cobá and the Mayan centers in Belize and Guatemala. A 15-foot-wide sacbe, built during the Late Postclassical period (1250–1600), extended from the city to the mangrove swamp (today the remains of the sacbe get flooded during the rainy season). Structures were erected at 400-foot intervals along the white road, and almost all of them faced west. At the beginning of this century, the ancient stones were used to build a chicle (gum) plantation, which was managed by one of the leaders of the War of the Castes. Today, all that stands are the remains of a 56-foot **temple-pyramid**—one of the tallest on the Quintana Roo coast—at the center of a big patio. From its summit you can see the Caribbean, 15 kilometers (9 miles) in the distance. Chunyaxché sits on the edge of a deep blue lagoon and is surrounded by a nearly impenetrable jungle inhabited by wildcats, white-tailed deer, wild boars, raccoons, badgers, pheasants, wild turkeys, ducks, herons, and parakeets. You can swim or fish in the lagoon, and there is a small restaurant on the highway next to the dirt road leading to the ruins. *Admission: $4. Open Tues.–Sun. 9–6.*

Twenty-four kilometers (15 miles) to the south, at Km 73 on Route 307, is **Felipe Carrillo Puerto**, named for a local hero who preached rebellion. In 1920 Carrillo Puerto eventually became governor of Yucatán and instituted a series of reforms that led to his assassination by the henchman of the presidential candidate of an opposing party. This town, formerly known as Chan Santa Cruz, also played a central role in the 19th-century War of the Castes, during which it was not only a significant political and military center but also a religious capital. It was here that the Talking Cross first appeared—carved into a cedar tree near a cenote. The Indian priest Manuel Nahuat, translating from behind a curtain, interpreted the cross as a sign for the Indians to attack the *dzulob* (white Christians) under the protection of the cross. Although Mexican soldiers cut down the tree and destroyed the cross, the Indians made other crosses from the trunk and placed them in neighboring villages, including Tulum. The last messages were given in 1904; by then half the local population had been annihilated in the war.

Today, the town exists primarily as the hub of three highways, and the only vestige of the momentous events of the last century is the small, uncompleted temple (located on the edge of town in an inconspicuous, poorly marked park) begun by the Indians in the 1860s and now a monument to the War of the Castes. The church where the Talking Cross was originally housed also stands. Several humble hotels, some good restaurants, and a gas station may be incentives for stopping here on your southbound trek.

Route 307, a dreary and monotonous road to Belize, continues south for another 112 unremarkable kilometers (69 miles), until the sudden appearance of the spectacularly vast and

⑲ beautiful **Laguna de Bacalar.** Also known as the Lake of the Seven Colors, this is the second largest lake in Mexico (56 kilometers/35 miles long) and is frequented by scuba divers and other lovers of water sports. Seawater and fresh water mix in the lake, intensifying the aquamarine hues, and the water contrasts starkly with the dark jungle growth. If you drive along the lake's southern shores, you'll enter the affluent section of the town of Bacalar, with elegant turn-of-the-century waterfront homes. Also in the vicinity are a few simple hotels and campgrounds.

Bacalar appears to be the oldest settlement in Quintana Roo, having been founded in AD 435. Of some historical interest is the **Fuerte de San Felipe,** a stone fort built by the Spaniards during the 18th century to ward off marauding pirates and Indians and later used by the Maya during the War of the Castes. The monolithic structure is right on the zócalo and overlooks the lake. Presently it houses government offices and a museum with exhibits on local history. *Admission free. Open daily 8–5.*

Just beyond Bacalar exists the largest sinkhole in the world,

⑳ the **Cenote Azul,** 607 feet in diameter, with clear blue waters that afford unusual visibility even at 200 feet below the surface. Surrounded by lush vegetation and underwater caves, the cenote attracts divers who specialize in this somewhat tricky type of dive. Other recreational areas on the water are to be found at **Laguna Milagros,** a lovely lagoon with an island in the center and a shoreline graced by palms and bougainvillea, and at **Xul-Ha,** a rustic spa. Restaurants and rental shops are in the vicinity, too.

㉑ **Chetumal**—38 kilometers (24 miles) farther along Route 307— is the last Mexican town on the southern Caribbean. It was founded in 1898 as Payo Obispo in a concerted and only partially successful effort to gain control of the lucrative traffic in the region's precious hardwoods, arms, and ammunition, and also to put down the rebellious Indians. The city, which overlooks the Bay of Chetumal at the mouth of the Río Hondo, was devastated by a hurricane in 1955 and rebuilt as a modern state capital and major port. Because of its status as a free port (in the past it was a haven for smugglers), Mexican merchants come to buy imported goods not found elsewhere in the country. In ancient times it was one of the major Mayan ports.

Overall, Chetumal feels more Central American than Mexican; this is not surprising, given its proximity to Belize, with which there is both commercial and tourist traffic. Chetumal's streets are also vaguely reminiscent of some parts of the American South, with monotonous rows of run-down (but often charming) clapboard houses interspersed with low-lying ramshackle commercial establishments. The mixed population includes many black Caribbeans and Middle Easterners, and the arts reflect this eclectic combination—the music includes reggae, salsa, calypso, and Belizean bruckdown; there is not much mariachi. The cuisine represents an exotic blend of Yucatecan, Mexican, and Lebanese.

The town's most attractive thoroughfare, the wide **Boulevard Bahía,** runs along the waterfront and is a popular gathering spot at night (though on the weekend Chetumal practically shuts down). The main plaza sits between the boulevard and Avenidas Alvaro Obregón and Héroes; unremarkable modern government buildings and some especially bland patriotic statues and monuments to local heroes wall in the plaza on two sides. Brackish bay waters lapping at the dock create a melancholy rhythm, but if you sit at one of the sidewalk cafés by the square, you will have an appealing view of this huge, placid bay.

Downtown Chetumal contains a small zoo, a few discos, and a cultural institute; the reasonably priced hotels, which seem to cater mostly to the modest needs of traveling salesmen, are generally clean. For shopping, you can stroll along Avenida Héroes, where most of the stores are located, but the merchandise tends to be a humdrum, functional miscellany. Although Chetumal's provisions are modest, the town presents a pleasant waterfront, since the city is surrounded by water on three sides. The area's clean, white bayfront beaches can compete with any of the beaches along the coast.

Surrounding attractions offer alternatives to downtown ㉒ Chetumal. **Banco Chinchorro,** a 42-kilometer (26-mile) coral atoll and national park (fishing prohibited), is situated two hours offshore and littered with shipwrecks. The reef, which is popular with divers, is accessible by boat from the fishing vil- ㉓ lage of **Xcalak,** near the tip of the Xcalak peninsula, which divides the bay from the ocean. The peninsula is accessible from Highway 307 by way of the Majahual exit, north of Laguna Bacalar. The road is paved to Majahual on the coast, then turns to dirt, sand, and ruts running south to Xcalak—about a one-hour drive. A few small resorts cater to the divers and explorers willing to make the long trek. This area is full of mangrove swamps, tropical flowers, birds and other wildlife, and wonderfully deserted beaches.

Chetumal's major water attractions, however, sit farther inland. The **Río Hondo** runs alongside the borders between Mexico and Belize and Guatemala; in its wildest parts, alligators roam the riverbeds and manatees breed. The **Palmar** and **Obregón springs** by the river, just outside Chetumal, have rustic resorts.

Sixty-eight kilometers (42 miles) west of Chetumal, off Route
24 186, lies **Kohunlich,** renowned for the giant stucco masks on its
principal pyramid, for one of the oldest ball courts in Quintana
Roo, and for the remains of a great hydraulic system at the
Stelae Plaza. The masks—about 5 feet tall—are set vertically
into the wide staircases; apparently they played a part in ceremonies dedicated to the sun god. Archaeologists believe that
Kohunlich was built and occupied during the Early Classical
period, about AD 300–600. This site is usually deserted, and in
the vicinity are scores of unexcavated mounds, stelae, and
thriving flora and fauna. *Admission: $4. Open daily 8–5.*

What to See and Do with Children

Croco-Cun, near Playa del Carmen, is a crocodile farm and
miniature zoo located 29 kilometers (18 miles) south of Cancún.
The biologists running Croco-Cun have collected specimens of
most of the animals and reptiles indigenous to the area, and
offer immensely informative tours to visitors willing to spend
an hour or two learning about the jungle's wildlife. Self-guided
tours, a restaurant, and a gift shop are also available. *Rte. 307
at Km 30, tel. 98/841709. Admission: $2.50. Open Tues.–Sun. 9–6;
closed Mon.*

Shopping

There aren't many high-quality crafts available along the Caribbean coast, although stands on the road leading to the ferry
in Playa del Carmen and in the parking lot at the Tulum ruins
do their best to unload a mediocre and overpriced selection of
embroidered clothing, schlock reproductions of ancient carvings and statues, knickknacks made from shells, and hammocks. Several roadside artisans' markets have sprung up
along Route 307; most feature a repetitive display of cotton
rugs. If you drive, stock up on groceries, pharmacy items, hard-
ware, and auto parts in Puerto Morelos, Playa del Carmen,
Felipe Carrillo Puerto, or Chetumal. As for Chetumal, while
Mexicans go there to buy imported and black-market appli-
ances, North Americans will find the merchandise inferior and
the prices no bargain. Save your shopping dollars for Mérida
or Cozumel.

Sports and Fitness

Water Sports Diving, snorkeling, and fishing are among the most popular
activities along the coast. Quintana Roo attracts scuba divers
and snorkelers with its transparent turquoise and emerald waters strewn with rose, black, and red coral reefs and sunken
pirate ships. Schools of black, gray, and gold angelfish, lumi-
nous green-and-purple parrotfish, earth-colored manta rays,
and scores of other jewel-toned tropical species seem oblivious
to the clicking underwater cameras. The visibility in these waters reaches 100 feet, so you can see the marine life and topography without even getting wet. There is particularly good
diving in Akumal and Laguna de Bacalar. For details, *see* Exploring, *above.*

For fly-fishing, boats can be rented from locals who run beachside stalls. If you're interested in deep-sea fishing in the Car-

ibbean, where catches such as marlin, bonito, and sailfish can be found, many local marinas run charters. Generally, larger hotels have dive shops on the premises. The following is a brief list of outfitters. For details about where to dive, *see* Exploring, *above.*

Akumal **Kapaalua Dive Shop** (tel. 800/351–1622), **Akumal Dive Shop** (tel. 987/22453, 987/41259, or 800/777–8294), and **Cedam Dive Centers** (tel. 987/22211) rent diving equipment.

Chetumal **Casa Lucy** (Av. Héroes No. 52, between Plutarco Elias and Ignacio Zaragoza) rents diving gear.

Puerto Aventuras **Mike Madden's CEDAM Dive Centers** (in the Club de Playa hotel, tel. 987/22233, fax 987/41339) is a full-service dive shop with certification courses; cave and cenote diving is a specialty. There is another Mike Madden shop at the Diamond Resort in Playa del Carmen (tel. 987/30340).

Puerto Morelos Scuba gear is available from the **Ojo de Agua Dive shop** (no phone) and at the dive stand on the beach by the plaza.

Punta Bete **La Posada del Capitan Lafitte** and **Shangri La Caribe** (tel. 800/538–6802 for both), located on Carretera 307 just north of Playa del Carmen, run deep-sea fishing trips and have full-service dive shops on the premises.

Xcalak Situated about 164 kilometers (100 miles) from Chetumal, and reached by boat, plane, or car, the little fishing village of Xcalak makes a good point of departure for deep-sea fishing and diving. The **Costa de Cocos Hotel** (Box 316, Bloomingdale, IL 60108, tel. 800/443–1123) runs trips.

Dining and Lodging

Dining Most of the restaurants along the Mexican Caribbean coast are simple beachside affairs with outdoor tables and palapa roofs. Little attention is paid to the niceties of decor you find in such resort destinations as Cancún, Cozumel, and even Isla Mujeres. In addition to their generally casual ambience, restaurants here offer bargains, especially when it comes to seafood, provided it is fresh and local, such as grouper, mojarra, snapper, shad, and seabass. Shrimp, lobster, oysters, and other shellfish are usually flown in frozen from the Gulf or Pacific coast, and often you can taste the difference. A number of places that cater to the North American palate have sprung up where tourists congregate, especially in Playa del Carmen and Akumal; their menus include such items as pizza and spaghetti. The few luxury hotels in the area have fancy restaurants offering Continental cuisine, elegant service, and of course high prices—almost as high as those in Cancún. Many of the restaurants have limited hours or close down in summer (off-season) and during the hurricane season (September–November). Generally, all restaurants maintain a casual dress code and do not accept reservations.

Highly recommended restaurants are indicated by a star ★.

Category	Cost*
Very Expensive	over $20
Expensive	$15–$20

Category	Cost*
Moderate	$8–$15
Inexpensive	under $8

*per person excluding drinks and service

Lodging Accommodations on the Caribbean coast run the gamut from campsites to simple palapas and bungalows to middle-range functional establishments to luxury hotels and condominiums. Many of these hotels include two or three meals in their prices. The fanciest accommodations are in Playa del Carmen, Akumal, and Puerto Aventuras, while the coastline (including the Tulum area) is sprinkled with small campgrounds and hotels on solitary beaches. Note that hotel rates drop as much as 25% in the low season (June–October).

In Chetumal, you will probably not find much to impress you in the way of accommodations. Hotels tend to be older, functional, and lacking in character. Accommodations reflect the town's origin as a pit stop for traders en route to or from Central America. Consider using Laguna Bacalar as your base for explorations in the area.

Highly recommended hotels are indicated by a star ★.

Category	Cost*
Very Expensive	over $90
Expensive	$60–$90
Moderate	$25–$60
Inexpensive	under $25

*All prices are for a standard double room in the high season (Nov.–June), excluding service and the 10% tax.

Akumal **Luna Chueca.** "The Broken Moon" is the official name of this
Dining tiny restaurant, but locals call it Katie's Place. Owner Katie Robinhawk has taken a one-bedroom condo at Half Moon Bay and turned it into a cult café, where locals and enterprising tourists congregate at the three indoor tables and tiled bar, or on the patio by the sea, and savor Katie's creative cuisine. Maya cooks prepare authentic tortillas, licuados, panuchos and flan, vegetarian chili rellenos, fried onion rings, thick French toast, and whatever else strikes Katie's fancy, especially at dinner. You'll need a car, a cab, or strong legs to reach Katie's, but it's worth it. *Go through the entranceway at Club Akumal Caribe, then turn left at the dirt road heading north to Half Moon Bay to the Hacienda de la Tortuga, tel. 987/22421 (condo office). No credit cards. Open Mon.–Sat. 7–10, 5:30–8. Moderate.*

Lodging **Haciendas de la Tortuga, Mirage, and Iguana.** Several condominium projects line the shores of Half Moon Bay north of Akumal, with various individuals handling rentals. These three small complexes on the beach have one-bedroom units with tiled kitchens and baths, with housekeeping service. The dive shops and restaurants at Club Akumal Caribe are within walking distance. *On the dirt road about 10 minutes north of Club Akumal Caribe. For reservations: Box 522, Cancún, Quintana Roo, 77500, tel. 987/41294 in Akumal, fax 988/73074 in Cancún.*

Facilities: restaurant, pool, kitchens. No credit cards. Expensive.

Villas de las Palmas. Expatriate Americans Daniel Mincey and Karen Jenkins handle reservations and assist guests at several condominiums and private homes along the beach just south of Club Aventuras. The area is peaceful, and the units are a reasonably priced alternative for those wanting privacy, comfort, and the sense of being in a home away from home. *For reservations: Box 124, Playa del Carmen, Quintana Roo, 77710, tel. and fax 987/41886. 8 houses and condo complexes. No credit cards. Expensive.*

Dining and Lodging **Club Aventuras Akumal.** An all-inclusive luxury hotel managed by the Spanish hotel group Oasis, this sprawling property started as the private preserve of millionaire Pablo Bush Romero, a friend of Jacques Cousteau. Today the beautiful beach—protected by an offshore reef—and the pier are used as the starting point for canoeing, snorkeling, diving, fishing, and windsurfing jaunts. The U-shaped building, with nautical decor, features handsome mahogany furniture and sunken blue-tile showers between Moorish arches (no doors!). All rooms have balconies (you can choose a sea view or a garden view) and air-conditioning or ceiling fans (same price). The condominium units are much larger and include living rooms and kitchenettes. The clientele consists primarily of Americans and Canadians on package deals, though non-group guests are also welcome. Guests staying in nearby condos can pay a daily or weekly fee to use the hotel's pools and other facilities. *For reservations: Adventure Tours, 111 Avenue Rd., 5th floor, Toronto M5R 3J8, tel. 416/967–1112 or, in Akumal, 987/22887. 44 rooms plus 49 condominium units and penthouses. Facilities: restaurant, indoor and outdoor bar, beach, 2 pools, game room, dive shop, tennis court, boutiques, travel agency, car rental. AE, MC, V. Very Expensive.*

Club Akumal Caribe & Villas Maya. Accommodations at this resort, situated on the edge of a cove overlooking a small harbor, range from rustic but comfortable bungalows with red tile roofs and garden views (Villas Maya) to beachfront rooms in a modern three-story hotel building. All have air-conditioning, ceiling fans, and refrigerators. Also available are the more secluded one-, two-, and three-bedroom condominiums called the Villas Flamingo, on Half Moon Bay and a half-mile from the beach. The bungalows and hotel rooms are cheerfully furnished in rattan and dark wood, with attractive tile floors; the high-domed condominium units, Mediterranean in architecture and room decor, have kitchens and balconies or terraces overlooking the pool and beach. The property began as a few thatched cottages built for CEDAM, the Mexican divers' organization, and it still emphasizes diving. Two on-property dive shops offer resort courses, PADI certification, and cenote or cave diving; snorkeling, windsurfing, kayaking, and deep-sea fishing are also available. The best of the three restaurants is Lol Ha: Breakfasts come with a basket of fresh sweet breads, and the grilled steak and seafood dinner entrées are bountiful. An optional meal plan includes breakfast and dinner. *Km 104, Carretera Cancún–Tulum, no phone. For reservations: Akutrame, Box 13326, El Paso, TX 79913, tel. 915/584–3552 or 800/351–1622. 40 bungalows, 21 rooms, 4 villas, 3 condos. Facilities: 3 restaurants (Moderate–Expensive), snack bar, ice cream* parlor, pizza parlor, bar, pool, beach, 2 dive shops, boutique, grocery. AE, DC, MC, V. Expensive.

Bacalar **Rancho Encantado.** On the shores of Laguna Bacalar, five
Lodging minutes north of Chetumal, the Rancho comprises six private
casitas (cottages), each with its own patio and hammocks,
kitchenette, sitting area, and bathroom. The casitas and public
areas feature hand-carved hardwood furnishings, woven Oaxacan rugs, and sculptures of Maya gods; lush green lawns border the water, where a gaggle of snow-white geese honk at
passersby. Both breakfast and dinner are included in the room
rate, and guests applaud the homemade breads and ice creams,
curries, gumbo, lasagna, and other exotic fare (no red meat is
served). You can swim and snorkel off the private dock leading
into the lagoon. When traveling by car on Route 307, watch for
the road sign on your left. *For reservations: Turquoise Reef
Group, Box 2664, Evergreen, CO 80439, tel. 303/674–9615 in CO
or 800/538–6802 outside CO, fax 303/674–8735. 6 units. Facilities:
restaurant, bar, lagoon excursions. No credit cards. Expensive.*

Boca Paila **Boca Paila Fishing Lodge.** This enclave of eight spacious
Lodging thatched cottages sits in the midst of the Sian Ka'an Biosphere
Reserve. Clean, bright, and cheerful accommodations include
the basics: bed, dresser, and nightstand on tile floors and within
white walls. Catering principally to anglers, the lodge provides
boats and guides for fly-fishing (bonefish, tarpon, snook, and
barracuda), as well as for billfishing off Cozumel; guests should
bring their own tackle. The staff also arranges six-day fishing
packages and day trips to the lagoons and flats at Ascensión
Bay, 72 kilometers (45 miles) south. Mayan specialties, such as
pollo pibil (chicken baked in banana leaves), are served at meal-
time. If you're flying in from Cozumel or Playa del Carmen,
arrange in advance for the lodge staff to pick you up; drivers
are available for day trips as well. *For reservations: Frontiers,
Box 959, Wexford, PA 15090, tel. 412/935–1577 or 800/245–1950.
8 cottages. Facilities: restaurant, fishing packages. Deposit required. No credit cards. Very Expensive.*

★ **Caphé-Ha.** Orginally built as a private home by an American
architect, this small guest house—located between a lagoon
and the ocean—is a perfect place to stay if you're interested in
bonefishing and birding. A private two-bedroom house, with a
kitchen, private bath, and living room, and a two-unit bungalow
(with shared baths) are your choices; though neither has fans
or electricity, all the windows have screens and catch the ocean
breeze. A caretaker/chef from Mérida cooks meals that are
served in the solar-powered community palapa; he will prepare
vegetarian meals upon request. Fishing tackle and snorkeling
gear are available from the property's small dock, but there's
an extra charge for bonefishing. The room rates include breakfast and dinner; advance reservations must be accompanied by
a 50% deposit, and a three-day or longer stay is required during
high season. Caphé-Ha is located 30 kilometers (19 miles) south
of Tulum, on the road to Sian Ka'an, 5 kilometers (3 miles) past
the bridge at Boca Paila and around the next rocky point. *For
reservations: tel. 99/213404 in Mérida or 212/219–2198 in NY. 1
villa, 1 bungalow. Facilities: fishing packages. No credit cards.
Very Expensive.*

Casa Blanca Lodge. Punta Pájaros is reputedly one of the best
places in the world for light-tackle saltwater fishing, to which
this new, remote fishing resort provides unique access. The

American-managed, all-inclusive lodge—just 100 feet from the ocean—is set on a rocky outcrop covered with palm trees. Bonefish swarm in the mangrove swamps, flats, and shallow waters. The lodge's seven large, modern guest rooms, painted white with turquoise trim, and with slatted windows and tile and mahogany bathrooms, provide a pleasant tropical respite at dusk. An open-air thatched bar and a large living and dining area welcome anglers with drinks, fresh fish dishes, fruit, and vegetables at the start and end of the day. The lodge offers weekly fishing packages and shorter itineraries during June–July and October–December. Rates include three meals, fishing, and a round-trip charter flight from Cancún to the Punta Pájaros airstrip. Those coming by land must make the three-hour drive to Punta Allen and then take a one-hour boat trip across the bay. *For reservations: Frontiers, Box 959, Wexford, PA 15090, tel. 412/935–1577 or 800/245–1950. 7 rooms. Facilities: restaurant/bar, open-air bar, fishing packages. Prepayment required. No credit cards. Very Expensive.*

★ **Sol Pez Maya.** An idyllic fishing resort smack in the middle of the Boca Paila peninsula and the Sian Ka'an Biosphere Reserve, this property consists of only seven cabañas and a small restaurant. The simply furnished bungalows, with small patios, are set back slightly from the expanse of white beach, palm trees, and sea pines. Table fans are provided for morning and evening use, but the generator shuts down in the daytime and after 11 PM, when you must rely on the screen door to let in the sea breeze and keep out the fierce mosquitoes. Manager Nestor Erazo can arrange boat trips for bonefishing, fly-fishing, deep-sea fishing, birding, or exploring the savannah and the mangrove swamps and even an obscure Mayan ruin, Chunyaxché. Turtles come to the beach to lay their eggs between May and July. Sol Pez Maya is well worth the price, since fabulous fresh meals, daily fishing, and transfers to and from Cancún or Playa del Carmen are included. Follow the dirt road south of the Tulum ruins for about 24 kilometers (15 miles); the hotel is another kilometer (⁶⁄₁₀ mile) beyond a small wooden bridge that cuts the peninsula in two. This road is very difficult to maneuver, and the trip takes about one hour. Call the reservations number for road conditions. *For reservations: Box 9, Cozumel, Quintana Roo 77600, tel. 987/20072 or 800/336–3542, fax 987/21599. 7 bungalows. Facilities: restaurant, beach, fishing boats. No credit cards. Very Expensive.*

Chemuyil
Dining and Lodging

Chemuyil. This gorgeous little cove and coconut grove surrounding a very quiet beach has its own campground and restaurant. Facilities include hammock rentals (for sleeping under palm trees) and tiny open-air palapas with mosquito netting and hammocks. At Marco Polo, the restaurant, you can sit at the bar or at a small table, or you can lounge on a hammock under the palapa as you sip a delicious freshly squeezed limonada. The seafood- and chicken-based cuisine is much the same as you'd find at any of a number of palapa eateries in the area. *Km 110, Carretera Cancún–Chetumal, no phone. 6 rooms. Facilities: restaurant (Moderate). Inexpensive.*

Chetumal
Dining

Casablanca. This informal, air-conditioned restaurant is one of the favorite local hangouts. Overall, the food—mostly Mexican dishes—is good and the wine list is better. *Av. Madero 293, tel. 983/22355. AE, MC, V. Moderate.*

Mandinga. The best place in town for the freshest seafood, Mandinga is best known for its octopus and conch seafood soup, a spicy blend of the daily catch. *Av. Belice 214, tel. 983/21824. No credit cards. Moderate.*

Sergio's. This popular pizza parlor is situated in a small, simply decorated frame house. Locals rave about the grilled steaks. *Av. Alvaro Obregón 182 at Av. 5 de Mayo, tel. 983/22355. AE, MC, V. Moderate.*

Lodging **Hotel Continental Caribe.** The modern architecture sets the tone for this downtown property, conveniently located across the street from the municipal market. Highlighting the atrium is a small fountain that gushes from the angular pool. Inside, rooms are carpeted and decorated in a yellow and orange color scheme that could use updating. The public areas are run-down and shabby, but the rooms are clean. The hotel's restaurant, La Cascada, features international fare and bargain breakfasts. *Av. Héroes 171, Box 1, 77000, tel. 983/21100. 64 rooms, 10 suites. Facilities: restaurant, bar, air-conditioning, disco, cafeteria, minibar, TV, travel agency. AE, MC, V. Moderate.*

Príncipe. The best three-star hotel in Chetumal is located between the bus station and downtown. The rooms are air-conditioned, clean, and modern, with satellite TV. There is also a restaurant-bar on the premises. *Av. Héroes 326, 77000, tel. 983/24799 or 983/25167. 52 rooms. Facilities: restaurant-bar, color TV, parking. AE, MC, V. Moderate.*

Cobá **Villa Arqueólogica Cobá.** This Club Med property, a three-
Dining and Lodging minute walk from the entrance to the Cobá ruins, overlooks
★ one of the region's vast lakes, where turtles swim to the hotel's dock for a breakfast of bread and rolls. Tastefully done in white stucco and red paint, with bougainvillea hanging from the walls and museum pieces throughout the property, the hotel has a clean, airy feel; corridors in the square, two-story building face a small pool and bar. Although the air-conditioned rooms are small, they feel cozy. A handsome library, housing books on the Maya and paperback novels, features a large VCR and a pool table. Dining choices near the isolated Cobá ruins are quite limited, so the restaurant here is an attractive option, though it should not be judged by the rather large, impersonal, and formal dining room. The food—although pricey—is very good. For regional fare, try the grouper, ceviche, shrimp, chicken píbil, or enchiladas. On the more international side are pâtés, salad nicoise, marinated artichokes, and a superb chocolate mousse. *For reservations: tel. 800/CLUB-MED. 40 rooms. Facilities: restaurant (Expensive), bar, pool, tennis court, gift shop. AE, MC, V. Moderate.*

El Bocadito. Though nowhere near as lavish as the Villa, El Bocadito is a friendly, satisfactory budget alternative and only a five-minute walk from the ruins. The simple, tiled rooms fill up quickly—if you're thinking of spending the night, stop here first before visiting the ruins. There is no hot water, and only fans to combat the heat, but the camaraderie of the clientele and staff make up for the discomforts. The restaurant is decent, clean, and popular with tour groups. *On the road to the ruins, APDO 56, Valladolid, Yucatán, Mexico 97780, no phone. 8 rooms. No credit cards. Inexpensive.*

Felipe Carrillo **El Faisán y El Venado.** Given the paucity of hotels in Felipe
Puerto Carrillo Puerto, this one is your best bet. It's bare-bones, but
Dining and Lodging you can choose between air-conditioned rooms or rooms with

ceiling fans. The rooms also come with color or black-and-white TV and refrigerators. The pleasant restaurant does brisk business with locals at lunchtime because it is so centrally located. Yucatecan specialties such as poc chuc, *bistec a la yucateca* (Yucatecan-style steak), and pollo píbil are served in a simple but rustically decorated setting. *Av. Juárez 781, 77200, tel. 983/40043. 21 rooms. Facilities: restaurant. No credit cards. Inexpensive.*

Playa del Carmen
Dining

Chicago Connection Sports Bar & Grill. As the name implies, this joint caters to the I-can't-leave-home-for-long-without-a-hamburger crowd. Replete with nautical decor, it makes a good show of re-creating an American-style eatery. This is a fun, informal place that especially hops when live music is played. *Av. 5a at Calle 6, tel. 987/21230, ext. 166. AE, MC, V. Expensive.*

Albatros. This beachfront palapa restaurant-bar is owned by Americans, and it rates high with compatriots who come to hang out as well as to sample the food. Suggestions for lunch include fish or sandwiches; breakfasts are also very good. *6 blocks north of ferry pier, tel. 987/30001. MC, V. Moderate.*

★ **Limones.** Probably the most romantic place in town, this restaurant offers dining by candlelight, either alfresco in a courtyard or under the shelter of a palapa indoors. Candles on the tables, wine bottles hanging from the ceiling, and guitar music make this place all the more romantic. House favorites include copious entrées such as fettuccine, lasagna, and lemon-sautéed beef scaloppini. Appetizers might be home-baked pizza bread or salads. The daily dinner special is the best bargain in town. *Av. 10a at Calle 2, 3 blocks north of the pier, no phone. AE, V. Moderate.*

★ **Máscaras.** The wood-burning brick oven here produces exceptionally good thin-crusted pizzas and homemade pastas and breads. Fresh-squeezed, sweetened lime juice, margaritas, wine, and beer help wash down the rich Italian fare. Be sure to try to calamari in garlic and oil, and mashed potatoes with sautéed mushrooms. Masks from throughout the world cover the walls; jazz plays in the background. The café is very popular with locals and the workers from the hotels, and is a central gathering spot with a view of the goings-on at the zócalo. *Av. Juárez (on the plaza), tel. 987/21300. MC, V. Moderate.*

Rick's Caribbean Dreams Café. Located upstairs at the Blue Parrot Inn, this trendy place has an excellent view. Beach lovers thrive on the café's studiously hip, quasi-Caribbean ambience, and the food is decent, if a bit overpriced. Japanese tacos (a seafood dish with flour tortillas), lobster, shrimp, chicken kebabs, burgers, and vegetarian dishes are on the menu, and so is breakfast. Come late in the day to this simply decorated, contemporary Mexican-style restaurant with white walls and swinging seats at the bar for a sandwich and coffee. *7 blocks north of the pier, no phone. MC, V. Moderate.*

Doña Juanita. Juanita's daughter has now taken over the management of this simple, rustic restaurant on the outskirts of town. Fish dishes receive rave reviews for freshness, generous portions, and price. Try the fillet of red snapper. *Av. Juárez at Rte. 307, no phone. No credit cards. Inexpensive.*

El Tacolote. Opened in 1992, this fanciful, colorful restaurant specializes in traditional Mexican dishes and several varieties of tacos–try the beef and melted cheese. You can eat cheaply or splurge on a multicourse feast while watching the action on the plaza from an outdoor table. *Av. Juárez on the plaza, no phone. MC, V. Inexpensive.*

Tacos al Pastor. Fans of the wickedly delicious little pork tacos frequent this stand opposite the Posada Sian Ka'an. *Av. 5a at Calle 2, no phone. No credit cards. Inexpensive.*

Lodging **Albatros.** Owned and managed by Americans, the Albatros is
★ a set of 18 homey thatched cabanas situated on the beach and complete with hammocks hanging on the patios. The one-, two-, and three-bedroom cabanas are gaily painted in pastel colors and have hot water and ceiling fans. Purified water is available from large demijohns, and extra care is taken to keep the premises free of insects. *6 blocks north of ferry pier; Box 31, Playa del Carmen, Quintana Roo, 77710, tel. 987/30001 or 800/527–0022. 18 cabanas. Facilities: restaurant, bar. MC, V. Moderate.*

Blue Parrot Inn. This very cozy property is situated at the extreme northern end of the beach. Room options vary from a one-story structure on the sand to private bungalows, some of which contain kitchenettes, mosquito nets, and purified water. Choose among two-story bungalows, palapas, or beachfront villas, all of which are decorated with rustic Mexican furnishings such as hammocks, bentwood, and stucco. *7 blocks north of pier; for reservations: Box 64, Playa del Carmen, Quintana Roo, 77710, tel. 904/775–6660, fax 98/844564 (Cancún). 9 palapas, 4 beachfront rooms, 3 bungalows, 1 beachfront villa. Facilities: restaurant, water-sports equipment. MC, V. Moderate.*

Royale. Owned by the American operators of the Albatros, the Royale opened in 1991 directly on the beach. Offering a clean, comfortable alternative to its more tired and rundown neighbors, the two-story hotel has 23 bright rooms with hot-water showers, ceiling fans, and hammocks hanging on the balconies. *7 blocks north of ferry pier; for reservations: Box 31, Playa del Carmen, Quintana Roo, 77710, tel. 987/30001 or 800/527–0022. 23 rooms. No facilities. MC, V. Moderate.*

Alejari. The nicest hotel on Playa's north beach is this new two-story complex set amid lush gardens. Some rooms have kitchenettes and fans, others provide air-conditioning. A small market and a long-distance phone booth sit on the premises. *Calle 6N; for reservations: Box 166, Playa del Carmen, Quintana Roo, 77710, tel. 987/22754, fax 987/20155. 15 rooms. Facilities: store, kitchenettes. MC, V. Inexpensive.*

Costa del Mar. Large, white, and a bit antiseptic, this hotel consists of a newly built (in 1990) two-story motel block, an older motel-like unit, and four bungalows. The rooms in all facilities are clean and functional and done in sandy white with turquoise trim from the tile floors to the bedspreads and stucco walls. All the rooms but those in the bungalows have air-conditioning. *Calle Primera Norte, between 10 and 12, tel. and fax 987/20231. 31 rooms, 4 bungalows. Facilities: restaurant, small pool. AE, MC, V. Inexpensive.*

Posada Sian Ka'an. Located in town, three blocks north of the pier, the Posada features clean rooms with pine furnishings, plus kitchenettes, ceiling fans, and hot water, in a pleasant garden setting where you can hang up your own hammock by a natural cenote. *For reservations: Box 135, Quintana Roo, 77710, tel. in Mérida, 992/97422. 11 rooms. No facilities. No credit cards. Inexpensive.*

Dining and **Shangri-La Caribe.** Similar to Las Palapas next door, Shangri-
Lodging La's attractive whitewashed bungalows (some duplexes, some

suites), capped with palapa roofs, have hammocks out front and ceiling fans inside; some of the larger cabanas also feature sitting areas. Music blares from the palapa-covered bar, where the French, German, and American clientele gather around the pool table. You can order American or Mexican food à la carte at the spacious restaurant. *On a dirt road off Rte. 307, midway between Punta Bete and Playa del Carmen. For reservations: Turquoise Reef Group, Box 2664, Evergreen, CO 80439, tel. 303/674–9615 in CO or 800/538–6802 outside CO, fax 303/674–8735. 30 bungalows, 6 suites. Facilities: restaurant, bar, coffee shop, beach, pool, dive shop, water sports, gift shop, car rental. All reservations (minimum 3 nights) must be prepaid. No credit cards. Closed around Sept. 1–Nov. 1. Very Expensive.*

Continental Plaza Playacar. Playa del Carmen became a first-class tourism destination when the Playacar hotel opened in October 1991. The centerpiece of an 880-acre master-planned resort, Playacar faces the sea on the south side of the ferry pier. A pastel, blush-colored palace, it possesses all the amenities of its competitors at the larger resort towns. The tropical-style rooms have ocean views and balconies or patios, marble baths, blonde wood furnishings, satellite TV, and in-room safes. The beach is one of the nicest in Playa del Carmen, and far less crowded than those to the north. Mexican and international dishes are served at a restaurant in the main building and a palapa by the pool; the breakfast buffet is excellent. A shopping/dining/banking complex links the hotel with downtown Playa del Carmen via a pleasant pedestrian mall. A full-scale scuba and water-sports facility offers diving, snorkeling, sailing, and waterskiing. The resort development will eventually include an 18-hole golf course and private homes. *Fraccionamiento Playacar, tel. 987/21583 or 800/882–6684. 188 rooms, 16 suites. Facilities: 2 restaurants, bar, pool, dive shop, boutique, travel agency. AE, MC, V. Expensive.*

Las Molcas. This large, pretty hotel, situated in downtown Playa a half-block from the ferry pier and one block south of the plaza, has a colonial-style lobby and hallways with red tile floors. Pleasant, attractive rooms face the pool, the sea, or the street. The modern, unremarkable hotel dining room, with some outdoor tables overlooking the plaza, is a safe bet for standard international fare. *Box 79, Quintana Roo, 77710, tel. 987/21100 or 987/21200, ext. 109–111, 99/256990 in Mérida, 305/534–3716 for reservations. 35 air-conditioned rooms. Facilities: restaurant, bar, pool, gift shop. AE, MC, V. Expensive.*

Diamond Resort. Opened in 1992 as part of the Playacar development, Diamond is an all-inclusive resort that sprawls down a sloping hill to the sea. The 296 rooms are spread out in small thatch-roofed villas along winding paths; the dining room, bar, lobby, and entertainment areas are housed in a gigantic multipeaked, two-story palapa. Unlike many all-inclusives, Diamond's design allows peace and privacy. One pool is used for games and activities, while another is reserved for quiet lounging. Guests get a bit rowdy at the karaoke bar and outdoor stage, but the noise does not reach the guest rooms. Electric carts are available for getting around the grounds. Buffet-style meals are plentiful and imaginatively prepared. Playa del Carmen is a 20-minute walk or $5 cab ride north. *In the Playacar development, tel. 987/30340 or 800/858–2258, fax 987/30345. 296 rooms. Facilities: dining room, bar, 2 pools, dive shop, 4 tennis courts, gift shop, car rental, sports equipment. Expensive.*

★ **Las Palapas.** Las Palapas is an ideal get-away-from-it-all destination resort where many guests stay for 10 days or more. White cabanas with blue trim lend a rustic feel, and duplexes feature balconies or porches, palapas, and hammocks. The thatch roofs and hexagonal shape of the buildings enhances the ocean breezes, making air-conditioning unnecessary. The beach and pool are complemented by a shuffleboard area, clubhouse, beach bar, palapa bar, and attractive palapa restaurant, where Chef Roberto Kappes prepares spectacular Mexican buffets and German specialties as well as hamburgers, tacos, and other snacks. German tour groups keep the hotel's occupancy up to 80 percent year-round; make reservations early. Room rates include breakfast and dinner. *Km 292 on Rte. 307 (Box 116), Playa del Carmen, Quintana Roo, 77710, tel. 987/22977, fax 5/379–8041 in Mexico City. 50 cabanas. Facilities: restaurant, 2 bars, pool, beach, in-room safes. 3-night minimum stay. AE, MC, V. Expensive.*

Puerto Aventuras
Dining

Carlos 'n Charlie's. Having a branch of this popular restaurant chain on the grounds is a sign of true resort status. Carlos Anderson's restaurants are known for being wacky, wild, and rowdy and for serving ample portions of well-prepared barbecued ribs and chicken, enchiladas, carne asada, and other Mexican dishes, and powerful tequila drinks. The food isn't up to par here yet. *In the commercial center, no phone. MC, V. Moderate.*

Papaya Republic. The owners of this small gourmet restaurant refused to sell out to the developers of Puerto Aventuras, and continue doing business at the end of a dirt road to the south of the resort. Fresh ceviche, gazpacho, and local fish in almond sauce are among the offerings, which change with the availability of ingredients. *Off the main road into Puerto Aventuras, down a dirt road to the right marked by a sign, no phone. No credit cards. Moderate.*

Lodging

Club de Playa. A small 30-room hotel with stunning views of the Caribbean. The swimming pool seems to flow right into the sea, and guests have use of a health spa. The spacious rooms are decorated in pinks and greens, with first-class amenities. The Swiss-trained chef prepares international cuisine at the small dining room. *Near the marina, tel. 987/35100 or 800/44OASIS, fax 404/240–4513 in the U.S. 30 rooms. Facilities: restaurant, pool, marina, spa, water sports. AE, MC, V. Very Expensive.*

Oasis. A larger hotel at the other end of the marina (opened in 1992), the Oasis bustles with activity as European tour groups on great package deals fill the hotel. The rooms include kitchenettes with microwaves; some have whirlpool baths. The resort's excellent dive shop is on the premises, along with a great gift shop featuring folk art from throughout Mexico. A shuttle bus runs to both hotels, the golf course, commercial center, and marina. *On the beach at the north end of the complex, tel. 987/35051 or 800/44OASIS, fax 404/240–4513 in the U.S. 70 rooms. Facilities: 2 pools, 3 restaurants, dive shop, gift shop, tour desk. AE, MC, V. Very Expensive.*

Puerto Morelos
Dining

Los Pelícanos y las Palmeras. If you're looking for good fresh fish—fried, grilled, or steamed—stop by these two small thatched huts on the beach. *Puerto Morelos, no phone. No credit cards. Inexpensive.*

Lodging **Cabañas Playa Ojo de Agua.** This dive-oriented hotel is located on a lovely beach just north of town. The white guest rooms have kitchenettes, ceiling fans, and ocean views. A freshwater pool and a good restaurant that serves Yucatecan and American dishes are among the features here. *One block north of town. For reservations: Calle 12, No. 96, between 21 and 23, in Mérida, Yucatán, 97050, tel. 99/250292, fax 99/283405. 12 rooms. Facilities: restaurant, bar, pool, dive shop. No credit cards. Closed Sept. and Oct. Moderate.*

Los Arrecifes and Casa Miguel. Located on an isolated (and sometimes windy) beach, Los Arrecifes is an older hotel that's been remodeled and redecorated by Vicki Sharp, who is also creating a bed-and-breakfast inn called Casa Miguel across the street from the beach. Arrecifes has eight one-bedroom apartments with kitchenettes, large living rooms and balconies, in an ideal setting. Casa Miguel has four private bedrooms with private baths and a central kitchen and dining area; the house is available for use by families and groups or individuals. Sharp also has information on condo and house rentals in Puerto Morelos. *Arrecifes is 8 blocks north of town on the street closest to the beach; Casa Miguel is 6 blocks north of town on the same street. For reservations: Box 986, Cancún, Quintana Roo, 77500, tel. 98/871011, fax 98/832244. Facilities: kitchens. No credit cards. Moderate.*

Dining and **Caribbean Reef Club at Villa Marina.** This gorgeous white
Lodging condo complex is one of the nicest hideaways along the coast, especially because of its location on an isolated beach south of town. The colonial-style suites have marble floors, air-conditioning, ceiling fans, blue-tiled kitchenettes, floral pastel linens, and arched windows. Sliding glass doors lead to balconies outside, where you can slip in an afternoon nap on your own private hammock. The adjacent restaurant is easily the most picturesque in town, with a balcony overlooking the sea, hand-painted tile tables, and candlelight at night. The menu has a Texan flair, offering chicken-fried steak, BBQ ribs, fajitas, and key lime pie. *South of the ferry dock. For reservations: Box 1526, Cancún, Quintana Roo, 77500, tel. 98/832636, fax 98/832244 or 800/3–CANCUN. 21 suites. Facilities: restaurant, bar, pool water sports. AE, MC, V. Expensive.*

Posada Amor. This family-run hotel near the pier, one of Puerto Morelo's first hotels, has been operating for more than 15 years. The humble rooms, located in a two-story building behind the restaurant, have screened windows with dark blue drapes (helpful for late sleepers) and cement slab beds. Only 10 rooms have private baths. The restaurant, a neighborhood gathering spot, serves great home-style Mexican meals, but no alcohol. *Near ferry pier, no phone. 20 rooms. Facilities: restaurant. No credit cards. Inexpensive.*

Punta Bete **Posada del Capitán Lafitte.** Set on an invitingly long stretch of
Dining and Lodging beach just 10 kilometers (6 miles) north of Playa del Carmen
★ at Punta Bete, this lodging is known for its genuinely chummy, unpretentious atmosphere. This is no luxury resort, but a simple cluster of two-unit cabanas, each with its own private bath and ceiling fan. Breakfast, dinner, tax, and tips are included in the room rate, so you rarely need to carry money. In the evening the European and American clientele congregates around a small but pretty pool/bar decorated with red tiles and coral-pink stucco. A small hotel was under construction at press time. *On a dirt road (follow the signs), 2 8/10 km (1 2/5 mi) off Rte. 307.*

For reservations: Turquoise Reef Group, Box 2664, Evergreen, CO 80439, tel. 303/674–9615 in CO or 800/538–6802 outside CO, fax 303/674–8735. 39 rooms, 2-bedroom duplex cabin. Facilities: restaurant (Moderate), bar, beach, pool, dive shop, car rental. All reservations (minimum 3 nights) must be prepaid. No credit cards. Closed around Sept. 1–Nov. 1. Expensive.

Kai Luum Camptel. Owned and managed by the locally known Bilgore family, this "luxury" campground attracts a predominantly American clientele. Tents come with wooden platform floors and gas lanterns and are covered with palapas; hammocks hang from the support poles; rest rooms are within an easy walk from campsites. There is no electricity, so guests spend the evening lounging in the beach chairs in the bar. Diners sit at communal picnic tables and are served food from a fixed—but surprisingly eclectic—menu that features cuisine prepared by Mayan chefs. Breakfast and dinner are served, and tax and tip are included in the rate. The bar—little more than a palapa on the beach—runs on the honor system, and the gift shop—housed in a palapa and filled with exquisite handicrafts from throughout Mexico and Guatemala—has no locks or doors. To afford guests an even richer experience, Kai Luum shares some facilities with the Posada del Capitán Lafitte (a three-minute walk down the beach), as well as some group activities, including snorkeling trips, scuba certification and dives, fishing, and birding. *On a dirt road, 2⁸/10 km (1²/5 mi) off Rte. 307 (look for the Posada del Capitán Lafitte sign on the left). For reservations: Turquoise Reef Group, Box 2664, Evergreen, CO 80439, tel. 303/674–9615 in CO or 800/538–6802 outside CO, fax 303/674–8735. 40 tents. Facilities: restaurant, bar, beach, crafts shop, dive shop, hot tub. All reservations (minimum 3 nights) must be prepaid. No credit cards. Closed around Sept. 1–Nov. 1. Moderate.*

Tulum Dining ★ **Casa Cenote.** Don't miss this outstanding restaurant beside a large cenote—this one's a mini-pool of fresh and salt water full of tropical fish. In fact, take a swim in the cenote first. With luck you may spot one of the three resident manatees, bashful critters who would prefer to be left in peace. Follow up with a spot of snorkeling in the sea, then rest in the shade under the restaurant's uniquely designed palapa roof—note the absence of center support. The beef, chicken, and cheese are imported from the United States, and the burgers, chicken fajitas, and nachos are superb. On Sunday afternoon the expats living along the coast gather at Casa Cenote for a lavish barbecue featuring ribs, chicken, beef brisket, or lobster kebabs. The restaurant operates without electricity or a generator (perishables are packed in ice coolers) and closes at dark. *On a dirt road off Rte. 307, between Xel-Há and Tulum, 987/41–36–8. No reservations. No credit cards. Moderate.*

Lodging **Cabañas Tulum.** This property, nicely situated in a coconut grove on a beach, is 7 kilometers (4 miles) south of the Tulum ruins on the dirt road leading to Boca Paila. Eighteen palapa bungalows with private bathrooms (but without fans), and an indoor-outdoor restaurant, bar, and game room make a good package. *Tulum, 77780, no phone. 18 cabañas. Facilities: restaurant, bar, game room. No credit cards. Inexpensive.*

Dining and Lodging ★ **Osho Oasis.** On the site of the long-standing Cabañas Chac Mool along the dirt road south of the ruins now emerges a holistic, New-Age–style resort. Only four of the 22 cabanas have private baths, but all have hammock-like mattresses suspended from the ceiling, rock floors, and mosquito nets (the windows have no screens). Communal showers are equipped with hot water, and a generator provides electricity at night. The restaurant (Expensive) serves superb vegetarian meals, plus fish and lobster, and is worth visiting even if you aren't staying here. It's best to write or fax ahead for reservations. *For reservations: Box 99, Tulum, Quintana Roo, 77780, tel. 987/42772, fax 987/30230, reservations in the U.S. 415/381–9861 (Sun.–Thurs.5–7 PM).* No credit cards. Moderate.

Acuario. This hotel and restaurant opened in 1990 and was still undergoing additions and changes at press time. Situated at the turnoff for the Tulum ruins, the hotel has large, clean rooms with satellite TV, screen windows, ceiling fans, and hot water; the pool may be filled by the time you get there. The Acuario restaurant (Moderate) is well worth a visit because the owner takes pride in the preparation and quality of the food. Although the diner-like setting is unimpressive, Acuario offers a menu that includes above-average seafood, soup, tacos, nachos, guacamole, salads, and a really good coconut ice cream. Breakfast—beginning at 6:30 AM—is excellent. The management is accommodating and friendly, and the hotel is a good choice for those traveling the coast by bus. *Crucero de las Ruinas de Tulum, Km 127 Carretera Cancún–Chetumal, 77780, no phone. 11 rooms. Facilities: restaurant, bar, pool, parking, satellite TV, market, and gift shop. No credit cards. Inexpensive.*

Xcalak Lodging ★ **Costa de Cocos.** For the ultimate in privacy and scenery you can't beat the southern tip of the Xcalak peninsula, where divers and explorers congregate for trips to the famed Chinchorro Banks. Costa de Cocos is one of the precious few resorts in this area, and is easily the most hospitable and comfortable. Eight cleverly crafted cabanas have exquisite handcrafted mahogany furnishings, screened windows, tiled baths, and bookshelves stocked with an eclectic selection of paperbacks. The proprietors, Dave and Maria Randall, are immensely knowledgeable about the peninsula and the reef offshore. Small pangas (launches) transport divers to the nearby reefs, and day trips by boat to Belize can be arranged. The on-site dive shop has a compressor for air, and rents tanks, weights, and other equipment. While guests must rely on the two or three restaurants in town for full meals, coffee, homemade muffins, and fresh fruit are served under the resort's central palapa for breakfast, and cold drinks are available throughout the day. It's best to have reservations in advance; if you plan to drop by unannounced, be sure to start out for Xcalak early in the day so you can make it back to the main road before dark if the cabanas are full. *Xcalak Peninsula, 56 kilometers (35 miles) south of Majahual. For reservations: Box 316, Bloomingdale, IL 60108, tel. 800/443–1123, fax 983/21676. 8 cabanas. Facilities: dive shop, airstrip. No credit cards. Moderate.*

Xcaret Dining **Restaurant Xcaret.** This small palapa restaurant, with walls lined with photos from diving expeditions, serves conch ceviche, lobster, poc chuc, and french fries. *Off Rte. 307, Xcaret, no phone. No credit cards. Inexpensive.*

Nightlife

There isn't much in the way of nightlife along the coast, unless you happen upon some entertainment in a luxury hotel bar. If you're staying in Akumal, try **Discoteca Akumal** at the Hotel Akumal Cancún; if you're in Playa del Carmen, try **Ziggy's** or **Bambu.** At Puerto Aventuras **Carlos 'n Charlie's** is the most happening place at night.

7 Campeche

Updated by
Maribeth Mellin

Most of the State of Campeche is flat—never higher than 1,000 feet above sea level—but more than 60% of its territory is covered by jungle, where the precious mahogany and cedar abound. The Gulf Stream keeps temperatures at about 26°C (78 °F) year-round; the humid, tropical climate is eased by evening breezes. Campeche's economy is based on agriculture, fishing, logging, salt, tourism, and—more recently—hydrocarbons, of which it is the largest producer in Mexico. But most of the oil industry is concentrated at the southern end of the state, near Ciudad del Carmen.

The city of Campeche has a run-down but lovely feel to it: No self-conscious, ultramodern tourist glitz here, just an isolated, friendly city (population 250,000) content to rest on its staid old laurels. That good-humored, lackadaisical attitude is enshrined in the Spanish adjective *campechano*, meaning easygoing, hearty, genial, cheerful. The city gets only about 20,000 tourists a year, its strongest attraction being its sense of history. You can easily imagine pirates attacking the formidable stone walls that surround the downtown, and several Mayan ruins and undisturbed Mayan towns are within driving distance. The city's coastline is cluttered with commercial fishing operations, and there are a few popular public beaches. It is possible to see much of Campeche City in a day or two, but you will probably want to stay longer to absorb the traditional lifestyle, whiling away the hours at a café near the plaza.

The city of Campeche's location on the gulf has played a pivotal role in its history. Ah-Kin-Pech (Mayan for "serpent chigger")—from which the Spanish name of Campeche is derived—was the capital of an Indian chieftainship long before the Spaniards arrived in 1517. Earlier explorers had visited the area, but it was not until 1540 that the conquerors—led by Francisco de Montejo and, later, his son—established a real foothold at Campeche (originally called Salamanca), using it as a base for their conquest of the peninsula.

Because Campeche City was the only port and shipyard on the gulf, the Spanish ships, with their rich cargoes of plunder from the Mayan, Aztec, and other indigenous civilizations, dropped anchor here en route from Veracruz to Cuba, New Orleans, and Spain. News of this wealth spread, and soon the shores were infested with pirates. From the mid-1500s to the early 1700s, such notorious corsairs as Diego the Mulatto, Lorencillo, Peg Leg, Henry Morgan, and Barbillas swooped down repeatedly from their base on Tris—or Isla de Términos, as Isla del Carmen was then known—pillaging and burning the city and massacring its people.

Finally, after appealing for years to the Spanish crown, the citizens of Campeche received funds that enabled them to build a protective wall (with four gates and eight bastions). For some time thereafter, the city thrived on its exports, especially *palo de tinte*—a dyewood used by the nascent European textile industry—but also hardwoods, chicle, salt, and henequen. However, when the port of Sisal on the northern Yucatán coast opened in 1811, Campeche's monopoly of the gulf traffic ended, and its economy fell into decline.

The shape of modern-day Campeche is still defined by history. Remnants of the wall and other military structures divide it into two main districts, intramural (the old city) and extramural (the new). Because the city was long preoccupied with defense, colonial architecture is less developed here than elsewhere in Mexico. Churches are more somber; streets (still paved with cobblestones) are narrow because of the confines of the walls; houses are more practical than aesthetic in their design. Although the face of the city has altered over the centuries, as landfill was added and walls and bastions demolished to make room for expansion, it still retains a tenor of antiquity.

The state as a whole has a population of only about 620,000, most of it scattered through villages and small towns. Mayan traditions still reign in the countryside, which is dotted with windmills and fields of tobacco, sugarcane, rice, indigo, maize, and cocoa. Wildlife flourishes here, too: Jaguars, tapirs, and armadillos roam free, while the sea provides fishing boats with shrimp, barracuda, swordfish, and other catch. Thousands of Guatemalan refugees now make their home in Campeche, where they have been settled into two camps, one of which is involved in excavating the Mayan archaeological site of Edzná. Smaller, more obscure Mayan ruins exist throughout the state.

Essential Information

Important Addresses and Numbers

Tourist Information The **main tourist office** is located at Plaza Moch Cohuo (Av. Ruíz Cortines, tel. 981/66068 or 981/66767), near the Baluarte San Carlos, and is open weekdays 9–3 and 4–9; volunteers sometimes staff the office on Saturday morning. There are also **information modules** at the bus station (Av. Gobernadores 289 at Calle 45, tel. 981/60663 or 981/60419) and the airport (same phone). Modules are open Monday–Saturday 8–noon and 4–8.

Emergencies **Red Cross** (Av. Resurgimiento s/n, tel. 981/60666 or 981/65202).

Police (Calle 12 between Calles 57 and 59, tel. 981/62111, 981/62329, or, in town, 06).

Medical Clinics **Hospital General** (Av. Central at Circuito Baluartes, tel. 981/60920 or 981/64233) has a 24-hour emergency room.

Social Security Clinic (Av. Central at Circuito Baluartes, tel. 981/61855 or 981/65202) is open 24 hours for emergencies.

Late-night Pharmacies **Farmacia Ah-Kin-Pech** (Calle Pedro Sainz de Baranda 100, Centro Comercial Ah-Kin-Pech Local 113, tel. 981/68602) is open 24 hours and delivers to hotels.

Banks Campeche banks are open weekdays 9–1:30, but hours for changing traveler's checks are 10–1. Those where you can exchange money include **Banamex** (Calle 53 No. 15 at Calle 10, tel. 981/60730) and **Bancomer** (Av. 16 de Septiembre 120, tel. 981/66622).

Telephones There are two public booths for making long-distance calls: one at Avenida Gobernadores s/n (open 8 AM–10 PM) and one at the corner of Calle 12 at Calle 59 (open 9 AM–10 PM).

Mail The **post office** (Av. 16 de Septiembre, between Calles 53 and 55; tel. 981/64390) is open Monday–Friday 9–6.

Travel Agencies and Tour Operators The major Campeche-based operators are **American Express/VIPs** (Prolongación Calle 59, Edificio Belmar, Depto. 5, tel. 981/11010 or 981/68333) and **Agencia de Viajes Campeche** (Calle 10 No. 339, tel. 981/65233 or 981/62844).

Arriving and Departing by Plane, Car, Train, and Bus

By Plane **Aeromexico** (tel. 981/66656 in Campeche or 800/237–6639) has one flight daily from Mexico City.

By Car Campeche can be reached from Mérida in about 1½ hours along the 160-kilometer (99-mile) *via corta* (short way, Rte. 180). The alternative route, the 250-kilometer (155-mile) *via larga* (long way, Rte. 261), takes at least three hours but crosses the major Mayan ruins of Uxmal, Kabah, and Sayil. From Chetumal, take Rte. 186 west to Francisco Escárcega, where you pick up Rte. 261 north; the drive takes about seven hours. Villahermosa is about six hours away driving inland via the town of Francisco Escárcega, but longer if you hug the gulf and cross the bridge at Ciudad del Carmen.

By Train The **Mexican National Railroad** (Av. Héroes del Nacozari, s/n, tel. 981/62009 or 981/61433) has routes to Campeche from Mérida and Mexico City, but the lines are not among those that have been recently upgraded. It may be difficult to book a sleeper on the Mexico City line (the trip is 24 hours long), so this journey is recommended only for the most stoic traveler. Two trains depart daily from Campeche, at 8 AM and 11 PM, for the 10-hour trip to Palenque.

By Bus There is generally a big difference between first- and second-class bus service throughout Mexico. The former offers fewer stops and more comfortable coaches; the price difference is negligible. **ADO** (Av. Gobernadores 289 at Calle 45, along Rte. 261 to Mérida, tel. 981/60002), a first-class bus line, runs service to Campeche from Coatzacoalcos, Ciudad del Carmen, and Mérida every half hour, and from Mexico City, Puebla, Tampico, Veracruz, and Villahermosa regularly, but less frequently. There is second-class service on **Autobuses del Sur** (tel. 981/63445) from Chetumal, Ciudad del Carmen, Escárcega, Mérida, Palenque, Tuxtla Gutiérrez, Villahermosa, and intermediate points throughout the Yucatán Peninsula.

Getting Around

By Bus The municipal bus system covers the entire city, but you can easily visit the major sights on foot. Public buses run along Avenida Ruíz Cortines and cost under $1.

By Car Rental agencies include **Hertz** (Hotel Baluartes, Av. Ruíz Cortines s/n, tel. 981/63911 or 981/68848) and **AutoRent** (Ramada Inn, Calle 57 No. 1, tel. 981/62714 or 981/62233).

By Taxi Taxis can be hailed on the street, or—more reliably—commissioned from the **taxi stand** (Calle 8 between Calles 55 and 53, tel. 981/62366 or 981/65230) or at stands by the bus stations and market.

Guided Tours

There are no organized tours of Campeche. Ask at the tourist office for a guide, who will set his or her price. You should be able to take a three-hour walking tour for about $10.

Exploring

Because it has been walled since 1686, most of historic Campeche is neatly contained in an area measuring just five blocks by nine blocks. Today, for the most part, streets running north–south are even-numbered, and those running east–west are odd-numbered. The city is easily navigable (on foot, at least); the historical monuments and evocative name plaques above street numbers serve as handy guideposts.

On eight corners in the old city, or Viejo Campeche, stand *baluartes,* or bastions, in various stages of disrepair or reconstruction. These were once connected by a 3-kilometer (2-mile) wall in a hexagonal fortification that protected the city against the pirates who kept ransacking it. When the wall and bastions were completed (in 1717), the pirates were driven away for good. Only short stretches of the wall are extant. Two stone archways—one facing the sea, the other the land—are all that remain of the four gates that provided the only means of access to Campeche. There are also four outlying forts and 10 churches.

Campeche was one of few walled cities in North or Central America and was built along the traditional lines of defensive Spanish settlements, such as Santo Domingo (in the Dominican Republic), Cartagena (in Colombia), and Portobelo (in Panama). The walls also served as a class demarcation. Within them lived the ruling elite. Outside were the barrios of the Indians who aided the conquistadores, and whose descendants continued to serve the upper class. The mulattoes brought as slaves from Cuba also lived outside.

Campeche City

Numbers in the margin correspond to points of interest on the Campeche City map.

Our Campeche itinerary highlights attractions in Campeche City then takes you into the countryside. While it may sound dauntingly ambitious to accomplish the city tour in one day, many of the sights described here can be seen in just a few minutes; the more leisure-minded visitor, however, should schedule two days. Traveling throughout the State of Campeche could take from two to four days, depending on how much time you devote to some of the towns that are farther off the beaten path.

1 The **Centra de Información de Turistica** (between Av. 16 de Septiembre and Av. Ruíz Cortines, tel. 981/66068 or 981/66767) is housed in a modern red and white building on the Plaza Moch Cohuo (after the *cacique,* or chief, responsible for the Spaniards' first defeat in Mexico, which took place in 1517 in nearby Champotón). It is situated on a piece of landfill along the waterfront boulevard. Here you can pick up maps of the city and its environs.

2 Across the way, what appears to be a flying saucer is actually the **Congreso del Estado,** the State Congress building, where government activities take place. Across Calle 8, notice the rather handsome neoclassical Municipal Palace, built in 1892.

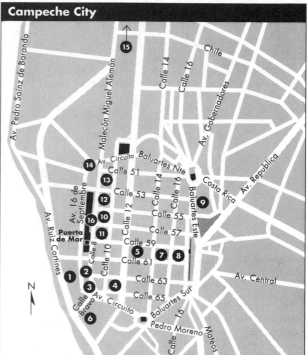

Campeche City

Continue southeast on Avenida 16 de Septiembre; on your left,
where the avenue curves around and becomes Circuito
Baluartes, you'll arrive at the first bastion, the **Baluarte San
Carlos.** Because this one contains only scale models of the original defense system, you may prefer to save your energy for
some of the more elaborate installations. The dungeon, however, is interesting and can be visited. The Sala de las Fortifi-
caciones (Chamber Fortifications) contains the Museo de la
Ciudad, or City Museum, with photographs of the city as it
developed. *Small admission fee. Open Tues.–Sat. 8–8, Sun. 8–1.*

One block east, occupying the full city block between Calles 10
and 12 and Calles 63 and 65, stands the **Ex-Templo de San José.**
The Jesuits built this fine Baroque church in 1756, and today
its facade stands as an exception to the rather plodding architectural style of most of the city's churches. Its immense portal
is completely covered with blue talavera tiles and crowned by
seven narrow, stone finials that resemble the roofcombs on
many Mayan temples. The convent-school next door is now
used for cultural events and art exhibitions. Campeche's first
lighthouse, built in 1864, sits atop a brick pillar next to the
church. *Admission free. Open Tues.–Fri. 9–2 and 5–10.*

Now head north on Calle 12 for two blocks, then turn right onto
Calle 59, where you will pass the tiny **Iglesia de San Francisquito,** whose architecture and ambience do justice to the historic street's old-fashioned beauty. Behind the genteel lace curtains of some of the homes, you can glimpse equally genteel
scenes of Campeche life, with faded lithographs on the dun-col-
ored walls and plenty of antique furniture and clutter. Along

Calle 59 once stood some of Campeche's finest homes, many of them two stories high, with the ground floors serving as warehouses and the upper floors as residences. Geometric motifs decorate the cornices, and the windows are gaily adorned with iron latticework. The richest inhabitants built as close to the sea as possible, in case escape became necessary. Beneath the city a network of tunnels crisscrossed, linking the eight bastions and providing temporary refuge from the pirates.

6 Take Calle 10 south to Calle Bravo, home of the **Iglesia de San Román.** Generally, contemporary Campeche lacks the old city's character, but this exception—which sits just outside the intramural boundary in the barrio of the same name—suggests the old charm. San Román, with a bulbous bell tower typical of other Yucatán churches, was built to house the *naboríos* (Indians brought by the Spaniards to aid in the Conquest and later used as household servants), and the barrio, like other neighborhoods, grew up around the church. Though it went up in the 16th century, the church became central to the lives of the Indians only when an ebony image of Christ, the "Black Christ," was brought in about 1565. The Indians had been skeptical about the Christian saints, but this Christ figure came to be associated with miracles. The legend goes that a ship that refused to carry the tradesman and his precious statue was wrecked, while the ship that did take him on board reached Campeche in record time. To this day, the Feast of San Román—when the icon is carried through the streets as part of a colorful and somber procession—is the biggest such celebration in Campeche. People still come to see the black wood Christ mounted on a silver filigree cross. *Calle 10 s/n, no phone. Open Mon.–Sat. 7–noon and 4–8:30; Sat. Mass at 7:30 PM, Sun. Mass at 10 AM and 7:30 PM.*

Time Out The best breads and sweet rolls in town are baked fresh every day at the **Panadería Nueva España** (Calle 10 between Calles 57 and 59). Stop by after 5 PM, when the fresh *bolillos* are set out in large bins.

7 One block beyond San Francisquito, at the corner of Calle 59 and Calle 14, is the **Museo Regional,** for which you should allow at least two hours. The museum occupies the former Casa del Teniente del Rey, or House of the King's Governor, who lived here between 1804 and 1811. His official's stature entitled him to build a house with architectural flourishes not permitted to less eminent citizens, including entrances flanked by columns or framed by portals, and the central atrium surrounded by Moorish archways leading off to numerous corridors and rooms. The ground floor comprises the archaeological museum, which is devoted primarily to the Maya. Jewels and jade masks from the tomb of Calakmul; figurines from Jaina; giant stone masks from Edzná; and plentiful illustrations, photographs, and models are on exhibit. The historical museum on the second floor covers the 18th century and includes religious art, weapons, manuscripts, and a superb carved ebony rudder shaped like a greyhound around which a serpent is entwined. *Admission $4.50. Open Tues.–Sat. 8–8, Sun. 8–1.*

8 Old Campeche ends one block east of the museum at the **Puerta de Tierra,** the only one of the four city gates that still stands with its basic structure intact; the walls, arches, and gates were refurbished in 1987. This stone arch intercepts a long stretch of the partially crenelated wall, 26 feet high and 10 feet thick, that once encircled the city; looking through it, you can just barely see across town to its counterpart, the **Puerta de Mar,** through which all seafarers were forced to pass. Because the latter stands alone, without any wall to shore it up, it looks like the Arc de Triomphe. The wall that is standing today around the Puerta de Tierra was built in 1957 to replace the one demolished in 1893. A light-and-sound show here highlights the city's history on Friday at 8 PM. *Admission: $3.*

To take in the heart of a true Mexican inner city, walk north on Calle 16 for three blocks, then turn east (right) onto Calle 53, which leads to the **Mercado Municipal,** where locals congregate en masse to shop for seafood, produce, and housewares. Beside the market is a small bridge aptly named Dog Bridge—two bright yellow plaster dogs guard the area. The market is open daily from dawn to dusk. Try to arrive early, before it gets uncomfortably crowded.

After browsing through the market, walk four blocks west on Calle 55 to an exquisite mansion highlighted by Moorish arcades. In 1865 Empress Carlotta, wife of the doomed Maximilian, stayed here briefly, but it was long enough for the town to celebrate her visit with all due pomp and circumstance. It was during the short-lived reign of Maximilian that Campeche, besieged by French troops, was forced to become part of Yucatán; at his death it became an independent state.

Just opposite the mansion stands the **Parque Principal,** the southern side of which—Calle 57—is lined with several agreeable cafés and hotels; the park is the focal point for the town's activities. Concerts are held on Sunday evening, when it seems all the city's residents come out for a stroll.

Time Out | **Café Literario El Murmillo,** a somewhat unusual, bohemian-style hangout along Calle 57, is the kind of starkly furnished and poorly lit gathering place that seems more typical of Paris or Madrid than of a Mexican town. This café offers a scholarly ambience in which to take some refreshment before continuing on.

Also situated across from the Parque Principal on Calle 57 is the **Campeche hotel** (*see* Lodging, *below*), a dilapidated but likable inn with colorful tile floors, an iron balustrade, and what must once have been a striking courtyard.

Across the street from the north side of the park—on Calle 55 between Calles 8 and 10—is another exception to the generally somber architecture rule of colonial Campeche. The **Catedral** took two centuries (from 1650 to 1850) to build and incorporates Neoclassical and Renaissance elements. (The present cathedral occupies the site of Montejo's original church, which was built in 1540.) The simple exterior lines terminate in two bulbous towers rising to each side of the gracefully curved stone entrances, the fluted pilasters echoing those on the towers. Sculptures of saints set in niches recall the French Gothic cathedrals. The interior is no less impressive, with a single limestone nave, supported by Doric capitals and Corinthian columns, arching toward the huge octagonal dome above a black-and-white marble floor. The pièce de résistance, however, is the magnificent Holy Sepulcher, carved from ebony.

Walk one block north of the cathedral to the corner of Calles
⓮ 10 and 53, where you'll find the eclectic **Mansión Carvajal.** Built in the early 20th century by one of the wealthiest plantation owners in Yucatán, this structure did time as the Hotel Señorial before arriving at its present role as a government office center and headquarters for the state governor's wife and her staff. Take a stroll: The black-and-white tile floor, Art Nouveau staircase with Carrara marble steps and iron balustrade, and blue and white Moorish arcades speak volubly of the city's heyday, when Campeche was the peninsula's only port. *Calle 10 s/n, between Calles 53 and 55, no phone. Admission free. Open Mon.– Sat. 8–2:30 and 5–8:30. Closed Sun.*

Just a short block north on Calle 8 (which becomes Malecón
⓯ Miguel Alemán) is the **Baluarte Santiago,** the last of the bastions to be built (1704). It has been transformed into a botanical garden. A film explaining the garden's 250 plant species is shown throughout the day (when the projector is working). The original bastion was demolished at the turn of the century, but it was rebuilt in the 1950s. Architecturally this fort looks much the same as the others in Campeche: a stone fortress with thick walls, watchtowers, and gunnery slits. *Calle 8 at Calle 49, tel. 981/66829. Admission free. Open Tues.–Sat. 9–1 and 4:30–8, Sun. 9–1.*

At this point, devotees of religious history may wish to venture three long blocks north, away from the city center and into a
⓰ residential neighborhood, to the ruins of the **Iglesia de San Francisco** (1546), the oldest church site in Campeche. Possibly more significant is that it marks the spot where—in 1517—the first Mass on the North American continent was said. One of Cortés's grandsons was baptized here, and the baptismal font still stands.

Campeche has one other bastion museum that warrants visit-
⓱ ing: the **Baluarte de la Soledad,** otherwise known as the **Museo de los Estelas.** The largest of the bastions, this one has comparatively complete parapets and embrasures that offer a sweeping view of the cathedral, the municipal buildings, and the Gulf of Mexico. Artifacts housed inside include 10 Mayan stelae and other pieces from the Late Classical period (AD 600–900), such as a sculpture of a man wearing an owl mask. *Calle 8 at Calle 57, no phone. Admission: 50¢; free on Sun. Open Tues.– Sat. 8–8, Sun. 8–1.*

State of Campeche

After touring Campeche's churches and museums, you may want to drive through the State of Campeche, stopping at some of the archaeological sites and beaches. These attractions also nicely break up a trip to Mérida, Villahermosa, or Chetumal.

Numbers in the margin correspond to points of interest on the State of Campeche map.

Along Route 180 The so-called short route to or from Mérida takes you past
toward Mérida several villages and minor archaeological sites. Although the
⓲ pretty 15th-century town of **Hecelchakán,** 75 kilometers (56 miles) north of Campeche, boasts a lovely church and former convent, it is known primarily for the **Museo Arqueológico del**

Camino Real. This museum holds an impressive collection of clay figurines from the island of Jaina and stelae from the Puuc region. It is difficult to visit Jaina, because the archaeological zone is being restored, so many of Jaina's intricate sculptures, most of which have been removed from the island, are on display here. *Rte. 180 to Hecelchakán, no phone. Admission: less than 25¢; free on Sun. Open Tues.–Sat. 8–8, Sun. 8–2; closed Mon.*

⑱ Some 24 kilometers (15 miles) north, you'll come to **Calkiní** and its fortress-monastery built by the Franciscans between 1548 and 1776. Inside the building is an exquisite cedar altarpiece on which the four Evangelists have been carved, and the columns and cornices adorning the convent have been painted in rich gold, red, and black. The portal is plateresque (resembling fine silverwork), while the rest of the structure is Baroque. Interestingly enough, Calkiní dates back much earlier, to the Ah-Canul dynasty. According to a local codex, the Ah-Canul chieftainship was founded here in 1443 beneath a ceiba, a tree sacred to the Maya and frequently mentioned in their legends. The Ah-Canul was the most important dynasty at the time of the Conquest; the fighters rebelling against Montejo were put down in Mérida giving the coup de grace to the Maya spirit.

⑲ The neighboring village of **Becal** is noted for the famous *jipi-japa* (Panama-style) hats made here by local Indians. The Indians weave reeds of the jipi plant or the guano palm in caves beneath their houses, because the humidity there keeps the reeds flexible. First produced in the 19th century by the García family, the hats have become a village tradition. Just across the **⑳** Yucatán state line, in **Halachó**, townspeople weave motifs from central Mexico into their baskets. The rest of the way to Mérida consists of relatively monotonous terrain, with the occasional clusters of white, thatched-roof huts, speed bumps, windmills, and spearlike henequen plants.

Along Route 261 toward Mérida **㉑** This is by far the longer—and more interesting—way to reach the Yucatán capital. The first ruin, **Edzná,** deserves more fame than it has. Archaeologists consider it one of the peninsula's most important ruins because of the crucial transitional role it played among several architectural styles. Its obscurity can be attributed to at least three factors: It is relatively difficult to reach; excavation began here only recently (in 1943); and it has been difficult to acquire funds for the restoration work. Excavation, which had continued fitfully until 1987, stopped completely in early 1990, when international funding dried up. In 1992, European archaeologists began working at the site, and the Guatemalan refugees who live 23 kilometers (14 miles) southeast of the site in the village of Quetzal-Edzná are once again being paid to assist with the restoration.

The site, occupied from 300 BC to AD 900, was discovered in 1927. The 6-square-kilometer (2-square-mile) expanse of savanna and occasional tall trees is situated in a broad valley prone to flooding and surrounded by low hills. It comprises two main complexes: the ceremonial center, which has been excavated, and the Grupo de la Vieja, which has not. Surrounding the site are vast networks of irrigation canals and moats, the remnants of a highly sophisticated hydraulic system that channeled rainwater into human-made *chultunes,* or wells.

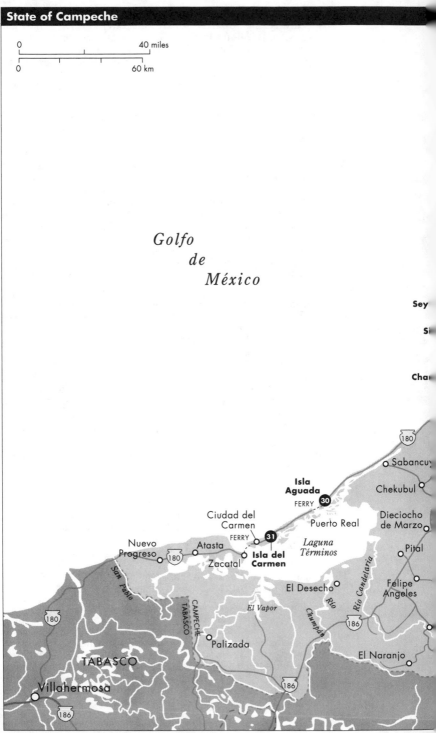

State of Campeche

0   40 miles
0   60 km

*Golfo
de
México*

Sey

S

Cha

180

Sabancuy

Chekubul

**Isla
Aguada**
FERRY **30**

Ciudad del
Carmen
FERRY **31**

Puerto Real

Dieciocho
de Marzo

Nuevo
Progreso   180   Atasta

Zacatal

**Isla del
Carmen**

*Laguna
Términos*

Pital

San Pablo

TABASCO
CAMPECHE

El Vapor

El Desecho

Rio Candelaria

Rio Champán

Felipe
Angeles

180

Palizada

186

El Naranjo

TABASCO

Villahermosa

186

186

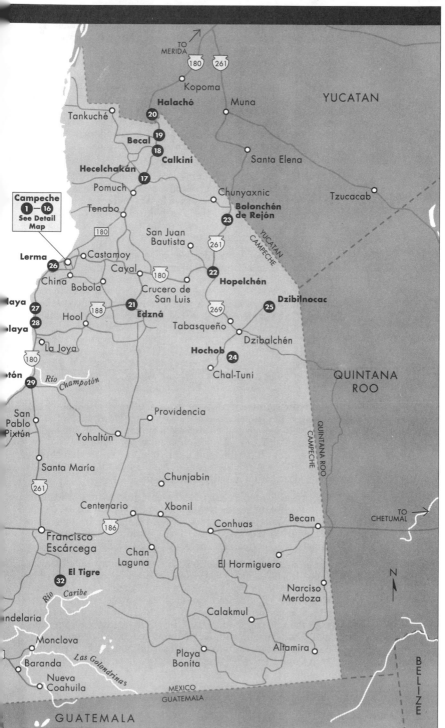

TO MERIDA

(180) (261)

Kopoma

Halachó 20

Muna

YUCATAN

Tankuché

Becal 19

18 **Calkiní**

Santa Elena

Hecelchakán

17

Pomuch

Chunyaxnic

Tzucacab

Tenabo

Bolonchén de Rejón

23

YUCATAN
CAMPECHE

Campeche
1 — 16
See Detail Map

180

San Juan Bautista

261

Lerma

26

Castamoy

Cayal

180

22

Hopelchén

Dzibilnocac

China

Bobola

Crucero de San Luis

269

25

laya 27

21 **Edzná**

Hool

188

Tabasqueño

Dzibalchén

laya 28

La Joya

Hochob

24

QUINTANA
ROO

180

Chal-Tuni

tón 29

Río Champotón

Providencia

San Pablo Pixtún

Yohaltún

QUINTANA ROO
CAMPECHE

Santa María

Chunjabin

261

Centenario

Xbonil

186

Conhuas

Becan

TO CHETUMAL

Francisco Escárcega

Chan Laguna

El Hormiguero

N

El Tigre

32

Río Caribe

Narciso Merdoza

ndelaria

Calakmul

Altamira

Monclova

Las Golondrinas

Baranda

Playa Bonita

Nueva Coahuila

MEXICO
GUATEMALA

B
E
L
I
Z
E

GUATEMALA

Commanding center stage in the complex is the **Five-Story Pyramid,** which rises 102 feet over the Great Acropolis. The man-made platform consists of five stories, each narrower than the one below it, terminating in a tiny temple crowned by a roofcomb. The architecturally innovative roof of the gallery comprising each story functioned as a terrace for the story above. Hieroglyphs carved into the vertical face of the 15 steps between each story describe astronomy and history, while the numerous stelae depict the opulent attire and adornment of the ruling class—quetzal feathers, jade pectorals, and skirts of jaguar skin. Over the course of several hundred years, Edzná grew from a humble agricultural settlement into a major politico-religious center.

Carved into Building 414 of the Great Acropolis are some grotesque masks with huge and sinister protruding eye sockets, the effect of which is enhanced by the oversize incisors or tongues extending from the upper lips. Local lore holds that Edzná, which means the House of the Gestures, or Grimaces, may have been named for these images.

A variety of architectural styles have been discerned at this site. The Petén style of northern Guatemala and Chiapas is reflected in the use of acropoli as bases for pyramids, of low-lying structures that contrasted handsomely with soaring temples, and of corbeled arch roofs, richly ornamented stucco facades, and roofcombs. The Río Bec style, which dominated much of Campeche, can be seen in the slender columns and exuberant stone mosaics. The multistory structures, arched passageways, stone causeways, and hieroglyph-adorned stairways represent both the Chenes and Puuc styles. *Take Rte. 180 east for 44 km (27 mi) to Cayal and then Rte. 188 southeast for 18 km (11 mi). Admission: $4.50. Open daily 8–5.*

㉒ Return to Route 180 and continue another 41 kilometers (25 miles) east to **Hopelchén,** the Place of the Five Wells. Noted for the lovely Franciscan church built in honor of St. Francis of Padua in 1667, this is a rich agricultural region where corn, beans, tobacco, fruit, and henequen are cultivated. From Hopelchén, you can travel either north or south, depending on which destination most appeals to you.

㉓ About 34 kilometers (21 miles) north, just short of the state line, lies **Bolonchén de Rejón,** named for the adjacent Cave of the Nine Wells, where legend says a distressed Maya girl took refuge from the vagaries of love. (In Mayan, the caves are called Xtacumbinxunán, meaning "hidden lady.")

㉔ ㉕ To the south of Hopelchén, off Route 261, are two small Mayan ruins: **Hochob,** about 25 kilometers (16 miles) away, and **Dzibilnocac,** 61 kilometers (38 miles) away. Both are excellent examples of the Chenes architectural style, which peaked in the Classical period from about AD 200 to 900. Closely associated with the Puuc style and found throughout eastern Campeche and southern Yucatán, it is characterized by columns, ornamental friezes, frontal roofcombs, and multistory structures with sloping sides. Platforms, stairways, vaulted ceilings, and mounds are about all you will see, but if you have your own vehicle and a little time to spare, it can be fun to venture into this hinterland.

Route 180 to Villahermosa Heading south from Campeche, Route 180 hugs the coast, offering a wonderful view of the gulf. The deep green sea is so shallow that the continental shelf is almost visible at low tide, and because waves and currents are rare, the gulf resembles a lake more than the vast body of water that it is. The first **㉖** beach—presently under development—is near **Lerma** at Playa Bonita, which can be reached by public buses. The buses depart daily (6 AM–11 PM) from the market (Circuito Baluartes, between Calles 53 and 55). You would be better off, however, if **㉗** you continue south for 33 kilometers (21 miles) to **Seybaplaya,** a fishing port. A couple of kilometers beyond lies **Payucán,** a beach with fine white sand, moderate waves, palapas, and restaurants (but no dressing rooms). Off this beach, you can fish, dive, or take a boat trip out to sea. A little farther on Route 180 **㉘** is **Sihoplaya,** an attractive resort with one hotel operating and several others in the planning stages. Buccaneer Henry Morgan is said to have hidden here before attacking Campeche.

㉙ Traveling about 60 kilometers (37 miles) farther down, through a hilly region with curving roads, will bring you to **Champotón's** immensely satisfying vista of open seas. Champotón is a charming little town with a bridge, palapas right on the water, and plenty of swimmers and launches in sight. The Spaniards dubbed the outlying bay the *Bahía de la Mala Pelea,* or Bay of the Evil Battle, because it was here that the Spanish conqueror and explorer Hernández de Córdoba's troops were trounced in 1517 by belligerent Indians armed with arrows, slingshots, and darts.

The 17th-century **Church of Nuestra Señora de las Mercedes** and the ruins of the **San Luis fort** still stand in Champotón. This area, ideal for fishing and hunting, teems with shad and bass as well as deer, wild boar, doves, and quail, and is sustained by an economy based largely on chicle, water coconut, sugarcane, bananas, avocados, corn, and beans.

㉚ Some 105 kilometers (65 miles) southwest, you'll come to **Isla** **㉛** **Aguada,** surrounded by the Términos Lagoon. **Isla del Carmen,** a barrier island protecting the lagoon from the gulf, is the place the pirates who raided Campeche hid from 1663 until their expulsion in 1717. The island has served as a depot for everything from dyewoods and textiles to hardwoods, chicle, shrimp, and lately, oil. Its major development is at **Ciudad del Carmen,** on the eastern end, now connected by a bridge to the mainland.

There is a surprising variety of things to do on Isla del Carmen, which has several fine white-sand beaches with palm groves and shallow waters, excellent fishing (sailfish, swordfish, shrimp, oyster, and conch), water sports, restaurants, hotels, and even some nightlife. Catamarans regularly ply the inner canals, dolphins can be spotted at Zacatal, a Moorish 18th-century pavilion marks the center of Zaragoza Park, and the **Museum of Anthropology and History** (Av. Gobernadores 289, no phone) displays pre-Hispanic and pirate artifacts. Archaeological sites on the island include Xicalango, where Cortés's mistress, Malinche, eventually lived, and Itzankanac, where the last Aztec emperor, Cuauhtémoc, supposedly met his demise (although other sources place Itzankanac on the mainland, near Tabasco). Good bets for accommodations include the bare-bones **Hotel Zacarias** (Calle 24 No. 58, tel. 938/20121) and the considerably pricier, five-star **Eurotel** (Calle 22 No. 208, tel. 938/21030). The best beaches for swimming are **El Playon** and **Playa Benjamin.**

To Chetumal (off The vestiges of at least 10 little-known Mayan cities lie hidden
Route 186) off Route 186 between Francisco Escárcega and Chetumal,
though in this section we cover only El Tigre. Four sites lie near
the highway, but the others are more difficult to reach; a four-
wheel-drive—and much enthusiasm—are required. The Campeche tourist office can recommend guides and direct you to
the more obscure sites.

㉜ The ruins known as **El Tigre,** near the Tabasco border, may
have been the Postclassical site of Itzankanac, capital of the
province of Acalán, where Spanish conquistador Cortés
hanged Cuauhtémoc, the last Aztec emperor. This enormous
site has barely been explored and is difficult to reach. Topog-
raphically, the region is unlike northern Campeche: Tall forests
compete with dense jungle foliage, including hanging vines and
orchids, and both are washed by waterfalls and the river
(where boats can be rented to fish for haddock and bass or to
watch the exotic water birds). El Tigre comprises a 656-foot-
long ceremonial plaza closed in by three huge pyramid bases.
Dozens of mounds crowd around smaller plazas and patios, and
a 33-foot-wide *sacbe*, or white limestone causeway, leads off toward a swamp. *30 km (19 mi) southeast of Francisco Escárcega
(on a dirt road). Admission: $4.50. Open daily 8–5.*

Shopping

Folk art in Campeche is typical of the rest of Yucatán's handicrafts: basketry, gold and silver filigree, leather goods, embroidered cloth, clay trinkets, and tortoiseshell (which is illegal to
import into the U.S., because the animals from which the shells
come are an endangered species).

Shopping The city has two large, modern shopping malls: the **Plaza
Districts/Malls Comercial Ah-Kin-Pech** (between Calles 51 and 49), on the
stretch of the waterfront boulevard known as Avenida Pedro
Sáinz de Baranda, and **Super Plaza,** on Avenida Lopez Mateos.
The variety of establishments at both malls includes a super-
market, pastry shop, beauty salon, pharmacy, money exchange, perfumery, sporting-goods store, and clothing shops.
Visit the **municipal market** (Circuito Baluartes at Calle 53), at
the eastern end of the city, for crafts and food.

Local Crafts For handicrafts, try **Artesanía Típica Naval** (Calle 8 No. 259,
tel. 981/65708), where craftsman David Pérez's miniature
boats and prize-winning regional costumes can be found. Another shop selling folk art, particularly wicker baskets, is
México Lindo (Calle 57 No. 30, tel. 981/67206). Regional folk
art is exhibited and sold at **Baluarte San Pedro** (Calle 51 at
Calle 18, no phone), which was a prison during the Inquisition.

Sports

Hunting, fishing, and birding are popular throughout the State
of Campeche. Contact the **Hotel Castelmar** (Calle 61 No. 2, tel.
981/65186) for information regarding the regulations and the
best areas for each sport. Licenses and gun permits are required for big game, so make your inquiries well in advance.

Dining

There is nothing fancy about Campeche's restaurants, but its regional cuisine is renowned throughout Mexico—particularly the fish and shellfish stews, shrimp cocktails, squid and octopus, crabs' legs, *panuchos* (tortillas stuffed with beans and diced fish), and Yucatecan specialties. Other unusual seafood delicacies include pompano wrapped in paper, red snapper in banana leaves, shark casserole, and crayfish claws. *Botanas*, or canapés, include fried eggs, prunes in syrup with chile, *ceviche* (raw marinated fish), and *chicharrón* (fried pork rind). The addition of cumin, marjoram, bay leaf, cayenne pepper, and allspice imparts an exotic flavor to entrées. Fruits are served fresh, made into breads or liqueurs, or blended with rum or vinegar. Look for mango, papaya, *zapote* (sapodilla), mamey, guanabana, tamarind, watermelon, jícama, melon, pineapple, and coconut, to name only a few. Because regional produce is plentiful, most restaurants—including those listed below—fall into the inexpensive (under $15 for a three-course meal excluding drinks and tips) category. Restaurants throughout Campeche have casual dress codes (no shorts) and do not require reservations.

Highly recommended restaurants are indicated by a star ★.

Campeche City

Barbillas. The relaxed atmosphere, accented by creamy white walls and tropical touches, makes this mostly seafood restaurant a good spot for a lunch break. Specializing in fish (pompano and snapper) and shellfish (shrimp, oysters, conch, and crabs' legs), this restaurant offers a real taste of Yucatecan fare. Located on the edge of town, Barbillas is somewhat out of the way, but the excellent service and extensive menu are worth the trip. *Av. Lázaro Cárdenas Fracc. 2000 at Av. López Portillo, no phone. AE, MC, V. Closed for dinner.*

★ **La Pigua.** A favorite with local professionals lingering over long lunches, La Pigua is perhaps the best seafood restaurant in town, with the most pleasant ambience. The long, glass-walled dining room is surrounded by trees and plants. A truly ambitious lunch would start with a seafood cocktail or plate of cold crab claws, followed by *pescado relleno*, a fish fillet stuffed with finely diced shellfish, and then local peaches drenched in sweet liqueurs. The restaurant was featured in Mexico's exhibit at the 1992 Expo in Sevilla, Spain. *Malecón Miguel Alemán 197-A, tel. 981/13365. MC, V. Closed for dinner.*

Marganzo. This rustically furnished restaurant, conveniently situated a half block south of the plaza, is a popular tourist spot. It's impeccably clean and has a colorful decor and dependable, if somewhat unexciting, cuisine. Lunch and dinner menus include several seafood dishes as well as such specials as *pan de casón* (tortillas with chili peppers). Waitresses dressed in colonial Mexican–style skirts and embroidered blouses and wearing gold and coral accessories keep in step with Marganzo's regional theme. *Calle 8, tel. 981/13898. AE, MC, V. Closed for breakfast.*

Miramar. These two restaurants—one across from Hotel Castelmar and one near the town hall building—attract locals and foreign visitors with their fabulous *huevos motuleños* (fried eggs served on corn tortillas and topped with ham, beans, peas, and cheese), red snapper, shellfish, soups, and meat dishes. The wooden tables and chairs and the paintings of the coat-of-arms of the Mexican Republic give Miramar a colonial feel. *Calle 20 No. 8, tel. 981/20923; and Calle 8 No. 73, tel. 981/62883. MC, V.*

Video Taco. The young folk of Campeche hang out at this small café, where inexpensive tacos are served to the beat of music videos. *Av. Madero s/n. No phone. No credit cards.*

Lodging

Most of Campeche City's hotels are old (and several are in disrepair), reflecting the city's lackadaisical attitude toward tourism. Hotels tend to be either luxury accommodations along the waterfront, with air-conditioning, restaurants, and other standard amenities, or basic downtown accommodations offering only ceiling fans and a no-credit-card policy. Those in the latter category tend to be either seedy and undesirable or oddly charming, with some architectural and regional detail unique to each.

Highly recommended hotels are indicated by a star ★.

Category	Cost*
Moderate	$40–$90
Inexpensive	Under $40

All prices are for a standard double room, excluding service and the 10% tax.

Campeche City

Moderate **Alhambra.** A great choice away from the bustle of the city, the Alhambra is a modern hotel facing the waterfront near the university. A wide screen TV plays softly in the lobby; TVs in the rooms get U.S. stations, sometimes including CNN. Rooms are carpeted and clean, with king- and double-size beds. Bathtubs are a welcome addition, rare in these parts. *Av. Resurgimiento 85 between Av. Universidad and Av. August Melgar, tel. 981/66800, fax 981/66132. 98 rooms. Facilities: restaurant, bar, pool. MC, V.*

Debliz. Those traveling by car may wish to stay outside town at this modern hotel in a residential area north of the city. The four-story, elevator-equipped property is refreshingly decorated with cream color walls, beige carpets, dark wood furnishings, and paintings of flowers. Room amenities include color TV, reading lamps, and double beds. The bar and garden are popular gathering places for hotel guests. The Debliz can seem deserted and lonely, until the tour buses that frequent the place pull into the parking lot. *Av. Las Palmas 55, off Av. Pedro Sainz de Baranda, near the baseball stadium, tel. 981/10111, fax 981/61611. 120 rooms. Facilities: restaurant, cafeteria, bar, pool. AE, MC, V.*

★ **Ramada Inn.** A whitewashed, four-story modern hotel right on the seafront, the luxurious Ramada offers a relaxing pool area with greenery and a bar. Fairly large rooms, with all the necessary amenities, are decorated in blues with rattan furnishings; balconies overlook the pool or the bay. The lobby restaurant,

El Poquito, is extremely popular with locals at breakfast and at night before the disco Atlantis opens. *Av. Ruíz Cortines 51, tel. 981/62233 or 800/228–9898, fax 981/11618. 119 rooms. Facilities: restaurant, coffee shop, pool bar, gift shop, disco, travel agency. AE, MC, V.*

Inexpensive **Campeche.** A classic run-down Mexican hotel with colorful tile floors, thin mattresses, and peeling paint, this property has managed, in spite of it all, to retain its personality. The inner courtyard, trimmed with red tiles and iron balustrades, suggests the hotel's former loveliness. *Calle 59 No. 2, tel. 981/65183. 42 rooms. No facilities. No credit cards.*

Castelmar. Though modest, this hotel has certain colonial touches such as beautiful tiles and quasi-Moorish architecture. The rooms are huge, with high ceilings and ceiling fans, but have peeling walls and smell of the sea. *Calle 61 No. 2, tel. 981/65186. 18 rooms. No facilities. No credit cards.*

Colonial. This building—the former home of a high-ranking army lieutenant—dates back to 1850 but was made over as a hotel in the 1940s, when its wonderful tiles were added. Pastel-colored rooms with ceiling fans (only some of the units are air-conditioned) are clean and functional, but the hotel's public areas have become extremely run-down. *Calle 14 No. 122, tel. 981/62222 or 981/62630. 30 rooms. No facilities. No credit cards.*

Lopez. Pink, yellow, and white walls reflect the airy ambience found in this small, pleasant, two-story accommodation. Standard rooms include colonial-style desks and armoires, luggage stands, and easy chairs. Although the restaurant serves basic Continental fare, it's a convenient enough stop for breakfast, lunch, or dinner. *Calle 12 No. 189, tel. 981/63344. 39 rooms. Facilities: restaurant (closed Sun.). AE, MC, V.*

Nightlife

For entertainment, check out the sound-and-light show at the **Puerta de Tierra** (Calle 59 at Calle 18 and Circuíto Baluartes, no phone) every Friday evening at 8:30 ($2). If you're in the mood to dance, try Campeche's one disco, **Atlantis,** in the Ramada Inn.

Campeche has five movie theaters. Two of the most conveniently located are: **Cine Estelar** (Malecón Miguel Alemán and Calle 49-B) and **Cine Selem** (Calle 12 and Calle 57), but both show only Spanish-language films.

8 Mérida and the State of Yucatán

*Updated by
Maribeth Mellin*

There is a marvelous eccentricity about Mérida. Fully urban, with maddeningly slow-moving traffic, it has a self-sufficient, self-contented air that would suggest a small town more than a state capital of some 600,000 inhabitants (locals say there are 850,000). Gaily pretentious turn-of-the-century buildings have an Iberian-Moorish flair for the ornate, but most of the architecture is low-lying and although the city sprawls, it is not imposing. Grandiose colonial facades adorned with iron grillwork, carved wooden doors, and archways conceal marble tiles and lush gardens; horse-drawn carriages hark back to the city's heyday as the wealthiest capital in Mexico.

Mérida is a city of subtle contrasts, from its opulent yet faded facades to its residents, very Spanish yet very Mayan. The Indian presence is unmistakable: People are short and dark-skinned, with sculpted bones and almond eyes; women pad about in *huipiles* (hand-embroidered, sacklike white dresses), and craftsmen and vendors from the outlying villages come to town in their huaraches. So many centuries after the conquest, Yucatán remains one of the last great strongholds of Mexico's indigenous population. To this day, in fact, many Maya do not even speak Spanish, primarily because of the peninsula's geographic and, hence, cultural isolation from the rest of the country. Additionally, the Maya—long portrayed as docile and peace-loving—for centuries provided the Spaniards and the mainland Mexicans with one of their greatest challenges. As late as the 1920s and 1930s, rebellious pockets of Mayan communities held out against the outsiders, or *dzulobs.* Yucatecos speak of themselves as *peninsulares* first, Mexicans second.

The Mayan civilization—one of the great ancient civilizations—had been around since 1500 BC, but it was in a state of decline when the conquistadores arrived in AD 1517, burning defiant warriors at the stake, severing limbs, and drowning and hanging women. Ironically, Yucatán offered neither gold nor fertile land, but it became a strategic administrative and military foothold, the gateway to Cuba and to Spain. (Mérida still is the gateway to Cuba: Americans who cannot get to Cuba by other means take little-publicized charter flights.) Francisco de Montejo's conquest of Yucatán took three gruesome wars, a total of 24 years. "Nowhere in all America was resistance to Spanish conquest more obstinate or more nearly successful," wrote the historian Henry Parkes. In fact, the Maya were responsible for the deaths of more Spaniards than were any other tribe in the Americas—more than during the conquest of the Aztecs and the Incas combined. By the 18th century, huge maize and cattle plantations flourished throughout the peninsula, and the wealthy *hacendados* (plantation owners), left largely to their own devices by the viceroys in faraway Mexico City, accumulated fortunes under a semifeudal system. As the economic base shifted to the export of dyewood, henequen, and chicle, the social structure—based on Indian peonage—barely changed.

Insurrection came during the War of the Castes in the mid-1800s, when the enslaved indigenous people rose up with religious fervor and massacred thousands of whites. The United States, Cuba, and Mexico City finally came to the aid of the ruling elite, and between 1846 and 1850 the Indian population of Yucatán was effectively halved. Those Mayans who did not escape into the remote jungles of Quintana Roo or get sold into slavery in Cuba found themselves worse off than before under the dictatorship of Porfirio Díaz, who brought Yaqui prisoners to the peninsula as forced labor under the rapacious grip of the hacendados. Díaz's legacy is still evident in the pretentious French-style mansions that stretch along Mérida's Paseo de Montejo.

Yucatán was then and still is a largely agricultural state, although oil, tourism, and the *maquiladora*, or in-bond industry (usually foreign-owned assembly plants), now play more prominent roles in the economy. Some 93 offshore platforms dot the continental shelf surrounding the peninsula, and soon there will be as many as 50 in-bond plants. The capital accounts for about half the state's population, but the other half lives in villages, maintaining conservative traditions and lifestyles.

Physically, Yucatán, too, differs from the rest of the country. Its geography and wildlife have more in common with Florida and Cuba—with which it was probably once connected—than with the central Mexican plateau and mountains. A mostly flat limestone slab possessing almost no bodies of water, it is riddled with underground cenotes, caves with stalactites, small hills, and intense jungle. Wild ginger and spider lilies grow in profusion, and vast flamingo colonies nest at swampy estuaries on the northern and western coasts, where undeveloped sandy beaches extend for 370 kilometers (230 miles). Deer, turkeys, boars, ocelots, tapirs, and armadillos flourish in this semitropical climate (the average temperature is 82°F, or 28°C).

But it is, of course, the celebrated Mayan ruins, Chichén Itzá and Uxmal especially, that bring most tourists to Mérida. The roads rank among the best in the country, and the local travel agencies are adept at running tours. At Chichén, visitors flock to see El Castillo pyramid, surrounded by recumbent stone figures of Chac Mool (the rain god); and the Puuc hills south of Mérida, where most of the ruins are situated, have more archaeological sites per square kilometer than anywhere else in the hemisphere. Yucatecan craftsmen also produce some of the finest crafts in Mexico, notably hammocks, filigree jewelry, huaraches, and huipiles. And small towns such as Progreso and Valladolid, while bereft of star-quality sightseeing attractions, charm visitors with their very unpretentiousness.

High season generally corresponds to high season in the rest of Mexico: Thanksgiving week, the Christmas period, Easter week, and the month of August. Rains fall heaviest between May and November, bringing with them an uncomfortable humidity. Levels of service differ drastically between the high and low seasons, so you should be prepared for a trade-off.

Essential Information

Important Addresses and Numbers

Tourist Information The main **Tourist Information Center** (Teatro Peón Contreras, corner of Calles 60 and 57, tel. 99/249290 or 99/249389) is open daily 8–8 and will provide you with free information and brochures including "Yucatán Today," "Mérida Tips," and "Discover It! Mérida" (also available at many hotels). Kiosks, open 8–8, can be found at the airport (tel. 99/246764), the ADO bus terminal (no phone), and next to the Palacio Municipal on Calle 62 (no phone).

Consulates **United States** (Paseo de Montejo 453, tel. 99/255011, 99/258677, or 99/255409); **United Kingdom** (Calle 58, No. 450, at Calle 53, tel. 99/216799 or 99/283962); **Canada** (in Mexico City, tel. 5/254–3288).

Emergencies **Police** (tel. 99/233456); **Red Cross** (Calle 68, No. 583, at Calle 65, tel. 99/212445); **Fire** (tel. 99/214122).

Hospital **Hospital O'Horan** (Calle 59-A at Av. Itzaes, tel. 99/238711 or 99/213056).

Late-night **Farmacia Yza Aviación** (Calle 71 at Av. Aviación, tel.
Pharmacies 99/238116); **Farmacia Yza Tanlum** (Glorieta Tanlum, tel. 99/251646); and **Farmacia Canto** (Calle 60, No. 513, at Calle 63, tel. 99/210106).

Banks If you need to exchange money, banks throughout Mérida are open weekdays 9–1:30. **Banamex** has its main offices in the handsome Casa de Montejo, on the south side of the main square, with a branch at the airport. Several other banks can be found on Calle 65 between Calles 62 and 60 and on Paseo Montejo.

Money There are two exchange houses: **Del Sureste** (Calle 56 at Calle
Exchange 57), open weekdays 9–5 and Saturday 9–1; and **Canto** (Calle 61 at Calle 52), open weekdays 9–1 and 4–7.

English-language **Librería Dante** has several branches around town (Calle 59 at
Bookstores Calle 68; Parque Hidalgo; in the Teatro Peón Contreras, at the corner of Calles 60 and 57; and on the main square, next to Pizza Bella), all of which carry a small selection of English-language books. **Libeco** (Calle 57, No. 500-5, at Calle 60) sells used books and magazines, some of them in English, and sets up a stall in Parque Santa Lucía on Sunday. For newspapers and magazines from Mexico City and the United States, visit **Discolibros Hollywood** (Calle 60, No. 496).

Spanish-language Intensive Spanish classes for foreigners are available through
School the **Centro de Idiomas** (Calle 14, No. 106, at Calle 25, Col. Mexico 97128, Mérida, Yucatán, Mexico, tel. 99/261155, fax 99/269020). Classes last a minimum of two weeks; advanced classes in special areas of study are available. Students stay with local families or in hotels.

Travel Agencies Mérida's local agencies and operators include **Achach Ortíz**
and Tour Operators (Calle 60, No. 457, tel. 99/242290), **American Express** (Calle 56-A, No. 494, tel. 99/244222), **Buvisa** (Paseo de Montejo, No. 475, tel. 99/277922), **Ceiba Tours** (Calle 60, No. 495, tel. 99/244477, fax 99/244588; Holiday Inn, tel. 99/244477), **Intermar Caribe** (Prolong. Paseo de Montejo 74 at Calle 11, tel. 99/260037), **Mayaland Tours** (Av. Colon 502, tel. 99/252122), **Turismo Aviomar** (Calle 60, No. 469, tel. 99/256990, fax 99/246887), **Viajes Novedosos** (Calle 58, No. 488, tel. 99/239073), and **Yucatán Trails** (Calle 62, No. 482, tel. 99/282582).

Arriving and Departing by Plane

Airport The Mérida airport is 7 kilometers (4 miles) west of the city's
and Airlines central square, about a 20-minute ride. The following airlines serve Mérida: **Aeromexico** (tel. 99/279000 or 800/237–6639) flies nonstop from Miami, Cancún, New Orleans, and Mexico

City; **Mexicana's** (tel. 99/241362 or 800/531–7921) nonstops are from Mexico City and Havana; **Aerocaribe** (tel. 99/230002 in Mérida), a subsidiary of Mexicana, has flights from Cancún, Chetumal, Cozumel, Oaxaca, and Tuxtla Guitierrez; **Aviateca** (tel. 99/249477), a Guatemalan carrier, flies from Houston and Guatemala City; **Taesa** (tel 99/239133) flies from Cozumel and Mexico City; and **Continental** (tel. 99/46–1359 or 800/231-0856) flies from Houston.

Between the Airport A private taxi costs about $10; collective service (usually a Volk-
and City Center swagen minibus), about $6. For both services, pay the taxi-ticket vendor at the airport, not the driver. If you're driving into town, take the airport exit road, make a right at the four-lane Avenida Itzaes (the continuation of Route 180), and follow it to the one-way Calle 59, just past El Centenario Zoo. Turn right on Calle 59 and go straight until you reach Calle 62, where you again turn right, and drive a block to the main square. (Parking is difficult here.) By bus, there is the irregular but inexpensive No. 79.

Arriving and Departing by Car, Bus, and Train

By Car Route 180, the main road along the Gulf Coast from the Texas border to Cancún, runs into Mérida. Mexico City lies 1,550 kilometers (960 miles) to the west; Cancún, 320 kilometers (200 miles) due east.

Driving from Cancún, you'll pass Valladolid, Chichén Itzá, and numerous villages along the way. From Campeche, it takes less than two hours to reach Mérida via Route 180. This is the fastest route. Another option is the three-hour drive along Route 261 from Campeche, which passes the ruins of Uxmal and other ancient Mayan sites as well as present-day Mayan villages. From Chetumal, the most direct way—it takes approximately nine hours—is Route 307 to Felipe Carrillo Puerto, then Route 184 to Muna, continuing north on Route 261. These paved highways are in good shape.

By Bus The **main bus station** (Calle 69, No. 544, between Calles 68 and 70, tel. 99/247880) offers frequent first- and second-class service to Akumal, Cancún, Chichén Itzá, Playa del Carmen, Puerto Morelos, Tulum, Uxmal, Valladolid, and Xel-Há. One bus a day stops throughout the Puuc region, with 20-minute stops at Uxmal, Kabah, Sayil, and Labná. It also serves Campeche, Felipe Carrillo Puerto, Palenque, Puebla, Veracruz, and Villahermosa. The **Progreso bus station** (Calle 62, No. 524, between Calles 65 and 67, tel. 99/283965) has departures for Progreso and Dzibilchaltún. Buses to Celestún, Izamal, Oxkutzcab, Sisal, Ticul, and Uxmal depart from the second-class station on Calle 50, No. 531, at Calle 67.

By Train What with the uncomfortable, inadequate train service and the high incidence of robberies, not even the tourist office recommends taking trains in Yucatán, though the station itself is worth a look. All the same, you can get second-class train service (at Calle 55 between Calles 46 and 48, tel. 99/230960) to Mexico City via Campeche ($10). The train to the capital takes about 36 hours—twice as long as the bus. Train service to Progreso has been restored after a 20-year hiatus; it runs twice a day, once on Sunday.

Telephones

Local phone numbers are gradually changing throughout Mérida, causing much confusion. New phone books have yet to be printed; if you need information talk with the operator or your hotel staff. There are several long-distance **Ladatel phone booths** around town: at the airport; at all bus stations; at Avenida Reforma and Avenida Colón; Calle 57 at Calle 64; Calle 59 at Calle 62; and at Calle 60 between Calles 55 and 53. Both local and international direct calls can be made at some of these public phones, which accept 100-peso coins (at press time, they had not yet been changed to new peso coins). Some phones accept Ladatel cards, phone cards of varying worth that can be purchased at some hotels and at the newsstands by the Plaza Principal on Calle 61.

Mail

In addition to the **main post office** (Calle 65 at Calle 56, tel. 99/212561), there are branches at the airport (tel. 99/211556) and at the main bus station (Calle 69 between Calles 68 and 70, no phone), all open Mon.–Fri. 8–5, Sat. 8–2.

Getting Around Mérida

By Bus Mérida's municipal buses run daily from 5 AM to midnight, but service is somewhat confusing until you master the system. In the downtown area, buses go east on Calle 59 and west on Calle 61, north on Calle 60 and south on Calle 62. You can catch a bus heading north to Progreso on Calle 56.

By Car Driving in Mérida can be hell because of the one-way streets (many of which end up being one-lane because of the parked cars), and because traffic is dense. But having your own wheels is the best way to take excursions from the city. Prices are sometimes lower if you arrange your rental in advance through one of the large international companies. There are almost 20 car-rental agencies in town, including **Avis** (Calle 57, No. 507, tel. 99/282096), **Budget** (Paseo Montejo 497, tel. 99/255453), **Hertz** (Calle 55, No. 479, tel. 99/249333), and **Arrendadora de Mexico** (Calle 60, No. 495, tel. 99/274916).

By Taxi Taxis don't cruise the streets for passengers; instead, they are available at 12 taxi stands around the city, or from the main taxi office (tel. 99/214347). Individual cabs cost between $4 and $5; collective service, about $1.

By Carriage Horse-drawn *calesas* (carriages) that drive along the streets of Mérida can be hailed along Calle 60. A ride to the Paseo de Montejo and back will cost about $10.

Guided Tours

There are more than 50 tour operators in Mérida, and they generally offer the same destinations. What differs is how you go—in a private car, a van, or a bus—and whether the vehicle is air-conditioned. A two- to three-hour city tour, including museums, parks, public buildings, and monuments, will cost between $7 and $20; or you can pick up an open-air sightseeing bus at Parque Santa Lucía. A day trip to Chichén Itzá, with guide, entrance fee, and lunch, runs approximately $40. For about the same price you can see the ruins of Uxmal and Kabah in the Puuc region, and for a few more dollars you can add on the neighboring sites of Sayil, Labná, and the Loltún Caves. Afternoon departures to Uxmal allow you to take in the sound-and-light show at the ruins and return by 11 PM, for $40–$50 (including dinner). There is also the option of a tour of Chichén Itzá followed by a drop-off in Cancún for about $50. Most tour operators take credit cards (*see* Travel Agencies and Tour Operators, *above*).

Special-Interest Several of the tour operators run overnight excursions to ar-
Tours chaeological sites farther afield, notably Cobá, Tulum, Edzná, and Palenque. Tours of the Ruta Maya including sites in Mexico, Guatemala, and Belize are offered by **VN Travel** (Calle 58, No. 488, tel. 99/245996), **Vagabonder Tours** (Box 2664, Evergreen, CO 80439, tel. 303/674–9615 or 800/538–6802), and **Mayaland Tours** (Av. Colon 502, tel. 99/252122 or 800/235–4079, fax 99/252397), which also offers self-guided tours with economical rental car rates. **Ecoturismo Yucatán** (tel. 99/251844, fax 99/259047) specializes in nature tours, including bird-watching, natural history, anthropology, and the Mundo Maya. Owners Roberta and Alfonso Escobedo are especially adept at organizing group and individual trips to out-of-the-way archaeological sites and natural parks in Yucatán, Campeche, Chiapas, Tabasco, Belize, and Guatemala.

Exploring

Mérida

Travelers to Mérida are a loyal bunch, content to return again and again to favorite restaurants, neighborhoods, and museums. The city's traffic and noise are frustrating, particularly after a peaceful stay on the coast or at one of the archaeological sites, but its merits far outweigh its flaws. Mérida is the cultural and intellectual center of the peninsula, with museums, schools, and attractions that greatly enhance the traveler's insights into the history and character of Yucatán. Consider making it one of the first stops in your travels, and make sure your visit includes a Sunday, when traffic is light and the city seems to revert to a more gracious era.

Numbers in the margin correspond to points of interest on the Mérida map.

Most streets in Mérida are numbered, not named, and most run one way. North–south streets have even numbers, which ascend from east to west; east–west streets have odd numbers, which ascend from north to south. Street addresses are confusing because they don't progress in even increments by blocks; for example, the 600s may occupy two or even 10 blocks. A particular location is therefore usually identified by indicating the street number and the nearest cross street, as in "Calle 64 at Calle 61" (the "at" may appear as "x") or "Calle 64 between 61 and 63."

 Begin at the **Plaza Principal,** which the Meridanos do *not* call the *zócalo* but rather the *plaza grande.* Ancient, geometrically pruned laurel trees and *confidenciales*—*S*-shaped benches designed for tête-à-têtes—invite lingering. The plaza was laid out in 1542 on the ruins of T'hó, the Mayan city demolished to

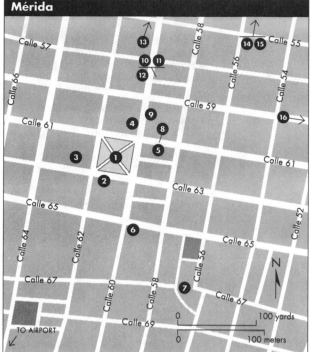

Mérida

make way for Mérida, and is still the focal point around which the most important public buildings cluster. The plaza is bordered to the east and west by Calles 60 and 62, and to the north and south by Calles 61 and 63. (Studying a map might be a good idea.)

❷ The tan stucco **Casa de Montejo** (which appeared to be receiving a coat of white paint at press time) sits on the south side of the plaza, on Calle 63. Montejo—father and son—conquered the peninsula and founded Mérida in 1540; they built this stately palace 10 years later. The property remained with the family until the late 1970s, when it was restored by Agustín Legorreta (designer of the Hotel Camino Real in Mexico City) and converted into a bank. Built in the French style during Mérida's heyday as the world's henequen capital, it now represents the city's finest—and oldest—example of colonial plateresque architecture, which typically features elaborate ornamentation and *porfiriato* (refers to the reign of dictator Porfirio Díaz, and the architecture he inspired, which mimicked 19th-century French style in such traits as broad boulevards, heroic statues, mansard roofs, gilded mirrors, and the use of marble). A bas-relief on the doorway—which is all that remains of the original house—depicts Francisco de Montejo the younger, his wife and daughter, and Spanish soldiers standing on the heads of the vanquished Maya. Even if you have no banking to do, step into the building weekdays between 9 and 1:30 to glimpse the lushly foliated inner patio.

③ Continue around to the west side of the square, occupied by the 17th-century **Palacio Municipal** (Calle 62, between Calles 61 and 63)—the city hall—which is painted yellow and trimmed with white arcades, balustrades, and the national coat of arms. Originally erected on the ruins of the last surviving Mayan structure, it was rebuilt in 1735 and then completely reconstructed along colonial lines in 1928. It remains the headquarters of the local government.

④ Occupying the northeast corner of the square is the **Palacio del Gobierno,** or Governor's Palace (Calle 61, between Calles 60 and 62), built in 1885 on the site of the Casa Real (Royal House). The upper floor of the Governor's Palace contains murals that depict the history of Yucatán, which Fernando Castro Pacheco painted in 1978. On the main balcony stands a reproduction of the Bell of Dolores Hidalgo, where Mexican independence was rung out on September 15, 1821. Every year on that date, the state governor tolls the bell to commemorate the great occasion.

Time Out | Just to the left of the Palacio Municipal is **Jugos California** (Calle 61 between Calles 60 and 62), a popular juice bar where you can get delicious tropical fruit concoctions. **Pan Montejo,** next door, is one of the best bakeries in town.

⑤ The oldest **Catedral** on the North American mainland stands catty-corner from the Palacio del Gobierno. Begun in 1561, it took several hundred Mayan laborers, working with stones from the pyramids of the ravaged Mayan city, 36 years to complete. Designed in the somber Renaissance style by an architect who had worked on the Escorial in Madrid, its facade is stark and unadorned, with gunnery slits instead of windows, and faintly Moorish spires. Inside, the **Cristo de las Ampollas** (black Christ of the Blisters), now occupying the place of honor in the chapel next to the altar, is a replica of the original, which was destroyed during the Revolution (which was also when most of the gold that typically burnished Mexican cathedrals was carried off). According to legend, the Christ figure was carved from a tree that had burned all night yet appeared the next morning unscathed. A later fire left the statue covered with the blisters for which it is named. For those who are fond of near-superlatives, the crucifix above the main altar is reputedly the second largest in the world.

Continue 1½ blocks south from the cathedral along Calle 60 to Calle 65, Mérida's main shopping street. This bustling heart of the commercial quarter is lined with, among other businesses, **⑥** banks and perfumeries. Turn left to the **Mercado de Artesanías "García Rejón,"** a market where you'll find local handicrafts and souvenirs. Shops selling dry goods, straw hats, and hammocks occupy both sides of Calle 65. A block farther east, between Calles 56 and 58, stand two picturesque 19th-century edifices housing the **main post office** and **telegraph buildings.** **⑦** Behind them sprawls the pungent, labyrinthine **Mercado Municipal,** where almost every patch of ground is occupied by Indian women selling chilies, herbs, and fruit. On the second floor of the main building is the **Bazar de Artesanías Municipales,** the principal handicrafts market, where you can buy jewelry, pottery, embroidered clothes, hammocks, and straw bags.

History lovers should stop in at the small but informative

8 **Museo de la Ciudad,** on Calle 61 between Calles 60 and 58. Once a hospital chapel for the only convent in the entire bishopric, it now houses prints, drawings, photographs, and other displays that recount the history of Mérida. *Calle 61 at Calle 58, no phone. Admission free. Open Tues.–Sun. 8–8.*

North of the square on **Calle 60** there are many noteworthy parks and historic buildings, including, only half a block away,

9 the small, cozy **Parque Hidalgo,** or Cepeda Peraza, as it is officially known. Dilapidated mansions-turned-hotels and sidewalk cafés stand at two corners of the park. Opposite, you'll find the **Café Express,** a gathering place that attracts primarily local men, though others are welcome.

10 Just north of the park, on Calle 60 is the Italianate **Teatro Peón Contreras,** designed in 1908 along the lines of the grand European turn-of-the-century theaters and opera houses. A restoration in the early 1980s retained the marble staircase and the dome with frescoes. Today, in addition to performing arts, the theater also houses temporary art exhibits and the main

11 **Centro de Información Turística** (tel. 99/249290), which is located to the right of the lobby. The center distributes maps and can provide information about local attractions.

12 Opposite the theater, the arabesque **Universidad Autonoma de Yucatán** plays a major role in the city's cultural and intellectual life. The folkloric ballet performs on the patio of the main building (*see* Mérida for Free, *below*). A Jesuit college built in 1618 previously occupied the site; the present building, dating from 1711, recalls the Moorish style, with its scalloped, crownlike upper reaches and uncloistered archways.

13 Heading north on Calle 60, you'll pass the **Parque Santa Lucía** on your left, at Calle 55. The rather plain park draws crowds to its Thursday-night serenades, performed by local musicians. The small church opposite the park dates from 1575 and was built as a place of worship for the African and Caribbean slaves who lived here; the churchyard functioned as the cemetery until 1821.

14 The 10-block-long street known as the **Paseo de Montejo** exemplifies the Parisian airs the city took on in the late 19th century, when wealthy plantation owners were building opulent, impressive mansions. The broad boulevard, lined with tamarinds and laurels, is sometimes wistfully referred to as Mérida's Champs-Elysées. Inside the mansions, the owners typically displayed imported Carrara marble and antiques, opting for the decorative and social standards of New Orleans, Cuba, and Paris over styles that were popular in Mexico City. (At the time there was more traffic by sea via the Gulf of Mexico and the Caribbean than there was overland across the lawless interior.) Although the once-stunning mansions fell into a disrepair from which few have recovered, their stateliness is still evident under the dowdiness.

15 The most compelling of these mansions, the pale peach **Palacio Cantón,** presently houses the **Museum of Anthropology and History.** Its grandiose airs seem more characteristic of a mausoleum than a home, but in fact it was built for a general between 1909 and 1911 and was designed by Enrique Deserti, who also did the blueprints for the Teatro Peón Contreras.

Marble shows up everywhere, as do Doric and Ionic columns and other Italianate Beaux-Arts flourishes. From 1948 to 1960 the mansion served as the residence of the state governor; in 1977 it became a museum. The seven-room museum now houses one of the finest Mayan collections in the country; bilingual legends accompany the displays. (Lengthier explanations, however, are in Spanish only; private guides are available for hire.) Exhibits explain the Mayan practice of dental mutilation and incrustation. A case of "sick bones" shows how the Maya suffered from osteoarthritis, nutritional maladies, and congenital syphilis. The museum also houses vivid, original mural paintings, reproductions of pyramids and sculptures, and various objects—such as conch shells, stones, and quetzal feathers—that were used as money. Other features include exhibits on Chichén Itzá, henequen production, and colonial religious art, and an excellent bookstore. *Calle 43 at Paseo de Montejo, tel. 99/230557. Admission: $4.50. Open Tues.–Sat. 8–8; Sun. 8–2; bookstore open weekdays 8–3.*

The Paseo de Montejo continues for a couple of kilometers, eventually becoming the road to Progreso. Before turning back from the museum, walk a few blocks north; you'll pass numerous restaurants and several hotels. To get back to the city center, you have your choice of buses, taxis, or walking.

Time Out   If you're hungry, **Soberanis Montejo** (Paseo de Montejo 468, between Calles 39 and 37)—the uptown branch of a seafood restaurant chain—offers fish, conch, lobster, and shrimp at moderate prices in a more modern and attractive setting than the one downtown.

If you love Mexican crafts, you may want to trek several blocks **16** east of the plaza, along Calle 59, to the **Museo de Arte Popular,** which is housed in a fine old mansion. The ground floor, devoted to Yucatecan arts and crafts, displays weaving, straw baskets, filigree jewelry, carved wood, beautifully carved conch shells, exhibits on huipil manufacture, and the like. The second floor focuses on the popular arts of the rest of Mexico. *Calle 59, between Calles 50 and 48, no phone. Admission free. Open Tues.– Sat. 8–8.*

At the far south of the city, about nine blocks south of the square, stands the **Ermita de Santa Isabel** (circa 1748), part of a Jesuit hermitage also known as the Hermitage of the Good Trip. A resting place in colonial days for travelers heading to Campeche, the restored chapel is an enchanting spot to visit at sunset and perhaps a good destination for a ride in a calesa. Next door there's a little garden with a waterfall and footpaths bordered with bricks and colored stones. *Calles 66 and 77. Admission free.*

Before leaving Mérida, there are a couple of small museums that may be of interest to you, including the **Gottdiener Museum** (Calle 59 between Calles 60 and 58), which presents masterpieces by the sculptor Enrique Gottdiener; and the **Juan Gamboa Guzmán State Painting Museum** (Calle 59 between Calles 60 and 58), where 19th-century oil paintings, colonial wood carvings, and photographs are displayed.

You can leave the city of Mérida by several routes: east toward Chichén Itzá and Valladolid; south to Uxmal; north to Progreso and the north coast; or west to Celestún.

To Chichén Itzá and Valladolid

Numbers in the margin correspond to numbers on the State of Yucatán map.

Although it's possible to reach Chichén Itzá (120 kilometers/75 miles east of Mérida) along the shorter Route 180, it's far more scenic to follow Route 80 until it ends at Tekantó, then head south to Citilcúm, east to Dzitas, and south again to Pisté. These roads have no signs, but are the only paved roads going in these directions. Ask directions frequently. A new eight-lane toll highway (still unnumbered) has been constructed from Mérida to Valladolid, and work continues on the extension of this highway to Cancún (the section between Cancún and Chichén Itzá is now open). Access to the toll highway is off Highway 180, about 15 miles east of Mérida.

Chichén Itzá attracts a large number of visitors who come for the famous ruins. For those traveling by car, the trip can be enhanced by stopping at several villages on the way. Route 80 passes through **Tixkokob,** a Mayan community famous for its hammock weavers. By cutting south at Tekantó and east again at Citilcúm (the road has no number, and there are few road signs), you'll reach **Izamal,** nicknamed Ciudad Amarillo (Yellow City) for the painted earth-tone-yellow buildings. In the center of town stands an enormous 16th-century **Franciscan monastery** perched on—and built from—the remains of a pre-Columbian pyramid. One of the largest and oldest religious structures in Mexico, the church boasts a gigantic atrium and rows of 75 yellow arches. The pyramid, called Kinich Kakmó, is difficult to climb because of the crumbling steps, but once you're on top you'll have a wonderful view of the surrounding countryside, with its flat fields of maguey cactus and henequen broken only by occasional clumps of trees. On clear days it's even possible to spot Chichén Itzá.

Probably the best-known Mayan ruin, **Chichén Itzá,** the Maya-Toltec center, was the most important city in Yucatán from the 11th to the 13th century. The architectural mélange encapsulates Mexican history, showing foreign domination and the intermingling of cultures. Chichén was altered by each successive wave of inhabitants, and archaeologists are able to date the arrival of new inhabitants by the changes in the architecture; however, they have yet to explain the long gaps of time when the buildings seem to have been uninhabited. The site is believed to have been first settled in AD 432, abandoned for an unknown period of time, then rediscovered in 964 by the Maya-speaking Itzás from the Tabasco region, who gave the site its name; *Chichén Itzá* means "the mouth of the well of the Itzás." The Itzás also abandoned the site, and in 1185 it was rediscovered by the central-Mexican Toltecs, who abandoned it forever in 1224. Francisco de Montejo established a short-lived colony here in the course of his conquest of Yucatán in the mid-1500s. At the beginning of this century, U.S. Consul General Edward Thompson carried out some of the earliest excavations at the site, basing himself at a hacienda (now the Hacienda Chichén)

State of Yucatán

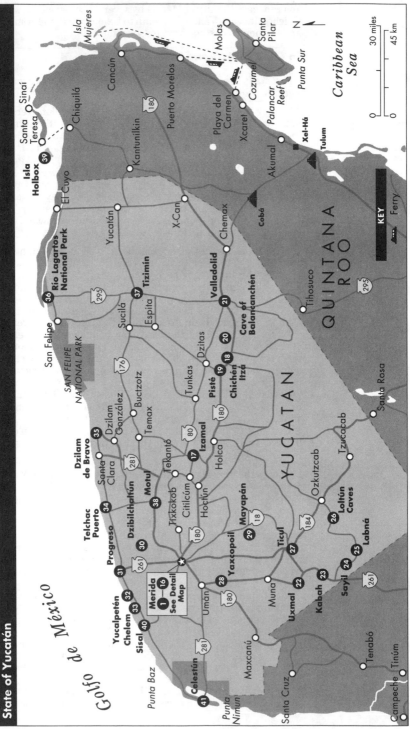

Golfo de México

Caribbean Sea

30 miles
45 km

QUINTANA ROO

YUCATÁN

SAN FELIPE NATIONAL PARK

Río Lagartos National Park

KEY
Ferry

Isla Mujeres
Santa Pilar
Molas
Cozumel
Punta Sur
Palancar Reef
Xcaret
Playa del Carmen
Akumal
Cobá
Xel-Há
Tulum
Puerto Morelos
Cancún
Chiquilá
Kantunilkin
X-Can
Chemax
Valladolid
Cave of Balancanchén
Tihosuco
Santa Rosa

Sinaí
Santa Teresa
El Cuyo
Yucatán
Isla Holbox
San Felipe
Tizimín
Sucilá
Espita
Dzitas
Tunkas
Pisté
Chichén Itzá
Holca
Izamal
Temax
Buctzotz
Dzilam González
Dzilam de Bravo
Santa Clara
Telchac Puerto
Progreso
Yucalpetén
Chelem
Sisal
Celestún
Punta Baz
Punta Nimun
Maxcanú
Umán
Muna
Santa Cruz
Tenabó
Tinúm
Campeche
Uxmal
Kabah
Sayil
Labná
Loltún Caves
Ozkutzcab
Tzucacab
Ticul
Mayapán
Yaxcopoil
Tixkokob
Citilcúm
Hoctún
Tekantó
Motul
Dzibilchaltún
Santa Teresa

Merida
1—16
See Detail Map

Tihosuco

36
37
21
20
18
19
17
35
34
30
31
32
33
40
41
28
29
22
23
24
25
26
27
38
39

18

N

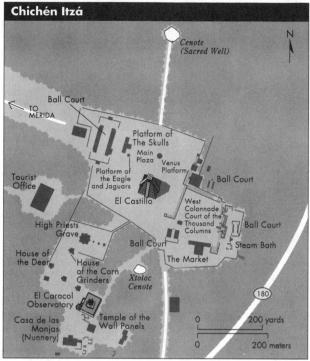

Chichén Itzá

Cenote (Sacred Well)

N

Ball Court

TO MERIDA

Platform of The Skulls

Main Plaza

Venus Platform

Tourist Office

Platform of the Eagle and Jaguars

El Castillo

Ball Court

West Colonnade

Court of the Thousand Columns

Ball Court

High Priests Grave

Ball Court

Steam Bath

House of the Deer

House of the Corn Grinders

Xtoloc Cenote

The Market

180

El Caracol Observatory

Casa de las Monjas (Nunnery)

Temple of the Wall Panels

| 0 | 200 yards |

| 0 | 200 meters |

and carting most of the treasure away to the Peabody Museum at Harvard University.

The majesty and enormity of this site are unforgettable. An architectural hybrid, it incarnates much of the fascinating and bloody history of the Maya, from the steep temple stairways down which sacrificial victims were hurled, to the relentlessly ornate beauty of the smaller structures. Its audacity and vitality are almost palpable. Chichén Itzá encompasses approximately 6 square kilometers (2 square miles), though only 20 to 30 buildings of the several hundred at the site have been fully explored. These buildings include the often-photographed Mayan pyramid, a sprawling colonnade evoking imperial Rome, the largest ball-playing court in Mesoamerica, a sacrificial well once filled with precious offerings, and one of the only round buildings in the Mayan lands. Stone sculptures of the feathered serpent god, reclining *Chac Mools* (rain gods, associated with human sacrifice), steam baths for ritual purification, ruined murals, astronomical symbols, and broad *sacbeob* (white roads usually used for ceremonial purposes or as trade arteries) leading to other ancient centers endow the site with nearly all the celebrated visual elements of the Mayan civilization.

Chichén Itzá is divided into two parts—Old and New—though architectural motifs from the classical period are found in both sections. A more convenient distinction is topographical, since there are two major complexes of buildings separated by a dirt path. The martial, imperial architecture of the Toltecs and the more cerebral architectural genius and astronomical expertise of the Maya are married in the 98-foot-tall pyramid called **El Castillo** (The Castle), which dominates the site and rises above all the other buildings.

Atop the castle is a temple dedicated to Kukulcán (known as Quetzalcóatl in central Mexico), the legendary leader-turned-deity who was incarnated by the plumed serpent. According to ancient lore, Kukulcán led the Toltecs on their migration to Yucatán, then disappeared to the east, promising to return one day; the Spaniards—whom the Toltecs mistook for gods—transformed that prophecy into a nightmarish reality. Four stairways, each facing a different cardinal point, provided access to the temple; only one is used today. Those who fear heights can hold on to a rusty chain running down the center. Each access way consists of 91 very steep and narrow steps, which, when one adds the temple platform itself, makes a total of 365 (one for each day of the Mayas' extraordinarily accurate solar calendar). Fifty-two panels on the sides stand for the weeks of the secular (as opposed to the religious) calendar, while the 18 terraces symbolize the months of the year. An open-jawed plumed serpent rests on the balustrade of each stairway, and serpents reappear at the top of the temple as sculptured columns.

At the spring and fall equinoxes (March 21 and September 21), the afternoon light and shadow strike one of these balustrades in such a way as to form a shadow representation of Kukulcán undulating out of his temple and down the pyramid to bless the fertile earth. The sound-and-light show in the evening is not as well done as the one at Uxmal, but the engineering is astounding and the colored lights that enhance the wall carvings of El Castillo provide after-dark entertainment. The accompanying narration is drawn from the works of Bishop de Landa—one of the first Spaniards to write about the Mayan religion and life—and from the few surviving Mayan texts, including the Books of Chilam Balam and Popul Vuh. Thousands of people travel to Chichén Itzá for the equinoxes, particularly in the spring when there is little likelihood of rain. Hotel reservations for the event should be made well in advance; a year ahead is not unreasonable (*see* Lodging, *below*). *Sound-and-light show in Spanish, $1, 7 PM; in English, $2, 9 PM.*

In 1937, archaeologists discovered a more ancient temple inside the Castillo. A humid, slippery stairway leads upward to an altar that once held two statues: a Chac Mool and a bejeweled red tiger. The tiger wears a mosaic disc of jade and turquoise and is now housed in the Anthropology Museum in Mexico City. The inner temple is open to the public for only a few hours in the morning and again in the afternoon. Claustrophobes should think twice before entering: The stairs are narrow, dark, and winding, and there is often a line of tourists going both ways, making the trip somewhat frightening.

The temple rests on a massive trapezoidal square, on the west side of which is Chichén Itzá's largest **ball court,** one of seven on the site. Its two parallel walls are each 272 feet long, with two stone rings on each side, and 99 feet apart. The game was something like soccer (no hands were used), but it had religious as well as recreational significance. Bas-relief carvings at the court depict a player being decapitated, the blood spurting from his severed neck fertilizing the earth. Acoustics are so good that someone standing at one end of the court can hear the whispers of another person clearly at the other end. Sadly, the western wall of the court has been blackened by acid rain blown eastward from the oil fields on the Gulf of Mexico.

Between the ball court and El Castillo stands a **Tzompantli,** or stone platform, carved with rows of human skulls. In ancient times it was actually covered with stakes on which the heads of enemies were impaled. This Aztec motif was otherwise unknown in the Mayan region, though a similar platform was found at Tenochtitlán, the Aztec capital (modern-day Mexico City). The influence of the Toltecs, who preceded the Aztecs in the Valley of Mexico, is once again apparent.

The predilection for sacrifice was once believed to have come from the Toltecs, but recent research suggests that the pre-Toltec Maya had already been indulging in their own forms of the ritual. The **Sacred Well,** a cenote 65 yards in diameter that sits half a mile north of El Castillo at the end of a 900-foot-long *sacbe* (a white stone causeway usually used for ceremonial purposes or as a trade artery), was used only for sacrifices; another cenote at the site supplied drinking water. Skeletons of men, women, and children were found in the first well; they were thrown in to placate the rain gods and water spirits. The slippery walls were impossible to scale, and most of the victims could not swim well enough to survive until noon, when those who did hang on were fished out to recount what they had learned. (Hunac Ceel, the notorious ruler of Mayapán in the 1450s, hurled himself into its depths to prove his divine ascendancy, and survived.) Thousands of gold, jade, and other artifacts, most of them not of local provenance, have been recovered from the brackish depths of the cenote. Long on display at Harvard's Peabody Museum, many of the finds have now been returned to the Mexican government. Trees and shrubs have washed into the well over the centuries, and their remains have prevented divers from getting to the bottom; because the cenote is fed by a network of underground rivers, it cannot be drained. More treasure undoubtedly remains. (The well's excavation launched the field of underwater archaeology, later honed by Jacques Cousteau.)

Returning to the causeway, on your left is the **Group of the Thousand Columns** with the famous **Temple of the Warriors,** a masterful example of the Toltec influence at Chichén Itzá. This temple so resembles Pyramid B at Tula—the Toltecs' homeland, north of Mexico City—that scholars believe the architectural plans must have been carried 1,280 kilometers (800 miles) overland. Indeed, they can cite no other case in the pre-Columbian world of identical temples built by two such distant tribes. Nonetheless, until more work is done at Chichén Itzá, controversy will continue as to whether the influence was exercised from Tula to Chichén Itzá or in the opposite direction. Masonry walls carved with feathered serpents and frescoes of vultures and jaguars consuming human hearts are among the unmistakably Toltec details. Using columns and wood beams instead of the Mayan arches and walls to divide space enabled the Toltec–Mayan architects to expand the interior and exterior spaces dramatically. Another anomaly is the murals of everyday village life and scenes of war: Such realism was rare in pre-Columbian art. The first artistic representation of the defeat of the Maya can be found on the interior murals of the adjacent **Temple of the Jaguar.**

To get to the less visited cluster of structures at Chichén Itzá—often confused with Old Chichén Itzá—take the main road south from the Temple of the Jaguar past El Castillo and turn right onto a small path opposite the ball court on your left. You'll pass several thatched huts (as well as young children and turkeys) en route. The ancient edifices here, overgrown with flowering vines, are as intriguing as the more visited ones, but the astronomical observatory dubbed **El Caracol** is the most impressive. The name, meaning "snail," refers to the spiral staircase at the building's core. Built in several stages, El Caracol is possibly the sole round building constructed by the Maya. Although definitely used for observing the heavens (judging by the tiny windows oriented toward the four cardinal points, and the alignment with the planet Venus), it also appears to have served a religious function, since the related Toltec cults of Kukulcán and the god of wind often involved circular temples.

After leaving El Caracol, continue south several hundred yards to the beautiful **Casa de las Monjas** (Nunnery) and its annex, which have long panels carved with flowers and animals, latticework, hieroglyph-covered lintels, and Chac masks (as does the nunnery at Uxmal). It was the Spaniards who gave the structure this sobriquet; no one knows how the Maya used it.

At Old Chichén Itzá, south of the remains of Thompson's hacienda, "pure Mayan" style—a combination of Puuc and Chenes styles, with playful latticework, Chac masks, and gargoyle-like serpents on the cornices—dominates. (This style also crops up at Uxmal, Kabah, Labná, and Sayil, among other sites.) Highlights include the Date Group (so named because of the complete series of hieroglyphic date inscriptions), the House of the Phalli, and the Temple of the Three Lintels. Mayan guides will lead you down the path by an old narrow-gauge railroad track to even more ruins, barely unearthed, if you ask. A fairly good restaurant and great ice-cream stand are located in the entrance building, and there are refreshment stands by the cenote and on the pathway near El Caracol. *Admission to site and museum: $6, free on Sunday and holidays. Parking: $1. Use of video camera $8. Open daily 8–5.*

⑲ The town of **Pisté,** about 1 kilometer (⅗ mile) west of the ruins on Route 180, serves mainly as a base camp for travelers to Chichén Itzá. Hotels, campgrounds, restaurants, and handicrafts shops tend to be cheaper here than south of the ruins. At the west end of town are a Pemex station and a bank.

Time Out   On the outskirts of Pisté, a short walk from the ruins, **Pueblo Maya,** a psuedo Maya village, provides a shopping and dining center for tour groups. The restaurant serves a bountiful buffet at lunch ($10).

From Chichén Itzá, drive east along Route 180 for about 4 kilometers (2½ miles), then turn left at the first dirt road you come **⑳** to and continue for about ½ kilometer (³⁄₁₀ mile) to the **Cave of Balancanchén.** This shrine, whose Mayan name translates as "hidden throne," remained virtually undisturbed from the time of the Conquest until its discovery in 1959. Within the shrine is the largest collection of artifacts yet found in Yucatán—mostly vases, jars, and incense burners once filled with offerings. You'll walk past tiers of stalactites and stalagmites forming the image of sacred ceiba trees until you come to an underground lake. The lake is filled with blindfish (small fish with functionless eyes), and an altar to the rain god rises above it. In order to explore the shrine you must take one of the guided tours, which depart almost hourly, but you must be in fairly good shape, because some crawling is required; claustrophobes should skip it, and those who go should wear comfortable shoes. Also offered at the site is a sound-and-light show that fancifully recounts Mayan history. *Caves can also be reached by bus or taxi from Chichén Itzá. Admission to caves, including tour: $6, free on Sunday; show: $5. Open daily 9–4; tours Mon.–Sat. 9–4, Sun. 8–11. Sound-and-light show in English, 11 AM, 1 and 3 PM; in Spanish, 9 and 10 AM, noon, 2 and 4 PM.*

Following Route 180 east for another 40 kilometers (25 miles) will take you to the second-largest city in the State of Yucatán, **②** **Valladolid.** This picturesque, pleasant, and provincial town (population 50,000) is enjoying growing popularity among travelers en route to or from Río Lagartos (*see below*) who are harried by more touristy towns. Montejo founded Valladolid in 1543 on the site of the Mayan town of Zací. The city suffered during the Caste War, when it was besieged by the rebellious Maya (who killed all the Europeans they could find), and again during the Mexican Revolution.

Today, however, placidity reigns in this agricultural market town. The center is mostly colonial, although it has many 19th-century structures. The main sights are the **colonial churches,** principally the large **cathedral** on the central square and the 16th-century **San Bernardino church and convent of Sisal,** three blocks southwest. The latter were pillaged during the insurrection.

A briny, muddy **cenote** in the center of town draws only the most resolute swimmers; instead, visit the adjacent **ethnographic museum** or the **Cenote Dzitnup** outside town. Cenote Dzitnup is dark and slightly forbidding, but you can swim here. Valladolid is renowned for its cuisine, particularly its sausages. Try one of the restaurants within a block of the square, which also has two very good and reasonably priced hotels. You can also find good buys on sandals, baskets, and the local liqueur, Xtabentún.

To Uxmal and the Puuc Route

If you opt for the southward journey from Mérida, follow Route 180 south and turn onto Route 261 at Umán; 80 kilometers (50 **②** miles) farther south you'll reach **Uxmal.** If Chichén Itzá is the most impressive Mayan ruin in Yucatán, Uxmal is arguably the most beautiful. Where the former has a Toltec grandeur, the latter seems more understated and elegant—pure Maya. The architecture reflects the late classical renaissance of the 7th–9th centuries and is contemporary with that of Palenque and Tikal, among other great Mayan metropolises of the southern highlands. Although the name translates as "thrice built," the site was actually rebuilt, abandoned, and reoccupied in several stages, for reasons still unknown. Toltec (Itzá) invaders briefly

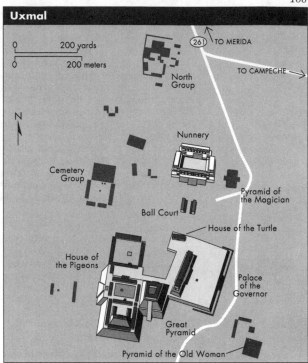

occupied Uxmal in the 10th century; the site reemerged as a
Mayan ceremonial center in the postclassical era and was deserted for the last time some 90 years before the Conquest.
When John Lloyd Stephens came upon Uxmal in 1840, it was
owned by a descendant of the same Montejo family that had
conquered Yucatán three centuries earlier.

In any case, the site is considered the finest and largest example of Puuc architecture, which embraces such details as ornate
stone mosaics and friezes on the upper walls, intricate cornices
with hooked noses, rows of columns, and soaring vaulted
arches. Lines are clean and uncluttered, with the horizontal—
especially the parallelogram—preferred to the vertical. Many
of the flat, low, elongated buildings were built on artificial platforms and laid out in quadrangles. The cult of Chac, the ele-
phant-snouted rain god whose image appears throughout
Yucatán, became obsessive in this parched region. But the area
lacks cenotes; though the Maya dug cisterns, called *chultunes*,
for collecting rainwater, drought may be the reason that Uxmal
was so often occupied and then abandoned. Phallic figures—
rare in Mayan art—are abundant, too.

While most of Uxmal remains unrestored, three buildings in
particular merit attention. The most prominent, the **Pyramid
of the Magician,** is, at 92 feet high, the tallest structure at the
site. Unlike most Mayan pyramids, which are stepped and angular, it has a strangely elliptical design. Built five times, each
time over the previous structure, the pyramid has a stairway
on its western side that leads through a monster-shaped doorway to two temples at the summit. The monster or mask motif

is repeated on one side of the stairs. You get a magnificent panoramic view of Uxmal and the hills by climbing up to the top. According to legend, the pyramid derived its name from the magical dwarf who built it overnight; it is especially lovely at night, when its pale beige slope glows in the moonlight.

West of the pyramid lies the **Nunnery,** or Quadrangle of the Nuns. You may enter the four buildings; each comprises a series of low, gracefully repetitive chambers that look onto a central patio. The building on the southern side is broken by a tall corbeled arch that is formed by placing ceiling stones increasingly close to and on top of one another until they meet at a central supporting capstone. Elaborate decoration—in the form of stone latticework, masks, geometric patterns, representations of the classic Mayan thatched hut (*na*), coiling snakes, and phallic figures—blankets the upper facades, in contrast with the smooth, sheer blocks that face the lower walls.

Continue walking south; you'll pass the ball court before reaching the **Palace of the Governor,** which archaeologist Victor von Hagen considered the most magnificent building ever erected in the Americas. Interestingly, the palace faces east while the rest of Uxmal faces west. Archaeologists believe this is because the palace was used to sight the planet Venus. Covering five acres and rising over an immense acropolis, the palace lies at the heart of what must have been Uxmal's administrative center. Its 320-foot length is divided by three corbeled arches, which create narrow passageways or sanctuaries. Decorating the facade are intricate friezes (along the uppermost section), geometrically patterned carvings overlaid with plumed serpents, stylized Chac masks, and human faces. These mosaics required more than 20,000 individually cut stones.

First excavated in 1929 by the Danish explorer Frans Blom, the site served in 1841 as home to John Lloyd Stephens, who wrote of it: "The whole wears an air of architectural symmetry and grandeur. If it stood at this day on its grand artificial terrace in Hyde Park or the Garden of the Tuileries, it would form a new order . . . not unworthy to stand side by side with the remains of Egyptian, Grecian, and Roman art." Today a sound-and-light show recounts Mayan legends, including the kidnapping of an Uxmal princess by a king of Chichén Itzá, and focuses on the people's dependence on rain. The artificial light brings out details of carvings and mosaics that are easy to miss when the sun is shining—for example, the stone replicas of *nas,* which bear a remarkable resemblance to contemporary huts, on one facade of the nunnery. The show is performed nightly in Spanish and English and is one of the better such productions. *Admission to site and museum: $6, free on Sunday and holidays. Parking: $1. Use of video camera $8. Open daily 8–5. Sound-and-light show in Spanish, $2, 7 PM; in English, $2.50, 9 PM.*

Four smaller Puuc sites near Uxmal are also worth visiting, and en route you pass through beautiful hilly jungles. **Kabah,** 23 kilometers (14 miles) south of Uxmal on Route 261, lies almost entirely in ruins; its mounded landscape has a soft, almost Grecian beauty. Linked to Uxmal by a *sacbe,* at the end of which looms a great independent arch, is the 151-foot-long **Palace of the Masks,** so called because of the huge number of Chac masks with their hooked noses. Another 270 can be seen at the Codz-Poop temple, located on the east side of the road.

Five kilometers (3 miles) to the south you'll see the turnoff to **(24) Sayil,** the oldest site of the group, renowned primarily for its majestic three-story **palace** with 100 rooms. The structure recalls Palenque in its use of multiple planes, its columned porticos and sober cornices, and in the play of its long, solid horizontal masses, heightened by colonnades. *Admission: $4, free on Sunday and holidays. Open daily 8–5.*

Another 9 kilometers (6 miles) beyond Sayil, on Route 261, **(25)** rests the monumental arch at **Labná.** While most Mayan arches linked inner passageways at door height, this one is more characteristic of the great imperial arches of classical antiquity except for the corbels. Another factor that makes it atypical of the Mayan style is that this arch—adorned with lavish friezes, latticework, stepped frets, and, of course, the snouty Chac masks—dominates the entire facade. One of the curiosities of Mayan civilization is that the Maya never discovered the true, or curved, arch. *Admission: $4, free on Sunday. Open daily 8–5.*

Continue along the road from Labná for another 18 kilometers **(26)** (11 miles) to the **Loltún Caves,** a 500-meter (³⁄₁₀-mile) series of caverns containing Mayan and neolithic remains and stalactites and stalagmites. *Admission: $4. Open Tues.–Sun. 9–5; guided tours at 9:30, 11, 12:30, 2, and 3.*

From Loltún, drive 10 kilometers (6 miles) northeast to **Oxkutzcab,** where, to the left, you can pick up Route 184. An **(27)** additional 17 kilometers (10½ miles) will bring you into **Ticul,** where most of the Yucatecan pottery is produced, along with huipiles and shoes. Many descendants of the Xiu dynasty, which ruled Uxmal before the Conquest, still live here. One of the larger towns in Yucatán, Ticul boasts a handsome 17th-century church.

Time Out If you save your appetite for **Los Almendros Restaurant,** in Ticul, you'll be rewarded by what is considered the best regional restaurant in Yucatán.

From this point you can either head back to Mérida or continue on to Mayapán, about 49 kilometers (30 miles) to the east (*see below*).

If you wish to get back to Mérida, turn right off Route 184 at Muna onto Route 261 and follow Route 261 back to Route 180. Along Route 261, about 62 kilometers (38 miles) north of **(28)** Uxmal, you may want to stop at **Yaxcopoil,** a restored 17th-century hacienda that offers a nice change of pace from the ruins. The building, with its distinctive Moorish double arch out front, has been used as a film set and is the best-known henequen plantation in the region. Visit the museum inside, which displays archaeological pieces and machinery used in the processing of henequen. *Km 33, Rte. 261. Admission free. Open Mon.–Sat. 8–sunset, Sun. 9–1.*

Those who are really enamored of Yucatán and the ancient **(29)** Maya can detour at Ticul on Route 18 to the ruined city of **Mayapán,** the last of the great city-states on the peninsula. There have been few excavations here, however, so archaeological evidence of past glory is limited to a few fallen statues of Kukulcán, and today the site is mainly of historical interest. *Just before Telchaquillo, Mayapán is off the road to your left; follow signs.*

To Progreso and the North Coast

If you have decided to take the easterly course toward Progreso and the north coast, follow the Paseo de Montejo north out of Mérida, where it becomes Route 261. After 14 kilometers (9 miles) you'll come to the ruins of **Dzibilchaltún** ("the place where there is writing on flat stones"), which is thought to have been the capital of the Mayan states at one time. The site occupies more than 65 square kilometers (25 square miles) of land cluttered with thousands of mounds, low platforms, piles of rubble, plazas, and stelae. It was established around 2000 BC and is now surrounded by a national preserve. Inhabited until shortly before the Conquest, it appears to be the oldest continuously occupied Mayan ceremonial center. The national and state governments have targeted the site for further restoration, and in 1992 plans for the creation of an outdoor museum called Pueblo Maya were announced.

For now, Dzibilchaltún's significance lies in the stucco sculpture and ceramics, from all periods of Mayan civilization, that have been unearthed here. The **Temple of the Seven Dolls** (circa AD 500), the only structure excavated on the site to date, is the only Mayan temple known to have windows. Low and trapezoidal, the temple exemplifies the late preclassical style, which predates such Puuc sites as Uxmal. The remains of stucco masks adorn each side, and there are vestiges of sculptures of coiled serpents. The stone cube atop the temple and the open chapel built by the Spaniards for the Indians are additional peculiarities. Twelve sacbeob lead to various groups of structures. The **Xlacah cenote**—at 144 feet one of the deepest in Yucatán—apparently supplied ceremonial as well as drinking water. Bones and ceremonial objects unearthed by divers from the National Geographic Society indicate that this cenote was used for sacrifices.

A small **museum** at the entrance to the site displays the seven vulcanized-rubber deformed male "dolls"—thought to be used against sickness—that were found deep inside the temple. The dolls, dating to the 13th and 14th centuries, are unusual because rubber is virtually unknown in the region, though the Lacandón Indians in Chiapas (descendants of the ancient Maya) make similar ones. The collection also includes thousands of figurines, bones, jewelry, and potsherds found in the cenote. There is a small refreshment stand. *Admission: $4, free on Sunday and holidays. Open daily 8–8.*

About 16 kilometers (10 miles) farther north on Route 261 is **Progreso,** the waterfront town closest to Mérida. Progreso, which is not particularly historical, is noisy with traffic and not at all picturesque. On weekdays during most of the year the town is deserted, but when school is out (Easter week, July, and August) and on summer weekends it becomes a popular vacation destination for families from Mérida. Progreso has fine sand and shallow waters that extend quite far out, making for nice walks, although its beaches are inferior to those of Quintana Roo. Because it is so close to Mérida and because its interest is limited, there is really no reason to spend the night here, but a couple of attractions in the small town may interest you.

The approach requires crossing some very foul-smelling swamps, and these remind you of Progreso's main raison d'être: It has been the chief port of entry for the peninsula since its founding in 1872, when the shallow port at Sisal, to the southwest, proved inadequate for handling the large ships that were carrying henequen cargo. In 1989 the 2-kilometer (1-mile) long pier was extended 7 kilometers (4 miles) out to sea to accommodate the hoped-for cruise-ship business and to siphon some of the lucrative tourist trade from Cozumel, but at the moment it looks as though all the millions invested have produced a white elephant because most cruise ships require deeper waters.

Progreso's attractions include its **malecón** (main square), Calle 19, which is lined with seafood restaurants. Fishermen sell their catch on the beach east of the city between 7 and 8 AM, so it's a good place to come for fresh fish. Some 120 kilometers (75 miles) offshore are the **Alacranes Reef,** where divers can explore sunken ships, and **Pérez Island,** which supports a sizeable population of sea turtles and seabirds. Sportfishing, for such catch as grouper, red snapper, dogfish, sea bass, and pompano, is popular at the **marina** in nearby Yucalpetén (*see below*).

For more information on the town and on guides who provide service to the reef, visit the **tourist office,** where representatives are friendly and helpful. *Calle 80, No. 176, at Calle 37, tel. 993/50104. Open Mon.–Sat. 9–1 and 3–7.*

③② Three kilometers (2 miles) west of Progreso, at the end of the narrow, marshy promontory, is **Yucalpetén.** Along the approach you'll pass a number of dead palm trees that were obliterated by the yellowing palm disease that has swept the peninsula in recent years. The harbor here dates only from 1968, when it was built to provide shelter for small fishing boats during the hurricane season. Little goes on here other than some activity at the yacht marina and the fancy Fiesta Inn, though more hotels are planned for the future. Just beyond Yucalpetén **③③** is the even tinier village of **Chelem,** which has a few beachfront bungalow hotels.

③④ A short drive (43 kilometers/27 miles) to the east of Progreso along the same road and past time-shares in progress, palm groves, henequen fields, and tiny villages, sits **Telchac Puerto,** now known as Nuevo Yucatán—the state government's latest venture in tourism development. One reason for this location is its proximity to **Laguna Rosada,** where the flamingos come to nest; another is its lovely, empty (at least that's how they were at this writing) beaches. More and more foreigners are getting wind of the inexpensive rental homes in the nearby fishing village of **Chicxulub Puerto,** with its inviting beach and low winter rates.

③⑤ If you continue east on the coastal road, eventually you'll get to **Dzilam de Bravo,** where a better road—Route 281—heads back toward Mérida and points south. The pirate Jean Laffite supposedly lies buried just outside this village; at least there's a grave so marked, and two locals claim to be his descendants. Stop here for a swim in the gentle waters.

If you're a flamingo fan (flamingo season runs from April to May), take Route 281 13 kilometers (8 miles) to Dzilam González, then follow the unpaved road to Buctzotz, where you'll **36** pick up Route 176 to Route 295 to Río Lagartos and **Río Lagartos National Park.** Actually a long estuary, not a river, the park was built with ecotourism in mind, though the alligators for which it and the village were named have long since been hunted into extinction. In addition to flamingos, birders can spot egrets, herons, ibis, cormorants, pelicans, and even peregrine falcons flying over these murky waters; fishing is good, too, and hawksbill and green turtles lay their eggs on the beach at night. **Hotel Nefertiti**—the only hotel in town—offers boat tours, or you can hire a boat from the docks near the hotel.

If you wish to extend this tour rather than return to Mérida, continue 104 kilometers (64 miles) south of Río Lagartos on Route 295 to Valladolid and then westward to Chichén Itzá (*see above*).

To return to Mérida, you'll have to backtrack, but you may want to make a brief stop in two villages to break up the monotony **37** of the drive. **Tizimín,** renowned as the seat of an indigenous messianic movement during the 1840s Caste War, is situated at the junction of Highways 176 and 295. The town boasts a 17th-century church dedicated to the Three Kings, who are honored here during a festival that is held December 15–January 15.

38 Farther along Route 176 is **Motul,** for which *huevos motuleños* are named. This is the birthplace of the Indian rebel leader Felipe Carrillo Puerto, whose former house is now a museum containing displays on the life and times of the Socialist governor of Yucatán. *Open daily 8–noon and 4–6.*

39 Even farther afield is **Isla Holbox,** a tiny island (25 kilometers/16 miles long) at the eastern end of the Río Lagartos estuary and just across the Quintana Roo state line. A fishing fan's heaven because of the pompano, bass, barracuda, and shark thronging its waters, the island also pleases seekers of tranquillity who don't mind rudimentary accommodations (two hotels, plus rooms and hammocks for rent) and simple palapa restaurants. Seabirds populate the air, the long sandy beach is strewn with seashells, and the swimming is good on the gulf side. To get there, take Route 176 to Kantunilkin, then head north on the unnumbered road for 44 kilometers (27 miles) to Chiquilá. Continue by ferry (schedules fluctuate but it runs twice daily; one-hour crossing) to the island. Isla Holbox can also be reached from Valladolid.

Sisal and Celestún

Traveling westward from Mérida, take an hour-long drive on **40** Route 25 to the town of **Sisal,** which gave its name to the henequen that was shipped from the port in great quantity during the mid-19th century. With the rise of Progreso, Sisal dwindled into little more than a fisherman's wharf. Today the attractions are few: a **colonial customs house** and the private 1906 **lighthouse.** Sisal livens up a bit in July and August when Méridanos come to swim and dine. **Hotel Felicidades,** a few minutes' walk up the beach east of the pier, caters to tourists during the vacation months and can be fun when a crowd arrives, although it is a bit dingy. **Club de Patos,** farther up the beach, is open only during the peak summer season. **Madagascar Reef,** one of three offshore reefs, offers excellent diving.

④ To reach the fishing town of **Celestún,** take Route 180 southwest to Umán, then Route 281 west for 92 kilometers (57 miles). The town sits at the end of a spit of land separating the Celestún estuary from the gulf on the western side of Yucatán. It is the only point of entry to the **Parque Natural del Flamenco Mexicano,** a 147,500-acre wildlife reserve with one of the largest colonies of flamingos in North America. From September through April clouds of pink wings soar over the pale blue backdrop of the estuary, which also features rocks, islets, cenotes, and mangroves, and make for stunning scenery; cormorants, ducks, and herons also fly overhead. There is good fishing in both the river and the gulf; and you can see deer and armadillo roaming the surrounding land.

Popular with Mexican vacationers, the park's sandy beach is pleasant during the day but tends to get windy in the afternoon, with choppy water and blowing sand. To see the birds, hire a fishing boat at the dock outside town. And take advantage of one of the several seafood restaurants on the beach strip.

Mérida for Free

Nearly every day of the week the Instituto de Cultura de Yucatán sponsors free performances of regional music and dance in the city parks, including the following:

Vaquerías, a traditional dance performed at regional haciendas after the cattle are branded. *In front of the Municipal Palace, on Calle 62 between Calles 61 and 63. Mon. 9 PM.*

Musical Memories from North, Central, and South America. *Parque Santiago, Calles 59 and 72. Tues. 9 PM.*

Yucatecan folkloric ballet, with guitar trios and poetry. *Casa Cultural Mayab on Calle 63 between Calles 64 and 66. Wed. 9 PM.*

Yucatán Serenade, including music, song, poetry, and costumes at the Palacio de Gobierno. *Parque Santa Lucía, Calle 60 at Calle 55. Thurs. 9 PM.*

University folkloric ballet. *Patio of the University of Yucatán's main building, Calles 60 and 57. Fri. 9 PM.*

Mérida en Domingo, comprising five separate special events: jazz, semiclassical, and folkloric music at 11 AM, in front of the Municipal Palace; Yucatecan music by the police orchestra, also at 11 AM, in Parque Santa Lucía (Calles 60 and 55); a traditional *mestizo* wedding celebration, performed by the city's folkloric ballet and the police orchestra at 1 PM in front of the Municipal Palace on the main square; marimba concerts on Sunday at 11:30 AM in Parque Hidalgo (Calles 60 and 59); and music and entertainment for children, at 10 AM in Parque de la Madre (Calle 60 between Calles 59 and 57).

What to See and Do with Children

El Centenario Zoological Park, Mérida's great children's attraction, is a large, somewhat tacky amusement complex consisting of playgrounds, rides (including ponies and a small train), a roller skating rink, snack bars, and cages with more than 300 marvelous native monkeys, birds, reptiles, and other animals, as well as pleasant wooded paths, a small lake where you can hire rowboats, and picnic areas. Come on Sunday if you enjoy the spectacle of people enjoying themselves. The French Renaissance–style arch (1921) commemorates the 100th anniversary of Mexican independence. *Av. Itzaes between Calles 59 and 65 (entrances on Calles 59 and 65). Admission free. Open daily 9–6.*

Parque Natural del Flamenco Mexicano (*see* Celestún in Exploring, *above*).

Museum of Anthropology and History (*see* Mérida in Exploring, *above*).

Museum de Arte Popular (*see* Mérida in Exploring, *above*).

Shopping

Throughout the Exploring section we noted towns known for specific crafts, but for the most part Mérida is the best place in Yucatán to buy local handicrafts at reasonable prices. The main products include *hamacas* (hammocks), *guayaberas* (short, loose shirts), huaraches, huipiles, *ternos* (hand-embroidered dresses), baskets, *jipis* or Panama hats, leather goods, gold and silver filigree jewelry, masks, painted gourds, vanilla, and piñatas. A word about hammocks, one of the most popular craft items sold here: They are available in cotton, nylon, and silk as well as in the very rough and scratchy henequen fiber. Silk, which is very expensive, is unquestionably the best choice. Double-threaded hammocks are sturdier and stretch less than single-threaded ones, a difference that can be identified by studying the loop handles. Hammocks come in different sizes: *sencilla*, for one person; *doble*, very comfortable for one but crowded for two; *matrimonial*, which will decently accommodate two; and *familiares* or *matrimoniales especiales*, which can theoretically sleep an entire family. Unless you're an expert, avoid the hammocks sold by street vendors and head for one of the specialty shops (*see* Specialty Stores: Crafts, *below*).

Shopping Districts/Streets/Markets/Malls

On the second floor of the **central municipal market** (between Calles 65 and 56 and Calles 54 and 59) you'll find crafts, food, flowers, and live birds, among other items.

On Sunday in Mérida, you will find an array of wares at three bazaars: the **Handicraft Bazaar,** in front of the Municipal Palace across from the main square, starting at 9; the **Popular Art Bazaar,** a flea market in Parque Santa Lucía, at the corner of Calles 60 and 55, also at 9; and the **Book Bazaar,** in the Callejón del Congreso, Calle 60, starting at 10.

Lining the streets north of the main square, especially **Calle 60,** are crafts and jewelry stores.

Mérida now has several shopping malls; the largest and newest is **Plaza Fiesta** (Calles 21 and 6), on the northeast edge of the city near the Jardines de Mérida, with about 75 shops.

Specialty Stores **El Alcatraz** (Calle 58 between Calles 47 and 49, half a block
Crafts from Parque Santa Ana) specializes in Oaxacan crafts. The best
places for hammocks are **La Poblana** (Calle 65, No. 492) and **El
Aguacate** (Calle 58, No. 492); for guayaberas, **Camisería Canul**
(Calle 59 No. 496); and for jipis, **La Casa de los Jipis** (Calle 56,
No. 526). Handicrafts are also on sale at the handicrafts mar-
ket, **Bazar García Rejón** (corner of Calles 65 and 62); and **Casa
Cultural Mayab** (Calle 63 between Calles 64 and 66), where folk
art from throughout Mexico is displayed. **Mayakat** (Paseo de
Montejo 498, tel. 99/236385) specializes in handpainted tiles.

Galleries The **Teatro Daniel Ayala** (Calle 60 between Calles 59 and 61)
features contemporary paintings and photography and is open
weekdays 9–2 and 5–9, weekends 9–2. Local painters and sculp-
tors also show their work at **Galería de Arte Art'Ho** (Calle 60,
No. 477-A, between Calles 53 and 55). **Galería Manolo Rivero**
(Calle 60 at Calle 51, tel. 99/232463) features exotic, and occasionally erotic, paintings and sculptures by avant-garde artists. **Galería Teyer** (Calle 60, No. 469, between Calles 55 and 53,
tel. 99/233007) features exquisite wooden carvings of Mayan
gods and designs.

Jewelry Probably the largest and finest selection of crafts—particularly silver jewelry—is at **Sonrisa del Sol** (Calle 62, No. 500
Altos, between Calles 61 and 59, almost on the main square, tel.
99/281255). Good selections of earrings and onyx beads can be
found at **El Paso** (Calle 59, No. 501). **Las Palomas** (Calle 60,
between Calles 53 and 55) has case after case of silver jewelry,
plus a full selection of tacky and tasteful souvenirs.

Sports and Fitness

Participant Sports

Fishing Fishing has become an increasingly popular pastime as the
passion for hunting declines because of the new concern for
preservation. Those interested in sportfishing for such catch
as grouper, red snapper, and sea bass, among others, will be
sated in **Yucalpetén,** west of Progreso. **Río Lagartos** also offers
good fishing in its murky waters. In the Parque Natural del
Flamenco Mexicano in **Celestún,** you have your choice of river
or gulf fishing.

Golf There is an 18-hole championship golf course (and restaurant,
bar, and clubhouse) at **Club Campestre de Mérida** (Calle 30, No.
500, tel. 99/71100 or 99/71700), 16 kilometers (10 miles) north
of Mérida on the road to Progreso.

Hunting Hunting has always been popular in Yucatán, but as more species become endangered the sport is attracting fewer enthusiasts. The best hunting area is on the northwest coast around
Sisal, 51 kilometers (32 miles) northwest of Mérida, and November–March remain the most successful months for hunting
duck and other waterfowl. The importation of firearms and
other arrangements can be complicated, so it's best to go
through a specialist and take part in a group expedition. **Ceiba
Tours** (Holiday Inn, tel. 99/256389) is well versed at cutting
through red tape and setting up expeditions.

Tennis The **Holiday Inn** (Av. Colón 498 at Calle 60, tel. 99/256877) has
tennis courts, as do the **Club Campestre de Mérida** (*see* Golf,

above), the **Centro Deportivo Bancario** (Carr. a Motul s/n, Frac. del Arco, tel. 99/60500 or 99/77819), and the **Deportivo Libanés Mexicano** (Calle 1-G, No. 101, tel. 99/70669).

Spectator Sports

Baseball　Baseball is played with enthusiasm from February or March to July at the stadium in the **Kukulcán Sports Center** (Calle 14, No. 17), next to the Carta Clara brewery.

Bullfights　Bullfights are most often performed from November to January, or during other holiday periods at the **bullring** (Paseo de la Reforma), near Avenida Colón. Contact the travel desk at your hotel or one of the tourist information centers; prices range from $7 to $11 for seats in the sun and from $11 to $17 for seats in the shade.

Dining and Lodging

Dining　Dining out is a pleasure in Mérida. The city's 50-odd restaurants offer a superb variety of cuisine—primarily Yucatecan, of course, but also Lebanese, Italian, French, Chinese, and Mexican—at very reasonable prices. Generally, reservations are advised for those places marked "Expensive," but only during the high season. Neat but casual dress is acceptable at all Mérida restaurants.

Pisté, the village nearest to Chichén Itzá, is not a gourmand's town: The food in most of its restaurants is simple, overpriced, and only fair. For the most part, the hotel restaurants are even worse. Most of the restaurants in town have been set up to handle tour-bus crowds and are empty the rest of the time. If you prefer to dine inexpensively, try one of the palapa-covered cafés along the main road. The small markets and produce stands can provide the makings for a modest picnic.

The restaurants near the ruins in Uxmal are nothing to write home about either. The exception is Los Almendros, in Ticul, which is well worth the 15-minute drive.

All restaurants are open for breakfast, lunch, and dinner unless otherwise noted. People who like eating with the locals might stop in at one of the many *loncherías* (diners) in the small towns and downtown districts of cities for panuchos, *empanadas* (meat-filled turnovers), tacos, or *salbutes* (which are like panuchos without the beans). As in Mérida, neat but casual dress is acceptable.

Highly recommended restaurants are indicated by a star ★.

Category	Cost*
Very Expensive	over $20
Expensive	$15–$20
Moderate	$8–$15
Inexpensive	under $8

per person, excluding drinks and service

Lodging　Outside of Mérida you'll find that accommodations fit the low-key, simple pace of the region. Internationally affiliated properties are the exception rather than the rule; instead, charmingly idiosyncratic old mansions offer visitors a base from which to explore the countryside and Mérida itself—which merits at least a two-day stay.

Mérida's 60-odd hotels offer a refreshingly broad range, from the chain hotels at the top end and the classic, older hotels housed in colonial or turn-of-the-century mansions (suffused with genteel charm and full of warm touches) to fleabags adequate only for the budget traveler unconcerned with creature comforts. As in the rest of Mexico, the facade rarely reveals the character of the hotel behind it, so check out the interior before turning away. Properties in Mérida have a 97000 postal code.

Location is very important in your choice of hotels: If you plan to spend most of your time enjoying Mérida, stay in the vicinity of the main square or along Calle 59. If you're a light sleeper, however, choose a hotel away from the plaza (traffic makes the noise level unbearable) or along Paseo de Montejo, about a 20-minute stroll from the Plaza Mayor. If you're a real stickler for hot water, test the faucets before renting a room. In general, the public spaces in Mérida's hotels are better maintained than the sleeping rooms. All hotels have air-conditioning unless otherwise noted.

Highly recommended hotels are indicated by a star ★.

Category	Cost*
Very Expensive	over $90
Expensive	$60–$90
Moderate	$25–$60
Inexpensive	under $25

All prices are for a standard double room, excluding service and the 10% tax

Chichén Itzá
Dining and Lodging
★

Hacienda Chichén. A converted 17th-century hacienda, this hotel once served as the home of archaeologist Edward S. Thompson and later as the headquarters for the Carnegie expedition. The rustic cottages have been modernized, and all rooms, which are simply furnished in colonial Yucatecan style, have private bathrooms, ceiling fans, and verandas. An enormous old pool sits in the midst of the landscaped gardens. Fairly good meals are served at set hours on the patio overlooking the grounds; stick with the Yucatecan specialties. *Carretera Mérida–Cancún, Km 120, tel. in Mérida 99/248844 or 800/223-4084, fax 99/245011. 20 rooms. Facilities: restaurant (Expensive), bar, pool. No air-conditioning. AE, DC, MC, V. Closed May–Oct. Expensive.*

★ **Mayaland.** The hotel closest to the ruins, this charming 1920s property belongs to the Barbachano family, whose name is practically synonymous with tourism in Yucatán. Accommodations include a wing and several bungalows set in a large garden on a 100-acre site. The observatory is visible from the alcoves on the road side of the hotel. Colonial-style rooms in the main building feature decorative tiles, ceiling fans, air-conditioning, television, and mosquito netting; bungalows do not have television or air-conditioning. The hot water often runs cold. Tour buses fill the road in front of the hotel, so choose a room at the back. Light meals served poolside and at tables overlooking the garden are a far better choice than the fixed-price meals served in the dining room. *Carretera Mérida–Cancún, Km 120, tel. in Chichén Itzá, 985/62777; in Mérida, Mayaland Tours, Av. Colón 502, tel. 99/252122, 99/252133, or 800/235–4079, fax 99/257022. 65 rooms. Facilities: restaurant (Expensive), bar, pool. AE, MC, V. Expensive.*

Pirámide Inn Resort and RV Park. This slightly tacky, American-owned two-story motel in Pisté features rooms with white walls, white tile floors, and modern furniture. The garden contains a small Mayan pyramid and a tennis court, and adjoining the inn are 30 RV hookups. The restaurant is one of the best in Piste. *1 km before Chichén Itzá, Box 433, Mérida, Yucatán (for reservations), or 800/262–9696 in the U.S. 44 rooms. Facilities: restaurant (Moderate), pool, satellite TV, lending library, tennis court, tours. AE, MC, V. Moderate.*

Dolores Alba. The best low-budget choice near the ruins is this family-run hotel, a long-time favorite in the country south of Pisté. The rooms are simple, clean, and comfortable; some have air-conditioning. Hammocks hang by the small pool, and breakfast and dinner are served family-style in the main building. Free transportation to the ruins is provided. *Carretera Pisté-Cancún, 1½ mi. south of Chichén Itzá, reservations in Mérida Calle 63, No. 464, tel. 99/285650, fax 99/283163. 28 rooms. Facilities: dining room, pool. MC, V. Inexpensive.*

Mérida **Alberto's Continental Patio.** You can probably find this restau-
Dining rant praised in just about every guidebook and it merits the
★ kudos: The setting is romantic and the food is excellent. The building, which dates from around 1727, is adorned with such fine details as mosaic floors from Cuba. Two beautiful dining rooms are tastefully decorated with dark wood trim, copper utensils, stone sculpture, and candles in glass lanterns on the tables. An inner patio surrounded by rubber trees is suitable for starlit dining. Most of the guests are tourists, but that need not detract from the surroundings or the food. If you order Lebanese food, your plate will be heaped with servings of shish kebab, fried kibi, cabbage rolls, hummus, eggplant, and tabbouleh, accompanied by pita bread, almond pie, and Turkish coffee. Black bean soup, enchiladas, fried bananas, and caramel custard make up the Mexican dinner; there are also a Yucatecan dinner, an Italian dinner, and à la carte appetizers and entrées. *Calle 64, No. 482, at Calle 57, tel. 99/285367. AE, MC, V. Open daily 11–11. Very Expensive.*

★ **La Bella Epoca.** For a truly special dinner, nothing matches the elegance and style of this second-story dining room, the former ballroom of an old mansion that has been restored well beyond its original grandeur. Crystal chandeliers sparkle over tiny balcony tables overlooking Parque Cepeda Peraza. An ambitious menu includes French, Mexican, Middle Eastern, Yucatecan, vegetarian, and unusual Maya dishes—try the *sikil-pak*, a dip with ground pumpkin seeds; the charcoal-broiled tomatoes and onions; or the succulent *pollo píbil* (chicken baked in banana leaves). Arrive for dinner before 8 PM to claim one of the small balcony tables overlooking the street. *Calle 60, between Calles 57 and 59, tel. 99/281928. AE, MC, V. Open daily 12 PM–1 AM. Expensive.*

La Casona. This pretty mansion-turned-restaurant near Parque Santa Ana has an inner patio, arcade, red tile roof, and ceiling fans. The accent is Italian, and the specialties include homemade pasta—ravioli, manicotti, and linguine. Calzones stuffed with cheese or spinach, osso buco, chicken, fish, and píbil are other good bets. Vegetable soup accompanies most orders. The restaurant offers live music on weekends. *Calle 60, No. 434, between Calles 47 and 49, tel. 99/238348. AE, MC, V. Open daily 1 PM–midnight. Expensive.*

Pancho's. The waiters in this steak and seafood restaurant—Mérida's version of the Carlos 'n' Charlie's chain—dress in what looks like Hollywood's idea of "Bandito" costumes. The bar, with its fancy drinks, attracts the international singles set; dancing is possible some nights on the outdoor patio. *Calle 59, No. 509, between Calles 60 and 62, tel. 99/230942. AE, MC, V. Closed for lunch. Expensive.*

Alameda. Middle Eastern and vegetarian specialties share the menu with standard Yucatecan fare at this side-street café, where businessmen linger over grilled beef shishkabob, pita bread, and coffee at breakfast. The street action is visible from tables at the front; those in the back patio are quieter. Everything is served without side dishes—if you want beans or potatoes with your eggs you must ask for them. Meat-free dishes include tabbouleh and spinach and cauliflower casseroles. *Calle 58, No. 474, across the street from the Posada Toledo, tel. 99/283635. No credit cards. Open Mon.–Thurs. 8–8, Fri.–Sat. 8–10, Sun. 8–5. Moderate.*

Express. Young and middle-aged Méridano men in guayaberas spend hours in this plain café-style restaurant that reeks of Madrid café ambience (and of cigar smoke as well). That ambience is reinforced by the paintings of old Spain (and old Mérida) on the walls, the ceiling fans, and the old-fashioned globe lights. On the menu are broiled garlic chicken, sandwiches, shrimp, and red snapper. Service can be slow, but then Express is a place for lingering. *Calle 60, No. 502, at Calle 59, tel. 99/281691. No credit cards. Moderate.*

Los Almendros. Another Mérida classic, this chain restaurant credits itself with the invention of poc chuc, and though perhaps overrated, it does know how to cater to the tourists and businesspeople who frequently fill its chairs and tables to the limit. The two dining rooms have both ceiling fans and air-conditioning. The food tends to be on the greasy, oily side, and sometimes the taste of the food itself is all but drowned in wonderful local spices. Nonetheless, the restaurant provides a more than passable introduction to the variety of Yucatecan cuisine, including cochinita píbil, panuchos, pork sausage, papadzules, and *pollo ticuleño* (boneless, breaded chicken in tomato sauce, accompanied by fried beans, peas, red peppers, fried bananas, and ham and cheese). All dishes are described in English with pictures on the paper menus. The sangria—with or without alcohol—washes it all down. *Calle 50-A, No. 493, between Calles 57 and 59, tel. 99/212851. AE. Moderate.*

Pizza Bella. This pizza place on the main square next to Librería Dante also serves Mexican and American breakfasts, espresso, and cappuccino. Checkered tablecloths atop wooden tables and an eclectic collection of posters (maps to beer advertisements) adorning the walls add atmosphere to this otherwise pizza-joint-style restaurant. *Calle 61, No. 500, Depto. E-2, tel. 99/236401. No credit cards. Moderate.*

★ **Pórtico del Peregrino.** The name means "pilgrim's porch," and this colonial-style restaurant has the decor to match: A red tile floor, iron grillwork, and copious plants set the tone in both the indoor and outdoor patio sections. The menu features lime soup, baked eggplant with chicken, shrimp, chicken píbil, shish kebob, mole enchiladas, seafood stew, chicken liver brochettes, and spaghetti. For dessert, try the coconut ice cream with Kahlúa. *Calle 57, No. 501, tel. 99/216844. AE, MC, V. Closed for breakfast. Moderate.*

★ **Santa Lucía.** Locals crowd this small dining room, a few steps below the sidewalk, at lunch time, when the bountiful *comida corrida* is served. The bargain three-course lunch usually includes such Yucatecan specialties as *sopa de lima* (lime soup) and *pollo píbil.* Before you order, browse through the book of guests' comments to get tips on favorite meals—the pepper steak constantly wins rave reviews. Soft tropical music plays in the background, and the service is friendly and efficient. *Calle 60, No. 481, next to Parque Santa Lucía, tel. 99/285957. MC, V. Closed for breakfast. Moderate.*

Ananda Maya Ginza. One of a handful of vegetarian restaurants in town, this one is light on the decor, which includes wood tables, white walls, and stone floors, and heavy on the health drinks, made mostly with local vegetables, fruit, and herbs. Regular coffee and Yucatecan beers are also served, and the salads are made with fresh local vegies washed with purified water. The terrace of this old historic home provides a quiet dining atmosphere beneath a big tree. *Calle 59, No. 507, between Calles 60 and 62, tel. 99/282451. No credit cards. Open Mon.–Sat. 9–10; closed Sun. Inexpensive.*

Café Louvre. Catty-corner from the main square, this popular café occupies a front room looking out to the plaza and a cavernous back room bustling with family activity. The service tends to be indifferent, but that doesn't seem to bother the locals, who come here for the sandwiches, *huevos motuleños,* hot cakes, fried bananas with cream, and iced tea. *Calle 62, No. 499-D, at Calle 61, tel. 99/213271. No credit cards. Inexpensive.*

★ **Cafetería Pop.** A favorite with the student crowd (the university is across the street), this place—with some 12 white-linoleum-covered tables—resembles a crowded American diner. The busiest time is 8 AM–noon, but for late risers the breakfast menu can be ordered à la carte all day and the noteworthy coffee is freshly brewed round the clock. In addition, sandwiches, hamburgers, spaghetti, chicken, fish, beef, and tacos are featured. Beer, sangria, and wine are served only with food orders. *Calle 57, No. 501, at Calle 62, tel. 99/216844. MC, V. Inexpensive.*

Nicte-Ha. Metal chairs and tables with plastic tablecloths sit under an arcade right on the main square, making this modest eatery a fine place for people-watching. A good selection of Yucatecan fare—soups, huevos motuleños, poc chuc, seafood, *antojitos* (appetizers), and a combination platter—is offered at budget prices. Afterward, stop in at the *sorbetería* next door for a sherbet. *Calle 61, No. 500, at Calle 60, tel. 99/230784. No credit cards. Inexpensive.*

Lodging **Casa del Balam.** This very pleasant hotel on well-heeled Calle
★ 60 (opposite the Opera House) was built 60 years ago as the home of the Barbachano family, pioneers of Yucatán tourism. Today the hotel—owned and managed by Carmen Barbachano—has a lovely courtyard ornamented with a fountain, arcades, ironwork, and a black-and-white tile floor; rocking chairs in the hallways impart a colonial feeling, as do the mahogany trimmings and cedar doorways. The rooms are capa-

cious and well maintained, featuring painted sinks, wrought-iron accessories, and minibars. The suites are especially agreeable, with large bathrooms, tiny balconies, arched doorways, and mahogany bureaus. *Calle 60, No. 488, Box 988, tel. 99/248844, 99/248044, or 800/437–9607, fax 99/245011. 54 rooms. Facilities: restaurant, 2 bars, minibars, pool, sun deck, travel agency, car rental, gift shop. AE, MC, V. Very Expensive.*

Holiday Inn. A deluxe, modern hotel at the fashionable north end of the Paseo de Montejo—too far from the center if you are on foot, fine if you have a car—this chain hotel is wholly Americanized. Rooms are decorated in typical Holiday Inn fashion and include simple, functional furnishings. Mexicans hold business meetings and conventions here. At press time, two new high-rise hotels were under construction near the Holiday Inn, with all the accompanying noise and traffic congestion. *Av. Colón 498 at Calle 60, tel. 99/256877 or 800/465–4329. 214 rooms. Facilities: 3 restaurants, 4 bars, disco, minibars, pool, lighted tennis court, shops, parking. AE, DC, MC, V. Very Expensive.*

Los Aluxes. A good choice within walking distance of the plaza but somewhat removed from the traffic noise, Los Aluxes is a modern, six-story hotel with all the first-class amenities. Fountains, trees, and an abundance of plants soften the anonymous decor, and the pool's garden offers a peaceful respite from city hustle and bustle. The carpeted rooms are comfortably decorated in pale peach and blue. Underground parking is a major plus, and the hotel has one of the best dining rooms in town. *Calle 60 at Calle 49, tel. 99/242199 or 800/782–8395, fax 99/233858. 109 rooms. Facilities: pool, restaurant, bar, travel agency, shop, satellite TV in rooms. AE, MC, V. Very Expensive.*

María del Carmen. A modern Best Western hotel, the María del Carmen caters to business travelers, bus groups, and those traveling by car who desire secured parking. The plaza, market, and other major sights are within easy walking distance. The modern rooms are decorated with Oriental lamps and furniture. *Calle 63, No. 550, between Calles 68 and 70, tel. 99/239233 or 800/528–1234, fax 99/239290. 89 rooms. Facilities: pool, restaurant, bar, travel agency, satellite TV in rooms. AE, MC, V. Very Expensive.*

Mérida Misión. Part of the city's landscape for decades (in its earlier incarnation it was the Hotel Mérida), the Misíon has two major assets: an excellent location in the heart of downtown and a genuine colonial ambience, with chandeliers, wood beams, archways, patios, fountains, and a pool. Handsome public areas make it a pleasure to spend time here; it is not just a place to retire for the night. *Calle 60, No. 491, tel. 99/237665 or 800/221–6509, fax 99/239500. 145 rooms. Facilities: restaurant, nightclub, snack bar, pool, travel agency, gift shop. AE, DC, MC, V. Expensive.*

Montejo Palace. Although the seven-story Montejo Palace situated only a block from the Anthropology Museum—is perfectly adequate and functional, it is a bit short on character. At press time, however, the hotel was undergoing a thorough renovation (which should be completed by 1994), with rooms on the first floor redecorated in modern violet and aqua. The ornate European style so popular along Paseo Montejo is still in evidence, but heavy furnishings become less oppressive when balanced with light floral linens. The hotel's neighborhood is far more serene and less congested than central Mérida, with good restaurants and a few nice shops nearby. *Paseo de Montejo 483-C,* *tel. 99/246046 or 800/437–9607, fax 99/280388. 88 rooms. Facilities: restaurant, cafeteria, bar, nightclub, pool, travel agency, gift shop. AE, DC, MC, V. Expensive.*

Casa Mexilio. One would never guess that behind the drab exterior of this guest house sits the most exquisitely decorated bed-and-breakfast in all Mérida, if not the entire country. Two partners—one Mexican, one American—have brought the best of their respective architectural and decorating traditions to bear on this small house with seven guest rooms (one on each floor), which is being restored to something beyond its original splendor. From the dark entrance you approach a tiny pool adjacent to a charming kitchen, painted as extravagantly as the kitchen that belonged to Frida Kahlo, the celebrated Mexican painter and the wife of the even more famous muralist Diego Rivera. At the top of the narrow stairs is a sun deck laden with cacti; one entire wall of the house is covered with vines. Middle Eastern wall hangings, French tapestries, colorful tile floors, black pottery, tile sinks, rustic furniture, loft beds, and white walls make up the eclectic decor, which reaches its pinnacle in an immensely cozy sitting room on the second floor, complete with stereo, TV, and bookshelves. The price includes breakfast. *Calle 68, No. 495, tel. 99/282505; for reservations tel. 303/674–9615 or 800/538–6802, fax 303/674–8735. 7 rooms. Facilities: restaurant, pool. AE, MC, V. Moderate.*

Caribe. The Caribe has all the makings of an authentic colonial hotel, including tile floors, dark wood furniture, and a large inner courtyard with arcades. It is located on Parque Hidalgo, but most of its rooms overlook the inner courtyard and restaurant, as do the open balconies, which are lined with comfortable chairs. The rooftop sun deck and swimming pool have a great view of the plaza and downtown. The hotel's café, El Meson, is one of the better restaurants in Parque Hidalgo. *Calle 60, No. 500, tel. 99/249022 or 800/826–6842, fax 99/248733. 56 rooms. Facilities: restaurant, outdoor cafeteria, pool, travel agency, parking. AE, DC, MC, V. Moderate.*

Del Gobernador. A modern stucco exterior and simple air-conditioned lobby match the clean rooms painted in white, cream, and light pinks and decorated with hanging plants. The hotel and its dining room are extremely popular with Mexican travelers, who are more concerned with modern comforts than with colonial charm. Most rooms have tiled baths, carpeting, and balconies. *Calle 59, No. 535, tel. 99/237133, fax 99/281590. 61 rooms. Facilities: restaurant/bar, pool, travel agency. AE, MC, V. Moderate.*

★ **Gran Hotel.** Cozily situated on Parque Hidalgo, this 1901 hotel is the oldest in the city, and it still lives up to its name. The five-story neoclassical building, with an Art Nouveau courtyard complete with wrought-iron bannister, variegated tile floors, Greek columns, and a myriad of potted plants, exudes charm. High ceilings in rooms drenched in cedar provide a sense of spaciousness. All units have balconies and some have air-conditioning. Ask for a room overlooking the park. Porfirio Díaz, Fidel Castro, and Sandino stayed in sumptuous Room 17, and Room 12½ has an enormous sitting room. TVs are available upon request. The Patio Español restaurant, although separately owned, is situated in the hotel. *Calle 60, No. 496, tel. 99/236963 or 99/247633, fax 99/247622. 34 rooms. Facilities: restaurant, sun roof. MC, V. Moderate.*

Posada Toledo. This slightly musty inn occupies a beautiful old colonial house with high ceilings, floors of patterned tile, and old-fashioned carved furniture that evoke its former elegance. The dining room, where breakfast is served, is particularly fine, with stained-glass door frames. Antiques clutter the halls, along with warm, faded portraits of 19th-century family life, so that one feels more like a personal guest of the establishment than another nameless hotel client. The rooms have the same bright tile floors; glass doors on the dining room cabinets reveal family heirlooms; and the inner patio—with marble columns enclosing a tropical garden—is a study in Mexican refinement. You have a choice of a ceiling fan or air-conditioning. *Calle 58, No. 487, at Calle 57, tel. 99/231690 or 99/232256. 20 rooms. No facilities. MC, V. Moderate.*

Residencial. Location is the major draw at this bright pink hotel, opened in 1991. It sits on Calle 59, the main entrance to town, and has a gated parking lot. The decor's French Colonial theme is most evident in the small dining room with its silken drapes, linen cloths, and high-backed chairs. Rooms have powerful showers, comfortable beds, and mirrored doors on the spacious closets. While the bar and small swimming pool in the central courtyard are pleasant for encountering fellow guests, they are far from private. *Calle 59, No. 589, at Calle 76, tel. 99/243899 or 99/243099, fax 99/212230. 66 rooms. Facilities: restaurant, bar, pool, parking. AE, MC, V. Moderate.*

Dolores Alba. A comfortable, friendly standby in the budget range, the Dolores Alba is owned by the Sanchez family, who also have the budget hotel Janiero in Mérida and the Dolores Alba at Chichén Itzá. The basic rooms, some with air-conditioning, frame a courtyard where guests' cars can be parked. A full $3.50 breakfast is served in the dining room; guests can keep cold drinks in the lobby refrigerator. *Calle 63, No. 464, tel. 99/285650, fax 99/283163. 40 rooms. Facilities: pool, restaurant (breakfast only). Inexpensive.*

Galería Trinidad. Eccentricity holds sway at this impossibly original, slightly ramshackle, bizarre little hotel, nearly unidentifiable unless you are looking specifically for it. In its previous lives it has been a hacienda, an auto rental shop, and a furniture store, but in the late 1980s owner Manolo Rivero made it into a hotel. An adjacent and still browsable gallery houses leftovers from the Galería Trinidad's days as a furniture store. The large, chaotic lobby is filled with plants, a fountain, and yellow wicker furniture; making your way through the maze that is the rest of the hotel, you'll encounter painted wooden angels, curved columns, and even a green satin shoe mounted on a pedestal. The rooms are small and equally odd. (Rivero has a second 17-room hotel, the Trinidad, a block away; guests have access to the Galería's swimming pool.) *Calle 60 at Calle 51, tel. 99/232463. 30 rooms. Facilities: pool, gallery. AE, MC, V. Inexpensive.*

Progreso Dining

Capitán Marisco. This large and pretty restaurant-bar on the malecón features a nautical motif, with a ship's rudder in the center of the main dining room and a fountain adorned with seashells. The house specialty is *filete a la hoja de plátano* (fish fillet—usually grouper, sea bass, or pompano—cooked in a banana leaf), but the entire menu is dependable. For a superb view of the sea, visit the outdoor terrace on the second floor. *Malecón between Calles 10 and 12, tel. 993/50639. AE, MC, V. Expensive.*

Soberanis. This branch of a respected Mexican chain of seafood houses is a dependable choice for fish dishes and traditional Mexican meals. *Calle 30, No. 138, between Calles 27 and 29, tel. 993/50582. AE, MC, V. Moderate.*

Lodging **Fiesta Inn Mérida Beach.** This unlikely luxury chain hotel and time-share (affiliated with Posadas de México) sits in Yucalpetén, a tiny fishing village 35 kilometers (22 miles) north of Mérida and very close to Progreso. The two-story hotel's attractive pastel stucco exterior and lobby are complemented by rooms with teal carpets, orange curtains, and coral-and-oyster-white walls. Some rooms have sofa beds; all have balconies. The pretty pale-green-and-purple cafeteria features a nautical decor. The pool—alongside which mariachis play on weekends—is right on the beach, which is separated from the property by a small lawn. The inn surrounds a little harbor filled with boats, and the jetty leads to a tiny lighthouse. *Calle 19, No. 91, Col. Reparto Costa Azul, Progreso 97320, tel. 993/50300, 993/50222, fax 993/50699 or 800/FIESTA–1. 88 rooms. Facilities: cafeteria, pool bar, cable TV, 2 pools, 4 tennis courts, surfing, marina, gift shop, bicycle rental, beauty salon. AE, DC, MC, V. Very Expensive.*

Sian Ka'an. These four whitewashed, thatched-roof, two-story villas, right on the beach in Chelem (just west of Yucalpetén and near Progreso) all come with kitchenettes, ceiling fans, and terraces that overlook the water. Decorated in rustic Mexican-Mediterranean style, the suites feature handwoven bedspreads, *equipales* (leather chairs from Jalisco), and handblown glassware. Prices include breakfast. Ask about discounts, which can be significant in the off-season. *Calle 17, s/n, tel. in Mérida, 99/282582, fax 99/244919; in Chelem, tel. 993/54017. 8 suites. Facilities: restaurant, beach, pool. AE, DC, MC, V. Expensive.*

Progreso. This clean, modest-but-tasteful three-star hotel in the heart of Progreso opened in 1990. The rooms, some with balconies, are furnished in pine, with arched window frames and tiled baths. *Calle 29 at Calle 28, tel. 993/50038. 9 rooms. Facilities: restaurant, air-conditioning or ceiling fans. MC, V. Inexpensive.*

Uxmal **Los Almendros.** Located in Ticul, a small town 28 kilometers
Dining (17 miles) east of Uxmal (turn left at Santa Elena), this restau-
★ rant offers fresher and juicier foods than do the other members of the Los Almendros chain. Although the interior is simple and clean, with whitewashed walls, the scenery behind the restaurant gives you a real taste of Yucatán: It's not unusual to see old Mayan women in their huipiles and baseball hats patting corn tortillas by hand. As for the menu, the prices are the same as in the other branches, and poc chuc and cochinita píbil are good choices. This is one place, however, where you can expect to wait in line for a table, especially during high season. *Calle 23, No. 196, tel. 99/20021. MC, V. Moderate.*

Nicte-Ha. This café beside the Hacienda Uxmal hotel is the least expensive dining option by the ruins, serving pizzas, sandwiches, and a large buffet lunch. Diners are welcome to use the swimming pool by the restaurant. Stop by after your morning tour, have lunch and a swim, and return to the ruins in late afternoon when the groups are gone and the sun is less intense. *At the Hacienda Uxmal, on Hwy. 261, tel. 99/247142. MC, V. Moderate.*

Las Palapas. A great alternative to the hotel dining rooms at Uxmal, this family-run restaurant specializes in delicious Yucatecan dishes served with homemade tortillas. When tour groups request it in advance, the owners prepare a traditional feast, roasting the chicken or pork píbil style in a pit in the ground. If you see a tour bus in the parking lot stop in—you may chance upon a memorable fiesta. *Hwy. 261, 5 kilometers (3 miles) north of the ruins, no phone. No credit cards. Inexpensive.*

Lodging **Hacienda Uxmal.** The oldest hotel at the site, built in 1955 and still owned and operated by the Barbachano family, this pleasant colonial-style building has lovely floor tiles, ceramics, and iron grillwork. The rooms—all with ceiling fans and air-conditioning—are tiled and decorated with worn but comfortable furniture. Inside the large courtyard are a garden and pool. Across the road and about 100 yards south you'll find the ruins. Ask about packages that include free or low-cost car rentals for the nights you spend at Uxmal and at the Mayaland hotel in Chichén Itzá. *Within walking distance of the ruins, tel. in Uxmal, 99/247142; in Mérida, Mayaland Tours, Av. Colón 502, tel. 99/252122, 99/252133, or 800/235–4079; fax 99/252397. 80 rooms. Facilities: restaurant, bar, pool, gift shop. AE, DC, MC, V. Expensive.*

Villa Arqueológica Uxmal. The hotel closest to the ruins is this two-story Club Med property built around a large Mediterranean-style pool. The functional rooms have cozy niches for the beds, tiled bathrooms, and powerful air conditioners. Mayan women in traditional dress serve well-prepared French cuisine in the restaurant, and large cages located around the hotel contain tropical birds and monkeys. For a fee, day-trippers can use the pool, then dine in the restaurant. *Within walking distance of the ruins, tel. 99/247053; in the U.S., tel. 800/CLUB–MED. 44 rooms. Facilities: restaurant, bar, pool, tennis court, gift shop. AE, MC, V. Expensive.*

Valladolid **El Mesón del Marqués.** This building, on the north side of the
Dining and Lodging main square, is a well-preserved, very old hacienda built around a lovely courtyard. Rooms in the modern addition at the back of the hotel have air-conditioning and are attractively furnished with rustic and colonial touches; rooms in the older section have ceiling fans. Unusually large bathrooms boast bathtubs—a rarity in Mexican hotels. As an added draw, El Mesón features a pool, a crafts shop, and a restaurant that serves local specialties. *Calle 39, No. 203, tel. 985/62073, fax 985/62073. 25 rooms, plus 9 suites. Facilities: restaurant (Moderate), bar, gift shop, pool. MC, V. Moderate.*

María del Luz. Another choice by the main plaza, this hotel is built around a small swimming pool and courtyard. The rooms have been recently renovated with new floors, fresh paint, and tiled bathrooms. Air-conditioning and televisions are being added to all the rooms. The street-side restaurant is attractively furnished with high-backed rattan chairs and linen cloths; Mexican dishes are predictable and inexpensive. *Calle 2, No. 195, tel. 985/62071, fax 985/62098. 30 rooms. Facilities: restaurant (Inexpensive), bar, pool. MC, V. Inexpensive.*

The Arts and Nightlife

The Arts

Mérida Mérida enjoys an unusually active and diverse cultural life, including free government-sponsored music and dance performances nightly in local parks (*see* Mérida for Free, *above*). For information on these and other performances, consult the tourist office, the local newspapers, or the billboards and posters at the Teatro Peón Contreras (Calle 60 at Calle 57) or Café Pop (Calle 57 between Calles 60 and 62).

Among a variety of performances presented at the **Teatro Peón Contreras** is "The Roots of Today's Yucatán," a combination of music, dance, and theater presented by the Folkloric Ballet of the University of Yucatán. *Admission: $4. Tues. 9 PM.*

Another theater that regularly hosts cultural events is the **Teatro Daniel Ayala** (Calle 60 between Calles 59 and 61).

Nightlife

Mérida Downtown movie theaters include **Cine Aladino** (Calle 60, No.
Film 514), **Cine Apolo** (Calle 60, No. 487), **Cine Fantasio** (Calles 59 and 60), **Cine Mérida** (Calle 62), **Cine Rex** (Calle 57, No. 553).

Events The **Hotel Calinda Panamericana** (Calle 59, No. 455, tel. 99/239111 or 99/239444) stages folkloric dances most nights by the pool. **Tulipanes** (Calle 46, No. 462-A, tel. 99/270967), a restaurant and nightclub built over a cenote, stages a folkloric ballet and "Mayan ritual" performance that ends with a "sacrifice" nightly at 8.

Music A number of restaurants feature live music and dancing, including **El Tucho** (Calle 60, No. 482, between Calles 55 and 57, tel. 99/242323), **La Prosperidad** (Calle 53 at Calle 56, tel. 99/240764), and **Pancho's** (Calle 59 between Calles 60 and 62, tel. 99/230942).

Discos There are discos that appeal to both locals and tourists at the **Holiday Inn** (Av. Colón, No. 498, at Calle 60) and the **Hotel Calinda Panamericana** (Calle 59, No. 455). **Excess** (Prolongación Paseo de Montejo 301), Mérida's most exclusive disco, is in the conspicuous lavender building.

State of Yucatán Both Chichén Itzá and Uxmal offer elaborate nighttime sound-and-light shows accompanied by narrations of Mayan legends (*see* Exploring, *above*).

Spanish Vocabulary

Note: *Mexican Spanish differs from Castilian Spanish.*

Words and Phrases

	English	Spanish	Pronunciation
Basics	Yes/no	Sí/no	see/no
	Please	Por favor	pore fah-**vore**
	May I?	¿Me permite?	may pair-**mee**-tay
	Thank you (very much)	(Muchas) gracias	(**moo**-chas) **grah**-see-as
	You're welcome	De nada	day **nah**-dah
	Excuse me	Con permiso	con pair-**mee**-so
	Pardon me/what did you say?	¿Como?/Mánde?	pair-**doan/mahn**-dey
	Could you tell me?	¿Podría decirme?	po-**dree**-ah deh-**seer**-meh
	I'm sorry	Lo siento	lo see-**en**-toe
	Good morning!	¡Buenos días!	**bway**-nohs **dee**-ahs
	Good afternoon!	¡Buenas tardes!	**bway**-nahs **tar**-dess
	Good evening!	¡Buenas noches!	**bway**-nahs **no**-chess
	Goodbye!	¡Adiós!/¡Hasta luego!	ah-dee-**ohss/ah**-stah-**lwe**-go
	Mr./Mrs.	Señor/Señora	sen-**yor**/sen-**yore**-ah
	Miss	Señorita	sen-yo-**ree**-tah
	Pleased to meet you	Mucho gusto	**moo**-cho **goose**-to
	How are you?	¿Cómo está usted?	**ko**-mo es-**tah** oo-**sted**
	Very well, thank you.	Muy bien, gracias.	**moo**-ee bee-**en**, **grah**-see-as
	And you?	¿Y usted?	ee oos-**ted**?
	Hello (on the telephone)	Bueno	**bwen**-oh
Numbers	1	un, uno	oon, **oo**-no
	2	dos	dos
	3	tres	trace
	4	cuatro	**kwah**-tro
	5	cinco	**sink**-oh
	6	seis	sace
	7	siete	see-**et**-ey
	8	ocho	**o**-cho
	9	nueve	new-**ev**-ay
	10	diez	dee-**es**
	11	once	**own**-sey
	12	doce	**doe**-sey
	13	trece	**tray**-sey
	14	catorce	kah-**tor**-sey
	15	quince	**keen**-sey
	16	dieciséis	dee-es-ee-**sace**
	17	diecisiete	dee-**es**-ee-see-**et**-ay
	18	dieciocho	dee-**es**-ee-o-cho
	19	diecinueve	**dee-es**-ee-new-**ev**-ay
	20	veinte	**vain**-tay
	21	veinte y uno/veintiuno	**vain**-te-oo-no

30	treinta	**train**-tah
32	treinta y dos	train-tay-**dose**
40	cuarenta	kwah-**ren**-tah
43	cuarenta y tres	kwah-**ren**-tay-**trace**
50	cincuenta	seen-**kwen**-tah
54	cincuenta y cuatro	seen-**kwen**-tay **kwah**-tro
60	sesenta	sess-**en**-tah
65	sesenta y cinco	sess-**en**-tay **seen**-ko
70	setenta	set-**en**-tah
76	setenta y seis	set-**en**-tay **sace**
80	ochenta	oh-**chen**-tah
87	ochenta y siete	oh-**chen**-tay see-**yet**-ay
90	noventa	no-**ven**-tah
98	noventa y ocho	no-**ven**-tah **o**-cho
100	cien	see-**en**
101	ciento uno	see-en-toe **oo**-no
200	doscientos	doe-see-**en**-tohss
500	quinientos	keen-**yen**-tohss
700	setecientos	set-eh-see-**en**-tohss
900	novecientos	no-veh-see-**en**-tohss
1,000	mil	meel
2,000	dos mil	dose meel
1,000,000	un millón	oon meel-**yohn**

Colors	black	negro	**neh**-grow
	blue	azul	ah-**sool**
	brown	café	kah-**feh**
	green	verde	**vair**-day
	pink	rosa	**ro**-sah
	purple	morado	mo-**rah**-doe
	orange	naranja	na-**rahn**-hah
	red	rojo	**roe**-hoe
	white	blanco	**blahn**-koh
	yellow	amarillo	ah-mah-**ree**-yoh

Days of the Week	Sunday	domingo	doe-**meen**-goh
	Monday	lunes	**loo**-ness
	Tuesday	martes	**mahr**-tess
	Wednesday	miércoles	me-**air**-koh-less
	Thursday	jueves	who-**ev**-ess
	Friday	viernes	vee-**air**-ness
	Saturday	sábado	**sah**-bah-doe

Months	January	enero	eh-**neh**-ro
	February	febrero	feh-**brair**-oh
	March	marzo	**mahr**-so
	April	abril	ah-**breel**
	May	mayo	**my**-oh
	June	junio	**hoo**-nee-oh
	July	julio	**who**-lee-yoh
	August	agosto	ah-**ghost**-toe
	September	septiembre	sep-tee-**em**-breh
	October	octubre	oak-**too**-breh
	November	noviembre	no-vee-**em**-breh
	December	diciembre	dee-see-**em**-breh

Useful phrases	Do you speak English?	¿Habla usted inglés?	ah-blah oos-**ted** in-**glehs**?
	I don't speak	No hablo español	no **ah**-blow

Spanish		es-pahn-**yol**
I don't understand (you)	No entiendo	no en-tee-**en**-doe
I understand (you)	Entiendo	en-tee-**en**-doe
I don't know	No sé	no **say**
I am American/ British	Soy americano(a)/ inglés(a)	soy ah-meh-ree-**kah**-no(ah)/ in-**glace**(ah)
What's your name?	¿Cómo se llama usted?	**koh**-mo say **yah**-mah oos-**ted**?
My name is ...	Me llamo ...	may **yah**-moh
What time is it?	¿Qué hora es?	keh **o**-rah es?
It is one, two, three ... o'clock.	Es la una; son las dos, tres	es la **oo**-nah/sone lahs dose, trace
Yes, please/No, thank you	Sí, por favor/No, gracias	**see** pore fah-**vor**/no **grah**-see-us
How?	¿Cómo?	**koh**-mo?
When?	¿Cuándo?	**kwahn**-doe?
This/Next week	Esta semana/ la semana que entra	**es**-tah seh-**mah**-nah/lah say-**mah**-nah keh **en**-trah
This/Next month	Este mes/el próximo mes	**es**-tay mehs/el **proke**-see-mo mehs
This/Next year	Este año/el año que viene	**es**-tay **ahn**-yo/el **ahn**-yo keh vee-**yen**-ay
Yesterday/today/ tomorrow	Ayer/hoy/mañana	ah-**yair**/oy/mahn-**yah**-nah
This morning/ afternoon	Esta mañana/tarde	**es**-tah mahn-**yah**-nah/**tar**-day
Tonight	Esta noche	**es**-tah **no**-cheh
What?	¿Qué?	keh?
What is it?	¿Qué es esto?	keh es **es**-toe
Why?	¿Por qué?	pore **keh**
Who?	¿Quién?	kee-**yen**
Where is ... ?	¿Dónde está ... ?	**dohn**-day es-**tah**
the train station?	la estación del tren?	la es-tah-see-**on** del **train**
the subway station?	la estación del Metro?	la es-ta-see-**on** del **meh**-tro
the bus stop?	la parada del autobús?	la pah-**rah**-dah del oh-toe-**boos**
the post office?	la oficina de correos?	la oh-fee-**see**-nah day koh-**reh**-os
the bank?	el banco?	el **bahn**-koh
the ... hotel?	el hotel ... ?	el oh-**tel**
the store?	la tienda ... ?	la tee-**en**-dah
the cashier?	la caja?	la **kah**-hah
the ... museum?	el museo ... ?	el moo-**seh**-oh
the hospital?	el hospital?	el ohss-**pea**-**tal**
the elevator?	el ascensor?	el ah-**sen**-sore
the bathroom?	el baño?	el **bahn**-yoh

Here/there	Aquí/allá	ah-**key**/ah-**yah**
Open/closed	Abierto/cerrado	ah-be-**er**-toe/ ser-**ah**-doe
Left/right	Izquierda/derecha	iss-key-**er**-dah/ dare-**eh**-chah
Straight ahead	Derecho	der-**eh**-choh
Is it near/far?	¿Está cerca/lejos?	es-**tah** sair-kah/ **leh**-hoss
I'd like . . .	Quisiera . . .	kee-see-air-ah
a room	un cuarto/una habitación	oon **kwahr**-toe/ **oo**-nah ah-bee-tah-see-**on**
the key	la llave	lah **yah**-vay
a newspaper	un periódico	oon pear-ee-**oh**-dee-koh
a stamp	un timbre de correo	oon **team**-bray day koh-**reh**-oh
I'd like to buy . . .	Quisiera comprar . . .	kee-see-**air**-ah kohm-**prahr**
cigarettes	cigarrillo	ce-gar-**reel**-oh
matches	cerillos	ser-**ee**-ohs
a dictionary	un diccionario	oon deek-see-oh-**nah**-ree-oh
soap	jabón	hah-**bone**
a map	un mapa	oon **mah**-pah
a magazine	una revista	**oon**-ah reh-**veess**-tah
paper	papel	pah-**pel**
envelopes	sobres	**so**-brace
a postcard	una tarjeta postal	**oon**-ah tar-**het**-ah post-**ahl**
How much is it?	¿Cuánto cuesta?	**kwahn**-toe **kwes**-tah
It's expensive/ cheap	Está caro/barato	es-**tah kah**-roh/ bah-**rah**-toe
A little/a lot	Un poquito/ mucho . . .	oon poh-**kee**-toe/ **moo**-choh
More/less	Más/menos	mahss/**men**-ohss
Enough/too much/too little	Suficiente/de masiado/muy poco	soo-fee-see-**en**-tay/ day-mah-see-**ah**-doe/**moo**-ee **poh**-koh
Telephone	Teléfono	tel-**ef**-oh-no
Telegram	Telegrama	teh-leh-**grah**-mah
I am ill/sick	Estoy enfermo(a)	es-**toy** en-**fair**-moh(ah)
Please call a doctor	Por favor llame un médico	pore fa-**vor ya**-may oon **med**-ee-koh
Help!	¡Auxilio! ¡Ayuda!	owk-**see**-lee-oh/ ah-**yoo**-dah
Fire!	¡Encendio!	en-**sen**-dee-oo
Caution!/Look out!	¡Cuidado!	kwee-**dah**-doh

On the Road

Highway	Carretera	car-ray-**ter**-ah
Causeway, paved highway	Calzada	cal-**za**-dah
Route	Ruta	**roo**-tah
Road	Camino	cah-**mee**-no
Street	Calle	**cah**-yeh
Avenue	Avenida	ah-ven-**ee**-dah
Broad, tree-lined boulevard	Paseo	pah-**seh**-oh
Waterfront promenade	Malecón	mal-lay-**cone**
Wharf	Embarcadero	em-bar-cah-**day**-ro

In Town

Church	Templo/Iglesia	**tem**-plo/e-**gles**-se-ah
Cathedral	Catedral	cah-tay-**dral**
Neighborhood	Barrio	**bar**-re-o
Foreign Exchange Shop	Casa de Cambio	**cas**-sah day **cam**-be-o
City Hall	Ayuntamiento	ah-yoon-tah-mee **en**-toe
Main Square	Zócalo	**zo**-cal-o
Traffic Circle	Glorieta	glor-e-**ay**-tah
Market	Mercado (Spanish)/ Tianguis (Indian)	mer-**cah**-doe/ tee-**an**-geese
Inn	Posada	pos-**sah**-dah
Group taxi	Colectivo	co-lec-**tee**-vo
Group taxi along fixed route	Pesero	pi-**seh**-ro

Items of Clothing

Embroidered white smock	Huipil	whee-**peel**
Pleated man's shirt worn outside the pants	Guayabera	gwah-ya-**beh**-ra
Leather sandals	Huarache	wah-**ra**-chays
Shawl	Rebozo	ray-**bozh**-o
Pancho or blanket	Serape	seh-**ra**-peh

Dining Out

A bottle of ...	Una botella de ...	**oo**-nah bo-**tay**-yah deh
A cup of ...	Una taza de ...	**oo**-nah **tah**-sah deh
A glass of ...	Un vaso de ...	oon **vah**-so deh
Ashtray	Un cenicero	oon sen-ee-**seh**-roh
Bill/check	La cuenta	lah **kwen**-tah

Bread	El pan	el pahn
Breakfast	El desayuno	el day-sigh-**oon**-oh
Butter	La mantequilla	lah mahn-tay-**key**-yah
Cheers!	¡Salud!	sah-**lood**
Cocktail	Un aperitivo	oon ah-pair-ee-**tee**-voh
Dinner	La cena	lah **seh**-nah
Dish	Un plato	oon **plah**-toe
Dish of the day	El platillo de hoy	el plah-**tee**-yo day oy
Enjoy!	¡Buen provecho!	bwen pro-**veh**-cho
Fixed-price menu	La comida corrida	lah koh-**me**-dah co-**ree**-dah
Fork	El tenedor	el ten-eh-**door**
Is the tip included?	¿Está incluida la propina?	es-**tah** in-clue-**ee**-dah lah pro-**pea**-nah
Knife	El cuchillo	el koo-**chee**-yo
Lunch	La comida	lah koh-**me**-dah
Menu	La carta	lah **cart**-ah
Napkin	La servilleta	lah sair-vee-**yet**-uh
Pepper	La pimienta	lah pea-me-**en**-tah
Please give me	Por favor déme	pore fah-**vor** day-may
Salt	La sal	lah sahl
Spoon	Una cuchara	**oo**-nah koo-**chah**-rah
Sugar	El azúcar	el ah-**sue**-car
Waiter!/Waitress!	¡Por favor Señor/Señorita!	pore fah-**vor** sen-**yor**/sen-yor-**ee**-tah

Index

Personal Itinerary

Departure *Date*

            Time

Transportation

Arrival *Date*   *Time*

Departure *Date*   *Time*

Transportation

Accommodations

Arrival *Date*   *Time*

Departure *Date*   *Time*

Transportation

Accommodations

Arrival *Date*   *Time*

Departure *Date*   *Time*

Transportation

Accommodations

Personal Itinerary

Arrival *Date*   *Time*

Departure *Date*   *Time*

Transportation

Accommodations

Arrival *Date*   *Time*

Departure *Date*   *Time*

Transportation

Accommodations

Arrival *Date*   *Time*

Departure *Date*   *Time*

Transportation

Accommodations

Arrival *Date*   *Time*

Departure *Date*   *Time*

Transportation

Accommodations

Addresses

Name	Name
Address	Address
Telephone	Telephone
Name	Name
Address	Address
Telephone	Telephone
Name	Name
Address	Address
Telephone	Telephone
Name	Name
Address	Address
Telephone	Telephone
Name	Name
Address	Address
Telephone	Telephone
Name	Name
Address	Address
Telephone	Telephone
Name	Name
Address	Address
Telephone	Telephone
Name	Name
Address	Address
Telephone	Telephone

Addresses

Name	*Name*
Address	*Address*
Telephone	*Telephone*
Name	*Name*
Address	*Address*
Telephone	*Telephone*
Name	*Name*
Address	*Address*
Telephone	*Telephone*
Name	*Name*
Address	*Address*
Telephone	*Telephone*
Name	*Name*
Address	*Address*
Telephone	*Telephone*
Name	*Name*
Address	*Address*
Telephone	*Telephone*
Name	*Name*
Address	*Address*
Telephone	*Telephone*

Escape to ancient cities and exotic

islands  *with CNN Travel Guide, a*

wealth of valuable advice. Host Valerie Voss will take you

to all of your favorite destinations,

including those off the beaten path.

 *Tune into your passport to the world.*

CNN TRAVEL GUIDE
SATURDAY 10:00 PMpt   SUNDAY 8:30 AMet

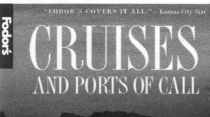

Announcing the only guide to explore a Disney World you've never seen before:

The one for grown-ups.

This terrific new guide is the only one written specifically for the millions of adults who visit Walt Disney World each year <u>without</u> kids. Upscale, sophisticated, packed full of facts and maps, *Walt Disney World for Adults* provides up-to-date information on hotels, restaurants, sports facilities, and health clubs, as well as unique itineraries for adults, including: a Sporting Life Vacation, Day-and-Night Romantic Fantasy, Singles Safari, and Gardens and Natural Wonders Tour. Get essential tips and everything you need to know about reservations, packages, annual events, banking service, rest stops, and much more. With *Walt Disney World for Adults* in hand, you'll get the most out of one of the world's most fascinating, most complex playgrounds.

At bookstores everywhere, or call 1-800-533-6478

Fodor's Travel Guides

U.S. Guides

Alaska

Arizona

Boston

California

Cape Cod, Martha's
Vineyard, Nantucket

The Carolinas & the
Georgia Coast

Chicago

Disney World & the
Orlando Area

Florida

Hawaii

Las Vegas, Reno,
Tahoe

Los Angeles

Maine, Vermont,
New Hampshire

Maui

Miami & the Keys

New England

New Orleans

New York City

Pacific North Coast

Philadelphia & the
Pennsylvania Dutch
Country

San Diego

San Francisco

Santa Fe, Taos,
Albuquerque

Seattle & Vancouver

The South

The U.S. & British
Virgin Islands

The Upper Great
Lakes Region

USA

Vacations in New York
State

Vacations on the
Jersey Shore

Virginia & Maryland

Waikiki

Washington, D.C.

Foreign Guides

Acapulco, Ixtapa,
Zihuatanejo

Australia & New
Zealand

Austria

The Bahamas

Baja & Mexico's
Pacific Coast Resorts

Barbados

Berlin

Bermuda

Brazil

Budapest

Budget Europe

Canada

Cancun, Cozumel,
Yucatan Penisula

Caribbean

Central America

China

Costa Rica, Belize,
Guatemala

Czechoslovakia

Eastern Europe

Egypt

Euro Disney

Europe

Europe's Great Cities

France

Germany

Great Britain

Greece

The Himalayan
Countries

Hong Kong

India

Ireland

Israel

Italy

Italy's Great Cities

Japan

Kenya & Tanzania

Korea

London

Madrid & Barcelona

Mexico

Montreal &
Quebec City

Morocco

The Netherlands
Belgium &
Luxembourg

New Zealand

Norway

Nova Scotia, Prince
Edward Island &
New Brunswick

Paris

Portugal

Rome

Russia & the Baltic
Countries

Scandinavia

Scotland

Singapore

South America

Southeast Asia

South Pacific

Spain

Sweden

Switzerland

Thailand

Tokyo

Toronto

Turkey

Vienna & the Danube
Valley

Yugoslavia

Fodor's Travel Guides

Special Series

Fodor's Affordables

Affordable Europe

Affordable France

Affordable Germany

Affordable Great
Britain

Affordable Italy

**Fodor's Bed &
Breakfast and
Country Inns Guides**

California

Mid-Atlantic Region

New England

The Pacific Northwest

The South

The West Coast

The Upper Great
Lakes Region

Canada's Great
Country Inns

Cottages, B&Bs and
Country Inns of
England and Wales

The Berkeley Guides

On the Loose in
California

On the Loose in
Eastern Europe

On the Loose in
Mexico

On the Loose in the
Pacific Northwest &
Alaska

**Fodor's Exploring
Guides**

Exploring California

Exploring Florida

Exploring France

Exploring Germany

Exploring Paris

Exploring Rome

Exploring Spain

Exploring Thailand

Fodor's Flashmaps

New York

Washington, D.C.

Fodor's Pocket Guides

Pocket Bahamas

Pocket Jamaica

Pocket London

Pocket New York
City

Pocket Paris

Pocket Puerto Rico

Pocket San Francisco

Pocket Washington,
D.C.

Fodor's Sports

Cycling

Hiking

Running

Sailing

The Insider's Guide
to the Best Canadian
Skiing

**Fodor's Three-In-Ones
(guidebook, language
cassette, and phrase
book)**

France

Germany

Italy

Mexico

Spain

**Fodor's
Special-Interest
Guides**

Cruises and Ports
of Call

Disney World & the
Orlando Area

Euro Disney

Healthy Escapes

London Companion

Skiing in the USA
& Canada

Sunday in New York

**Fodor's Touring
Guides**

Touring Europe

Touring USA:
Eastern Edition

Touring USA:
Western Edition

**Fodor's Vacation
Planners**

Great American
Vacations

National Parks of the
West

**The Wall Street
Journal Guides to
Business Travel**

Europe

International Cities

Pacific Rim

USA & Canada

WHEREVER YOU TRAVEL, HELP IS NEVER FAR AWAY.

From planning your trip to replacing
lost Cards, American Express® Travel Service
Offices* are always there to help.

CANCUN
Av. Tulum and Brisas, Suite A
98-841999

Hotel Camino Real
98-830824

Hotel Intercontinental
98-850755

COZUMEL
Fiesta Cozumel S.A. de C.V.
Ave. Rafael Melgar, No. 27
98-720925
98-720433

MERIDA
Paseo de Montejo #494
Por La 43 Y 45
99-284222

INTRODUCING

**AT LAST, YOUR OWN PERSONALIZED
LIST OF WHAT'S GOING ON IN THE
CITIES YOU'RE VISITING.**

**KEYED TO THE DAYS WHEN YOU'RE
THERE, CUSTOMIZED FOR YOUR
INTERESTS, AND SENT TO YOU
BEFORE YOU LEAVE HOME.**

**EXCLUSIVE FOR PURCHASERS OF
FODOR'S GUIDES...**

Fodor's WORLDVIEW
TRAVEL UPDATE

Introducing a revolutionary way to get customized, time-sensitive travel information just before your trip.

Now you can obtain detailed information about what's going on in each city you'll be visiting <u>before</u> you leave home—up-to-the-minute, objective information about the events and activities that interest you most.

This is a special offer for purchasers of Fodor's guides – a customized Travel Update to fit your specific interests and your itinerary.

Travel Updates contain the kind of time-sensitive insider information you can get only from local contacts – or from city magazines and newspapers once you arrive. But now you can have the same information before you leave for your trip.

The choice is yours: current art exhibits, theater, music festivals and special concerts, sporting events, antiques and flower shows, shopping, fitness, and more.

The information comes from hundreds of correspondents and thousands of sources worldwide. Updated continuously, it's like having your own personal concierge or friend in the city.

You specify the cities and when you'll be there. We'll do the rest — personalizing the information for you the way no guidebook can.

It's the perfect extension to your Fodor's guide and the best way to make the most of your valuable travel time.

Your Itinerary:
Customized reports available for 160 destinations

t
99
Rege
The a
in this
domain
tion as Joe
worthwhile.
the performan
Tickets are usu
venue. Alterna
mances are cancel
given. For more info
Open-Air Theatre, Inn
NW1 4NP Open Air T
Tel: 935-5756. Ends: 9-11
International Air Tattoo
Held biennially, the worl
military air display
demostra
tions, mi
bar

June 1

Fodor's/Worldview presents a Travel Update for:

Mr. Gavin Lynch
201 East 50th Street
New York, New York, 10022

Fodor's
WORLDVIEW

LONDON, UK

ARRIVE 23 Jun DEPART: 21 Jul

HIGHLIGHTS—EVENTS

Wimbledon Lawn Tennis Championships

Seats for the Wimbledon championships, especiall
those for the men's and women's finals in Lon
Centre Court, are the hottest tickets in Lon
summer. Each winter there is a ballot
No. 1 Court seats for the foll
ent. Through this ballot, to
ance of securing a ticket.
r top matches are included
bining hotel accommodati
ailable from the tourname
r, NAA Events Internation
4.

pen Air Theatre Season

n of open-air theater produ
d lovely park, once the
dandies, is as much of an
adway in the Park and e
bring your largest unbre
en interrupted by showe
le for the almost 1,200-seat
re offered when perfor-
ain, but refunds are not
ntact Sheila Benja
gent's Park
gent'

Ordering is easy.

You can order a Travel Update up to three months
before you leave. Of course, the closer to your trip
that you order, the more current the information.

You'll find a handy order form at the end of this eight-
page section. Choose your destinations and interest
categories from the lists included, fill out all sections
of the order form and mail or fax it back to us.

Or if you prefer, you can call us toll-free. We'll send
you a full, personalized report, similar to the samples
shown here, within 48 hours of receipt of your completed order.

Special concerts—
who's performing
what and where

One-of-a-kind,
one-time-only events

Special interest,
in-depth listings

Children — Events
Angel Canal Festival
The festivities include a children's funfair, entertainers, a boat rally and displays on the water. Regent's Canal. Islington. N1. Tube: Angel. Tel: 267 9100. 11:30am-5:30pm. 7/04.
Blackheath Summer Kite Festival
Stunt kite displays with parachuting teddy bears and trade stands. Free admission. SE3. BR: Blackheath. 10am. 6/27.
Megabugs
Children will delight in this infestation of giant robotic insects, including a praying mantic 60 times life size. Mon-Sat 10am-6pm; Sun 11am-6pm. Admission 4.50 pounds. Natural History Museum, Cromwell Road. SW7. Tube: South Kensington. Tel: 938 9123. Ends 10/01.
Childminders
This establishment employs only women, providing nurses and qualified nannies to

Music — Jazz & Blues
Tito Puente's Golden Men of Latin Jazz
The father of mambo and Cuban rumba king comes to town. Royal Festival Hall. South Bank. SE1. Tube: Waterloo. Tel: 928 8800. 8pm. 7/15.
Georgie Fame and The New York Band
Riding a popular tide with his latest album, the smoky-voiced Fame and his keyboard are on a tour yet again. The Grand. Clapham Junction. SW11. BR: Clapham Junction. Tel: 738 9000. 7:30pm. 7/07.
Jacques Loussier Play Bach Trio
The French jazz classicist and colleagues. Kenwood Lakeside. Hampstead Lane. Kenwood. NW3. Tube: Golders Green, then bus 210. Tel: 413 1443. 7pm. 7/10.
Tony Bennett and Ronnie Scott
Royal Festival Hall. South Bank. SE1. Tube: Waterloo. Tel: 928 8800. 8pm. 7/11.
Santana
Royal Festival Hall. South Bank. SE1. Tube: Waterloo. Tel: 928 8800. 8pm. 7/12.
Count Basie Orchestra and Nancy Wilson Trio
Royal Festival Hall. South Bank. SE1. Tube: Waterloo. Tel: 928 8800. 8pm. 7/14.
King Pleasure and the Biscuit Boys
Royal Festival Hall. South Bank. SE1. Tube: Waterloo. Tel: 928 8800. 6:30 and 9pm. 7/16.
Al Green and the London Community Gospel Choir
Royal Festival Hall. South Bank. SE1. Tube: Waterloo. Tel: 928 8800. 8pm. 7/13.
BB King and Linda Hopkins
Mother of the blues and successor to Bessie Smith, Hopkins meets up with "Blues Boy" Smith, Hopkins meets up with "Blues Boy"
Hall. South Bank. SE

Music — Classical
Marylebone Sinfonia
Kenneth Gowen conducts music by Puc and Rossini. Queen Elizabeth Hall. So Bank. SE1. Tube: Waterloo. Tel: 928 8 7:45pm. 7/16.
London Philharmonic
Franz Welser-Moest and George Benja conduct selections by Alexander Go Messiaen, and some of Benjamin's own positions. Queen Elizabeth Hall. South SE1. Tube: Waterloo. Tel: 928 8800. 8pr
London Pro Arte Orchestra and Forest C
Murray Stewart conducts selection Rossini, Haydn and Jonathan Willcocks. Queen Elizabeth Hall. South Bank. Tube: Waterloo. Tel: 928 8800. 7:45pm.
Kensington Symphony Orchestra
Russell Keable conducts Dvorak's D

Here's what you get . . .

Detailed information about what's going on — precisely when you'll be there.

Show openings during your visit

Reviews by local critics

Exhibitions & Shows—Antique & Flower
Westminster Antiques Fair
Over 50 stands with pre-1830 furniture and other Victorian and earlier items. Thu-Fri 11am-8pm; Sat-Sun 11am-6pm. Admission 4 pounds, children free. Old Royal Horticultural Hall. Vincent Square. SW1. Tel: 0444/48 25 14. 6-24 thru 6/27.

Royal Horticultural Society Flower Show
The show includes displays of carnations, summer fruit and vegetables. Tue 11am-7pm; Wed 10am-5pm. Admission Tue 4 pounds, Wed 2 pounds. Royal Horticultural Halls. Greycoat Street and Vincent Square. SW1. Tube: Victoria. 7/20 thru 7/21.

Hampton Court Palace International Flower Show
Major international garden and flower show taking place in conjunction with the British

Theater — Musical
Sunset Boulevard
In June, the four Andrew Lloyd Webber musicals which dominated London's stages in the 1980s (Cats, Starlight Express, Phantom of the Opera and Aspects of Love) are joined by the composer's latest work, a show rumored to have his best music to date. The 1950 Billy Wilder film about a helpless young writer who is drawn into the world of a possessive, aging silent screen star offers rich opportunities for Webber's evolving style. Soaring, aching melodies, lush technical effects and psychological thrills are all expected. Patti Lupone stars. Mon-Sat at 8pm; matinee Thu-Sat at 3pm. In-person sales only at the box office; credit card bookings, Tel: 344 0055. Admission 15-32.50 pounds. Adelphi Theatre. The Strand. WC2. Tube: Charing Cross. Tel: 836 7611. Starts: 6/21

Leonardo A Portrait of Love
A new musical about the great Renaissance artist and inventor comes in for a London premiere tested by a brief run at Oxford's Old Fire Station autumn. The work explores the relations Vinci and the woman

Spectator Sports — Other Sports
Greyhound Racing: Wembley Stadium
This dog track offers good views of greyhound racing held on Mon, Wed and Fri. No credit cards. Stadium Way. Wembley. HA9. Tube: Wembley Park. Tel: 902 8833.

Benson & Hedges Cricket Cup Final
Lord's Cricket Ground. St. John's Wood Road. NW8. Tube: St. John's Wood. Tel: 289 1611. 11am. 7/10.

Business-Fax & Overnight Mail
Post Office, Trafalgar Square Branch
Offers a network of fax services, the Intelpost system, throughout the country and abroad. Mon-Sat 8am-8pm, Sun 9am-5pm. William IV Street. WC2. Tube: Ch

Fodor's WORLDVIEW TRAVEL UPDATE

Alberquerque • Atlanta • Atlantic City • N Baltimore • Boston • Chicago • Cincinnati Cleveland • Dallas/Ft.Worth • Denver • De • Houston • Kansas City • Las Vegas • Los Angeles • Memphis • Miami • Milwaukee • New Orleans • New York City • Orlando • Springs • Philadelphia • Phoenix • Pittsburg Portland • Salt Lake • San Antonio • San Di San Franc • Seattle • St. Louis • Tamp Oslo • Wash • Honolulu • Island of Hawaii • Kauai • Maui • Abacos • Bimini Exuma • Anguilla • Countryside • Hamilton Berl Antigua & B • Nevis • Tort Virgin Gorda • Barbados • Dominica • Gren Lucia • St. Vincent • Trinidad &Tobago Caymans • Puerto Plata • Santo Doming Aruba • Bonaire • Curacao • St. Ma Quebec City • Montreal • Ottawa • Toron Vancouver • Guadeloupe • Martiniqu St. Barthelemy • St. Martin • Kingston • Ixta Montego Bay • Negril • Ocho Rios • Ponce San • Grand Turk • Providenciales • S St. John • St. Thomas • Acapulco • & Isla Mujeres • Cozumel • Guadal La Paz • Los Cabos • Manzinillo • Mazatl Mexico City • Monterrey • Oaxaca • Puerto Laredo • Puerto Vallarta • Veracruz • V Amsterdam • Athens •

Interest Categories

For <u>your</u> personalized Travel Update, choose the categories you're most interested in from this list. Every Travel Update automatically provides you with *Event Highlights* – the best of what's happening during the dates of your trip.

1.	**Business Services**	Fax & Overnight Mail, Computer Rentals, Photocopying, Secretarial , Messenger, Translation Services

Dining

2.	**All Day Dining**	Breakfast & Brunch, Cafes & Tea Rooms, Late-Night Dining
3.	**Local Cuisine**	In Every Price Range—from Budget Restaurants to the Special Splurge
4.	**European Cuisine**	Continental, French, Italian
5.	**Asian Cuisine**	Chinese, Far Eastern, Japanese, Indian
6.	**Americas Cuisine**	American, Mexican & Latin
7.	**Nightlife**	Bars, Dance Clubs, Comedy Clubs, Pubs & Beer Halls
8.	**Entertainment**	Theater—Drama, Musicals, Dance, Ticket Agencies
9.	**Music**	Classical, Traditional & Ethnic, Jazz & Blues, Pop, Rock
10.	**Children's Activities**	Events, Attractions
11.	**Tours**	Local Tours, Day Trips, Overnight Excursions, Cruises
12.	**Exhibitions, Festivals & Shows**	Antiques & Flower, History & Cultural, Art Exhibitions, Fairs & Craft Shows, Music & Art Festivals
13.	**Shopping**	Districts & Malls, Markets, Regional Specialities
14.	**Fitness**	Bicycling, Health Clubs, Hiking, Jogging
15.	**Recreational Sports**	Boating/Sailing, Fishing, Ice Skating, Skiing, Snorkeling/Scuba, Swimming
16.	**Spectator Sports**	Auto Racing, Baseball, Basketball, Football, Horse Racing, Ice Hockey, Soccer

Please note that interest category content will vary by season, destination, and length of stay.

Destinations

The Fodor's/Worldview Travel Update covers more than 160 destinations worldwide. Choose the destinations that match your itinerary from this list. (Choose bulleted destinations only.)

United States (Mainland)
- Albuquerque
- Atlanta
- Atlantic City
- Baltimore
- Boston
- Chicago
- Cincinnati
- Cleveland
- Dallas/Ft. Worth
- Denver
- Detroit
- Houston
- Kansas City
- Las Vegas
- Los Angeles
- Memphis
- Miami
- Milwaukee
- Minneapolis/ St. Paul
- New Orleans
- New York City
- Orlando
- Palm Springs
- Philadelphia
- Phoenix
- Pittsburgh
- Portland
- St. Louis
- Salt Lake City
- San Antonio
- San Diego
- San Francisco
- Seattle
- Tampa
- Washington, DC

Alaska
- Anchorage/Fairbanks/Juneau

Hawaii
- Honolulu
- Island of Hawaii
- Kauai
- Maui

Canada
- Quebec City
- Montreal
- Ottawa
- Toronto
- Vancouver

Bahamas
- Abacos
- Eleuthera/ Harbour Island
- Exumas
- Freeport
- Nassau & Paradise Island

Bermuda
- Bermuda Countryside
- Hamilton

British Leeward Islands
- Anguilla
- Antigua & Barbuda
- Montserrat
- St. Kitts & Nevis

British Virgin Islands
- Tortola & Virgin Gorda

British Windward Islands
- Barbados
- Dominica
- Grenada
- St. Lucia
- St. Vincent
- Trinidad & Tobago

Cayman Islands
- The Caymans

Dominican Republic
- Puerto Plata
- Santo Domingo

Dutch Leeward Islands
- Aruba
- Bonaire
- Curacao

Dutch Windward Islands
- St. Maarten

French West Indies
- Guadeloupe
- Martinique
- St. Barthelemy
- St. Martin

Jamaica
- Kingston
- Montego Bay
- Negril
- Ocho Rios

Puerto Rico
- Ponce
- San Juan

Turks & Caicos
- Grand Turk
- Providenciales

U.S. Virgin Islands
- St. Croix
- St. John
- St. Thomas

Mexico
- Acapulco
- Cancun & Isla Mujeres
- Cozumel
- Guadalajara
- Ixtapa & Zihuatanejo
- Los Cabos
- Manzanillo
- Mazatlan
- Mexico City
- Monterrey
- Oaxaca
- Puerto Escondido
- Puerto Vallarta
- Veracruz

Europe
- Amsterdam
- Athens
- Barcelona
- Berlin
- Brussels
- Budapest
- Copenhagen
- Dublin
- Edinburgh
- Florence
- Frankfurt
- French Riviera
- Geneva
- Glasgow
- Interlaken
- Istanbul
- Lausanne
- Lisbon
- London
- Madrid
- Milan
- Moscow
- Munich
- Oslo
- Paris
- Prague
- Provence
- Rome
- Salzburg
- St. Petersburg
- Stockholm
- Venice
- Vienna
- Zurich

Pacific Rim Australia & New Zealand
- Auckland
- Melbourne
- Sydney

China
- Beijing
- Guangzhou
- Shanghai

Japan
- Kyoto
- Nagoya
- Osaka
- Tokyo
- Yokohama

Other
- Bangkok
- Hong Kong & Macau
- Manila
- Seoul
- Singapore
- Taipei

Fodor's WORLDVIEW Order Form

THIS TRAVEL UPDATE IS FOR (Please print):

Name			
Address			
City	**State**	**ZIP**	
Country	**Tel #** ( ) -		

Title of this Fodor's guide: _____

Store and location where guide was purchased: _____

INDICATE YOUR DESTINATIONS/DATES: Write in below the destinations you want to order. Then fill in your arrival and departure dates for each destination.

		Month	Day		Month	Day
(Sample) *LONDON*	From:	6 /	21	To:	6 /	30
1	From:	/		To:	/	
2	From:	/		To:	/	
3	From:	/		To:	/	

You can order up to three destinations per Travel Update. Only destinations listed on the previous page are applicable. Maximum amount of time covered by a Travel Update cannot exceed 30 days.

CHOOSE YOUR INTERESTS: Select up to eight categories from the list of interest categories shown on the previous page and circle the numbers below:

1 2 3 4 5 6 7 8 9 10 11 12 13 14 15 16

CHOOSE HOW YOU WANT YOUR TRAVEL UPDATE DELIVERED (Check one):

❏ Please mail my Travel Update to the address above **OR**

❏ Fax it to me at **Fax #** ( ) -

DELIVERY CHARGE (Check one)

	Within U.S. & Canada	Outside U.S. & Canada
First Class Mail	❏ $2.50	❏ $5.00
Fax	❏ $5.00	❏ $10.00
Priority Delivery	❏ $15.00	❏ $27.00

All orders will be sent within 48 hours of receipt of a completed order form.

ADD UP YOUR ORDER HERE. *SPECIAL OFFER FOR FODOR'S PURCHASERS ONLY!*

	Suggested Retail Price	Your Price	This Order
First destination ordered	~~$13.95~~	$ 7.95	$ 7.95
Second destination (if applicable)	~~$ 9.95~~	$ 4.95	+
Third destination (if applicable)	~~$ 9.95~~	$ 4.95	+
Plus delivery charge from above			+
		TOTAL:	$

METHOD OF PAYMENT (Check one): ❏ AmEx ❏ MC ❏ Visa ❏ Discover
❏ Personal Check ❏ Money Order

Make check or money order payable to: Fodor's Worldview Travel Update

Credit Card # _____ **Expiration Date:** _____

Authorized Signature _____

SEND THIS COMPLETED FORM TO:
Fodor's Worldview Travel Update, 114 Sansome Street, Suite 700, San Francisco, CA 94104

OR CALL OR FAX US 24-HOURS A DAY
Telephone **1-800-799-9609** • Fax **1-800-799-9619** (From within the U.S. & Canada)
(Outside the U.S. & Canada: Telephone 415-616-9988 • Fax 415-616-9989)

(Please have this guide in front of you when you call so we can verify purchase.)
Offer valid until 12/31/94.